The Doctrine of the Covenant of Redemption According to John Gill (1697–1771)

Monographs in Baptist History

VOLUME 32

SERIES EDITOR
Michael A. G. Haykin, The Southern Baptist Theological Seminary

EDITORIAL BOARD
Matthew Barrett, Midwestern Baptist Theological Seminary
Peter Beck, Charleston Southern University
Anthony L. Chute, California Baptist University
Jason G. Duesing, Midwestern Baptist Theological Seminary
Nathan A. Finn, North Greenville University
Crawford Gribben, Queen's University, Belfast
Gordon L. Heath, McMaster Divinity College
Barry Howson, Heritage Theological Seminary
Jason K. Lee, Cedarville University
Thomas J. Nettles, The Southern Baptist Theological Seminary, retired
James A. Patterson, Union University
James M. Renihan, Institute of Reformed Baptist Studies
Jeffrey P. Straub, Independent Scholar
Brian R. Talbot, Broughty Ferry Baptist Church, Scotland
Malcolm B. Yarnell III, Southwestern Baptist Theological Seminary

Ours is a day in which not only the gaze of western culture but also increasingly that of Evangelicals is riveted to the present. The past seems to be nowhere in view and hence it is disparagingly dismissed as being of little value for our rapidly changing world. Such historical amnesia is fatal for any culture, but particularly so for Christian communities whose identity is profoundly bound up with their history. The goal of this new series of monographs, Studies in Baptist History, seeks to provide one of these Christian communities, that of evangelical Baptists, with reasons and resources for remembering the past. The editors are deeply convinced that Baptist history contains rich resources of theological reflection, praxis and spirituality that can help Baptists, as well as other Christians, live more Christianly in the present. The monographs in this series will therefore aim at illuminating various aspects of the Baptist tradition and in the process provide Baptists with a usable past.

The Doctrine of the Covenant of Redemption According to John Gill (1697–1771)

WANG YONG LEE

Foreword by **Malcolm B. Yarnell III**

WIPF & STOCK · Eugene, Oregon

THE DOCTRINE OF THE COVENANT OF REDEMPTION ACCORDING TO JOHN GILL (1697–1771)

Copyright © 2025 Wang Yong Lee. All rights reserved. Except for brief quotations in critical publications or reviews, no part of this book may be reproduced in any manner without prior written permission from the publisher. Write: Permissions, Wipf and Stock Publishers, 199 W. 8th Ave., Suite 3, Eugene, OR 97401.

Pickwick Publications
An Imprint of Wipf and Stock Publishers
199 W. 8th Ave., Suite 3
Eugene, OR 97401

www.wipfandstock.com

PAPERBACK ISBN: 979-8-3852-2492-0
HARDCOVER ISBN: 979-8-3852-2493-7
EBOOK ISBN: 979-8-3852-2494-4

Cataloguing-in-Publication data:

Names: Lee, Wang Yong, author | Yarnell, Malcolm B., III, foreword

Title: The doctrine of the covenant redemption according to John Gill (1697–1771) / Wang Yong Lee.

Description: Eugene, OR: Pickwick Publications, 2024 | Monographs in Baptist History | Includes bibliographical references and index.

Identifiers: ISBN 979-8-3852-2492-0 (paperback) | ISBN 979-8-3852-2493-7 (hardcover) | ISBN 979-8-3852-2494-4 (ebook)

Subjects: LCSH: Gill, John, 1697–1771. | Reformed Baptists—Great Britain—Clergy—Biography. | Reformed Baptists—Great Britain—Doctrines—History—18th century. | Redemption. | Covenant theology.

Classification: BX6459 G57 2025 (paperback) | BX6459 (ebook)

07/08/25

Contents

Foreword by Malcolm B. Yarnell III | *vii*

Acknowledgments | *xi*

List of Abbreviations | *xiii*

Chapter 1	Introduction	1
Chapter 2	Time and Eternity According to John Gill	21
Chapter 3	The Covenant of Redemption According to John Gill	62
Chapter 4	The Doctrine of the Trinity According to John Gill	118
Chapter 5	The Doctrine of Jesus Christ According to John Gill	168
Chapter 6	Conclusion	216

Bibliography | 221

Names Index | 243

Scripture Index | 249

Foreword

Rediscovering the Profound Genius of John Gill

THE NEOLOGISM *RESSOURCEMENT* WAS coined by French theologians in the twentieth century to describe theological renewal via a "return to the sources." Those Catholic theologians sought to protect their tradition from dissolving in the acids of Modernity.[1] More recently, Evangelical Protestants, disappointed with the debilitating effect of the historical critical method upon scholarly readings of Holy Scripture, have likewise sought theological renewal by drawing ancient wisdom from their own fonts in the Patristic, Medieval, and Reformation periods.[2]

It is now time for Evangelicals, especially in the Reformed and Baptist traditions, to begin mending our badly damaged dogmatic declarations by rediscovering the genius of John Gill. Every theological library that apportions its shelf space properly must provide prime space for the significant contributions of that peerless eighteenth-century divine. And his works ought to be read again and again. Four reasons for rediscovering this Reformed Baptist giant include the benefits found in his biblical commentaries, in his polemical theology, in his systematic theology, and in his pastoral virtue.

First, wise preachers regularly consult Gill's biblical commentaries in preparing sermons. Gill occupied the pulpit of the most prestigious Baptist church in London for over five decades and provided the Wednesday academic lectures at Great Eastcheap for nearly three decades. The fruit of his diligent research for preaching and teaching resulted in a detailed commentary on every book in the Bible, informed by the best Jewish and Gentile scholarship. Even that master of voluminous biblical commentary,

---

1. Gabriel Flynn and Paul D. Murray, *Ressourcement: A Movement for Renewal in Twentieth-Century Catholic Theology* (Oxford University Press, 2014).

2. Matthew Barrett, *The Reformation as Renewal: Retrieving the One, Holy, Catholic, and Apostolic Church* (Zondervan Academic, 2023).

John Calvin, did not match Gill's monumental feat. The latter's nine-volume *Expositions* of the Old and New Testaments continue to possess great utility, offering valuable historical, grammatical, and canonical reflections. Gill had access to the same exploding amount of information then becoming available to modern critics. However, unlike the skeptics, Gill honored the brilliance of the divine Mind rather than his own.[3]

Second, the consultation of Gill's polemical works can help restore integrity to the contemporary theological academy. While historians typically focus on his participation in the soteriological debates over duty faith, Antinomianism, and Arminianism, Gill's thoughtful defense of God and Christ against Arianism, Socinianism, and Sabellianism are worth consultation today as we learn again to fend off contemporary versions of these perennial errors. The acids of modernity have affected even conservative evangelicals, as seen in the rise of the neo-Arian doctrine of eternal functional subordination and in the continuing appeal of kenotic Christology. Ancient heresy and modern error continue to undermine the most important dogmas of the Christian faith, and John Gill offers helpful solutions. His powerful biblical, historical, and systematic expositions of the doctrines of the Trinity and of the eternal generation of God the Son have not yet been matched among Baptists.[4]

Third, even if a theologian cannot entirely agree with Gill, and I speak personally here, his profound genius as a dogmatic theologian must be honored and emulated. *A Body of Doctrinal Divinity*, published in 1769, is a masterpiece that places truth after truth in a beautifully crafted dogmatic frame. It is also important to note how, exhibiting great wisdom, Gill only wrote his systematic theology after he finished writing commentaries on the whole of the canon. Moreover, Gill listened to and taught from within the existing doctrinal conversation of the broader Christian tradition. The current practice, wherein specialized academics write systematic theologies with either little preaching experience or little exposure to the long Christian tradition, or both, has given us popular systems which undermine the most fundamental dogmas. Modern theologians would be wise to emulate Gill's biblical and historical method and consult his systematic results.

John Gill knew and believed the biblical canon, and John Gill understood and embraced both the Reformed and the Baptist theological canons. As a systematic thinker in that dual tradition, Gill remained true both to his Reformed and his Baptist roots. But Gill was no slavish divine. He defended

---

3. Cf. https://www.biblestudytools.com/commentaries/gills-exposition-of-the-bible/.

4. John Gill, *Treatise on the Doctrine of the Trinity* (London, 1731); Gill, *A Dissertation concerning the Eternal Sonship of Christ* (London, 1768; reprint, 2022).

his tradition because he deemed it biblical and logical, but he modified it where he thought it might be improved. As the current volume demonstrates, he customized Reformed covenant theology in important ways. The same respect for yet readiness to advance tradition is seen in his Baptist doctrines. It takes a young pastor with no small courage and subtlety of mind to propose and successfully change the confession of the church of Benjamin Keach, the greatest Particular Baptist theologian before Gill.

Fourth and finally, contemporary evangelicals should respect his virtues. Gill knew how to engage Christianly in doctrinal discourse. He debated in writing and in speech against Arians and Socinians to defend the Trinity, against some fellow Baptists to correct their Antinomianism, and against the "low side" position on "the Modern Question" of the duty of faith. While he lamented his own personal defects, his well-meaning opponents respected him. John Wesley recognized Gill's virtuous character, even as the two stalwart theologians disagreed vehemently. Wesley told Augustus Toplady that while Gill "fights for his own opinions through thick and thin," the founder of Methodism found the defender of divine grace "a positive man."[5] John Rippon, the pastor who followed Gill at the same church which would eventually be pastored by Charles Haddon Spurgeon, said of Gill, "Notwithstanding his exalted attainments and usefulness, he was *meek, humble*, and of a *sympathizing* spirit."[6]

Dr. Wang Yong Lee's excellent book, which you hold in your hand, helps launch a Reformed and Baptist *ressourcement* through detailed engagement with critical aspects of Gill's high doctrines of God, Christ, and salvation. In tight prose packed with meaning Lee unveils Gill's doctrine of the covenant of redemption. He shows how Gill grounded his theology in the eternal nature of God, how his covenant of redemption engages with and develops the logic of Scripture, and how he sought to improve the Reformed theological tradition. Lee's chapters on Gill's doctrines of Trinity and Christ are alone worth the price of the book for contemporary readers concerned to find ways to correct current trajectories.

Perhaps allowing Gill to have the final word will encourage the reader to process Lee's book carefully and then take up and read Gill's biblical commentaries, polemical defenses of God and Christ, and *A Body of Doctrinal Divinity*, as well as *A Body of Practical Divinity*. It is estimated that the London pastor wrote some 10,000 pages of theology, continually protecting his study so that he might engage in this sacred work. Although he regretted

---

5. John Rippon, *A Brief Memoir of the Life and Writings of the Late Rev. John Gill, D. D.* (London, 1838), 65.

6. Italics his. Rippon, *A Brief Memoir*, 129.

the opposition he often encountered, Gill persistently worked for the sole purpose of advancing divine Truth:

> Upon the whole, as I suggested at the beginning of this Introduction, I have but little reason to think the following Work will meet with a favorable reception in general; yet, if it may be a means of preserving sacred Truths, of enlightening the minds of any into them, or of establishing them in them, I shall not be concerned at what evil treatment I may meet with from the adversaries of them; and be it as it may, I shall have the satisfaction of having done the best I can for the promoting TRUTH; and of bearing testimony to it.[7]

Gill emphasized reconciliation to God in Christ with his whole life, biblically, polemically, systematically, and personally.[8] And we should be thankful that he did so as we again and again consult his works to help us preserve, protect, and proclaim the faith once for all delivered to the saints. May the Evangelical, Reformed, and Baptist *ressourcement* continue with the rediscovery of John Gill, one of our tradition's most prominent, prolific, and profound theologians.

Malcolm B. Yarnell III
Research Professor
Southwestern Baptist Theological Seminary
December 10, 2024

---

7. John Gill, *A Body of Doctrinal Divinity; or A System of Evangelical Truths, Deduced from the Sacred Scriptures*, New ed. (London, 1839; reprint Baptist Standard Bearer), lii.

8. His first two sermons, preached in the first two weeks after his baptism, concerned the person of Jesus Christ (1 Cor. 2:2) and the gospel of Jesus Christ (Isa. 53). He maintained his Christological foundation to the end.

Acknowledgments

THIS VOLUME IS A PRODUCT of the grace and faithfulness of our Triune God. He was, is, and will be beyond the timeline. However, He is eternal. The wonderful God, the Trinity, who always lives made another remarkable history through the conviction, knowledge, experience, thoughts and writings, and the whole life of John Gill. It is a blessing that I have been able to get a chance to see who God is and what He has done for us through Gill's life during this long journey of writing. *Soli Deo Gloria*!

Malcolm B. Yarnell III, my supervisor, has always supported me since I entered the doctoral program. Being a mentor, friend, teacher, and above all, calling himself a brother in Christ, Dr. Yarnell has enormously contributed to this volume by sharing generously his incisive discernment and insight. His advice, guidance, and prayer helped me leap into the upper, breathing in fresh air when I reached the breaking point. I am so grateful to the Lord and blessed to have Dr. Yarnell as my supervisor. Dr. David S. Dockery, my second reader, with his deep, wide, and rich experience of Christian higher education, has supported me during the whole process of writing. Not only spending time reading my chapters thoroughly but also sharing his wisdom and praying for me throughout the process. I am also greatly thankful to Dr. Robert W. Caldwell III for readily accepting the role of my third reader. I have gained benefit from his expertise in the writings of Christian history, especially the historical background of the eighteenth century regarding the doctrine of the Trinity. Lastly, two words I have learned from these three professors are Christocentric and humble, which I have mostly gained through the program. It is a huge blessing to see such men in person and to learn from them. I am so much blessed.

My family deserves the whole appreciation. All the prayers of my mother have led me to sustain what I have to hold and where I stand. My three blessings from God, Immanuel, Irene, and Isaac, have always brought our family joy and made me smile. Finally, my beloved wife in Christ,

Acknowledgments

Hyeonah K. Lee, who has always been with me, loved me, sacrificed herself for the family, deserves my wholehearted covenantal love, gratitude, and respect. I dedicate this volume to my wife, Hyeonah, for her unwavering love, patience, and sacrifices she made throughout the process.

Wang Yong Lee
Fort Worth, Texas
June 2023

List of Abbreviations

ABR	Australian Biblical Review
BECNT	Baker Exegetical Commentary on the New Testament
BHS	Biblia Hebraica Stuttgartensia
CD	Church Dogmatics
CTR	Criswell Theological Review
ECNT	Exegetical Commentary on the New Testament
JAOS	Journal of the American Oriental Society
JES	Journal of Ecumenical Studies
JETS	Journal of Evangelical Theological Society
JMAT	Journal of Ministry and Theology
JRT	Journal of Reformed Theology
MJT	Mid-America Journal of Theology
NAC	New American Commentary
NIBC	New International Biblical Commentary
NICOT	New International Commentary on the Old Testament
NIGTC	New International Greek Testament Commentary
NSBT	New Studies in Biblical Theology
NSD	New Studies in Dogmatics
PNTC	Pillar New Testament Commentary
PRJ	Puritan Reformed Journal
SBJT	Southern Baptist Journal of Theology
SNTSMS	Society for New Testament Studies Monograph Series

SWJT	Southwestern Journal of Theology
TB	Tyndale Bulletin
TDNT	Theological Dictionary of the New Testament
TDOT	Theological Dictionary of the Old Testament
TMSJ	The Master's Seminary Journal
TNTC	Tyndale New Testament Commentary
WBC	Word Biblical Commentary
WTJ	Westminster Theological Journal

CHAPTER 1

Introduction

"*Quod prius est in intentione posterius est in executione & contra*: that which is first in the intention of God, is last in the execution; and that which is last in the intent, is first in the execution."[1] What is the presupposition that drives Patrick Gillespie to quote William Twisse in his work on the covenant of redemption ("*pactum salutis*" hereafter *pactum*)? Those who have ever struggled with the nature of the *pactum* appreciate why Gillespie quotes Twisse in this way. One may consider that Gillespie, while elucidating one aspect of the *pactum* in the order of the decrees of God, contemplates the relationship between what is hidden in God's plan in eternity and what is manifested in redemptive history in time. Practically, he explains: "We say that God first decreed the glorifying of his mercy and justice upon all mankind, before he decreed anything concerning his creation, or his fall: for the creation and fall of man, were first in execution before justice and mercy was glorified in him."[2]

However, such a concept, in the eyes of the critics of the *pactum*, seems to structure the doctrine strictly in the scholastic Reformed theological model. It appears that the eternal aspects of the decrees of the triune God, e.g., the *pactum*, are inextricably linked to or can be legitimately and fully apprehended by man's rational and logical order of a thought process of a limited system. Particularly, this is the case regarding redemptive history, without a valid examination of the biblical foundation, which brings about one of the significant reasons why the *pactum* is harshly criticized even by

---

1. Patrick Gillespie, *The Ark of the Covenant Opened: Or, A Treatise of the Covenant of Redemption between God and Christ, as the Foundation of the Covenant of Grace* (London: Tho. Parkhurst, 1677), 55.

2. Gillespie, *The Ark of the Covenant Opened*, 55.

Reformed scholars.³ Theologians acknowledge that this theological framework and reasonable hermeneutic process are good tools to provide helpful inferences of Scripture only in a proper understanding of the legitimate theological interpretation, informed by evidence and support of the biblical references.

With this important hermeneutical concept in mind, this work tries to find a balanced interpretation of the *pactum* in terms of biblical and theological aspects through the lens of John Gill (1697-1771). By examining Gill's works, especially focusing on *The Doctrine of the Trinity, A Body of Doctrinal Divinity*, and *An Exposition of the Old and New Testaments* in relevant research, this volume attempts to demonstrate that John Gill's *pactum* plays a critical role, namely occupying a central locus in his whole covenantal redemptive system in time and eternity in relation to other doctrinal explications such as the doctrine of God (the Trinity), Christology, and soteriology.

LITERATURE REVIEW

Biblical Covenants and the Pactum Salutis

The *pactum* is a covenant in terms of human redemption. First, we must ask: "What is a covenant?" This simple but fundamental question makes a significant difference in understanding the biblical covenants. After fifty years of working in the Scriptures, Daniel Block, affirming covenants as the frame of biblical revelation, defines a covenant as "a formally confirmed agreement between two or more parties that creates, formalizes, or governs a relationship that does not naturally exist or a natural relationship that may have been broken or disintegrated."⁴ In addition, suggesting two kinds of

---

3. The criticisms and negative points against the *pactum* are dealt with below by the next section of the theological trajectory on the *pactum*.

4. Daniel I. Block, *Covenant: The Framework of God's Grand Plan of Redemption* (Grand Rapids: Baker, 2021), 1. Regarding the "natural relationship" in Block's definition, Michael Horton explains, "No part of God's nature or knowledge coincided with the creature at any point. That is to say, God is transcendent. Therefore, any relationship that one might have with this God would have to be something other than a *natural* relationship – that is, the relationship could not be explained in terms of, say, a common spiritual essence shared by the Creator and a creature" in Michael Horton, *Introducing Covenant Theology* (Grand Rapids: BakerBooks, 2006), 29. For more significant concepts of a covenant, see O. Palmer Robertson, *The Christ of the Covenants* (Phillipsburg, NJ: P&R, 1980), 4. Robertson by focusing on the sovereignty of God and the idea of bond defines the covenantal relationship between God and his people, "A Covenant is a *bond in blood sovereignly administered*" (Italics original). In relation to the concept

scriptural covenants, i.e., parity and disparity in relation to the covenantal parties, Block asserts, "In the Scriptures all covenants involving God are fundamentally monergistic suzerain-vassal pacts."[5] Two notable phrases from the statement raise a question regarding the nature of the *pactum*: "in

---

of bond, Peter Lillback provides Calvin's idea of a covenant, "The essence of Calvin's conception of the covenant is the notion of the binding of God . . . The gracious self-binding of the infinite God whereby He condescends to enter into a mutual covenant with His fallen and unworthy yet sovereignly chosen people is eloquently portrayed by Calvin . . . " Peter A. Lillback, *The Binding of God: Calvin's Role in the Development of Covenant Theology* (Grand Rapids: Baker, 2001), 137. From a slightly different view, the concept of a covenant occupies a foundational principle in all human and social relationships, says Herman Bavinck, such as friendship and marriage based on agreements and obligations. In this regard, his definition of a covenant goes by, "a covenant is an agreement between persons who voluntarily obligate and bind themselves to each other for the purpose of fending off an evil or obtaining a good." More attention seizes the matter of the parties of a covenant in Scriptures. Bavinck sets the limit of the biblical covenantal parties by God and his people, "In Scripture 'covenant' is the fixed form in which the relation of God to his people is depicted and presented." This idea of the covenantal party brings up a question whether the Scripture does include the concept of the *pactum* within the divine persons even if Bavinck himself deals with the *pactum* in a different section. See Herman Bavinck, *Reformed Dogmatics*, vol. 2: God and Creation, ed. John Bolt and trans. John Vriend (Grand Rapids: Baker, 2004), 568-569. With regard to the origin of the concept of a covenant, Louis Berkhof, although the covenant idea had been used and developed before the biblical covenants with Noah and Abraham, affirms, "This does not mean, however, that the covenant idea originated with man and was then borrowed by God as an appropriate form for the description of the mutual relationship between Himself and man . . . the archetype of all covenant life is found in the trinitarian being of God, and what is seen among men is but a faint copy (ectype) of this" in Louis Berkhof, *Systematic Theology*, New Combined Edition (Grand Rapids: Eerdmans, 1996), 263. For more details of the general biblical covenants, see Robert Davidson, "Covenant," in *The Oxford Companion to Christian Thought*, ed. Adrian Hastings, Alistair Mason, and Hugh Pyper (Oxford University Press, 2000); Gerard Van Groningen, "Covenant," in *Evangelical Dictionary of Biblical Theology*, ed. Walter A. Elwell (Grand Rapids: BakerBooks, 1996); Irvin A. Busenitz, "Introduction to the Biblical Covenants; The Noahic Covenant and the Priestly Covenant," *TMSJ* 10, no. 2 (Fall 1999): 173-189; David W. Jones and John K. Tarwater, "Are Biblical Covenants Dissoluble?" *SWJT* 47, no. 1 (Fall 2004): 1-11; Jacob B. Agus, "The Covenant Concept – Particularistic, Pluralistic, or Futuristic?" *JES* 18, no. 2 (Spring 1981): 217-230. For the non-biblical covenants and its relation to the biblical covenants, see George E. Mendenhall, *Law and Covenant in Israel and the Ancient Near East* (Pittsburgh: The Biblical Colloquium, 1955); Delbert R. Hillers, *Covenant: The History of a Biblical Idea* (Baltimore: The Johns Hopkins University Press, 1969); Meredith G. Kline, *Treaty of the Great King: The Covenant Structure of Deuteronomy* (Eugene: Wipe&Stock, 1963), 13-44; M. Weinfeld, "The Covenant of Grant in the Old Testament and in the Ancient Near East," *JAOS* 90, no. 2 (1970): 184-203; J. A. Thompson, "Non-Biblical Covenants in the Ancient Near East," *ABR* 8, no. 1 (1960): 38-45; Roy Beacham, "Ancient Near Eastern Covenants," *JMAT* 15, no. 1 (Spring 2011): 110-128; Ada Taggar-Cohen, "Biblical Covenant and Hittite išḫiul reexamined," *Vetus Testamentum* 61, no. 3 (2011): 461-488.

5. Block, *Covenant*, 2.

the Scriptures," and "all covenants." Block's assertion seems to deliver a notion that the *pactum* does not belong to the biblical covenants in the sense that all covenants in relation to God in the Scriptures are disparity pacts, which looks on man as the only party of God's covenants. Such a question arises because of the definition of the *pactum*. According to John Fesko, a leading Reformed scholar, the *pactum* is "the *pre-temporal intra-trinitarian agreement* to plan and execute the redemption of the elect."[6] In light of

---

6. J. V. Fesko, *The Trinity and the Covenant of Redemption* (Fearn, Ross-shire, U.K.: Mentor, 2016), xvii, 131. Italics emphasized. Gillespie gives his definition by emphasizing on the concept "agreements" with which all covenants share their essentiality: "this is an eternal transaction and agreement betwixt Jehovah and the Mediator Christ, about the work of our Redemption." Gillespie, *The Ark of the Covenant Opened*, 51. Herman Witsius' concept of the *pactum* lies in the will of the Father and the will of the Son, "I thereby understand the will of the Father, giving the Son to be the Head and Redeemer of the elect; and the will of the Son, presenting himself as a Sponsor or Surety for them; in all which the nature of a compact and agreement consists." Herman Witsius, *The Economy of the Covenants Between God and Man: Comprehending A Complete Body of Divinity*, vol. 1, trans. William Crookshank (London: Baynes, 1882), 165. Bavinck, though giving no framed definition of the *pactum*, grasps the concept as "the intratrinitarian pact of salvation," "a stable, eternal foundation in the counsel of God ... conceived as aiming at the salvation of the human race ... as a covenant between the three persons in the divine being itself." Herman Bavinck, *Reformed Dogmatics*, vol. 3: Sin and Salvation in Christ, ed. John Bolt and trans. John Vriend (Grand Rapids: Baker, 2006), 212-213. Berkhof provides a clear definition of the *pactum*, "The covenant of redemption may be defined as *the agreement between the Father, giving the Son as Head and Redeemer of the elect, and the Son, voluntarily taking the place of those whom the Father had given Him.*" Berkhof, *Systematic Theology*, 271. Listing the *pactum*'s definitions by each representative of English Puritans, English Particular Baptists, Dutch Reformed theologians, and modern Reformed scholars (i.e., John Flavel, Second London Confession of 1689, Herman Bavinck, and J. V. Fesko), Thomas Parr finds four basic ideas in common concerning the *pactum*: (1) specific relations as covenantal; (2) three divine persons of the Trinity as the parties; (3) man's redemption as the subject; and (4) pre-temporal or eternal as the timing. See Thomas Parr, "Patrick Gillespie on the Covenant of Redemption: Exegetical Arguments," *PRJ* 13, no. 1 (2021): 49-50. Parr says, "The covenant of redemption is thus present in the same essential form in the writings of" the four different fields of scholars in history. However, it will not be exact to say that these all four are in the same vein in terms of the *pactum* because there is a different understanding regarding the covenant parties. Throughout the history of the *pactum*, as seen above by the difference between Bavinck (divine three persons) and Berkhof (the Father and the Son) in its definition, the Holy Spirit who is the third person of the Trinity has been easily ignored as the party of the *pactum* with the Father and the Son. For example, though Herman Witsius seemingly makes a quick mention of the Holy Spirit in the nature of the *pactum* ("with the approbation of the Holy Spirit"), his basic understanding of the *pactum* affirms the relationship between the Father and the Son as already defined above. Witsius, *The Economy of the Covenants*, 177. Fesko classifies this issue into two groups: christological and trinitarian, and then asserts, "These differences of opinion do not rise to the level of heterodoxy." Fesko, *The Trinity and the Covenant of Redemption*, 129-130. Cf. Thomas Parr, "English Puritans

Block's statement about God's covenants, the description of "pre-temporal intra-trinitarian" appears to denote that neither is the concept found in the narrative of the Scriptures in time nor could it be called a covenant because it does not occur between God and man, which posits a subtle nuance of the confliction between the biblical covenants and the *pactum*.[7]

Even in the situation of the conceptual and logical discrepancy happening necessarily by definitional differences between the *pactum* and the biblical covenants, the doctrine of the *pactum* was widely acknowledged during the sixteenth and seventeenth centuries among the English and Continental Reformed covenant theologians.[8] For example, the *pactum* scholarship, according to Guy Richard, the modern covenant scholar, won the people of those centuries not because of the doctrine's theoretical sophistication but because of its biblical basis. Richard makes three points regarding the biblical usage of the *pactum*: language of Scripture pointing

---

and the Covenant of Redemption: The Exegetical Arguments of John Flavel and William Strong," *PRJ* 12, no. 1 (2020): 56-58; Robert Letham, "John Owen's Doctrine of the Trinity in its Catholic Context," in *The Ashgate Research Companion to John Owen's Theology*, ed. Kelly M. Kapic and Mark Jones (London: Routledge, 2012), 196. This issue of exclusion of the Holy Spirit in the *pactum*, as one of the crucial points of John Gill's theology, will be carefully dealt with by Gill's theological system and understanding of the *pactum* in this work.

7. Such confrontation between the eternal and temporal aspects concerning the *pactum* becomes an issue and brings about tensions even among the Reformed theologians, e.g., Karl Barth and Robert Letham. The common criticism from both theologians lies in the argument that the *pactum* puts the basic and orthodox doctrine of the Trinity into trouble. Richard Muller also admits that the *pactum* appears to have speculation in itself, yet he sees a positive facet as well: "For all that this doctrine of eternal covenanting between Father and Son appears as the most speculative element in the covenant theology, it represents that most basic of issues in the Reformed system – the eternal, divine, and consistently gracious ground of the plan of salvation, the resolution of the seemingly unbridgeable gap between the eternal and the temporal, the infinite and the finite, undertaken redemptively and by grace alone from the divine side." Richard A. Muller, "Toward the Pactum Salutis: Locating the Origins of a Concept," *MJT* 18 (2007): 15.

8. Guy M. Richard, "The Covenant of Redemption," in *Covenant Theology: Biblical, Theological, and Historical Perspectives*, ed. Guy Prentiss Waters, J. Nicholas Reid, and John R. Muether (Wheaton: Crossway, 2020), 45. Also see Richard A. Muller, "pactum salutis," in *Dictionary of Latin and Greek Theological Terms: Drawn Principally from Protestant Scholastic Theology*, Second Edition (Grand Rapids: Baker, 2017), 252-253. Muller makes a distinction between the roots of the idea of the *pactum* (sixteenth) and the prominent usage of the terminology *pactum* (seventeenth) by naming figures who wrote about the doctrine such as Edward Fisher, Peter Bulkeley, John Owen, David Dickson, Johannes Cloppenburg, and Johannes Cocceius. Concerning the widespread historical development pertaining to the *pactum* by key covenant theologians, see J. V. Fesko, *The Covenant of Redemption: Origins, Development, and Reception* (Göttingen: Vandenhoeck & Ruprecht, 2015), 16-22, 29-46.

to the *pactum*, dialogues between the Father and the Son, and teaching of individual passages.⁹ He also continues to mention two theological grounds with which the biblical rationale behind the *pactum* is supplemented and reinforced in history: covenant of works and grace and the Trinity.

Moreover, from the historical and theological perspective, Richard Muller's sharp inquiry on the origin and legitimacy of the *pactum* should draw the attention of contemporary theologians:

> What is perhaps most remarkable about this chronological presentation of the early dogmatic history of the *pactum salutis* is the lack of opposition to what, at least on Witsius' testimony, was a relatively new idea with a rather shaky pedigree – an idea, moreover, that did not easily find clear dogmatic precedent, in Witsius' view, prior to Arminius ... the seemingly sudden appearance of the doctrine as a virtual truism within the space of four years itself raises questions. Worlds may arise *ex nihilo*, doctrinal formulae probably do not.¹⁰

While both acknowledge the lack of opposition to the *pactum* in history and at the same time cast doubt because there is no lack of opposition found, Muller's explication concerning the origin of the *pactum* begins. Considering the Reformed exegesis and theological discussion as the backdrop or groundwork of the *pactum*, Muller unfolds the origin of the doctrine's concept by examining both exegetical foundations and arguments and doctrinal formulation of the Reformed scholarship, which will make it possible for the later *pactum* theologians to move forward and develop the doctrine beyond the realm of speculation.¹¹

Any attempts to separate the *pactum* from the biblical covenants are not based on the substantive difference in terms of the biblical foundation or evidence to support the existence of the *pactum*. The *pactum* is a biblical covenant.¹² Scott Swain drawing Ephesians 1:11 provides a basic premise in approaching the *pactum*, "the divine decree is the internal work of the Triune God (*opera Dei interna*) that moves and directs the external works of the Triune God (*operationes Dei externae*)."¹³ As far as the being and work

---

9. Richard, "The Covenant of Redemption," 45-57.
10. Muller, "Toward the *Pactum Salutis*," 14.
11. Muller, "Toward the *Pactum Salutis*," 15-65.
12. This statement does not mean that the *pactum* shares the identity or intrinsic features with other biblical covenants e.g., covenant of works, covenant of grace. Rather, it connotes that the *pactum* is biblical, and grounded in the teaching of Scripture, not an artificially humanly constructed contract.
13. Ephesians 1:11 reads, "In him we have also received an inheritance, because we were predestined according to the plan of the one who works out everything in

of the Triune God, who is the author of the Bible and perfectly free in time and eternity, is related to and concerned with the *pactum*, the concept of the *pactum* cannot be separated from the biblical covenants though it is not explicitly manifested but implicitly signified.[14]

Theological Trajectory in the History of the Pactum Salutis[15]

With regard to the articulation of the *pactum*'s locus in relation to the biblical covenants and theological discussions in the church history, the first

---

agreement with the purpose of his will." Unless otherwise indicated, Scripture quotations are from Christian Standard Bible, Holman. Based on the statement regarding the relation of the internal works and the external works, Swain, focusing on the Christological end of the *pactum*, describes, "In other words, though the Scriptures are relatively reticent to speak of the Son's *eternal appointment* by the Father in covenantal terms, the Scriptures speak quite liberally about the Son's *historical execution* of that appointment in covenantal terms." See Scott R. Swain, "Covenant of Redemption," in *Christian Dogmatics: Reformed Theology for the Church Catholic*, ed. Michael Allen and Scott R. Swain (Grand Rapids: Baker, 2016), 107, 120.

14. First, by definition, the *pactum* is necessarily related to the Triune God himself in his being and internal works that happen in eternity. Thus, it is crucial to note that the understanding of eternity pertaining to God's attributes presupposes and provides the background of the entire arguments and biblical reasoning of the *pactum*. In accordance with the significance of the idea, this work will deal with Gill's understanding of eternity with God's attributes prior to delving into his concept of the *pactum*. Secondly, with regard to the biblical lucidity of the concept of the *pactum*, the burden of proof relies on the proponents, but it should not be impossible in terms of that the *pactum* is permeated as a widespread concept with various methods in the Scriptures, e.g., prosopological exegesis. For more about prosopological exegesis, see Madison N. Pierce, *Divine Discourse in the Epistle to the Hebrews: The Recontextualization of Spoken Quotations of Scripture*, SNTSMS 178 (Cambridge: Cambridge University Press, 2020). Cf. Andrew D. Streett, "New Approaches to the Use of the Old Testament in the New Testament," *SWJT* 64, no. 1 (2021): 11-14. Curt Daniel asserts, "Some dispensationalists use this argument but forget that the Bible does not explicitly use dispensational terms such as the *dispensation of innocence*. Even the words *rapture* and *Trinity* are extra-biblical in name but not in content." See Curt Daniel, *The History and Theology of Calvinism* (Darlington, U.K.: Evangelical Press, 2019), 362. Italics original.

15. This trajectory tries to avoid rehashing the historical and theological narratives of the *pactum* in previous works. Rather, this review tries to build up for the sake of its own arguments of the work based upon the shoulders of the *pactum* giants in covenant theology. For more historical and theological flow of the *pactum* in details, see Fesko, *The Covenant of Redemption: Origins, Development, and Reception*; Bertus Loonstra, *Verkiezing – Verzoening – Verbond: Beschrijving en beoordeling van de leer van het pactum salutis in de gereformeerde theologie* (Gravenhage: Uitgeverij Boekencentrum, 1990); B. Hoon Woo, *The Promise of the Trinity: The Covenant of Redemption in the Theologies of Witsius, Owen, Dickson, Goodwin, and Cocceius* (Göttingen: Vandenhoeck & Ruprecht, 2018); Joel R. Beeke and Paul M. Smalley, *Reformed Systematic Theology*, vol. 2: Man and Christ (Wheaton: Crossway, 2020), 584-609.

full-fledged work that devoted its contents fully to the doctrine of the *pactum* came with *The Ark of the Covenant Opened* (1677), a posthumous work, by Patrick Gillespie (1617-1675) a Scottish minister. While "very many learned and godly persons have laboured in the same subject unto the edification of the church," John Owen, Gillespie's "long Christian acquaintance," recognizes "that for order, method, perspicuity intreating, and solidity of argument, the ensuing discourse exceedeth whatsoever single treatise I have seen written with the same design."[16]

The first concern of Gillespie was to prove that there is such a covenant in eternity between the Father and the Son, which is ultimately the basis and foundation of the covenant made with man in time, i.e., the covenant of grace.[17] This proof, according to Gillespie, lies in the generally acknowledged feature of a covenant in the Scriptures:

> where there are Proposals, Commands, or Promises upon the one part, with conditions required upon the other, and a consent unto, or acceptance of these Proposals, with the conditions required upon the other part, or where there is a restipulation of conditions upon the other part, there must needs be a Contract or Covenant, not only *materially* and *virtually*, because there is all the essentials of a Covenant; but *formally* and explicitly, because there are all the formalities of explicit Covenanting.[18]

Finding such covenantal relationships between the Father and the Son manifested in the redemptive history of the Scripture, Gillespie applies this characteristic of a covenant to the relation of the Father to the Son in eternity, which points to a covenant between the Father and the Son regarding man's redemption.[19]

---

16. "To the Reader" by John Owen in Gillespie, *The Ark of the Covenant Opened*.

17. Gillespie, *The Ark of the Covenant Opened*, 1. It is interesting to see the logic that the attempt to prove the existence of the *pactum* in eternity itself has already a connection to the covenant of grace in time conceptually. The *pactum* as the foundation of the covenant of grace proves that the central concept to link both eternal and temporal is *redemption* of man as the term *pactum* signifies. Gillespie also calls the *pactum* as the covenant of suretiship because Christ is not only the one of the parties of the *pactum*, but he is also the representative or head of the elect who will be redeemed in Christ.

18. Gillespie, *The Ark of the Covenant Opened*, 6. The conditions of the relationship between the Father and the Son in the *pactum* e.g., sending, being sent, Suretyship, Mediatorship, are all derived from this principle of being a covenant between parties. For more explanations concerning the formal covenant, Father's proposal, Christ's consent, Christ's role as Mediator, see Parr, "Patrick Gillespie," 58-72.

19. The application of a generally acknowledged covenant in the Bible between God and man or man and man to the eternal relation of the Father and the Son, needs more considerations with regard to the covenant parties. The *pactum* happens among the

Introduction 9

Another important aspect in Gillespie's *pactum* comes with its nature in terms of the order of eternal acts of God: "All the acts of God's will, his decree, and eternal transaction with Christ, are in regard of God, *one most simple and pure act of his will*; but in regard of our conceptions of them, who cannot take up many particular acts together in one; they are distinguished and expressed so in the word, that we may take them up distinctly."[20] Gillespie signifies that due to the ontological difference between Creator and creature, the legitimate method to access the doctrine of the *pactum* is only possible through the knowledge of who God is and what God does: *one most simple and pure act of his will.*[21]

Acknowledging covenant as an analogy in God's accommodation for man's understanding, Samuel Willard (1640-1707), an American Puritan, in *The Doctrine of the Covenant of Redemption* (1693), explains that God's one divine will, both sending in the Father and being sent in the Son, remains incomprehensible in the same vein as Gillespie: "Although these are but one Will, yet it comes under a distinct consideration by us, though the manner of it be above our conception."[22] One of the significant articles of the *pactum*

Triune God, and all other covenants include man at least as one party. In this regard, Gill's understanding of the covenant itself helps for the better approach to the *pactum*. This work will also study Gill's covenant concept while working on his *pactum*.

20. Gillespie, *The Ark of the Covenant Opened*, 54. Italics added.

21. In other words, the order of eternal acts of God, says Gillespie, delivers a concept that there is no such a temporal order in eternity. The eternal acts that seemingly appear to have a kind of a temporal order are interpretations and understanding from man's perspective that cannot observe God's entire work as one. God himself as pure act is the lens to see the frame of eternity.

22. Samuel Willard, *The Doctrine of the Covenant of Redemption: Wherein is laid the Foundation of all our Hopes and Happiness: Briefly Opened and Improved* (Boston: Benj. Harris, 1693), 26-27. The will issue is directly related to the parties. Does each person of the Triune God, especially the Father and the Son, have a will? Is it implying tritheism? Then, how does it harmonize with the divine simplicity in the doctrine of the Trinity? Following the importance of the issue, this work also deals with Gill's understanding of the will in the *pactum* pertaining to the doctrine of the Trinity. Prior to the mention of God's one divine will whose issue occurs between the Father and the Son, Willard considers that the parties of the *pactum* consists of God and the Son, in which a meaningful question arises concerning whether this God, one of the parties, is to be understood as essentially or personally. Opposing the opinion of some who argue that this God in covenanting should be understood essentially because the Holy Spirit is to be included, Willard regards this God as the God the Father. Willard believes that the essential works are legitimate and possible only when the three persons of the Triune God get involved with the internal works without excluding of the other. See Willard, *The Doctrine of the Covenant of Redemption*, 20-23. Cf. For information about Willard's life, thoughts, and ministry in detail, see Seymour Van Dyken, *Samuel Willard, 1640-1707: Preacher of Orthodoxy in an Era of Change* (Grand Rapids: Eerdmans, 1972). Willard's answer to the question of the parties whether it should be understood essentially

in the proposal ("sending") and undertaking ("being sent") between the Father and the Son is incarnation. However, the concept of incarnation in the *pactum*, says Willard, is not necessarily to have a human nature assumed by the second person of the Triune God because it is sufficient for the person to be only designated by promise or covenant without being "looked upon as man."[23]

---

or personally, reminds readers of the critique by Karl Barth as if Willard already knew his question. Barth claims, "And if, in relation to that which He obviously does amongst us, we speak of His eternal resolves or decrees, even if we describe them as a contract, then we do not regard the divine persons of the Father and the Son as partners in this contract, but the one God – Father, Son, and Holy Spirit – as the one partner, and the reality of man as distinct from God as the other." See Karl Barth, *Church Dogmatics*, ed. G. W. Bromiley and T. F. Torrance, trans. G. W. Bromiley (Edinburgh: T&T Clark, 1956), IV/1: 65 (hereafter CD).

23. See Willard, *The Doctrine of the Covenant of Redemption*, 28-29. Willard reasons why the Son "could and did undertake for the doing of this work [incarnation], without the Humane Nature Assumed" is because "The Covenant of Redemption was an Eternal Covenant; and therefore the party as such must come under an Eternal consideration, and that could only be in regard of his being the Eternal Son of God, or with respect to his Divine Personality." One of the remarks to keep in mind from Willard's words is that of "The Covenant of Redemption was an Eternal Covenant." Though Willard's emphasis by this phrase is on 'eternal,' so there needs a clear understanding of what 'eternal' means, the phrase 'eternal covenant' itself is meaningful. The Bible never uses the term "covenant of redemption"; however, "eternal covenant" happens throughout the Scriptures. This biblical term "eternal covenant" is recognized in connection to the eternal plan of God in man's redemption, which is manifested and concretized by the covenants of works and grace. In this regard, the term is linked inextricably to the redemptive history led by the covenantal relationship between God and his people in his eternal plan. Incarnation is the initiation of the covenantal redemptive history playing a key role in connecting the promise of the Old Testament [OT] to the fulfillment of the New Testament [NT]. The works of Christ, e.g., death and resurrection, initiated by incarnation in time echo both in time and eternity by the eternal covenant. Cf. Hebrews 13:20. Peter Gentry and Stephen Wellum well picture the frame between the covenant theology and the works of the Son: "As covenant theology has contended, one cannot deny that Scripture teaches that our triune God has an eternal plan . . . a plan conceived before the foundation of the world, made known on the stage of human history, and involving the work of all three persons of the Godhead . . . In addition, in that plan, the divine Son, in relation to the Father and Spirit, is appointed as the mediator of his people. And the Son gladly and voluntarily accepts this appointment with its covenant stipulations and promises, which are then worked out in his incarnation, life, death, and resurrection. This eternal plan establishes Christ as mediator, defines the nature of his mediation, and assigns specific roles to each person of the Godhead, and this plan is accomplished in history through the covenants of works and grace." See Peter J. Gentry and Stephen J. Wellum, *Kingdom through Covenant: A Biblical-Theological Understanding of the Covenants*, Second Edition (Wheaton: Crossway, 2018), 78. Gill's understanding of Christology especially in the Son's incarnation that implies and connects the *pactum* to the other covenants in the Bible, therefore, is closely related to the *pactum* and its unfolding in the progressive covenantal system in the redemptive

Another interesting but ambiguous point Willard makes draws attention, "Christ, not only as he is Man, but also as he is Son, is in the *Oeconomical* Dispensation of things, *Subordinate* to his Father."[24] At first glance, it seems to deliver that Christ's humanity, not divinity, is subordinate to the Father in time, which sounds quite legitimate in the "Oeconomical Dispensation." Additionally, Willard obviously states that the Father and the Son are equal, in essence, by citing two biblical verses.[25] However, the expression "not only as he is Man, but also *as he is Son* . . . subordinate to his Father" might bring about a concern that, if translated literally as it is, Christ is subordinate to the Father not only as humanity in both existing and functioning in time but also as deity in the same regards in eternity, even if Willard adds a condition, "in the Oeconomical Dispensation."

This issue, the so-called "Eternal Functional Subordination (EFS)" of the Son to the Father or "Eternal Relations of Authority and Submission (ERAS)," is not just an unnecessary concern at all. Making negative points on the *pactum*, Robert Letham criticizes:

> Furthermore, inevitable problems arise in applying covenant concepts to God. There are two kinds of covenant in the Bible. The first kind is a one-sided imposition. Applied to the relations to the Father and the Son (leaving the Holy Spirit aside!), this would mean *subordination*. The other covenant type is a *quid pro quo*, a voluntary contract between two or more persons. This requires the parties to be autonomous agents. Applied to the Trinity, this type of covenant implies that each person has his own will, entailing something approaching Tritheism. Both of these elements are present in the *pactum salutis*. In short, in constructions like this its compatibility with classic Trinitarian theology is questionable. It veers toward either *subordinationism* or *tritheism*.[26]

---

history in time. In other words, Christology reflects the *pactum* that is both the biblical framework and theological foundation.

24. Willard, *The Doctrine of the Covenant of Redemption*," 27. Italics original.

25. John 14:28 reads, ". . . because the Father is greater than I"; and 10:30, "I and the Father are one." Moreover, Willard is careful to apply Christ's humanity to John 14:28, and Christ's divinity to John 10:30, which indicates so-called "double-hermeneutic." Malcolm Yarnell explains, "The key to understanding the natures of Jesus Christ is to remember that Scripture speaks both of his humanity and of His deity" in the Lecture Note on Christology in Spring 2021. Also, see Fred Sanders, *The Triune God*, NSD (Grand Rapids: Zondervan, 2016), 112-119.

26. Robert Letham, *Systematic Theology* (Wheaton: Crossway, 2019), 435-436, Italics added. The beginning of the vigorous discussion on this issue goes back to 2016 ETS Annual Conference in San Antonio, TX. The interactions through the dialogue and panel discussion on Submission and Subordination in the Trinity happened between

In other words, one necessarily opposes the classic and orthodox teaching of the doctrine of the Trinity and admits subordinationism and tritheism in an attempt to accept the covenantal idea of the *pactum*. In this case, the *pactum* would seem to have no choice but to take its concept from the 'explicit covenants' in the Bible.[27] Such a method of applying the explicit concept of the biblical covenants to the implicit eternal covenant, as Gillespie did, makes an error, which ignores the ontological difference between the Creator and creature with regard to God's transcendence.[28]

Commonly, covenant theologians establish their systematic formulation of the whole Scripture in a twofold covenant frame: the covenants of works and grace. This double covenant method to apprehend the Scripture seems to mirror that the focus of covenant theology lies in the redemption of man by grace and mercy of God rather than the glory of the Godhead himself, though man's redemption leads ultimately to God's glory. Herman Witsius (1636-1708), in a typical manner, follows the format of the double covenant method, putting the *pactum* "within the context of his treatment concerning the covenant of grace."[29] In *The Economy of the Covenants between God and Man* (1677), Witsius deals with the covenant of grace in Book III; however, his covenant of grace has the actual beginning in Book II, which is pertaining to the *pactum* "in order the more thoroughly to understand the nature of the covenant of grace."[30] Thus, highlighting the characteristics in the covenant of grace, Witsius unfolds the nature of the *pactum* focusing on the works of the Son: (1) the beginning of the *pactum*; (2) the law binding the Son; (3) the Son's engagement of the *pactum*; and (4) promised reward to the Son.[31]

Wayne Grudem/Bruce Ware (for EFS) and Millard Erickson/Kevin Giles (against EFS).

27. Jacob Rainwater's paper presented at the 2021 ETS Annual Conference titled "A Sub-Trinitarian Covenant?: The Covenant of Redemption and Divine Simplicity," shows the relation of the *pactum* to the EFS in terms of the will of God and the divine simplicity. Arguing that the *pactum* and the divine simplicity are compatible, Rainwater makes Robert Letham's trinitarian critiques in threefold: (1) multiple wills of the Godhead; (2) applying the concept of covenant into the Godhead; and (3) the exclusion of the Holy Spirit in the *pactum*.

28. Gill's emphasis on the transcendence and sovereignty of God in relation to the doctrine of the *pactum* will be a good argument point enough to correct the Letham's critical assumption on the concept of covenant.

29. See J. Mark Beach, "The Doctrine of the *Pactum Salutis* in the Covenant Theology of Herman Witsius," *MJT* 13 (2002): 121.

30. Witsius, *The Economy of the Covenants*, 165.

31. Witsius, *The Economy of the Covenants*, 177. The first section "the beginning of the *pactum*" that consists of three periods also emphasizes on the Son: (1) its commencement in eternity; (2) its constitution in Christ's intercession; (3) its execution in Christ's incarnation and mediatorial work. See Beach, "The Doctrine of the *Pactum*

Finally, in the twenty-first century, "trying to retrieve and recover classic Reformed covenant theology for the church," John Fesko approaches the *pactum* by the threefold balanced subjects: historical, biblical, and theological.³² In connection with the classic Reformed doctrines, namely the Trinity, predestination, imputation, and *ordo salutis*, Fesko, acknowledging the *pactum* being "the foundation of all of God's activity in time and history" following the previous theologians, navigates important issues pertaining to the *pactum*, e.g., divine will, election, the role of the Holy Spirit, and God's transcendence.³³

Salutis," 127.

32. Fesko, *The Trinity and the Covenant of Redemption*, xx. As Fesko points out, Christians had to wait for almost three hundred years after Samuel Willard's monograph on the *pactum*. See Fesko, *The Covenant of Redemption: Origins, Development, and Reception*, 20-22. The one who broke the silence of the long dark period is Bertus Loonstra who published *Verkiezing - Verzoening - Verbond* (Election - Atonement - Covenant) in 1990. Loonstra contributes to the *pactum* scholarship by examining historical context in bringing up almost every key theologian related to the theological and dogmatic issues on the *pactum*. Fifteen years later, Carol Williams writes "The Decree of Redemption is in Effect a Covenant: David Dickson and the Covenant of Redemption" as a doctoral dissertation in Calvin Theological Seminary in 2005. Williams, in the context of the international Reformed community of federal theology including British and continental, spotlights the development of the divine threefold covenants in the theology of David Dickson (1583-1662) whose formulation of the *pactum* was accepted as orthodoxy for the first time (viii-ix). Especially known for the Speech to the General Assembly against Arminianism, says Carol, Dickson believes: (1) the Father and the Son as parties; (2) the number and names of the elect specified in the pactum; (3) the pactum made in eternity with the Mediator's suretyship before the foundation of the world, and also affirms that the Scripture presupposes the *pactum* in its language and expression (175, 219). Another doctoral dissertation is written by Reita Yazawa in 2013 titled "Covenant of Redemption in the Theology of Jonathan Edwards: the Nexus between the Immanent and Economic Trinity" in Calvin Seminary again. Reita's concern with the work is related to the theological legitimacy or plausibility of the immanent Trinity if it could be examined in Scripture and be applied in the Christian life. It is because the immanent Trinity in eternity is regarded as an abstruse concept in which God's inner trinitarian relationship occurs. In this context, Reita draws the doctrine of the covenant of redemption in the theology of Jonathan Edwards as a valid tool to prove the connection between the immanent Trinity and the economic Trinity in order for the doctrine of the Trinity to be practical in the Christian life. The most recent monograph on the *pactum* comes from the updated version of the dissertation written by B. Hoon Woo titled "The Promise of the Trinity: The Covenant of Redemption in the Theologies of Witsius, Owen, Dickson, Goodwin, and Coccieus" in 2018. His argument is to "demonstrate that the doctrine formulated by Herman Witsius, John Owen, David Dickson, Thomas Goodwin, and Johannes Cocceius can not only overcome modern criticisms, but it can also provide highly practical applications from trinitarian, christological, pneumatological, and soteriological perspectives."

33. Fesko, *The Trinity and the Covenant of Redemption*, 358.

Opponents against the Pactum Salutis

The *Pactum* has not always found favor with theologians. Since the early twentieth century, it has been recognized that the *pactum* hurts the fundamental concept of God, even in the eyes of the Reformed scholars. "This is mythology," asserts Karl Barth, one of the formidable opponents, casting doubt regarding the *pactum*: "Can we really think of the first and second persons of the triune Godhead as two divine subjects and therefore as two legal subjects who can have dealings and enter into obligations one with another?"[34] The *pactum* essentially violates, according to Barth, the doctrine of God because "God is one God" who exists only with one will in the Godhead. In this regard, Keith Loftin agrees, "The idea is that, if a pact between the Father and the Son is postulated, then the logical possibility of a disintegrated divine will–a 'dualism'–is introduced."[35]

O. Palmer Robertson impugns the historical justification of the *pactum* because there is "no specific development in the classic creeds of the Reformers of the sixteenth and seventeenth centuries."[36] Robertson continues with regard to its 'newness' and the biblical evidence:

> A sense of artificiality flavors the effort to structure in covenantal terms the mysteries of God's eternal counsels. Scripture simply does not say much on the pre-creation shape of the decrees of God. To speak concretely of an intertrinitarian "covenant" with terms and conditions between Father and Son mutually endorsed before the foundation of the world is to extend the bounds of scriptural evidence beyond propriety.[37]

As aforementioned in terms of EFS, Robert Letham asserts that the *pactum* necessarily entails a risk of affirming subordinationism and tritheism.[38] He continues to point out that the biblical support of the *pactum* is all

---

34. Barth, *CD*, IV/1: 65.

35. R. Keith Loftin, "A Barthian Critique of the Covenant of Redemption," *TRINJ* 38, no. 2 (2017): 215. Loftin abridges Barth's critique in two categories: (1) "*in abstracto*" objection, which "challenges an orthodox conception of the divine nature by suggesting God is righteous *in abstracto*; (2) "Mythology" objection, which asks a crucial question, "if the will of God is eternally one of perfect unity, whence the need for a covenantal *agreement* in order to accomplish salvation?" See Loftin, 215-216, Italics original.

36. Robertson, *The Christ of the Covenants*, 54.

37. Robertson, *The Christ of the Covenants*, 54.

38. Pertaining to the Letham's criticism on the *pactum*, see Daniel Block's covenant idea on the note 5 and Jacob Rainwater's explanation on the note 27 above regarding the application of the concept and definition of the biblical covenants into the *pactum*. In other words, if Block's two types of the concept of biblical covenants, i.e., parity and disparity, are applied to the *pactum*, it causes two serious problems in the doctrine of

concerned with the incarnate Christ focusing on his works, which naturally results in the exclusion of the Holy Spirit.[39] Letham also catches a subtle nuance of the term 'covenant' itself, in which the *pactum* does not reflect the real meaning of a covenant in the Bible: "The focus of the *pactum salutis* on contractual agreement misses the heart of what God's covenant is about. Such a construction generally overlooks the point that central to the covenant is the promise of living fellowship, communion, and union."[40]

Herman Hoeksema approaches the *pactum* from a slightly different perspective. When he investigates the biblical evidence supporting the *pactum*, he finds all of them are related to the Christ, who is "the Servant of Jehovah" or "the head of the elect," not the Son, who is equal to the Father and the Holy Spirit in essence as the *pactum*'s definition indicates regarding the parties.[41] For Hoeksema, the point of criticism is the distinction between the divine nature and the human nature of the Son as a party of the *pactum*, in accordance with which there comes about two kinds of relationship: (1) the counsel of peace, or the *pactum*; (2) the covenant with Christ as the Servant of Jehovah. Thus, Hoeksema extrapolates no root of the *pactum* based on the biblical examination.[42]

God: (1) when the parity concept of a covenant is applied to the *pactum*, it results in a subordination of the Son to the Father in eternity, which violates the co-equal status of the three persons in the Godhead; (2) when the disparity concept of a covenant is applied to the *pactum*, each agent of the covenant to fulfill the conditions necessarily has a will, and it results in the error of tritheism, which also violates the one will in the Godhead. Thus, it is important to understand the concept of the biblical covenants in relation to the *pactum*. Letham makes this point directly in his other works as well, "... strong elements of subordinationism were introduced in the case of the Son. Tritheistic tendencies have also been noted." Robert Letham, *The Work of Christ: Contours of Christian Theology* (Downers Grove: IVP, 1993), 53. Also, see Robert Letham, *The Holy Trinity: In Scripture, History, Theology, and Worship* (Phillipsburg, NJ: P&R, 2004), 377-406; *Union with Christ: In Scripture, History, and Theology* (Phillipsburg, NJ: P&R, 2011), 64-65.

39. Letham, *Systematic Theology*, 436.

40. Letham, *Systematic Theology*, 437.

41. See Herman Hoeksema, *Reformed Dogmatics* (Grand Rapids: Reformed Free Publishing Association, 1966), 285-336. "Without exception," says Hoeksema, the biblical passages as proof for the *pactum* "refer to the covenant which God establishes with Christ as the Head of the elect."

42. However, one may wonder if Hoeksema fully denies the *pactum* because he mentions: "And He is the God of the covenant, not according to a decree or according to an agreement or pact, but according to His very divine Nature and Essence ... A God that is lonely does not know Himself and love Himself, does not live and is not blessed, is a cold and dead abstraction. But God is One in Being and Three in Persons: Father, Son, and Holy Spirit. And as the Triune God, He is the living God, Who lives the infinitely perfect covenant life in Himself." Hoeksema, *Reformed Dogmatics*, 319. In this regard, Steven Baugh is interested in Hoeksema's standpoints in twofold: (1)

Biblical Evidence of the Pactum Salutis

That the idea of the *pactum* lies in the Bible implicitly means that a specific verse or an explicit biblical passage does not draw a clear picture of the *pactum*.[43] Thus, it is quite important to infer the legitimate biblical passages altogether for the *pactum*, which dots the landscape of the whole Scripture with regard to covenantal redemptive history. Knowing this character of the *pactum*, Bavinck, who affirms the biblical root of the *pactum*, begins the logical verification of the theological process of the Son's being a Mediator with the relevant biblical passages. Mentioning defects of the typical biblical passages of the *pactum*, Bavinck shows the *pactum* is permeated in the redemptive work of the Triune God in the whole narrative of the Bible, especially focusing on the role of Christ.[44]

As Hoeksema points out above, however, the supportive passages of the *pactum* need to be identified to see whether they belong to the *pactum* or the "covenant with Christ in human nature," though with a slightly different meaning. In other words, one needs to answer the questions, "Do the biblical evidence of the *pactum* suggested by covenant theologians belong to eternity or time? How does one distinguish if the evidence is concerned with eternity or time? What is the relationship of eternity to time with regard to the *pactum*?"

RESEARCH QUESTIONS

Ever since the sixteenth century, as the short theological survey on the *pactum* above demonstrates, the doctrine of the *pactum* has been largely formulated and developed in and through the Reformed theological camp,

---

Hoeksema's investigation of the biblical evidence rather "substantiate the *pactum salutis* to be correct in many cases; (2) Hoeksema emphasizes on the three persons of the Godhead in understanding the *pactum* "rather than in his unity." Baugh, therefore, says, "Hoeksema does not thereby reject the *pactum salutis* but arrives at it by deduction from the doctrine of the triune character of God." See S. M. Baugh, "Galatians 3:20 and the Covenant of Redemption," *WTJ* 66, no. 1 (2004): 50-51. For more biblical explanation of the criticism on the *pactum*, see Paul R. Williamson, "The *Pactum Salutis*: A Scriptural Concept or Scholastic Mythology?" *TB* 69, no. 2 (2018): 259-281.

43. The major passages of the *pactum* by the covenant scholars are as follows: Psalm 2:7, 89:3-4, 110; Isaiah 59:20-21; Zechariah 6:13; Luke 22:29; John 17; Galatians 3:17; Ephesians 1; 2 Timothy 1:9-10; Hebrews 7:22.

44. Bavinck, *Reformed Dogmatics*, vol. 3, 213-214. Regarding the defect, for example, Bavinck brings up one of the most classic texts Zechariah 6:13 which "does not prove anything and only states that the Messiah, who unites in his person both the kingship and the priesthood, will consider and promote the peace of his people."

and the argument is still in the process, regardless of whether agreed or disagreed. However, it is not just regarding the *pactum* itself, but it is all about the grand narrative and the picture of the whole Bible described and explained by the biblical concept of a covenant, which has been worked on and investigated by the Reformed theological framework. If God, as Hoeksema asserts, is the covenant God in Himself, and the Bible is colored by the various covenantal images, there is no reasonable cause for the Baptists to be excluded by the rich benefit of the biblical covenant theology whose fundamental foundation is found in the doctrine of the *pactum*.[45]

Another inquiry comes with the locus and function of the *pactum* in the Reformed theological frame. The logical threefold covenantal system, i.e., redemption, works, and grace, has been a characteristic of the Reformed covenantal structure in which the *pactum* largely plays a role as the foundation of the covenant of grace. Do the Reformed covenantal threefold frame and the foundational function of the *pactum*, in particular, describe the *pactum* in the most effective and appropriate manner in the whole covenantal system of the Bible? Is it fine to say that the *pactum* has just a notion of the foundation theoretically and metaphysically and as the "supplement" for a better explanation of the nature of the covenant of grace?

COVENANTAL UNIQUENESS OF JOHN GILL

Though following traditional Calvinism in terms of theology, in consideration of the research questions above, Gill's systematic theology is not in line with the Reformed threefold covenantal frame in setting up his own *pactum* structure. The first unique point of Gill's covenantal theology comes with the one covenant of redemption, which embraces both realms, i.e., eternity and time, through his unique definition of the *pactum* in the everlasting council and the everlasting covenant of grace. Chapter three below will go deep into Gill's concept of the *pactum*.

Secondly, the energetically positive acknowledgment regarding the role of the Holy Spirit in the *pactum* as an active party with the Father and the Son is another unique point of his covenantal system. Contrary to most preceding covenant theologians, especially to the Reformed, Gill argued for the *pactum* defined and formulated by the three divine persons in the Godhead, not just made by the Father and the Son. Finding the role of the Holy Spirit participating in the *pactum* as a legitimate party through the biblical narrative and the theological inference reinforces the fact that the *pactum* is not fabricated by the wrong understanding of the Trinity; rather,

---

45. See note 42 above.

the *pactum* is a biblical doctrine based on the orthodox trinitarian theology in Christian history.

THESIS

John Gill, an eighteenth-century particular Baptist pastor, and theologian, unfolds his covenant-centered theological system based on a strong biblical foundation.[46] In Gill's system, the concept of the *pactum* is never limited to the Reformed threefold frame. Rather, Gill's *pactum* takes control of every part of the biblical narrative and the theological flow by occupying the central locus of the redemptive history of the Bible.

This volume attempts to demonstrate that John Gill's covenant of redemption plays a critical role, occupying a central locus in his systematic theology, with time and eternity carefully related to the various loci, especially the doctrine of God (the Trinity), Christology, and soteriology.

METHOD

John Rippon, reflecting on Gill's *A Body of Doctrinal Divinity* [Hereafter, *Divinity*] (1767), writes two short but important words, "Here is the Doctor's whole *creed*" and "He has *his* SYSTEM."[47] Gill's theological system in *Divinity* is exquisite and meticulous in its conviction of the doctrine of the Trinity based on strong biblical expositions. Thus, this work pursues the central locus and function of the *pactum* in *Divinity* while examining other key doctrines, which include the doctrine of eternity, the doctrine of God (the Trinity), Christology, and soteriology (eternal justification) with reference mainly to Gill's *The Doctrine of the Trinity, An Exposition of the Old and New Testaments*, and to Gill's other writings.

Gill's understanding of the simplicity, attributes, persons, and nature of God revealed in Scripture is organically linked to the acts and works of the immanent God. The works of the Triune God in eternity regarding man's redemption in Christ are manifested in the covenantal redemptive history in Christ as well. The *pactum* in Gill's system plays a central role in man's redemption in both time and eternity. With this notion in mind, this volume will explore each of Gill's major doctrines, i.e., the doctrine of God,

---

46. It is well known: (1) John Gill served a Baptist church for over fifty years as a pastor; (2) John Gill was the first Baptist theologian who wrote and completed the verse-by-verse commentary of the whole Bible.

47. John Rippon, *A Brief Memoir of the Life and Writings of the late Rev. John Gill* (London: John Bennett, 1838), 96-97. Emphases original.

Christology, and soteriology, in order to demonstrate how the *pactum* is organically related to other doctrines, effectively shaping the understanding of redemptive history in Gill's theological system.

OVERVIEW OF CHAPTERS

Chapter 2 will serve as a presuppositional chapter of the whole work by providing Gill's theological frame of time and eternity in the *pactum*. First, the three theological types of eternity will delimit what one understands in terms of eternity. Then, based on Gill's definition of eternity, i.e., without beginning, end, and succession, the rest of the chapter will show the transcendent and sovereign feature of eternity compared to time, through which Gill unfolds the eternal covenant in connection with the nature and existence of God.

Chapter 3 will explore Gill's unique understanding of the *pactum*, the everlasting council, the everlasting covenant of grace, and its relation to a covenant. This chapter delivers two key ideas: one is the distinct character of Gill's *pactum*. Gill pictures the *pactum* in working the overall redemption of man in time and eternity rather than treating it as a part of the redemptive counsel. The other is the "Will" issue in operating as three persons in one essence of the Godhead. Will, person, and nature are inseparable from one another. The investigation of the relations will lead one to a reasonable conclusion of the will issue for the *pactum*. In addition, the Holy Spirit is not excluded in Gill's *pactum*. Rather, man's "redemption" in time and eternity is impossible without the approbation and application of the Holy Spirit.

Chapter 4 will examine Gill's understanding of the doctrine of the Trinity with regard to its unity and plurality. God's being in one nature and three persons in the Godhead, as Gill says, is the utmost mystery to man. The purpose of this chapter is to investigate the relationship between God's inner being that exists in three persons in one nature and the working of the *pactum*. In making and formulating the *pactum* within the eternal and immanent Triune God, scholars perceive a potentiality that the Son is subordinated to the Father because of the inherent characteristic of the *pactum* by its definition and function, especially the term Son and Father. Gill establishes the perfect harmony and coequalness for the three persons to work for the *pactum*. Through this logical process, the *pactum* reveals the perfect being of God in three persons and one nature, who is a pure act. Finally, this chapter deals with the unique issue of the eternal justification of Gill and its relation to the *pactum* in view of the soteriology.

Chapter 5 will show that Christ is the substantive locus not only for election before the foundation of the world, which becomes the object of the *pactum* but also for the manifestation of the *pactum* in the redemptive history. Gill offers four categories regarding the role of the Son in the *pactum*. By the four major functions of the Son, Gill shows that Christ embodies the *pactum* in time, is directly connected to what happens in the temporal redemption of man, and involves himself in history by incarnation, life, death, and resurrection.

Finally, chapter 6 will conclude the central locus of the *pactum* in Gill's covenantal redemptive system by reflecting on Gill's contribution to Baptist theology and church life.

CHAPTER 2

Time and Eternity According to John Gill

THE DOCTRINE OF THE *pactum* necessarily considers the concept of eternity. Gill's *pactum* is not an exception, functioning as a grand presupposition in Gill's covenantal theological system with specific regard to his understanding of the *pactum*. Eternity, in Gill's system, does not exist or remain notional due to his high view of theology, i.e., eternity does not derive from its own abstract idea but from God's attributes, in particular, his infinity.[1]

Though the concept of eternity plays such a crucial role in the doctrine of the *pactum*, at least in Gill's system, the Bible does not appear to draw a clear picture of or articulate a lucid concept of eternity.[2] Two terms עוֹלָם ("olam") and αἰών ("aion") are well known in the Old and New Testaments [OT, NT] usage to deliver the meaning of eternity, which indicates "long time," "farthest, remotest time," and "an indefinite past or future,"

---

1. In addition to the eternal aspect of God, from the perspective of God's attribute of divine simplicity, it is beautiful to see how Gill's whole theological system is based on God himself. In other words, the Triune God is the unique presupposition for Gill to unfold his system. Thus, it seems that it is not an overstatement to aver that the Book I of Gill's *Divinity*, which is all about God's character and attributes along with the unity and personal relations in the Triune God, already embodies what is later to be unfolded as an actualization of each doctrinal statement.

2. Douglas Estes, "Eternity," in *The Encyclopedia of Christian Civilization*, vol. II, ed. George Thomas Kurian (Chichester, West Sussex: Wiley-Blackwell, 2009), states "The Bible never discusses or defines eternity, and the various concepts used to describe eternity in the original languages are poetic not explanatory." Also, see James Barr, *Biblical Words for Time*, Revised Edition (Naperville, IL: Alec R. Allenson, 1969), 138, who expresses "the very serious shortage within the Bible of the kind of *actual statement* about 'time' or 'eternity' which could form a sufficient basis for a Christian philosophical-theological view of time."

"extended" or "uninterrupted time," according to which eternity is qualitatively reckoned to be a kind of time.³ Do these meanings of eternity from the biblical terms solely imply that eternity belongs to the concept of time, which signifies unlimited, unending, or everlasting duration of time?⁴ In other words, does the concept of eternity only reside in the realm of time?⁵

3. See Neuendettelsau H. D. Preuss, "עוֹלָם," *TDOT*, ed. G. Johannes Botterweck, Helmer Ringgren, and Heinz-Josef Fabry, trans. Douglas W. Stott, 15 vols. (Grand Rapids: Eerdmans, 1999), 10:531; Hermann Sasse, "αἰών, αἰώνιος," *TDNT*, ed. Gerhard Kittel, trans. Geoffrey W. Bromiley, 10 vols. (1964; repr. Grand Rapids: Eerdmans, 2006), 1:198. Preuss also explains that the plural use of עֹלָם itself denotes "periods of time, ages." More interesting is that עֹלָם in making construct combinations with other terms such as love, possessions, covenant, makes an emphasis of "the highest possible intensification" in those expressions. Preuss also asserts that this typical role of עוֹלָם by "amplification and intensification" is found even in an extra-biblical source, i.e., Qumran writings. See Preuss, "עוֹלָם," 532, 544. Sasse also mentions, while seeing the concept of αἰών is "in the sense of prolonged time," the plural usage of αἰών is indicated to "emphasise the idea of eternity which is contained but often blurred in the sing. αἰών." Sasse brings εἰς τοὺς αἰῶνας to support the idea of emphasis in Matt 6:13; Lk 1:33; Rom 1:25, 9:5, 11:36; 2 Cor 11:31; and Heb 13:8. See Sasee, "αἰών, αἰώνιος," 199. Besides עוֹלָם, which means "a period of time that either stretches into the far past or far future," there are more terms to indicate eternity in the OT: (1) עַד ("ad"), which says lasting time or forever, emphasizing the length of 'forever'; (2) נֶצַח ("nechakh"), describing "the quality of something as eternal or enduring"; (3) קֶדֶם ("qedem"), meaning "ancient past" that shows "a time period in the past that was long ago, even possibly before creation; and (4) דּוֹר ("dor"), which does not indicate eternity by itself because it literally means generation, that is, "the span of time in a line of descent from parent to child (usually about 30 years). However, דּוֹר denotes long periods of time or eternity sometimes as in Gen 17:7. In the NT, except αἰών and αἰώνιος, a few more terms indicate eternity: (1) διηνεκής ("dienekes"), referring to the "eternal quality of something"; (2) ἀΐδιος ("aidios") "describes a continuing period of time." See J. A. McGuire-Moushon and Rachel Klippenstein, "Eternity," *The Lexham Theological Wordbook*, ed. Douglas Mangum, Derek R. Brown, Rachel Klippenstein, and Rebekah Hurst (Bellingham, WA: Lexham, 2014). Also, see Garrett J. DeWeese, *God and the Nature of Time* (Burlington, VT: Ashgate, 2004), 96-104; Henri Blocher, "Yesterday, Today, Forever: Time, Times, Eternity in Biblical Perspective," *Tyndale Bulletin* 52, no. 2 (2001): 186.

4. A definition goes with the concept, "Eternity is not the sum of all the individual periods, nor even this sum with something added to it; it is 'time' without subdivision, that which lies behind it, and which displays itself through all times." Johannes Pedersen, *Israel: Its Life and Culture*, vols. I-II (Oxford University Press, 1926), 491. Robert Yarbrough also supports, "The Old Testament does not seem to conceive of eternity in purely abstract terms, as a static state of timelessness . . . The Old Testament, then, encourage us to define eternity in terms of the duration of the revealed God's dealings with his people in times past, now, and always." Robert W. Yarbrough, "Eternal Life, Eternality, Everlasting Life," *Evangelical Dictionary of Biblical Theology*, ed. Walter A. Elwell (Grand Rapids: Baker Books, 1996), 209-10.

5. It appears that the understanding of eternity in the biblical terms in relation to the realm of time stems from the Hebrew thought and mindset of time and history, which regards time as "realistic and existential." Eric Rust, contrasting the Greek

The traditional and theological trajectory of the concept of eternity in Christian history has been pertaining to the attributes of God, e.g., divine immutability and simplicity, which has also caused complicated issues of the relationship between God and time. The argument that God is timeless has had significant implications in terms of God's ontological characteristics, such as who He is and His relation to the creatures. With regard to both the discrepancy and correlation between time and eternity, Antjie Jackelen provides three short but well-organized models of theological consideration concerning time and eternity: ontological, quantitative, and eschatological.[6] Thus, this chapter, prior to the explication of Gill's understanding of eternity, will briefly deal with these three theological models of eternity based on Jackelen's framework, which will establish the comprehensive conceptions and substratum for Gill's doctrine of eternity. A lot more ink will be spilled regarding the ontological model, which has well over one thousand years been the traditional position in church history and still has quite a few proponents, though some have been modified in various modes compared to the other two models.[7]

THEOLOGICAL CONCEPT OF ETERNITY IN THREE MODELS

Throughout human history, whether Christian or secular, the study of eternity has been one of the most fascinating topics in the fields of religion, philosophy, science, and so forth. What, then, is an understanding of eternity in Christian theology? In this section, the study goes back to the fourth century, through the Middle Ages, and to contemporary times so

---

view of time, reality, and God, explicates, "The Hebrew did not indulge in metaphysical speculation, nor did he believe that primarily a man could know ultimate reality by penetrating the deeps of becoming on the basis of logical processes of thought. The ultimate reality was hidden by the processes of time, and man's reason, misdirected by sin, was insufficient for him by searching to find out God." Rust continues regarding God's self-revelation, "At certain points of time, however, God had disclosed himself redeemingly. Such self-disclosures were acts of grace to which a man or a nation must respond in penitence and obedient faith." Eric C. Rust, "Time and Eternity in Biblical Thought," *Theology Today* 10, no. 3 (1953): 329. This approach, ironically, to the aspect of God's transcendence and the reality of time suggests that eternity in relation to God's attributes cannot be in the realm of time.

6. Antjie Jackelen, "Where Time and Eternity Meet," *Dialog* 39, no. 1 (2000): 15-20.

7. See Paul Helm, *Eternal God: A Study of God without Time* (Oxford: Clarendon Press, 1988); Brian Leftow, *Time and Eternity* (Ithaca, NY: Cornell University Press, 1991); William Lane Craig, *Time and Eternity: Exploring God's Relationship to Time* (Wheaton: Crossway, 2001).

as to briefly investigate the trajectory of eternity by looking into the related works of the major theologians.

Ontological Model

Jackelen terms the first model "ontological," whose notion is found in chapter eleven of Augustine's (354-430) *Confessions*, which indicates "time and eternity are essentially different from each other."[8] However, Augustine was not the only person who argued for the qualitative antithesis between time and eternity, which has a connection with the idea that God is timeless. The line of thought in this traditional view has flowed in a strong conjunction from Augustine to Boethius, Anselm, and Aquinas in church history.[9]

---

8. Jackelen, "Where Time and Eternity Meet," 18.

9. Throughout the history, the church has defended the timelessness of God even before Augustine. Peter Sammons expands the historical affirmation concerning eternity in understanding timelessness from the first century to the Middle Ages by listing some significant figures: Ignatius of Antioch, Justin Martyr, Clement of Alexandria, Irenaeus of Lyons, Tertullian, Cyril of Jerusalem, and Hilary of Poitiers. Interesting is Sammons' description of Justin Martyr who claimed that "the Greek philosophers owed much of their understanding [of the eternality of God] to Moses and the 'ancient Christian teachers.'" Sammons continues, "When Scripture says of God, 'I am the first,' and 'there is no other,' Martyr explains, 'But either of the expressions seems to apply to the ever-existent God. For He is the only one who eternally exists, and has no generation.'" See Peter Sammons, "The Eternal God of a Vanishing Creation: Recovering the Doctrine of Divine Timelessness," *TMSJ* 31, no. 2 (2020): 201-7. Justin Martyr's remark is both interesting and meaningful because the biblical and theological concept of eternity as timelessness has been criticized, claiming that the idea of timelessness does not derive from the Bible directly but originally from the Greek such as Plato and Plotinus. For example, in his *Timaeus*, Plato contrasts the unchanging eternality with the changeable and becoming world in time, which indicates time is a created thing. Plotinus delineating eternity as "unchanging life, all together at once, already infinite, completely unswerving," also contrasts time with eternity, "time and/or the soul always wants something more explained why it's never complete, never really what it is, but always one-thing-after-another. Eternity, by contrast, is already precisely what it is, and therefore has nothing further to seek for. Whereas eternity is the satisfied repose of something that already is all that can be, already possessing, all at once, everything it could ever desire, time is the headlong, endless pursuit of something more, since by definition it cannot possess everything it desires all at once." Michael Chase, "Time and Eternity From Plotinus and Boethius to Einstein," *Schole Ancient Philosophy and the Classical Tradition* 8, no. 1 (2014): 75-76. With regard to a Christian understanding of time and eternity by the Greek Fathers and Patristics, i.e., Saint Gregory of Nyssa, Saint Basil the Great, Saint Maximus the Confessor, and Saint John of Damascus, which was unlike the human Greek philosophers, see Michael Azkoul, "On Time and Eternity: The Nature of History According to the Greek Fathers," *St Vladimir's Seminary Quarterly* 12, no. 2 (1968): 56-77.

What, then, is time and eternity for Augustine? The kernel of Augustine's elucidation concerning the relation of time to eternity comes with unfolding the origin and foundation of creation. The ontological difference between the transcendent, immutable creator God and the temporal, transient creation explains time belongs to creation: "You created all times and you exist before all times. Nor was there any time when time did not exist."[10]

Regarding the concept of time, the inquiry "What was God doing before he made heaven and earth?" leads Augustine, more than just "You have made time itself," to deeply consider what time is.[11] Though Augustine has difficulty articulating the concept of time, he says, "But I confidently affirm myself to know that if nothing passes away, there is no past time, and if nothing arrives, there is no future time, and if nothing existed there would be no present time."[12] Such a flowing, passing notion describing the relations among past, present, and future characterizes the concept of time, based upon which Augustine answers rather by asking a question,

> You are the originator and creator of all ages. What times existed which were not brought into being by you? Or how could they pass if they never had existence? ... But if time did not exist before heaven and earth, why do people ask what you were then doing? There was no 'then' when there was no time.[13]

---

10. Saint Augustine, *Confessions*, trans. Henry Chadwick (Oxford University Press, 2009), 11.13.16. Timothy George stating what Augustine means by "God created the world not *in* time but *with* time," explicates, "If Augustine was original in positing the cocreation of time and the world, he was entirely traditional as a Christian in affirming the doctrine of creation out of nothing–*ex nihilo*–and *de nouveau*. For him this meant that neither time nor space could constitute a first principle alongside God." See Timothy George, "St. Augustine and the Mystery of Time," in *What God Knows: Time, Eternity, and Divine Knowledge*, ed. Harry Lee Poe and J. Stanley Mattson (Waco, TX: Baylor University Press, 2005), 38.

11. Augustine, *Confessions*, 11.13.15.

12. Augustine, *Confessions*, 11.14.17.

13. Augustine, *Confessions*, 11.13.15. The veiled criticism in the original question, "What was God doing before he made the heaven and earth?" implies the reasoning that "if he [God] was at rest, there was no reason for him not to continue resting. If from all eternity he had planned to create, then why isn't creation itself eternal, and why didn't he create before he did?" Thus, this criticism attempts, ultimately, to draw a conclusion that God is not eternal. John Feinberg well abstracts Augustine's point, "It [the question] is ill-founded because it doesn't recognize a difference between time and eternity and that God is eternal. Thus, the idea that God might not intend to create, and then later decides to create, is based on thinking that God's existence involves temporal succession. Once one recognizes that God is eternal and that there is no past or future in eternity, one sees that it makes no sense to talk of God not willing something 'for a certain amount of time' and then 'beginning to will it' at a later 'time.'" See John S. Feinberg, *No One Like Him: The Doctrine of God*, Foundations of Evangelical Theology

It is natural for Augustine to draw such an outcome when considering the concept of time because time and eternity share no common dimension or realm. While mentioning the Word in John 1:1, Augustine portrays the dominant feature of eternity: "It is not the case that what was being said comes to an end, and something else is then said so that everything is uttered in a succession with a conclusion, but everything is said in the simultaneity of eternity."[14] There can be no comparison between time and eternity because time is "constituted of many successive movements which cannot be simultaneously extended. In the eternal, nothing is transient, but the whole is present. But no time is wholly present."[15] Ultimately, Augustine's concept of eternity is inextricably linked to who God is in His divine perfection manifested by His unique attributes: divine transcendence and immutability.

The next person who is in line with Augustine regarding the concept of eternity is Anicius Manlius Severinus Boethius (480-524), whose celebrated definition of eternity still reverberates: "*Eternity, then, is the complete, simultaneous and perfect possession of everlasting life*; this will be clear from a comparison with creatures that exist in time."[16] Boethius more clearly ex-

---

(Wheaton: Crossway, 2001), 380.

14. Augustine, *Confessions*, 11.7.9.

15. Augustine, *Confessions*, 11.11.13. In other words, the difference between the transient created entities and the unchanging perfection of the creator clearly manifests "God is free from modification and free from distension, and thus epitomizes the tranquil rest that temporal creatures strive for yet never find on their own." See William W. Young III, "Toward an inclusive conception of eternity," *International Journal for Philosophy of Religion* 89, no. 2 (2021): 175. God's divine perfection does not allow any successive movements in His intrinsic nature. Thus, in order for "the whole is present" to make happen there needs no successive movements, i.e., divine immutability, which means "For God to be immutable in His being, Augustine thinks, He must be capable of directly knowing the whole of the past and the future all at once and this cannot be done temporally but eternally." Hyo-Nam Kim, "Eternal God and Temporal World: The Reformed Understanding of Divine Affections as an Evidence of Eternal God Walking in the Temporal World," *Korea Reformed Theology* 59 (2018): 180.

16. Boethius, *The Consolation of Philosophy*, trans. Victor Watts, Revised Edition (London: Penguin Books, 1999), 5.6. Italics added for emphasis. Regarding an inquiry concerning the 'everlasting life' in Boethius' definition whether it could have a kind of 'duration,' Paul Helm asserts, "Boethius says that this life, in God, is illimitable, and this means not, . . . , eternal duration, but a property modifying the other attributes of God – his power, goodness, wisdom, knowledge, and so forth. Each of these attributes is illimitable. Boethius, . . . , seems to be contrasting the possession all at once of illimitable life and the possession in temporal sequence or series of illimitable life . . . So what Boethius appears to be saying is that nothing in time can be illimitable in character. Hence this aspect of Boethius' definition has nothing to do with duration, and his definition does not require the introduction of the idea of eternal duration at any point." Helm, *Eternal God*, 39-40.

plains what he means by the definition of eternity in the conceptual contrast with the world or finite things:

> Its life may be infinitely long, but it does not embrace and comprehend its whole extent simultaneously. It still lacks the future, while already having lost the past. So that that which embraces and possesses simultaneously the whole fullness of everlasting life, which lacks nothing of the future and has lost nothing of the past, that is what may properly be said to be eternal.[17]

Boethius's concept of eternity is basically caused by being "overwhelmed by the problem of reconciling God's foreknowledge with man's free will."[18] In other words, the dilemma goes with these two questions, "How does foreknowledge surely know things that have not happened yet?" and "How does it make sense that dubious things are to be logically necessary?"[19] As a resolution, Boethius asserts that the notion of eternal presence that embraces "the complete, simultaneous and perfect possession" is "a far better definition of Providence than 'foreknowledge of the future'; it is 'a looking forth rather than a looking forward.'"[20] Boethius explains,

> God sees those future events which happen of free will as present events; so that these things when considered with reference to God's sight of them do happen necessarily as a result of the condition of divine knowledge; but when considered in themselves they do not lose the absolute freedom of their nature. All things, therefore, whose future occurrence is known to God do without doubt happen, but some of them are the result of free will.[21]

---

17. Boethius, *Consolation*, 5.6.

18. Frank Herbert Brabant, *Time and Eternity in Christian Thought: Being Eight Lectures Delivered before the University of Oxford, in the Year 1936, on the Foundation of the Rev. John Bampton, Canon of Salisbury* (London: Longmans, Green, 1937), 63. Boethius' question about the foreknowledge and free will happens in prose three of the *Consolation*. For further explication on Boethius' problem, see Michael D. Robinson, *Eternity and Freedom: A Critical Analysis of Divine Timelessness as a Solution to the Foreknowledge/Free Will Debate* (Lanham, MD: University Press of America, 1995), 28-31.

19. Robinson, *Eternity and Freedom*, 31.

20. Brabant, *Time and Eternity in Christian Thought*, 65.

21. Boethius, *Consolation*, 5.6. Feinberg's explanation well supports Boethius, so it is worth quoting in length: "He sees all of time at once; it is all there before him just as a whole parade is entirely in view of someone standing atop a mountain near the parade route. Things that are past, present, or future from our perspective, are all within God's view. This allows God to know what is future to us, but since all of this is present from his perspective, Boethius thought there really is no problem of *fore*knowledge

In this regard, therefore, Boethius is at least in the same line with Augustine's concept of eternity, which claims the ontological qualitative difference between time and eternity, though his manner of approaching eternity is a little different from Augustine's in terms of resolving the issue of foreknowledge and man's free will.

The third advocate of the ontological model of time and eternity, Anselm of Canterbury (1033-1109), begins with the so-called 'ontological argument' for God's existence in *Proslogion* in discussing eternity, which is known as his theological method: "something-than-which-a-greater-cannot-be-thought."[22] For Anselm, "the perfection of God" through the ontological argument for God's existence becomes the foundation to unfold God's attributes.[23] In the case of eternity, Anselm connects God's ontological definition to eternity:

> All that which is enclosed in any way by place or time is less than that which no law of place or time constrains. Since, then, nothing is greater than You, no place or time confines You but You exist everywhere and always. And because this can be said of You alone, You alone are unlimited and eternal.[24]

Anselm also pictures God's perfection clearly manifested by his simplicity in relation to God's eternity: "Since, then, neither You nor Your eternity which You are have parts, no part of You or of Your eternity is anywhere

---

and freedom. The future is still open from our perspective. This is so, in part at least, because what God knows doesn't cause anything to happen. Moreover, since we don't know what he knows about our future, we cannot be driven by that information when we make our choices in the future." Feinberg, *No One Like Him*, 742. Helen Barrett also helps, "The cardinal mistake men make in wrestling with the problem of Foreknowledge and Freedom is to forget the part which the knower's mind itself contributes to knowing, and to imagine that the Divine intelligence is confined within the limits of human capacity . . . Eternity is something quite other than perpetuity, duration, endlessness, and because God is eternal, because His knowledge is not conditioned as man's is by time, He has 'all-at-once' . . . What for man is successive for Him is simultaneous, what man experiences as past, present and future lies unrolled before the Divine intelligence as a changeless, eternal present." Helen M. Barrett, *Boethius: Some Aspects of his Times and Work* (New York: Russell & Russell, 1965), 100.

22. Saint Anselm, *St. Anselm's Proslogion with A Reply on Behalf of the Fool by Gaunilo and The Author's Reply to Gaunilo*, trans. M. J. Charlesworth (Notre Dame: University of Notre Dame, 1979), 2.

23. See Katherin A. Rogers, "Anselmian Eternalism: The Presence of a Timeless God," *Faith and Philosophy* 24, no. 1 (2007): 5. Mentioning Anselm's methodology of 'ontological argument' in *Proslogion*, Rogers says, "In analyzing the relationship of God to creation, and eternity to time, the starting point is the perfection of God, and the method is to unpack that concept."

24. Anselm, *St. Anselm's Proslogion*, 13.

or at any time, but You exist as a whole everywhere and Your eternity exists as a whole always."[25]

Moreover, one of the most apparent explications concerning the divine timelessness in *Proslogion* comes with contrasting eternity with time:

> You were not, therefore, yesterday, nor will You be tomorrow, but yesterday and today and tomorrow You *are*. Indeed You exist neither yesterday nor today nor tomorrow but are absolutely outside all time. For yesterday and today and tomorrow are completely in time; however, You, though nothing can be without You, are nevertheless not in place or time but all things are in You. For nothing contains You, but You contain all things.[26]

While placing emphasis on the absolute qualitative difference between time and eternity ("absolutely outside all time"), Anselm draws attention to the point that all things are contained in God, who is eternal. Does this mean that God must also be in all things so as to contain all things in himself? Such a question might arise because Anselm, in his first philosophical writing, *Monologion*, states, "The supreme nature exists in everything that exists, just as much as it exists in every place."[27] Rogers, however, replies that God "is 'in' no places or times if by 'in' we mean He is limited to a given place or time as spatio-temporal creatures are."[28] This concept of eternity that contains all time is well described not as God's 'must-be-in-things' but as 'eternal present' in his late work *De Concordia*:

> For in eternity a thing has no past or future but only an (eternal) present, though in the realm of time things move from past to future without any contradiction arising... Moreover, although in eternity there is only a present, nevertheless it is not a temporal present as ours is, only an eternal one in which all periods of

---

25. Anselm, *St. Anselm's Proslogion*, 18. In this regard, the conceptions of both God's perfection and simplicity cannot be thought as separated. Being 'perfect' necessarily entails no lacking, changing as well as no dividing by parts, which indicates the idea of simplicity. To look further on Anselm's understanding of the divine simplicity with regard to time and eternity, see DeWeese, *God and the Nature of Time*, 145-51.

26. Anselm, *St. Anselm's Proslogion*, 19.

27. Saint Anselm, "Monologion," in *Anselm of Canterbury: The Major Works*, ed. Brian Davies and G. R. Evans (Oxford: Oxford University Press, 2008), 23. For more on temporal omnipresence in *Monologion*, see Leftow, *Time and Eternity*, 203-9.

28. Rogers, "Anselmian Eternalism," 5. Rogers continues, "It is quite impossible that God should exist wholly at a single time, since He is simple and hence His being and His life are identical," and cites *Monologion* 20, "His eternity is nothing other than His very self... if His eternity has a past, present, and future, it would follow that His very being has a past, present, and future." The translation is Rogers' own.

time are contained. Indeed, just as our present time envelops every place and whatever is in every place, so in the eternal present all time is encompassed along with whatever exists at any time ... For eternity has its own unique simultaneity which contains both all things that happen at the same time and place and that happen at different times and places.[29]

For Anselm, therefore, the eternal present is manifest in the fact that no temporal succession is allowed in eternity because God is simple and the life of God has no past, present, and future as man has, i.e., for God, "every event is present, all at once."[30]

Finally, Thomas Aquinas (1225-1274) inherits the time-eternity antithesis and divine timelessness in line with Augustine, Boethius, and Anselm. Particularly, the so-called Boethian formula for the concept of eternity makes a deep impact on setting Aquinas' structure up on eternity in his writings, e.g., *Summa Theologiae* and *Compendium Theologiae*.[31] Taking a negative method in dealing with the time-eternity relationship pertaining to the attributes of God, Aquinas in *Summa Theologiae* begins with the concept of time as "the *numbering of before and after in change*" from Aristotle's *Physics*.[32] More focusing on the attributes of God rather than the interrelation between time and eternity, Aquinas grasps eternity in terms of divine immutability:

---

29. Saint Anselm, "De Concordia: The Compatibility of God's Foreknowledge, Predestination, and Grace with Human Freedom," in *Anselm of Canterbury: The Major Works*, ed. Brian Davies and G. R. Evans (Oxford: Oxford University Press, 2008), 1.5.

30. "God is identical with His eternity. Being simple, God has no parts. If God is identical with His eternity and God has no parts, His eternity has no parts. So it has no past or future parts. But any everlasting life in time always has past or future parts. So God's life, Anselm concludes, is atemporal." Brian Leftow, "Anselm's perfect-being theology," in *The Cambridge Companion to Anselm*, ed. Brian Davies and Brian Leftow (Cambridge: Cambridge University Press, 2004), 148.

31. Eleonore Stump, *Aquinas* (London: Routledge, 2003), 134. Stump deals with Aquinas' overall understanding on eternity focusing on explaining the feature of eternal-temporal simultaneity [ET-Simultaneity] and eternal life's acting and participating in time.

32. Saint Thomas Aquinas, *Summa Theologiae: Latin Text and English Translation, Introductions, Notes, Appendices and Glossaries* (Blackfriars: Eyre and Spottiswoode, 1964), 1a.10.1. Italics original. The similar concept is also stressed in Aquinas' another writing with the negative expression concerning God's attributes, "Everything that begins to be or ceases to be does so through motion or change. Since, however, we have shown that God is absolutely immutable, He is eternal, lacking all beginning or end." Saint Thomas Aquinas, *Summa Contra Gentiles*, Book One: God, trans. Anton C. Pegis, F.R.S.C. (Nortre Dame: University of Notre Dame Press, 1975), 1.15.2.

So just as numbering antecedent and consequent in change produces the notion of time, so awareness of invariability in something altogether free from change produces the notion of eternity ... Eternity therefore principally belongs to God, who is utterly unchangeable. Not only that, but God is his own eternity, whereas other things, not being their own existence, are not their own duration. God, however, is his own invariable existence, and so is identical with his own eternity just as he is identical with his own nature.[33]

The immutability of God is related to the notion that God is no succession, which necessarily entails no concept of *beginning and end* as well as *before and after*; however, "a thing which changes is always something to which one can assign a before and after in terms of change."[34] Time reflects all these characteristics of change or movement: "Time is a measurement of motion."[35] Aquinas emphasizes time's intrinsic limitation: "For even though time lasted for ever, it would be possible to mark off beginnings and ends in it by dividing it into parts, and so in fact we talk of the beginning and end of a day or year; and this cannot happen in eternity."[36] For Aquinas, time-eternity antithesis is obvious, which illuminates and reaffirms that God is eternal, simple, and immutable; namely, God is perfect.

---

33. Aquinas, *Summa Theologiae*, 1a.10.1-2. Aquinas adds a few concepts of simplicity and eternal present to eternity, "Eternity and God are the same thing. So calling eternal does not imply his being measured by something extrinsic; the notion of measurement arises only in our way of conceiving the situation. Verbs of different tenses are used of God, not as though he varied from present to past to future, but because his eternity comprehends all phases of time." Aquinas, *Summa Theologiae*, 1a.10.3. Also, see John C. Yates, *The Timelessness of God* (Lanham, MD: University Press of America, 1990), 39.

34. Brian Davies, *The Thought of Thomas Aquinas* (Oxford: Clarendon, 1992), 106. Italics added.

35. Brabant, *Time and Eternity in Christian Thought*, 67.

36. Aquinas, *Summa Theologiae*, 1a.10.4. Both concepts that eternity belongs to God who is immutable, and time as being marked off beginnings and ends is possible to be divided by parts, are also related to existence itself and further to creation *ex nihilo*. There is no entity which co-eternal with God because God is the only God who alone is immutable with regard to that which it is not "'the world was created in time,' but rather must intend 'that its initial moment initiate time as well.'" For more on the *ex nihilo* and creation in detail in connection to Aquinas' concept of eternity, see David B. Burrell, C.S.C.,"Aquinas and Islamic and Jewish thinkers," in *The Cambridge Companion to Aquinas*, ed. Norman Kretzmann and Eleonore Stump (Cambridge: Cambridge University Press, 1993), 71-75; Also, see Aquinas, *Summa Contra Gentiles*, 1.15.4.

Quantitative Model

The second model of theological consideration concerning time and eternity suggested by Jackelen stems from Oscar Cullmann's work *Christus und die Zeit* ("Christ and Time"), first published in 1946. Jackelen explains in a nutshell Cullmann's concept of eternity: "Eternity is nothing but infinite time; historical time is just a limited piece of God's infinite time. There is no God above time."[37] In other words, for Cullmann, eternity belongs to the realm of temporality, and thus, eternity is a kind of time that is quite the opposite of the first model, viz., the view of timelessness.

What is the reason that Cullmann takes the position of the linear concept of time in terms of the time-eternity relationship? Cullmann patently elucidates in the introductory chapter to the third edition of *Christ and Time*, "I am interested in this concept merely because it provides the New Testament *background* to that which is important to me: the present-future tension."[38] The foundational inquiry for Cullmann lies in no time concept itself; rather, he asks, "What is Christianity?" In other words, Cullmann's question is concretized: "Our object is the study of the nature of the *New Testament* message."[39] The core message of NT, says Cullmann, is rightly understood by the redemptive-historical perspective within whose frame the "already-not yet" tension is revealed in the most efficient manner.[40] Thus, Cullmann thinks of the linear time concept as the best framework fit to the

---

37. Jackelen, *Where Time and Eternity Meet*, 19.

38. Oscar Cullmann, *Christ and Time: The Primitive Christian Conception of Time and History*, trans. Floyd V. Filson, Revised Edition (Philadelphia: The Westminster Press, 1964), 9. Italics original.

39. Oscar Cullman, *Salvation in History*, trans. Sidney G. Sowers (New York: Harper & Row, 1967), 19. Italics original.

40. "Although *Christ and Time* was originally written with the positive purpose of determining the 'essence of the New Testament message,' it has been popularly looked upon as an attack on Bultmann's demythologizing and existential hermeneutic." Earle Hilgert, "Some Reflections on Cullmann's New Edition of *Christ and Time*," *Andrew University Seminary Studies* 2 (1964): 28. Hilgert correctly understands Cullmann by pointing out Cullmann's argument for the *kerygma*, which happens in a specific spatial-temporal ground not in a philosophical, metaphysical speculation. Concerning the 'present-future' or 'already-not yet' tension, Cullmann, bringing up the relation of eschatology to the temporal future as Schweitzer and Bultmann tries to show no relevance between them, asserting, "I have decided plainly in favor of temporariness being the essence of eschatology, not as Schweitzer saw it, but from the redemptive-historical perspective, in which there exists a tension between the present (the already accomplished) and the future (the not yet fulfilled)." Cullmann, *Christ and Time*, 3; For the issue of NT message between Cullmann and Bultmann, see Hilgert, "Some Reflections," 33-36. For further explanation about the meaning of the redemptive historical perspective ("salvation history"), see Cullmann, *Salvation in History*, 74-78.

NT's message of the already-not yet tension: "It is a frame, within which they [NT authors] spoke of God's deeds."[41]

Exploring the plural usage of αἰών, which is used when eternity appears in the Bible, Cullmann argues that "it does not signify cessation of time or timelessness. It means rather endless time and therefore an ongoing of time which is incomprehensible to men."[42] Because, as aforementioned, time and eternity have no qualitative distinction from each other, Cullmann claims that the NT's concern regarding the concept of time is not about time and eternity antithesis structure but about limited time and unlimited or endless time opposite formulation, which is ultimately found in the NT.[43] Cullmann, therefore, defines eternity as "the endless succession of the ages (αἰῶνες)."[44]

Eschatological Model

The last model of the time-eternity relationship is more ambiguous than either of the other two models. Empathizing with this eschatological model in which "time and eternity appear to be intertwined, yet separated," Jackelen

---

41. Cullmann, *Christ and Time*, 11. Cullmann affirms his presupposition on time and eternity: "I still maintain that the New Testament never speculates about God's eternal being, and since it is concerned primarily with God's redemptive activity, it does not make a philosophical, qualitative distinction between time and eternity. It knows linear time only." Cullmann, *Christ and Time*, 11-12. M. R. Playoust puts in another expression to help what Cullmann means, "If one approaches the Bible in an unbiased way, it is apparent that it is the proclamation of concrete historical events which took place at a particular time and in a particular place. It does not proclaim any of the following: metaphysical speculation, philosophy of any kind, 'eternal truths,' nor is it about man's 'authentic existence.' God's saving acts occur in time. The biblical concept of time is to be understood in analogy to a straight line (unlike the Hellenistic idea of circular time) . . . Our time is, therefore, a delimited portion of God's time which is qualitatively no different from ours." Marc R. Playoust, "Oscar Cullmann and Salvation History," *Heythrop Journal* 12, no. 1 (1971): 30. Such a rectilinear concept of time, for Cullmann, becomes the key framework to unfold the salvation history. Here is Cullmann's reason, "Because time is thought of as a progressing line, it is possible here for something to be 'fulfilled'; a divine plan can move forward to complete execution." Cullmann, *Christ and Time*, 53.

42. Cullmann, *Christ and Time*, 46.

43. Cullmann, *Christ and Time*, 46. Cullmann summarizes, "Time in its entire unending extension, which is unlimited in both the backward and the forward direction, and hence is 'eternity.'" However, when it comes to the adjective form αἰώνιος ("eternal"), which is normally used as an attribute of God, says Cullmann, "it [the adjective] has the tendency to lose its time sense and is used in the qualitative sense of divine-immortal." Cullmann, *Christ and Time*, 48, n. 21.

44. Cullmann, *Christ and Time*, 62.

thinks of the idea of relationality as the focal point of this model.[45] It "corresponds to a significant development in theology . . . namely the move away from a monolithic concept of God which treats the doctrine of the Trinity like a law of geometry toward a dynamic concept of God which depicts the Trinity as a mystery of relations, a creative dance of life."[46] The proponents of the eschatological model have tried to accomplish two purposes: "to *differentiate* eternity from creaturely temporality and to *relate* eternity to creaturely temporality."[47]

Jackelen, while considering time a "manifold phenomenon" as well as "open, dynamic, and relational," raises several questions regarding the eschatological model: "What happens to time when it is related to its other, to eternity?"; "What is it that turns present time into old time?"; "What allows new time to intervene and to interact with previous times?"; and finally, "How can it be that theology speaks of 'already' and at the same time of 'not yet'?"[48] These questions implicitly deliver distinctive facets between old time and new time, which is not meant by tense, i.e., present and future; in other words, for example, the eschatological model focuses more on the futuristic aspect, whereas the ontological model is on reality.[49]

Moreover, these questions pertain to the encounter or conjunction between time and eternity with reference to trinitarian theology. The bonding association of the divine eternity of the Creator with the temporality of creatures requires only one condition: God's self-revelation. In relation to God's making himself known, the incarnation of the second person of the Trinity is the unique and perfect locus of the encounter. Christoph Schwöbel well summarizes the point:

> How are we to account for the relationship of time and eternity with regard to God's reconciliation in Christ? The appropriation of reconciliation to God the Son has two related aspects. On the one hand, it points to the incarnation of the Creator-Logos

45. Jackelen, "Where Time and Eternity Meet," 19.
46. Jackelen, "Where Time and Eternity Meet," 20.
47. Michael Welker, "God's Eternity, God's Temporality, and Trinitarian Theology," *Theology Today* 55, no. 3 (1998): 320. Italics added.
48. Jackelen, "Where Time and Eternity Meet," 19.
49. Antjie Jackelen, "A Relativistic Eschatology: Time, Eternity, and Eschatology in Light of the Physics of Relativity," *Zygon* 41, no. 4 (2006): 967. Jackelen adds, "According to the eschatological model and its preference for potentiality we can imagine time as the future of the past, the future of the present, and the future of the future. We can think of what already is in the light of what is not yet but is promised to come." With regard to the old time and new time, Welker explains they each indicate "the old and the new aeon." Welker also says the old time is "merely creaturely time," which will "disappear or are destined to vanish." See Welker, "God's Eternity," 322-3.

in Jesus of Nazareth. This implies at least that an eternal divine person becomes incarnate, assumes humanity in its temporal structures at a specific point in time and space. This alone has considerable persuasive power to conceive of the eternity of the triune God as an inclusive eternity, not as the "bad eternity" of timelessness.[50]

Eternity revealed by the incarnation of the Creator-Logos in Jesus, which must be understood in the "Trinitarian way," is and derives from "the eternal unbreakable communion of the three Trinitarian persons, who are in their communion their own beginning and end, joined in their own mediation by the Son."[51] Due to the communion of the three persons who share the essence of Godhead, it is granted that God's work *ad extra* is the work of all three persons: the Father, Son, and Holy Spirit. Thus, as God's immanent eternal communion is reflected to the creatures by the incarnation in the Son, the triune God should be reckoned as *"eternally temporally present* for every creature within the time of creation in order to be in communion with his creatures."[52]

Ingolf Dalferth provides a conclusive summary regarding the eschatological model in terms of the trinitarian theology to eternity:

> God is related to creation, in triune fashion, as a differentiated unity of Father, Spirit, and Son: as the timeless foundation of everything, as the multi-temporal companion of everyone, and as the temporal mediator of salvation in the specific lifetime of Jesus Christ and of all who believe in him. God's eternity is the epitome of these time relationships and cannot be identified with any one of them as such.[53]

Summary

The first section of this chapter deals with the theological concept of eternity in three models: ontological, quantitative, and eschatological. The

---

50. Christoph Schwöbel, "The Eternity of the Triune God: Preliminary Considerations on the Relationship between the Trinity and the Time of Creation," *Modern Theology* 34, no. 3 (2018): 352.

51. Schwöbel, "The Eternity of the Triune God," 350.

52. Schwöbel, "The Eternity of the Triune God," 351.

53. Antjie Jackelen, *Time and Eternity: The Question of Time in Church, Science, and Theology* (Philadelphia: Templeton Faoundation Press, 2005), 100, quoted from Ingolf U. Dalferth, "Gott und Zeit," in *Religion und Gestaltung der Zeit*, ed. D. Georgi, H-G. Heimbrock, and M. Moxter (Kampen: Kok Pharos, 1994), 33.

ontological model examined the works and thoughts of Augustine, Boethius, Anselm, and Aquinas, which is the traditional view on the relationship between time and eternity, one stressing qualitative antithesis. The quantitative model is based on Oscar Cullmann's work *Christus und die Zeit*, which regards salvation history as the core message of NT. Thus, Cullmann prioritizes the rectilinear concept of time as the framework to unfold the NT from the redemptive-historical perspective, from which the concept of eternity comes as unlimited or endless time. The eschatological model begins with the question, "What happens to time when it is related to its other, to eternity?" Emphasizing the dynamic and irregular aspect of time as a manifold phenomenon, eternity as new time is related to creaturely old time. The triune God's self-revelation, especially in the incarnation of the second person in Jesus Christ, manifests God as eternally temporally present within creation and creatures for communion.

With this general trajectory of the theological concept of eternity as background, the rest of the chapter draws an important picture of John Gill's concept of eternity in order to provide the foundational ground of Gill's covenant of redemption, the locus of his theological system.

TIME AND ETERNITY ACCORDING TO JOHN GILL

Time binds history in which man's being, acting, and working are interpreted. In this regard, Cullmann's view on time and eternity has merit, understanding eternity as unlimited time. Cullmann believes his view is ultimately derived from the core NT message structured by the redemptive-historical perspective, i.e., salvation in history. For Gill, however, eternity frames time itself as well as the redemptive history in time, whose foundation is based on the Triune God and begins with his act of creation. Eternity, according to Gill, is inextricably linked to one of God's attributes, infinity, which "chiefly respects and includes the 'omnipresence' and 'eternity' of God."[54]

---

54. John Gill, *A Body of Doctrinal Divinity, Book I: Of God, His Word, Names, Nature, Perfections and Persons*, ed. David Clarke, Seven Books (Fareham, U.K.: Bierton Particular Baptists, 2020), 51. Gill also says the infinity of God is closely connected with God's spirituality and simplicity, which will be dealt with while following Gill's biblical and theological explanations of eternity. Interesting is that these two conceptions are deeply related to God's nature or essence. Gill in the same page continues to say, "God is infinite in all his attributes." In consideration that each part of God's attributes is never separated from God's nature, eternity as one of the branches of God's infinity has a very intimate relation to God's nature.

Trinitarian Concept of Eternity

When it comes to the definition of eternity, Gill illustrates an improper usage of the term from two biblical passages, i.e., Genesis 17:7-8 and 2 Samuel 7:12, 16, prior to giving his own definition. Each expression, says Gill--"the everlasting possession of the land of Canaan," and "the thrones of David and Solomon are said to be established for ever"--delivers an inappropriate signification by connoting the sense of eternity, which is "of a long duration, but limited, and have [has] both a beginning and an end."[55] In contrast to

---

55. Gill, *Divinity, Book I*, 55. Coincidently, Gill points to Genesis 17 and 2 Samuel 7 as improper usages of the concept of eternity, which are crucial biblical passages to understand the *pactum* pertaining to the person and work of Jesus Christ in terms of the covenant formula. Though using these two passages as an improper usage, Gill makes a different exegetical interpretation between the two in *Divinity, Book I*. Both the permanent covenant and the permanent possession in Genesis 17 are interpreted in a literal sense only as having an end, not everlasting, which means no more existence whereas the everlasting thrones of David and Solomon have not only the literal sense of having an end but it also has a chance to be "understood spiritually, as David's Son and Antitype, his throne will be for ever and ever" (the original term in Hebrew for permanent or everlasting in both Genesis 17 and 2 Samuel 7 is the same: עוֹלָם). However, Gill explicates in his exposition of Genesis 17:7-8 that the everlasting covenantal blessings to Abraham belong to both his natural seed and his spiritual seed: "for an everlasting covenant; to his natural seed, as long as they should continue in the true worship of God; and in their own land; or until the Messiah came, in whom the covenant of circumcision had its accomplishment, and was at an end; and to all his spiritual seed, with respect to the spiritual blessings of it, which are everlasting, and are never taken away, or become void." With regard to the everlasting possession of the land of Canaan, Gill continues, "this respects only the natural seed of Abraham, and those in the line of Isaac and Jacob, to whom this land was given to hold for ever, in case they were obedient to the will of God; and therefore whenever they were disobedient, they were carried captive from it, as they are at this day; but when shall be converted, they will return to this land and possess it to the end of the world; and which was a figure of the heavenly inheritance, which is an eternal one, and will be enjoyed by all his spiritual seed to all eternity." John Gill, *An Exposition of the Old Testament*, vols. 6 (London: Mathews and Leigh, 1810; reprint, Paris, AR: The Baptist Standard Bearer, 2006), 1:121. For the eternality of the everlasting covenant and the possession of the land of Canaan in connection with the concept of people of God in the New Jerusalem, see Paul M. Hoskins, *The Book of Revelation: A Theological and Exegetical Commentary* (North Charleston, SC: ChristoDoulos, 2017), 431-37. This eternal covenant concept with the covenant formula will be more fully examined in the chapter five in relation to the role of Jesus Christ the second person of the Trinity in the *pactum*. 2 Samuel 7:12-16 also plays an important role in the metanarrative of the everlasting covenant in the redemptive history. The conception of the eternal thrones of David and Solomon is connected with the Messiah, which results that the everlasting covenant makes everlasting. Gill notes with regard to the everlasting house and kingdom in the verse 16: "he [David] saw with his eyes in his son Solomon, and with an eye of faith in his greater son the Messiah, in whom only these words will have their complete fulfilment." Gill, *An Exposition of the Old Testament*, 2:593.

such a restricted and time-bounded character of eternity, Gill defines eternity from the perspective of the Creator-creature qualitative difference as Augustine's basic inference presented in the ontological model:

> Eternity, properly so called, is that which is without beginning and end, and is without succession, or does not proceed in a succession of moments one after another; and is opposed to time, which has a beginning, goes on in a succession, and has an end: it is the measure of a creature's duration, and began when creatures began to be, and not before, and is proper to them, and not eternity, which only belongs to God.[56]

Gill's demonstration regarding the definition of eternity stems from Psalm 90:2, "Before the mountains were brought forth, or ever thou hadst formed the earth and the world, from everlasting to everlasting, thou art God," which leads to the trinitarian concept of eternity in the frame of Gill's covenantal system in the *pactum*.[57] Gill claims,

---

56. Gill, *Divinity*, Book I, 55.

57. Gill, *Divinity*, Book I, 55. In his interpretation of Psalm 90:2, Gill puts the eternity of Christ the Son in the same level with the eternity of God the Father. God's ontological being from everlasting to everlasting is applied to both the Father and the Son in the same manner. Gill explicates that such claim can be made a conclusion "from his [the Son] name, the everlasting Father; from his having the same nature and perfections with his Father; from his concern in eternal election, in the everlasting covenant of grace, and in the creation of all things; and his being the eternal and unchangeable I AM, yesterday, to-day, and for ever, is matter of comfort to his people." Gill, *An Exposition of the Old Testament*, 4:88. First, Gill argues that the eternality of Christ the Son is proved by a name, "the everlasting Father" whose expression happens in Isaiah 9:6, "For a child will be born for us, a son will be given to us, and the government will be on his shoulders. He will be named Wonderful Counselor, Mighty God, Eternal Father, Prince of Peace." Gill clarifies in his exposition on Isaiah 9:6 that "there is but one Father in the Godhead, and that is the first person . . . Christ is not the Father . . . it is easy to make it appear Christ is not the Father, but is distinct from him, since he is said to be with the Father from eternity, to be the Son of the Father in truth and love, his own Son, his only-begotten and beloved Son." Regarding the meaning of "the everlasting Father" indicating Christ the Son, Gill expounds that "Christ is a Father with respect to chosen men, who were given him as his children and offspring in covenant; who are adopted into that family that is named of him, and who are regenerated by his spirit and grace: and to these he is an *everlasting Father* . . . adoption is an act of the will of God in covenant from eternity: and Christ is a Father to these unto everlasting; he will never die, and they shall never be left fatherless." See Gill, *An Exposition of the Old Testament*, 5:55-56. Gill's explication on the eternality of Christ with regard to the eternal adoption in covenant gives a logical but, at the same time, a touching mind, which pictures the seemingly arid, lifeless, and cold term eternity as a warmhearted notion that cares fatherless children in the everlasting, limitless, and abundant love of the Father. Christ is the everlasting Father who adopts and cares those who are given him by his Father the first person of the Trinity. Second, Gill argues that the eternality of Christ the Son

Eternity, in this sense, is peculiar to God; as he only hath immortality, so he only has eternity; which must be understood not of the Father, or first person only, but of the Son and Spirit also; who are, with the Father, the one God; and possess the same undivided nature; of which Eternity is an attribute.[58]

Eternity belongs only to God, the Trinity. Gill's equal emphasis on the nature of eternity in balance with the Father, the Son, and the Holy Spirit originates in his firm conviction that all things are derived from the triune God who manifested himself as pure revelation to his own creation in time by the incarnate Son (Col 1:17).[59]

---

is proved by another name, unchangeable "I AM," which happens in John 8:58, "Truly I tell you, before Abraham was, I am." Knowing the meaning of the usage "I AM" applied to God in Exodus 3:14, which "signifies the real being of God, his self-existence, and that he is the Being of beings; as also it denotes his eternity and immutability, and his constancy and faithfulness in fulfilling his promises, for it includes all time, past, present, and to come," Jesus applied the name to himself. Gill, affirming Christ's being eternal God with the Father, asserts, "Christ was before Abraham was in being, the everlasting I am, the eternal God, which is, and was, and is to come . . . and the covenant of grace was made with him . . . and he had a glory with his father before the world was; yea, from all eternity he was the son of God, of the same nature with him, and equal to him; and his being of the same nature proves his eternity, as well as his deity, that he is from everlasting to everlasting God . . . he is the invariable unchangeable I am." See Gill, *An Exposition of the Old Testament*, 1:329; John Gill, *An Exposition of the New Testament*, vols. 3 (London: Mathews and Leigh, 1809), 1:855. Malcolm Yarnell, while explaining the context of God the Trinity's total separation above creation, and "the Son and the Holy Spirit are perceived as being on the Godward side of that line from eternity," draws from John 8:58 with reference to the Son's preexistence pictured by "the covenant name, 'I am.'" Yarnell's unique parallel with Gill's trinitarian concept of eternity comes with his interpretation of the Gospel of John 14-16, the status of the trinitarian God the Father, the Son, and the Holy Spirit "are permanently differentiated from the others [believers and the world]," which remain a creature bounded in time. See Malcolm B. Yarnell III, *God the Trinity: Biblical Portraits* (Nashville: B&H, 2016), 141. Also, see D. A. Carson, *The Gospel According to John*, The Pillar New Testament Commentary (Grand Rapids: Eerdmans, 1991), 358; G. R. Beasley-Murray, *John*, Word Biblical Commentary, vol. 36 (Dallas: Word, 1999), 139-40.

58. Gill, *Divinity: Book I*, 55.

59. The importance of the doctrine of the Trinity to Gill, particularly in relation of the Trinity to the *pactum* being the root of his theological loci, will receive additional attention in chapter 4. Basically, without mentioning the doctrine of the Trinity and the distinctiveness of each person in the Trinity, Gill does not unfold his theological system. His emphasis on the importance of the Trinity is well described in the first paragraph of his work on the Trinity, "The ancient *Jews used* to call it [the Doctrine of the Trinity] the sublime mystery, and sometimes the *mystery of all mysteries*; which if a man did not endeavor to make him feel acquainted with, it would have been better for him if he had never been created." John Gill, *The Doctrine of the Trinity Stated and Vindicated Being the Substance of Several Discourses on that Important Subject* (originally published in 1731; Paris, AR: Baptist Standard Bearer, 1999), 4. Italics original.

In interpreting Proverbs 8:23-24, does Gill explain, "before all time, before the earth or any thing was created; this further confirms the eternal existence of Christ's person, the antiquity of his office."[60] Namely, Gill affirms that Christ, in regard to the redemption of men, is the perfect Redeemer, Mediator, and Savior from eternity. With regard to the eternity of the Holy Spirit, Genesis 1:1-2 testifies that the Holy Spirit is the Creator of the heavens and the earth, who must exist before all creatures and time.[61] In praising the Creator, Psalm 33:6 proves it, "By the word of the Lord the heavens were made and by the breath of His mouth all their host."[62] Gill, based on Psalm 33:6, explicitly affirms the Spirit's eternality, stating that "the Spirit of God, the third Person in the Trinity," works all things together with the Father and the Son. The Holy Spirit is not excluded by the unique works of eternal God, in particular, creation, redemption, and consummation in the divine economy: "They were all, Father, Word, and Spirit, jointly concerned in the whole."[63]

Thus, Gill's conception of eternity does basically pertain to who God is as never ceased being of three persons in one Godhead who is infinite in every attribute. In other words, as aforementioned by Gill's definition, an eternity that belongs solely to God, the Trinity, is everlasting and forever, and its characteristic includes three components: without beginning, without end, and without succession. The rest of this chapter will unfold how Gill expounds on the eternity of God the Trinity in demonstrating these three components on a biblical basis with theological considerations, which will lead to the essential understanding of the concept and location of eternity for the investigation of the role of the *pactum* in Gill's systematic theology.

The Eternity of God: Without Beginning

The most fundamental premise of this section in Gill's mind, when it comes to the first part of the definition of eternity "without beginning," is that the notion of knowledge in time, i.e., knowing and being known, is and cannot be fully applied to an entity in the realm of "without beginning." Thus, it

---

60. Gill, *An Exposition of the Old Testament*, 4:383. Christ's eternity is closely related to the doctrine of the Trinity, especially to the eternal generation of Christ. Gill in his exposition of Proverbs 8:22-30 considers the issue of eternal Sonship of Christ at some length against the claim of Arius, "Christ is a creature, and was the first creature that God made, not of the same but of a like nature with himself." See Gill, *An Exposition of the Old Testament*, 4:382.

61. Gill, *Divinity: Book I*, 55-56.

62. The biblical quotation is from the New American Standard Bible.

63. Gill, *An Exposition of the Old Testament*, 3:663.

is inevitable for Gill to begin with the essence or nature of God: "From his nature and being; as from his 'necessary self-existence': the existence of God is not arbitrary, but necessary."[64] The necessary self-existence is beyond a temporal being's episteme of thought process, whose being is defined and conceptualized by another being, and is also above a consequence through understanding by an intellectual and logical approach to certain knowledge, which, therefore, is called transcendent.[65]

God's Nature and Being

Thus, for Gill, the idea of "without beginning" begins with the concept of divine incomprehensibility, which is deeply related to the nature of God.[66]

---

64. Gill, *Divinity: Book I*, 56.

65. This transcendent mind can only be shared and communicated by those who have the same necessary self-existence, who are ultimately the divine persons alone, the Father, the Son, and the Holy Spirit in one nature. The existence is also "not from the will of another," continues Gill, "for then that other would be both prior and superior to him, and so be God, and not he: it remains, therefore, that he necessarily existed; and if so, then he must be eternal; since there was none before him; nor can any reason be given why he should necessarily exist at such an instant, and not before." Gill, *Divinity: Book I*, 56. In other words, terms like "beyond," "transcendent" are related to the high view of the triune God's ontological distinctiveness as Creator as whose necessary nature and being prove itself in creation. Tim Shimko also notes, "God cannot be known because of the sharp Creator/creature divide. To claim to know him in a direct, intellectual manner is to bring him from the realm of transcendence into the created realm. Such a claim is essentially presumptuous and arrogant." See Tim Shimko, "Divine Incomprehensibility in Eastern Orthodoxy and Reformed Theology," *Theological Reflections* 19, no. 1 (2021): 16. Regarding the divine incomprehensibility of Eastern and Western understanding in difference, Phillip Cary attempts to find a resolution of settlement between the two by focusing on the theology of Thomas Aquinas who tried "to reconcile them by affirming that the vision of God is indeed beyond the natural capacity of the created intellect, but not beyond the capacity of an intellect that is elevated above its own nature by the gift of supernatural grace." Cary continues, "Hence the proposition by which Aquinas attempts to reconcile East and West on this point is: 'seeing the essence of God belongs to the created intellect by grace and not by nature.'" See Phillip Cary, "The Incomprehensibility of God and the Origin of the Thomistic Concept of the Supernatural," *Pro Ecclesia* 11, no. 3 (2002): 341.

66. The doctrine of the divine incomprehensibility is inextricably linked to the concept of God's transcendence, which fixes the boundary between time and eternity. In describing men's ungodliness before God in interpreting Romans 1, Karl Barth points out that the real ungodliness is to make no demarcation between Creator and creation with a remark of sarcasm concerning the confusion, "We suppose that we know what we are saying when we say 'God.' We assign to Him the highest place in our world: and in so doing we place Him fundamentally on one line with ourselves and with things." Karl Barth, *The Epistle to the Romans*, trans. Edwyn C. Hoskyns, Sixth Edition (Oxford: Oxford University Press, 1968), 44. James Leo Garrett Jr. relates the concept

The interpretation of Job 11:7, "Can you fathom the depths of God or discover the limits of the Almighty?" clearly shows what Gill has in mind regarding divine incomprehensibility,

> God is perfect and entire, wanting nothing, and is possessed of all perfections, may be found out, or otherwise he would not be God; but his essence and attributes, being infinite, can never be traced and comprehended by finite minds; there are some perfections of God we have no idea of, but are lost in confusion and amazement as soon as we think of them and reason about them, as his eternity and immensity particularly; for, when we have rolled over in our minds millions and millions of ages, we are as far off from eternity as when we began; and when we have pervaded all worlds, and every space and place, we have got no further into immensity than at first; *we are confounded when we think of a Being without beginning and without bounds, unoriginated, and unlimited.*[67]

---

of transcendence to God's holiness in the OT usage: "Holiness meant that which was uniquely, distinctively, and transcendently other than humankind." See James Leo Garrett, Jr., *Systematic Theology: Biblical, Historical, and Evangelical*, Fourth Edition, 2 vols. (North Richland Hills, TX: Bibal, 2011), 1:240. In NT, Paul who is impressed by who God is with regard to the divine incomprehensibility in Romans 11:33-34a, "Oh, the depth of the riches both of the wisdom and of the knowledge of God! How unsearchable his judgments and untraceable his ways! For who has known the mind of the Lord?," articulates by giving a clear distinction between God and man in 1 Corinthians 2:10-11, "Now God has revealed these things to us by the Spirit, since the Spirit searches everything, even the depths of God. For who knows a person's thoughts except his spirit within him? In the same way, no one knows the thoughts of God except the Spirit of God." Paul, however, goes further in verse 12 saying, "Now we have not received the spirit of the world, but the Spirit who comes from God, so that we may understand what has been freely given to us by God." Wayne Grudem makes a subtle nuance regarding what Scripture means by knowability of God in giving a distinction between "unable to be *fully* understood" and "unable to be understood." See Wayne Grudem, *Systematic Theology: An Introduction to Biblical Doctrine*, Second Edition (Grand Rapids: Zondervan, 2020), 177-78. In other words, this affirms that men are allowed to know God by his self-revelation "in His Word by the Holy Spirit to be known as the truth" though not exhaustively. Millard Erickson also notes, "When we speak of the incomprehensibility of God, then, we do not mean that there is an unknown being or essence beyond or behind his attributes. Rather, we mean that we do not know his qualities or his nature completely and exhaustively. We know God only as he has revealed himself." Millard J. Erickson, *Christian Theology*, Third Edition (Grand Rapids: Baker, 2103), 237. Barth, emphasizing on the full grace of God, continues, "For it is by the grace of God and only by the grace of God that it comes about that God is knowable to us . . . God's revelation takes place among us and for us, in the sphere of our experience and of our thinking. But it has to be seriously accepted that it happens as a movement 'from God.'" See Barth, *CD*, II/1:63, 69.

67. Gill, *An Exposition of the Old Testament*, 3:282. Italics added. While asserting

In relation to this understanding of the incomprehensibility, Barth notes in short, "We confound time with eternity."[68]

In addition, drawing a connection between the essence of God and his "face" from Exodus 33, Gill stresses God's incomprehensibility by describing God's "face" in the same manner,

> which cannot be seen, (Exo. 33:20, 23) that is, cannot be perceived, understood, and fully comprehended, especially in the present state; and, indeed, though in the future state saints will behold the face of God, and 'see him face to face, and as he is,' so far as they are capable of, yet it is impossible for a finite mind, in its most exalted state, to comprehend the infinite Nature and Being of God.[69]

When God said to Moses, "You cannot see my face," Gill not only notes God's essence is his "face," but he also connotes this "face" is revealed in Jesus Christ, who is "his [God's] essence, his very nature, and the glory of it."[70] Based on Colossians 2:9 and Philippians 2:6, Gill clearly articulates that God's essence "resides in the human nature of Christ, in the highest and most exalted manner," which reveals "the fulness of the divine nature, of all the perfections of deity, such as eternity, immensity, omnipresence, omnipotence, omniscience, immutability, necessary and self-existence, and every other."[71]

"the nature of God is, indeed, incomprehensible," Gill does not miss an important point by allowing a possibility of knowing God partly, not fully: "This [incomprehensibility] does not forbid us searching and inquiring after him: though we cannot have adequate idea of God, yet we should endeavor to get the best we can, and frame the best conceptions of him we are able; that so we may serve and worship him, honour and glorify him, in the best manner." Gill, *Divinity: Book I*, 41.

68. Barth, *The Epistle to the Romans*, 44.

69. Gill, *Divinity: Book I*, 40.

70. Gill, *An Exposition of the Old Testament*, 1:521.

71. Gill, *An Exposition of the New Testament*, 3:186. In the same vein, Barth, claiming Jesus Christ is God's revelation as a "divine encroachment" in the grace of God, asserts, "In virtue of that encroachment it has been taken among us and for us. The result is that the truth of the being and nature of God stands actually and perceptibly before us in all its divine certainty, and it can genuinely be apprehended by us." Barth, *CD*, II/1:70, 75. The remark of Barth here rather proves God's incomprehensibility because there would be no "genuinely be apprehended by us" without the grace of God in Jesus Christ who is the revelation of God. Namely, the incarnate Christ is the grace of God, strong evidence of God's incomprehensibility. On the other hand, Erickson says, "While his self-revelation is undoubtedly consistent with his full nature and accurate, it is not an exhaustive revelation. Further, we do not totally understand or know comprehensively that which he has revealed to us of himself. Thus, there is, and always will be, an element of mystery regarding God." Erickson, *Christian Theology*, 237. Cf.

Gill's concept of God's incomprehensibility pertaining to "without beginning" leads necessarily to the ontological question of who God is. "God is a spirit" is where Gill's conviction of who God is takes place, cited from John 4:24. Namely, "God is a spirit" denotes "a true definition, description, and declaration of God, and of his nature," which was directly "given by the Son of God, who lay in his bosom, and perfectly knew his nature, as well as his will."[72] In his early work, *The Cause of God and Truth*, Gill uses a pattern of word combination, "spiritual and eternal." This expression functions as eternal nature contrasting with a "temporal nature" in many places: e.g., spiritual and eternal good, spiritual and eternal welfare, spiritual and eternal salvation, spiritual and eternal peace, and so forth.[73] Thus, God is a spirit, and his spiritual nature is directly linked to eternity.

From this concept that God is a spirit, Gill displays an ontological distinction between spiritual and corporeal. From the exposition of Isaiah 31:3a, "Egyptians are men, not God; their horses are flesh, not spirit," Gill portrays the feebleness of flesh "without an immortal soul or spirit . . . much less angelic spirits, or like them, which are incorporeal, invisible, and exceedingly mighty and powerful . . . these are God's cavalry."[74] Gill goes further to explain that God allows corporeal expressions to be attributed to himself: e.g., his "eyes" signifying his "omniscience and all-seeing providence," his "ears" his "readiness to attend unto," his "arms" and "hands" his "power and the exertion of it," and so forth.[75] Gill explains God's corporeal functions in Scripture, depicting the unique and humble "portrayal of God in human form," which is called anthropomorphism.[76] One of Gill's fascinating ideas

---

See note 56 above.

72. Gill, *Divinity: Book I*, 41. When Gill construes "God is a spirit" in John 4:24, he means that the Son and the Holy Spirit are not excluded due to his trinitarian concept of God. Gill states, "Father, Son, and Holy Ghost: for taking the words in this light, not one of the persons is to be understood exclusive of the other; for this description, or definition, agrees with each of them, and they are all the object of worship." Gill, *An Exposition of the New Testament*, 1:788.

73. John Gill, *The Cause of God and Truth: In Four Parts with A Vindication of Part IV*, A New Edition (London: Thomas Tegg and Son, 1838), 12, 17-18, 19, 20, 31, 35, 45, 56, 57, 60, 70, 85, 95, 132, 218-19, 285, 287, 288, and 297.

74. Gill, *An Exposition of the Old Testament*, 5:179.

75. Gill, *Divinity: Book I*, 42.

76. Murray A. Rae, "Anthropomorphism," in *Dictionary for Theological Interpretation of the Bible*, ed. Kevin J. Vanhoozer (Grand Rapids: Baker, 2005), 48. Lewis and Demarest explains, "Anthropomorhisms, which figuratively ascribe to God human features . . . , confirm that God is not an impersonal force but a personal being endowed with intellect, emotions, and the power of self-determination." Gordon R. Lewis and Bruce A. Demarest, *Integrative Theology, Volume 1: Knowing Ultimate Reality: The Living God*, 3 vols. (Grand Rapids: Zondervan, 1987), 185.

in this regard, while mentioning the biblical examples of a divine person's appearance, is below:

> Then these were appearances of the Son of God in an human form, and *were presages of his future incarnation*; for as for the Father, no man ever saw his shape, (John 5:37) and, it may be, the reason why the parts of an human body are so often ascribed to God, may be on account of Christ's incarnation, *to prepare the minds of men for it, to inure them to ideas of it, to raise their expectation of it, and strengthen their faith in it.*[77]

In consideration of anthropomorphism in connection with the Son's proleptic incarnation, Gill denotes that God's eternity is far from the idea of deism, according to which "God is distinct from everything in our world, and he does not interact with it. He initially created the universe but then withdrew from it to let it run on its own."[78] The "spiritual and eternal" God is beyond time, and thus, the creature's mind cannot grasp his nature, which is characterized by transcendence and incomprehensibility. However, the eternality of God is also compatible with the corporeal realm by virtue of God's self-revelation in the Son. Gill makes a theological balance in terms of God's eternity in transcendence and his love in condescension manifested in the temporal nature through Christ by the Holy Spirit.

---

77. Gill, *Divinity: Book I*, 42. Italics added. Rae also notes, "This [God's self-manifestation] takes place most especially in the incarnation. The divine Word takes human form. This is the most significant anthromorphism, for by this means God enables human beings, in speaking of one who is like them in all respects, but without sin, to speak truly of God himself." Rae, "Anthropomorphism," 49.

78. Feinberg, *No One Like Him*, 61. Feinberg further explains, "The deistic God does not act in the world or sustain it, but remains thoroughly aloof from it. From a practical standpoint this view is tantamount to atheism, but conceptually it is not, for it denies only God's interaction with our world, not his existence." Another helpful concept goes with, "Deism can only offer a mute God unwilling or incapable of speaking to his creatures." See Bruce Riley Ashford and Keith Whitfield, "Theological Method: An Introduction to the Task of Theology," in *A Theology for the Church*, ed. Daniel L. Akin, Revised Edition (Nashville: B&H, 2014), 42. For the history and critique of deism, see Garrett, *Systematic Theology*, 1:94, who mentions "Deism represents the truth of the transcendence of God at the expense of the immanence of God and represents the truth of divine revelation through the creation at the expense of divine revelation through history." Pertaining to the relation between transcendence and immanence in regard to deism, see John M. Frame, *The Doctrine of God* (Phillipsburg, NJ: P&R, 2002), 107-114.

God's Purposes, Counsels, Decrees, and the Pactum

Gill's idea of "without beginning" in eternity, which has been made known by God's nature and being in the concept of incomprehensibility, is also argued from God's "purposes, counsels, and decrees."[79] There is no room for the term "new" to take place within the immanent triune God's life and work because there is no "change" or "movement" in the triune God's existence, which is the necessary accompanying phenomenon caused by the term "new."[80] Gill asserts, "No new purposes and resolutions rise up, or are framed by him in his mind; for then there would be something in him which was not before; which would imply mutability."[81] In this regard, Gill clearly articulates the relation of time to eternity,

> Nothing that is in time can give futurity to things in eternity: for the futurity of things was from all eternity, or all things which are or shall be in time, were future from all eternity; which futurity could arise from nothing else but the will and decrees of God, which of things possible made them future.[82]

In working on "thy counsels of old are faithfulness and truth" in Isaiah 25:1, Gill expounds the inner works of God from eternity,

> The decrees and purposes of God, which are from eternity, are all truly and faithfully performed; this is an amplification of the wonderful things which are done according to the counsel of the divine will; not only the choice of men to salvation, the redemption of them by Christ, and their effectual vocation; but

---

79. Gill, *Divinity: Book I*, 57.

80. See Malachi 3:6; James 1:17; and Numbers 23:19. The following section will deal with this concept of divine immutability more.

81. Gill, *Divinity: Book I*, 57. The same context is found from saying, "If there is any ordination or appointment to it, it must be before men have a being, even from eternity, since no new appointment, decree, purpose, or ordination is made by God in time." Gill, *The Cause of God and Truth*, 139.

82. Gill, *The Cause of God and Truth*, 374. Regarding this time/eternity relation, Gill definitely recognizes Boethius's concept of eternity, and not oppose it, as he mentions Boethius's definition in his words, "Eternity is the interminable or unbounded and perfect possession of life whole together." See Gill, *Divinity: Book I*, 55. From this perspective, therefore, terms such as eternal 'past' and eternal 'future' in the theological usage appear inappropriate. If, as argued in Gill's demonstration, eternity belongs to God beyond the time limit, putting such tensed words together with God's unique word 'eternal' would be improper and be making a notion of eternity less than as it should be. Eternity is just eternal. Such terms might be helpful for men to see and understand the biblical economy of redemption in the Bible in their view, but it is only from the men's perspective, not God's.

the calling of the Jews and Gentiles, in particular, in the latter day, and all things relating to the church to the end of time; which, as they were fixed in the eternal purpose of God, they are punctually and exactly brought about in time; these are the true and faithful sayings of God.[83]

Of special interest comes from the description "the counsel of the divine will; not only the choice of men to salvation, the redemption of them by Christ," entailing the temporal economy of God. With regard to the counsel of the divine will, Gill's attention is directed to men's redemption by Christ from eternity. This concept of redemption from eternity has a strong association with the *pactum*, that is, the covenant of redemption, and is also called "the covenant of grace" or "the council of peace" in Gill's own expression. While interpreting Ephesians 3:11, in the same vein, Gill articulates the *pactum* is the core of the biblical redemptive narrative and, therefore, makes the very locus of revealing who the triune God is in the whole divine economy of the Bible, asserting,

> The whole of salvation, in which is displayed the great wisdom of God, is according to a purpose of his; *the scheme of it is fixed in the council of peace*; the thing itself is effected in pursuance of it; Christ, the Redeemer, was set forth in it; his incarnation, the time of his coming into the world, his suffering and death, with all their circumstances, were decreed by God . . . (which) are *all according to a divine purpose: and this purpose is eternal, or was in the mind of God from all eternity*; for no new will can arise in him; no purpose, resolution, or decree can be made by him in time . . . and his purpose concerning the salvation of men must be eternal, since a council of peace was held, a covenant of peace was made.[84]

The *pactum* considers Christ and his role as one of the most crucial aspects. The secret of the *pactum* is in Christ who "was foreknown before the foundation of the world but was revealed in these last times" for the sake of the believers.[85] Therefore, God's eternity or the concept of eternity is again made certain by the appointment of Christ as "Man and Mediator" in the *pactum*, says Gill, "to be Redeemer and Saviour of men, or the preordination of him to be the Lamb slain for the redemption of his people, was before the foundation of the world."[86]

---

83. Gill, *An Exposition of the Old Testament*, 5:139.
84. Gill, *An Exposition of the New Testament*, 3:81. Italics added.
85. 1 Peter 1:20.
86. Gill, *Divinity: Book I*, 57. Gill is consistent with the argument for the concept

The Eternity of God: Without End

The notion "Eternity is without end" takes the second part of Gill's full definition of eternity, "which is without beginning and end, and is without succession," as aforementioned in the previous section.[87] Gill unfolds the idea that eternity is "without end" by focusing on two critical themes in the doctrine of God, i.e., theology proper: divine simplicity and immutability.

Simplicity[88]

With regard to the doctrine of divine simplicity, Gill does not provide biblical passages directly to support his argument in *Divinity*.[89] Is it legitimate and justified, then, for Gill to draw the concept of simplicity for the biblical demonstration that eternity is without end? God's spirituality, based on John 4:24, as the essential ground of who God is, leads Gill to the point of simplicity in relation to eternity: "God being a Spirit, we learn that he is a simple and uncompounded Being, and does not consist of parts, as a body does; *his spirituality involves his simplicity*."[90] God's spirituality, in which

---

of eternity in his expositions. As already mentioned in Ephesians 3, the *Divinity Book I*, and *The Cause of God and Truth*, Gill grasps what eternity means in the Bible in connection with the divine incomprehensibility, faithfulness, and truthfulness. In an explanation of the expression "before the foundation of the world" in 1 Peter 1:20, Gill affirms, "all God's appointments, relating either to Christ, or his people, are eternal; no new thoughts, counsels, and resolutions, are taken up by him in time. The affair of redemption by Christ is no new thing; the scheme of it was drawn in eternity; the persons to be redeemed were fixed on; the Redeemer was appointed in the council and covenant of peace." Gill, *An Exposition of the New Testament*, 3:538.

87. See note 53 above.

88. Recently, scholars have begun to refocus on the doctrine of the divine simplicity. For the historical, exegetical, and theological understanding with reference to the divine simplicity, see Jonathan M. Platter, *Divine Simplicity and the Triune Identity: A Critical Dialogue with the Theological Metaphysics of Robert W. Jenson*, Theologische Bibliothek Töpelmann (Berlin: De Gruyter, 2021); Steven J. Duby, *Divine Simplicity: A Dogmatic Account*, T&T Clark Studies in Systematic Theology (London: Bloomsbury T&T Clark, 2018); Jordan P. Barrett, *Divine Simplicity: A Biblical and Trinitarian Account* (Minneapolis, MN: Fortress Press, 2017); Paul R. Hinlicky, *Divine Simplicity: Christ the Crisis of Metaphysics* (Grand Rapids: Baker, 2016).

89. Criticizing the practices of theological constructs, which is not based upon the biblical account and evidence, Robert Picirilli claims, "When theologians focus on God as defined in himself, in eternal immutability, they end up representing God as he is conceived, all too often, in rationalistic philosophy. They concentrate on things the Bible itself never aspires to define, on theological constructs that the inspired writers of Scripture might not even recognize. These constructs include attributes of God such as his impassibility or aseity or simplicity. Often these attributes are defined in terms that grew out of Greek philosophical logic." Robert E. Picirilli, *God in Eternity and Time: A New Case for Human Freedom* (Nashville: B&H, 2022), xii.

90. Gill, *Divinity: Book I*, 43. Italics added.

every attribute of God is the nature of God, does not allow parts within himself which truly reveals glorification in his perfection.[91] Gill's understanding of simplicity, i.e., lacking parts, is firmly wedded to the concept of perfectness. "Without end" in eternity indicates there is no being that can define the ontological entity without end; however, if God is not simple but made up of parts, there should necessarily be an entity prior to or at least co-existent with God the Creator, explains Gill:

> If God was composed of parts, he would not be 'eternal,' and absolutely the first Being, since the composing parts would, at least, co-exist with him; besides, the composing parts, in our conception of them, would be prior to the compositum; as the body and soul of man, of which he is composed, are prior to his being a man: and, besides, there must be a composer, who puts the parts together and therefore must be before what is composed of them: all which is inconsistent with the eternity of God.[92]

The concept of simplicity also stands with God's absolute independence with respect to the perfection of God. The perfect stands, dwells, and exists alone in complete satisfaction with no other being. No entity can add to or subtract from the perfect because an idea of degree or measure is not applied to the perfect. This notion reflects the part of Gill's definition of eternity "without end." "What is composed of parts, depends upon those parts, and the union of them, by which it is preserved" has zero possibility to "put an end" to the independent, self-existent who stands forever and exists eternal in perfection.[93]

---

91. Regarding God and nature, Alvin Plantinga explains, "God does indeed have a nature; but he is identical with it. God is somehow simple, utterly devoid of complexity. He has a nature; but he and it are the very same thing. But then of course it is not prior to him; and if he is dependent upon it, this is no more than a harmless case of self-dependence." Alvin Plantinga, *Does God have a Nature?*, The Aquinas Lecture, 1980 (Milwaukee, WI: Marquette University Press, 2007), 26-27. "Metaphysically speaking, perfect and absolute unity entails simplicity. It does so because anything that is not metaphysically 'simple' is in some way composite, and to be composite means to have parts of some kind – which entails limitation and finitude in being. A perfect unity can only be simple actuality, without any parts or limitation of being. Furthermore, metaphysical reflection can go further. A composite entity cannot be the source of all beings and cannot account for its own existence, since, as a composed reality, a composite entity would be necessarily limited and finite due to the limitation and finitude of its parts. The Creator therefore must be metaphysically simple." Matthew Levering and George Kalantzis, "Introduction: Why Think About Divine Simplicity?" *Modern Theology* 35:3 (July 2019): 412.

92. Gill, *Divinity: Book I*, 43-44.

93. Gill, *Divinity: Book I*, 44, 58. For consideration of the relationship between

Dealing with eternity in terms of divine simplicity, Gill demonstrates a clear demarcation between God the Creator and his creatures. Each attribute of the triune God in the first book of his *Divinity* points to the nature and perfection of God. In other words, at the beginning of writing *Divinity*, Gill recognizes first and foremost God's perfection in the perfect immanent life and fellowship of the triune God, which happens in eternity and who himself is eternity, i.e., an utterly different realm with ontological and epistemological transcendent dimension. God's other incommunicable attributes, e.g., immutability, also stand together with eternity in accordance with divine simplicity. With regard to creation's life and destiny, particularly men's redemption, however, the concept of eternity, in contrast to the temporal realm, provides an identifiable ground regarding the demarcation between the two. Thus, in this regard, eternity renders the framework and presupposition of men's redemption in which God's internal and external works are clearly pictured by eternal covenant, namely *pactum*, as a pure act.[94]

---

divine simplicity and independence, see Matthew Baddorf, "Divine Simplicity, Aseity, and Sovereignty," *Sophia* 56, no. 3 (September 2017): 403-418.

94. See Gill, *Divinity: Book II*, 8-9. Gill's usage of the term 'pure act' shows a presupposition that there is a clear demarcation between eternity and time by the concept itself, which means "there is nothing unrealized in him." That is, "there is nothing potential in God." These citations are from the Systematic Theology I lecture note of Malcolm Yarnell, fall 2022, at Southwestern Baptist Theological Seminary. In the first chapter of the second book in *Divinity*, Gill explains more about "God is 'actus purus et simplicissimus ("pure and simple act")'" while dealing with the acts and works of God in detail. The relation between eternity and time functions an important role as a presupposition in that chapter as well. This concept, "God is a pure act," might open the door to the connection between the divine simplicity and immutability in eternality of God in the sense that "complete and perfect in himself from eternity to eternity, God has no potential that is not already fully realized. God cannot be more infinite, loving, or holy tomorrow than today. If God alone is necessary and independent of all external conditions, fully realized in all of his perfections, then there is literally nothing for God to *become*. For us, change might be for better or worse, but for a perfect God, change can only yield imperfection." See Michael Horton, *The Christian Faith: A Systematic Theology for Pilgrims on the Way* (Grand Rapids: Zondervan, 2011), 235. Italics original. Emphasizing the significance of difference between the Creator and creature while handling immutability, which will be dealt with by the subsequent section, Bavinck also mentions regarding being and becoming, asserting, "the doctrine of God's immutability is highly significant for religion. *The difference between the Creator and the creature hinges on the contrast between being and becoming.* All that is creaturely is in process of becoming. It is changeable, constantly striving, in search of rest and satisfaction, and finds this rest only in him who is pure being without becoming. This is why, in Scripture, God is so often called the Rock." Bavinck, *Reformed Dogmatics*, 2:156. Italics added. Bavinck's sharp contrast between being and becoming in the analogy of "Rock" highlights God's being the unchanging Creator. Interesting point is that Gill puts more emphasis on the everlastingness or unchangeableness of his covenant than the "Rock,"

Immutability

The part of Gill's definition of eternity "without end" is also illuminated by another theological concept, immutability, which is "closely connected with his [God's] spirituality and simplicity . . . and is necessary to him as a spiritual, simple and uncompounded Being."[95] A couple of biblical passages, according to Gill, support the notion of immutability not as a separated idea from other attributes of God but as one that is intimately linked with them.[96]

Gill asserts his understanding of immutability: "God only is in and of himself immutable; and he is unchangeable in his nature, perfections, and purposes, and in his love and affections to his people, and in his covenant, and the blessings and promises of it; and even in his threatenings."[97] The feature of the terms in the list above in relation to both God's ontological and economic aspects is eternality. In other words, the common description of these terms shows their eternality according to Gill: e.g., eternal purpose (Eph 3:11), eternal covenant (2 Sam 23:5), and eternal love (Ps 103:17; John 17:24). On what basis does the Scripture declare that purpose, covenant, and love are eternal? Gill avers, "God is immutable, and therefore without

---

asserting, "His covenant is firm and sure; more immoveable than rocks and mountains; it stand fast, with Christ, for ever, and God commands it for ever." See Gill, *Divinity: Book I*, 58.

95. Gill, *Divinity: Book I*, 45.

96. See Mal 3:6; Ps 102:25-27; Jas 1:17; Job 23:13; 1 Pet 1:24-25. In explicating the relationship between simplicity and immutability pertaining to eternity, William Mann draws a predictable question into the conversation: "The doctrine of God's eternality is sufficient by itself to establish the DDI [the doctrine of divine immutability]. That is, if God is eternal (in Boethius's sense) then he is immutable. Thus we do not need the DDS [the doctrine of divine simplicity] to secure the DDI, and if we do not need it, why should we use it?" In defense of the correlationship of the concepts, Mann advocates the necessity of using these terms: "The doctrine of God's eternality does indeed entail the DDI, but that fact alone provides no reason for accepting either it or DDI. The explanatory necessity of the DDS emerges when we ask why we should accept the doctrine of God's eternality. The DDS highlights the fact that both the doctrine of God's eternality and the DDI are embedded in a more comprehensive theory about God's nature. If God were not eternal and immutable he would not be simple, and if he were not simple, he would not be perfect. It is ultimately the 'logic of perfection' which gives us the DDS and the DDI." William E. Mann, "Simplicity and Immutability in God," in *The Concept of God*, ed. Thomas V. Morris (Oxford: Oxford University Press, 1987), 261.

97. Gill, *Divinity: Book I*, 46; also, see Gill, *An Exposition of the New Testament*, 3:499. Erickson adds, "There is first no quantitative change. God cannot increase in anything, because he is already perfection. Nor can he decrease, for if he were to, he would cease to be God. There also is no qualitative change. God's nature does not undergo modification. Therefore, God does not change his minds, plans, or actions, for these rest on his nature, which remains unchanged no matter what occurs." Erickson, *Christian Theology*, 249.

end," which means God lives everlastingly, and no one can put an end to his existence.[98] Therefore, Gill answers the question based on the interrelationship between immutability and eternity:

> He is not only called the living God (Jer 10:10) but is often said to 'live for ever and ever' (Rev 4:9, 10, 10:6). Hence his purposes and decrees are never frustrated, *because he ever lives to bring them into execution*: men take up resolutions, and form schemes, which, by reason of death, are never executed; their purposes are broken, and their thoughts perish; but 'the counsel of the Lord stands for ever; and the thoughts of his heart to all generations' (Ps 33:11), and therefore he himself must endure for ever: his promises are all fulfilled; not only because he is able and faithful to perform, *but because he continues for ever to make them good*.[99]

In other words, all the promises, covenants, purposes, and decrees of God can never fail and be eternally fulfilled because the triune God who never changes continues to live and work everlastingly on what is in his mind of both internally and externally until all things are fulfilled.[100]

---

98. Gill, *Divinity*, Book I, 58.

99. Gill, *Divinity: Book I*, 58. Italics added.

100. In the context of Ps 102:27, which proclaims "But you are the same, and your years will never end," Gill supports, "now he [God], that made the heavens and the earth, and will be when they will not be, especially in the present form they are, must be able to rebuild his Zion, and being on the glory he has promised; and from his eternity and immutability may be concluded the continuance of his church and interest in the world, until all the glorious things spoken of it shall be fulfilled, as follows." Gill, *An Exposition of the Old Testament*, 4:132. Another interpretation of Ps 102 regarding divine immutability comes from the Creator/creature difference, "Psalm 102 instructs us in two crucial matters: first, whatever God's immutability consists in and however we proceed to speculatively explicate it, divine immutability is rooted in the distinction between Creator and creature, and second, this distinction is not merely a matter of the fidelity of the divine purpose or will, but concerns the form of existence, the being, of creature and Creator respectively." Jared Michelson, "Contemplating the One Who Remains the Same: Augustine, Swinburne, and Psalm 102 on the Relation between Divine Immutability and Theological Reason," *Modern Theology* 36:4 (October 2020): 810. Therefore, immutability and eternity are in the same vein, which means the distinction of the two attributes of God made by a human perspective is just a distinction in notion, not a distinction in reality in the nature of God. Gill claims, "God is before all creatures; they being made by him, and so before time; he was the same before the day was as now, and now as he was before; 'even the same today, yesterday, and for ever': though he is 'the ancient of days,' he does not become older and older; he is no older now than he was millions of ages ago, nor will be millions of ages to come; *his eternity is an everlasting and unchangeable 'now'*; 'He is the same, and his years shall have no end.'" Gill, *Divinity: Book I*, 46. Italics added.

A significant issue with respect to immutability comes with the interpretation of John 1:14 ("the Word became flesh") and Philippians 2:5-11 ("emptied himself"), the so-called *kenosis* theory in relation to the two natures in one person of the incarnate Christ. Kenoticism seeks to explain the concept of emptying ("*kenosis*") in Philippians 2:7, which means "when Jesus became man, he divested himself of some, or all, divine attributes."[101]

101. John M. Frame, *Systematic Theology: An Introduction to Christian Belief* (Phillipsburg, NJ: P&R, 2013), 881. Regarding *kenosis* theory, Garrett explains, "Arising in nineteenth-century German Lutheranism, this approach to Christology has provided for many Protestants an alternative to the Chalcedonian pattern. It centers in the sequence of preexistence, self-emptying, and re-ascent or glorification. Two stages, the downward self-emptying of the incarnation and the upward self-fulfillment of victory over temptation, resurrection, and ascension, constitute the main theme of Christology, not the two natures, human and divine." Garrett, *Systematic Theology*, 1:609. Recognizing its heresy, Bloesch asserts, "In some of its forms there is no doubt that kenoticism is heretical. If the divine attributes were renounced by Christ when he became man, as many kenoticists hold, it is difficult to see how he can still be regarded as God." Donald G. Bloesch, *Essentials of Evangelical Theology: Volume One: God, Authority, and Salvation*, 2 vols. (Peabody, MA: Prince Press, 2001), 1:137; also, Frame agrees, "But if Jesus, in his incarnation, divested himself of any essential divine attributes (*morphe*), as on this view, then during his incarnation (which continues without end!) he was and is not God at all. For God is not God without his essential attributes. But the idea that Jesus was not God when he was in the flesh contradicts a vast amount of biblical data . . . " Frame, *Systematic Theology*, 881-2. This kenoticism issue is, ultimately, derived from having a censorious criticism of the mystery of Christ's two natures in the second person of the Trinity. Historically, however, from the early church era, the teaching of two natures of Christ concerning his deity and humanity has been an orthodox tradition in spite of various heretical challenges. The Niceno-Constantinopolitan Creed first affirms the two natures of Christ: " . . . In one Lord Jesus Christ, the only Son of God; who was begotten from the Father before all the ages, light from light, true God from true God, begotten not made, one essence with the Father; through whom all things came into existence. Who, for us human beings and for our salvation, descended from heaven and took flesh by the Holy Spirit and the virgin Mary and became human . . . " See Yarnell, *God the Trinity*, 241. Then, as Bavinck mentions, "Chalcedon correctly pronounced that the union of the two natures was without division or separation and without confusion or change." Bavinck, *Reformed Dogmatics*, 3:237. It is worthy of citing the Chalcedonian text of which value Jaroslav Pelikan asserts, "fundamental ever since to the christological development of all of the Latin West, much of the Greek East, and some of the Syriac East." The Chalcedon Creed reads, "Following therefore the holy fathers, we confess one and the same our Lord Jesus Christ, and we all teach harmoniously [that he is] the same perfect in godhead, the same perfect in manhood, truly God and truly man, the same of a reasonable soul and body; homoousios with the Father in godhead, and the same homoousios with us in manhood, like us in all things except sin; begotten before ages of the Father in godhead; the same in the last days for us and for our salvation [born] of Mary the Virgin Theotokos in manhood, one and the same Christ, Son, Lord, unique; acknowledged in two natures without confusion, without change, without division, without separation [ἐν δύο φύσεσιν ἀσυγχύτως, ἀτρέπτως, ἀδιαιρέτως, ἀχωρίστως]--the difference of the natures being by no means taken away because of the union, but rather the distinctive character of each nature

However, Gill, affirming that God's unchangeableness in his divine nature is not affected by Christ's incarnation, asserts:

> For though he, a divine Person, possessed of the divine nature, was 'made flesh,' or became man; the divine nature in him was not changed into the human nature, nor the human nature into the divine, nor a third nature would have been changeable; but so it was not; for as it has been commonly said, 'Christ remained what he was, and assumed what he was not'; and what he assumed added nothing to his divine person; he was only 'manifest in the flesh'; he neither received any perfection, nor imperfection, from the human nature.[102]

In the exposition of Malachi 3:6, "For I, the Lord, do not change," Gill signifies the speaker here is Christ in the deity and confirms Christ's unchangeableness even in assuming the human nature: "he changed not in his divine nature and personality by becoming man; he took that into union with him he had not before, but remained the same he ever was."[103]

Both "without end" and "without beginning" have a notion in common that the ontological and essential being in eternity is qualitatively different from the creaturely being in time. Following Gill's biblical and theological way of "without end," one meets with the triune God who is immutable and thus necessarily simple in which eternity also reveals God himself "without beginning" utterly apart from the temporal view.

Gill's understanding of eternity, as aforementioned, is based on his trinitarian theology; that is, each person of the Father, the Son, and the Holy Spirit in the Godhead is eternal. Thus, this chapter has pursued the concept

---

being preserved, and [each] combining in one person and hypostasis--not divided or separated into two persons, but one and the same Son and only-begotten God, Logos, Lord Jesus Christ; as the prophets of old and the Lord Jesus Christ himself taught us about him, and the symbol of the fathers has handed down to us." Jaroslav Pelikan, *The Emergence of the Catholic Tradition (100-600)*, The Christian Tradition: A History of the Development of Doctrine, 5 vols. (Chicago: The University of Chicago Press, 1971; Paperback edition, 1975), 1:263-64; also, see Oliver D. Crisp, "Incarnation," in *The Oxford Handbook of Systematic Theology*, ed. John Webster, Kathryn Tanner, and Iain Torrance (Oxford: Oxford University Press, 2007), 162-3. Recently, the conversation concerning the kenosis theory is not just limited to the Christology but rather extended to the doctrine of the Trinity, and other theological constructions requiring "a simultaneous engagement with the complexities of biblical interpretation, historical theology, and constructive dogmatic theology." See Paul T. Nimmo and Keith L. Johnson, eds., *Kenosis: The Self-Emptying of Christ in Scripture & Theology* (Grand Rapids: Eerdmans, 2022), 1.

102. Gill, *Divinity: Book I*, 47.
103. Gill, *An Exposition of the Old Testament*, 6:768.

of eternality, focusing on God's unique attributes following Gill's definition of eternity. The notion of eternity is equivalent to knowing who God is. In this regard, Gill's first part of the definition of eternity, "without beginning," is related to God's nature and being, especially to divine incomprehensibility, and to God's purposes and decrees. The second part of Gill's definition of eternity, "without end," has dealt with God's incommunicable attributes: divine simplicity and immutability. Finally, this chapter will consider the third and last part of Gill's definition of eternity "without succession."

The Eternity of God: Without Succession

The last section of Gill's definition of eternity unfolds in the concept that eternity does not belong to the consecutive duration in succession, which completes the concept of eternity, that is, one of the attributes of God. Two theological terms, delivering one notion in the same context, take place in regard to Gill's demonstration of "without succession": accommodation and condescension. The idea of these two theological terms pertains not only to incomprehensibility, the first part of Gill's definition of eternity but also to simplicity and immutability, the second part of Gill's definition. The divine accommodation and condescension resolve the seeming discrepancy between the biblical descriptions and theological demonstrations in terms of God's being and act in time and eternity. Is it, indeed, impossible for men to know God? Then, how are all the anthropomorphic descriptions and narratives between God and men in the Bible to be explained?[104] Gill answers this predictable question by explaining the third and last concept of eternity "without succession."

Accommodation and Condescension

Gill's basic principle of articulating eternity pertaining to God is that eternity is without beginning and end and "without succession," which, especially for the last one, means beyond "any distinctions of time succeeding one

---

104. Bavinck mentions, "inasmuch as the revelation of God in nature and in Scripture is specifically addressed to humanity, it is a human language in which God speaks to us of himself. For that reason the words he employs the human words; for the same reason he manifests himself in human forms. From this it follows that Scripture does not just contain a few scattered anthropomorphisms but is anthropomorphic through and through. From the first page to the last it witnesses to God's coming to, and searching for, humanity." Bavinck, *Reformed Dogmatics*, 2:99-100.

another, as moments, minutes, hours, days, months, and years."[105] Based on Isaiah 43:13, "Even from eternity, I am He" (NASB), Gill argues that the notion of "succession," which indicates the distinctions of time, does not belong to eternity. Gill translates אוּה יָגֶא סוֹיִמ־סַג in Isaiah 43:13 to "Before the day was, I am he," in which his theological interpretation is reflective in the usage of "Before." Exegetically considered, the preposition מִן carries meanings of "out of," "from," "on account of," etc., implying its central connotation, i.e., "*separation* or *removal*, whether from a person or place or in any direction."[106] Therefore, Gill's translation "Before" is in line with the implication of the usage of מִן; namely, the realm or dimension of God's being is utterly separated from "the day," whose realm belongs to consecutive time. In this sense, Gill signifies his translation "before" in Isaiah 43:13 by saying, "Before there was a day, before the first day of the creation; that is, before time was, or from all eternity."[107]

Thus, eternity lacks consecutive succession because the realm of God is "before" the creation, which consists of distinctions of time. However, the anthropomorphic expressions in the Bible, e.g., eyes, arms, hands, and ears, which are ascribed to God who is eternal, seem to make no demarcation between "without successive duration" and distinctions of time. In addition, it appears that time-related terms like "days and years are ascribed to God," though God's "without successive duration" in eternity should in the same manner apply to the same God even when God is in duration through time.[108] At this point, Gill brings up the theological idea of accommodation and condescension to the conversation.

Then, what is accommodation?[109] To Gill, the divine accommodation manifests both God's transcendence and immanence at the same time,

105. Gill, *Divinity: Book I*, 58.

106. Francis Brown, S. R. Driver, and Charles Briggs, "מִן־," in *The Abridged Brown-Driver-Briggs Hebrew-English Lexicon of the Old Testament: From A Hebrew and English Lexicon of the Old Testament*, ed. Richard Whitaker (Boston, MA: Houghton, Mifflin and Company, 1906).

107. Gill, *An Exposition of the Old Testament*, 5:248.

108. See Gill, *Divinity: Book I*, 58.

109. Daniel Treier defines accommodation by saying, "traditionally, God's use of human author's language, cultural settings, and other limits to communicate understandably without compromising Scripture's truthfulness." Daniel J. Treier, *Introducing Evangelical Theology* (Grand Rapids: Baker, 2019), 367. In other words, "Throughout the Bible God accommodates himself to our limited capacity as finite and fallen creatures by revealing himself to us in human words–for those are the only kinds of words we have." See Timothy George, "The Nature of God: Being, Attributes, and Acts," in *A Theology for the Church*, 166. Also, see David S. Dockery, *The Doctrine of the Bible* (Fort Worth, TX: Seminary Hill Press, 2020), 59. Thus, the term accommodation is basically related to God's revelation in association with anthropomorphic expressions in

Scripture because God's perfection cannot be defined in this finite realm. Frame notes, "Scripture takes abstract attributes of God, no less than concrete images of him, from human life–words that have uses in our conversation about earthly things. This is the only kind of revelation there is. The purpose of revelation is communication, and so the very purpose of revelation is to get God's message into human terms." Frame, *The Doctrine of God*, 367; also, Bavinck adds, "Eternity cannot be defined except as a negative of time. Scripture never even attempts to describe these perfections of God positively in terms of their own essence and apart from any relation to the finite." Bavinck, *Reformed Dogmatics*, 2:100. This concept does not occur in a vacuum. Well-known user of this idea, Origen, against "Celsus' false accusations in his book against the Christians and the faith of the churches," explains, "just as when we are talking with little children we do not aim to speak in the finest language possible to us, but say what is appropriate to the weakness of those whom we are addressing, and, further, do what seems to us to be of advantage for the conversion and correction of the children as such, so also the Logos of God seems to have arranged the scriptures, using the method of address which fitted the ability and benefit of the hearers." Origen, *Contra Celsum*, trans. Henry Chadwick (Cambridge: University Press, 1953), 4.71. In the next book does Origen interestingly draw 1 Corinthians 1:21 regarding the foolishness of preaching God and the foolish things of the world pertaining to accommodation, saying, "just as some words are suitable for use with children and are appropriate for their tender age, in order to exhort them to be better, because they are still very young, so also with those whom the word calls 'the foolish things of this world and the base things and the things that are despised' the ordinary interpretation of punishments is suitable because they have not the capacity for any other means of conversion and of repentance from many evils, except that of fear and the suggestion of punishment." See Origen, *Contra Celsum*, 5.14-16. Augustine also mentioning God's unchangeableness notes, "But if Scripture were not to use such expressions as the above, it would not familiarly insinuate itself into the minds of all classes of men, whom it seeks access to for their good, that it may alarm the proud, arouse the careless, exercise the inquisitive, and satisfy the intelligent; and this it could not do, did it not first stoop, and in a manner descend, to them where they lie." Augustin, "The City of God," in *A Select Library of the Nicene and Post-Nicene Fathers of the Christian Church*, ed. Philip Schaff, Vol. II: St. Augustin's City of God and Christian Doctrine, 14 vols. (Edinburgh: T&T Clark, 1988), 15.25. Subsequently, John Calvin follows, "The Anthropomorphites, also, who imagined a corporeal God from the fact that Scripture often ascribes to him a mouth, ears, eyes, hands and feet, are easily refuted. For who even of slight intelligence does not understand that, as nurses commonly do with infants, God is wont in a measure to 'lisp' in speaking to us? Thus such forms of speaking do not so much express clearly what God is like as accommodate the knowledge of him to our slight capacity. To do this he must descend far beneath his loftiness." John Calvin, *Institute of the Christian Religion*, ed. John T. McNeill and trans. Ford Lewis Battles (Louisville, KY: Westminster John Knox, 2011), 120-21. Another significant aspect to consider regarding accommodation is the question, "Does God deceive men by accommodation?" Hanson, pointing out that Origen "extended it to the length of saying that God was ready to deceive men for their own good," cites Novatian, "The prophet was speaking about God at that point . . . in symbolic language, fitted to that stage of belief, not as God was, but as the people were able to understand . . . God therefore is not finite, but the people's understanding is finite; God is not limited, but the intellectual capacity of the people's mind is limited." R. C. P. Hanson, "Biblical Exegesis in the Early Church," in *The Cambridge History of the Bible: From the Beginnings to Jerome*, ed. P. R. Ackroyd and C. F. Evans, 3 vols. (London: Cambridge University

especially through the anthropomorphic expressions and circumstances in the biblical narrative. The application of biblical descriptions such as days and years toward God should not be the same as the one toward men. Drawing Job's deploration in an accommodation description, "Thy days as the days of man? Thy years as man's days?" (10:5), Gill clearly indicates God's transcendence of no succeeding moments, "but a thousand years with the Lord are but as one day; his days are days not of time, but of eternity: nor so mutable, or he so mutable in them; man is of one mind to-day, and of another to-morrow; but the Lord is in one mind one day as another; he is the Lord that changes not; immutable in his nature, purpose, promises, and affections."[110] Regarding "Ancient of Days," another description in Daniel 7:13, Gill asserts this ancient is not "'in' days, or 'through' them, as aged persons are said to be in years," rather it means "he is more ancient than days; he was before all days, and his duration is not to be measured by them."[111]

Going further, these anthropomorphic descriptions of duration toward God with regard to God's transcendence are also related to the knowledge of God in terms of past, present, and future, whose conceptions are only applied to men in time. Gill argues that the understanding of God's knowledge proves the last part of his definition of eternity, "without succession":

> ... these he knows at once, and all together, not one thing after another, as they successively come into being; all things are open and manifest to him at once and together, not only what are past and present, but he calls things that are not yet, as though they were; he sees and knows all in one view, in his all-comprehending mind: and as his knowledge is not successive, so not his duration.[112]

Agreeing with the traditional line of Augustine and Boethius regarding the theological understanding of time and eternity, Gill's concept of

---

Press, 1970), 1:451-2. Frame also says, "A mother who speaks baby talk to a child does not intend to deceive him, but to convey truth in a way suited to the child's understanding." Frame, *Systematic Theology*, 704. In a slightly difference angle, Treier mentions, "God's accommodation to human contexts and limits is traditionally part of Scripture's truthfulness, not an indication of error. Accommodation shows that apparent errors 'properly understood ... were not errors at all but were written in language adapted to the capacity of the common people.'" Treier, *Introducing Evangelical Theology*, 311.

110. Gill, *An Exposition of the Old Testament*, 3:273. Gill comment is from 2 Peter 3:8, which also firmly proves the "without successive duration" in God's eternity. Gill argues, "If his duration was successive, or proceeded by succeeding moments, days, and years; one day would be but one day with him, and not a thousand; and a thousand days would answer to a thousand days, and not be as one only." See Gill, *Divinity: Book I*, 58.

111. Gill, *Divinity: Book I*, 58.

112. Gill, *Divinity: Book I*, 59.

eternity as "without succession" and "eternal present" does not limit eternity to Cullmann's quantitative eternity.[113]

God's immanence in the divine accommodation is deeply relevant to the divine name (or names) in which God reveals his condescension to men. Basically, Gill implies that God's condescending mercy in his rich love is presented when his name is revealed: "Since God is incomprehensible, he is not nominable; and being but one, he has no need of a name to distinguish him."[114] Although God's various names consistently picture God as "the eternal, immutable, and almighty Being, the Being of beings, self-existent, and self-sufficient," they are also "the object of religious worship and adoration."[115] In other words, by revealing his name, God makes room for a personal and private relationship with his people; namely, in Gill's expression, "in his name, Jehovah . . . he co-exists, with all the points of time, in time."[116]

---

113. In this regard, the concept of foreknowledge is not acceptable because there is no order of former and latter in God's eternity. Norman Geisler notes, "Speaking of God as *fore*knowing is another example of anthropomorphic language. Of course, an eternal God does not really foreknow; He simply knows in His eternal present. The biblical speech presenting Him as *fore*knowing is simply speaking from a human perspective." Norman Geisler, *Systematic Theology: God and Creation*, 4 vols. (Minneapolis, MN: Bethany House, 2003), 2:75. Italics original. Anthony Thiselton also brings up Thomas Aquinas and mentions, "Thomas Aquinas rejects divine foreknowledge for a further and different reason. He argues that the concept of *foreknowledge imposes on God a chronological or human notion of time*, whereas God is *outside* time as we know it." Anthony C. Thiselton, *Systematic Theology* (Grand Rapids: Eerdmans, 2015), 77. Picirilli, while acknowledging of no foreknowledge of God because "there is no before and after, no succession of events in God's eternal, immutable, omniscient existence," notes, "It is proper, then, to speak of 'fore'knowledge, since we are speaking correctly out of our temporal existence . . . God himself may not have any succession of events within himself, or experience any duration of time, but he knows perfectly well what succession of events is really occurring in our world and can act with us within the framework of those events. That he created this world justifies this implication. So does the fact that he is sustaining or upholding the world and all its events. So does the fact that God the Son entered this world in time and space." See Picirilli, *God in Eternity and Time*, 78-79.

114. Gill, *Divinity: Book I*, 36.

115. Gill, *Divinity: Book I*, 40.

116. Gill, *Divinity: Book I*, 58. Garrett, bringing Emil Brunner's idea on the divine name, saying, "the name itself stands for the selfhood of God, and the manifestation of God's name stands for the action of God," abridges him in three statements: (1) "The name of God means the possibility of divine revelation; (2) The name of God manifests the nature of God as person; (3) The naming of God is designed to lead human beings into communion or fellowship with God." Garrett, *Systematic Theology*, 1:218-19. This relationship through God's name is most clearly manifested by God's establishing a covenant. Schoville notes, "Perhaps the most profound anthropomorphism is the depiction of God establishing a covenant . . . Theologically, the legal compact initiated by

Summary

For Gill, time is a result of the eternal God's act of creation. Thus, it is impossible for Gill to confine eternity to the realm of time. This relationship between the Creator and creature necessarily determines and characterizes where time and eternity stand, respectively.

Psalm 90:2 forms the basis of Gill's argument for the concept of eternity in relation to the nature of God. He notes, "Before the mountains were born, before you gave birth to the earth and the world, from eternity to eternity, you are God." Based on the trinitarian conception of eternity, Gill's definition of eternity as "without beginning, end, and succession" concerns the attributes of God, who exists in three persons: the Father, Son, and Holy Spirit.

The first part of Gill's definition of eternity, "without beginning," deals mainly with God's essence, purposes, and decrees, especially focusing on the incomprehensibility. In the second part, Gill handles the simplicity and immutability with regard to "without end." Finally, Gill invites the conceptions of accommodation and condescension to demonstrate the third part, "without succession." Gill's method of unfolding the definition of eternity by employing God's essential attributes highlights the important role the concept of eternity functioned in Gill's systematic theology as a presuppositional frame for the *pactum*, which takes place as the very next topic after God's internal nature and being in his *Divinity*.

CONCLUSION

This chapter has attempted to establish Gill's theological frame of time and eternity, which will function as a presupposition for the *pactum* that will be

---

God becomes the instrument through which he established an intimate and personal relationship with the people, both collectively and individually. Without anthropomorphic expressions, this theological reality would remain virtually inexplicable." Keith N. Schoville, "Anthropomorphism," in *Evangelical Dictionary of Biblical Theology*. Horton in the covenantal context of Exodus 3 pictures God's condescending by sharing his identity "I AM who I AM" as the Lord God. This anthropomorphic revelation of God who is eternal in "without succession," initiates a relationship with his people by giving himself an identification of the expressions with a "possessive genitive" such as "the God of Abraham, Isaac, and Jacob; the God of Sinai; the God of Zion; the God of Israel." Therefore, by the means of accommodation and condescension, "the God who is not intrinsically bound by any creaturely limit nevertheless binds himself freely to us in our times and places." See Horton, *The Christian Faith*, 224; also, see John C. Peckham, *Divine Attributes: Knowing the Covenantal God of Scripture* (Grand Rapids: Baker, 2021), 27-29.

explored in the remaining chapters of this volume. For Gill, eternity is not just a philosophical or scientific notion that is an object of study but rather a fundamental basis for making an argument for the *pactum*. Throughout the whole of Book I of *A Body of Doctrinal Divinity*, Gill tries to demonstrate the being of God, his nature, perfections, and his persons. Acknowledging that man's attempt to define God's essence is unattainable (Ex 33), Gill spends the entire Book I of his systematic theology investigating the attributes of God and his persons. On the basis of God's incomprehensibility, Gill maintains that God's simplicity and immutability are consistently associated with God's infinity, in which the eternity of God takes place as an aspect. In addition, Gill does not ignore the fact that other attributes of God are closely aligned with God's eternity. Every attribute of God, e.g., omnipotence, omniscience, wisdom, love, grace, mercy, goodness, wrath, holiness, etc., is always connected with and reflects one another because God is simple and immutable.[117] Thus, the concept of eternity cannot be thought of as a separate notion from other attributes of God. Therefore, to deal with eternity, for Gill, is tantamount to dealing with God himself, which results in the understanding of the triune God being the cornerstone, presupposition, and justification of his argument.

With this concept of eternity as groundwork in mind, chapter three will explore Gill's unique understanding of the *pactum*, i.e., the everlasting council and the everlasting covenant of grace.

---

117. For further explanations about the relation of God's attributes and simplicity, see Richard of Saint Victor, *On the Trinity*, trans. Ruben Angelici (Eugene, OR: Cascade Books, 2011), Book II.

CHAPTER 3

The Covenant of Redemption According to John Gill

THE PREVIOUS CHAPTER CONCERNING Gill's understanding of time and eternity opens the door for the *pactum* to navigate its own position in Gill's systematic theology. To Gill, the *pactum* happens in eternity; however, the scope and effect of the *pactum* permeate even the elect of the world in time.[1] Due to who God is, as Gill mentions: "God is 'actus purus et simplicissimus'; he is all act," or "he is a pure act," time and eternity harmonize with each other in regard to the act of God.[2] In a fine statement of the connection between the decrees and acts of God in time and eternity, Gill explains,

> God never was without the thoughts of his heart, the acts of his understanding, and the volitions of his will. The 'Sovereignty' of God over all, and his 'independency', clearly show, that *whatever is done in time, is according to his decrees in eternity*; for if anything comes to pass without the will of God, or contrary to it, or what he has not commanded, that is decreed, (Lam. 3:37) how is he a sovereign Being, that does according to his will in heaven and in earth, and works all things after the counsel of his will?[3]

Thus, Gill's systematic theology reveals that God's acts are both internal and external works in time and eternity, and they are closely connected and interact with each other by the *pactum*. In other words, the internal

---

1. Who is the elect? This question is important as Gill asserts, "The basis of the covenant, is God's election of men to eternal life; the foundation of God, which stands sure, and which laid a foundation for the covenant of grace." Gill, *Divinity: Book II*, 81-82. Gill's idea of the elect and its implications will be fully dealt with in chapter five.

2. Gill, *Divinity: Book II*, 8-9. Also, see note 92 in chapter two above.

3. Gill, *Divinity: Book II*, 9. Italics added.

realm of eternity that is represented by God's attributes, perfection in three persons, and decrees, and the external domain of time that is formed by God's creation, redemption, and consummation, these two aspects are bridged by the *pactum*.[4] The *pactum* takes the central locus in the whole redemptive system of Gill's theological development.[5] Gill always affirmed the notion of God himself as the Trinity and his attributes, i.e., grace, mercy,

---

4. The complete framework of the *Divinity*, Book I through Book VII, draws an appropriate picture that the *pactum* functions as an essential point of encounter between Creator and creation, the Holy and the sinful, and the Savior and the saved in the person and work of Jesus Christ, the second person of the Trinity. The image of the theological stream in doctrinal connections is like a water of grace flowing from the ultimate source of love, mercy, and grace, i.e., the triune God, to the sinful, wicked, and miserable men towards the unique goal of all the biblical and theological courses: God's glory through men's redemption. The *pactum* is the covenant from which all the effectual saving resources, schemes, and methods are created and applied. With regard to Gill's theological *system* based on the *pactum* in *Divinity*, Rippon beautifully articulates, "That Dr. Gill had *his* system also, and maintained it, is evident to all who are conversant with his character and writings; but it is a memorial to his praise, that it was *such* a system as *deserved* the most cordial embrace. Nothing is more conspicuous in it, than the harmony of *all* the ineffable perfections of Jehovah, and the Union of each of the *three* divine and equally glorious *Persons* of the sacred Trinity, in all the parts of the salvation of God's elect; and that this sovereign and gracious scheme, from its decree to its final consummation, primarily embraces the glory of Father, Son, and Holy Spirit, as its *ultimate* end, securing to its distinguished objects, not merely individual safety now, and felicity hereafter, but the *personal* HOLINESS of every one of them, in this life, by which they resemble Christ; and *perfect* PURITY beyond the grave, in the everlasting beatific vision of him. This is the evident *tendency* of the evangelical system he espoused." Rippon, *A Brief Memoir*, 98. Italics original.

5. "Of particular interest to Gill was the *pactum salutis*, the covenant of redemption. His treatment of this doctrine comprises an extended section of his systematic theology – almost the entirely of the second portion of the first volume – and references or allusions to it appear in his numerous polemical pieces." David Mark Rathel, "John Gill and the History of Redemption as Mere Shadow: Exploring Gill's Doctrine of the Covenant of Redemption," *JRT* 11, no. 4 (2017): 378-79. John Fesko in working with the thesis, "the intra-trinitarian processions, missions, and *ordo salutis* are interconnected," notes the *pactum* to be located in the main place of the theological doctrines: "The *pactum salutis* is where we find the connections between election, christology, pneumatology, soteriology, and the eternal covenantal roots of the historical covenant of grace. Questions of priority must rest, therefore, not upon the application of redemption but upon its design and trinitarian ontology in the *pactum salutis*." J. V. Fesko, "The Covenant of Redemption and the Ordo Salutis," *TMSJ* 33, no. 1 (Spring 2022): 19. Also, Daniel Scheiderer agrees, while dealing with three features of Gill's *pactum* in the *Divinity*, "Gill integrates the covenant of grace [the *pactum*] with his treatment of a variety of doctrines throughout both parts of his *A Body of Divinity*. Thus, one might especially consider the way Gill rests his treatments of Christology, soteriology, eschatology, Christian spirituality, and the doctrine of baptism on his particular understanding of the covenant of grace." Daniel D. Scheiderer, "John Gill and the Continuing Baptist Affirmation of the Eternal Covenant," *SBJT* 25, no. 1 (2021): 66.

love, sovereignty, holiness, and eternality of the triune God, all of which are manifested by and through the *pactum*. In this regard, the *pactum* in Gill's system, being a fundamental theological method, functioned as the ultimate resource to perceive who God is and what God does with regard to men's redemption. Gill's strong desire for the covenantal bonding with the love of God manifested in the *pactum*, led him to remain consistent to be John Gill as he is, even to the end of his life:

> *I depend wholly and alone upon the free sovereign, eternal, unchangeable, and everlasting love of God; the firm and everlasting covenant of grace, and my interest in the persons of the Trinity; for my whole salvation*: and not upon any righteousness of my own, nor any thing in me, or done by me under the influences of the holy Spirit; nor upon any services of mine, which I have been assisted to perform for the good of the church; but upon my interest in the persons of the Trinity, the person, blood and righteousness of Christ, the free grace of God, and the blessings of grace streaming to me through the blood and righteousness of Christ; as the ground of my hope. These are no new things with me; but what I have been long acquainted with; what I can live and die by. And this you may tell to any of my friends. I apprehend I shall not be long here.[6]

Is it an impetuous decision or making a hasty conclusion to regard the *pactum* as the central locus in Gill's whole theological system of men's redemption? This chapter specifically attempts to bring such a thought to an end by investigating Gill's conception of the *pactum* while the whole dissertation heads toward the legitimate resolution of this fundamental question. First, Gill's twofold definition of the *pactum*, i.e., the everlasting council and the everlasting covenant of grace, helps understand how the two realms of time and eternity harmonize in Christ in terms of human redemption. Moreover, while exploring Gill's theological method in the *pactum*, the never-ceasing work of the main protagonist of this redemptive drama, three divine persons in the Godhead, is never to be disregarded, especially the role of the Holy Spirit. Finally, the properties of the *pactum* denote that the triune God is the God of the covenant through which all his attributes are revealed to his creation and become the justification of men's salvation.

---

6. John Gill, "A Summary of the Life, Writings, and Character of the late Reverend and Learned John Gill, D. D.," in *A Collection of Sermons and Tracts*, 3 vols. (London: George Keith, 1773), 1:xxxii. Italics added.

TWOFOLD DEFINITION

The locus of Gill's *pactum* in the whole *Divinity* explains how the structure of the *Divinity* is associated with Gill maintaining a twofold concept of the *pactum*: the everlasting council and the everlasting covenant of grace.[7]

7. Regardless of the typical manner of unfolding covenant theology by the covenant of redemption, works, and grace in the Reformed camp, Gill makes a distinction between, prior to the classification of the threefold covenant, God's eternal council and eternal covenant of grace in terms of the *pactum* regarding men's salvation. While recognizing the difficulty to make a distinction between both, Gill clearly enunciates, "but I think they are to be distinguished, and the one to be considered as leading on, and as preparatory and introductory to the other, though both of an eternal date." Gill, *the Divinity: Book II*, 45. The confusing issue is the meaning and usage of the term, covenant of grace. Gill does not follow the frame of the Reformed threefold covenant theology; therefore, Gill's essential theological method, i.e., covenant of grace, is by definition different from the Reformed idea of the covenant of grace, which is obviously distinguished from the covenant of redemption. Gill's covenant of grace is one comprehensive covenant occurring in eternity among the three person of the Godhead, which includes or roots the Reformed threefold covenant of redemption, works, and grace. The typical confession of the Reformed clearly states, "Man by his fall having made himself incapable of life by that covenant (covenant of works), the Lord was pleased to make a second, commonly called the covenant of grace; wherein He freely offereth unto sinners life and salvation by Jesus Christ, requiring of them faith in Him that they may be saved, and promising to give unto all those that are ordained unto life His Holy Spirit, to make them willing and able to believe." *Westminster Confession of Faith* (Glasgow: Free Presbyterian Publications, 1994), chapter 7. For the Westminster Confession's debate, construction process in the making, and especially for the overview of the assembly's deliberative process on the section of "The Plan of Redemption," see John R. Bower, *The Confession of Faith: A Critical Text and Introduction* (Grand Rapids: Reformation Heritage Books, 2020), 49-74. Herman Witsius defines the covenant of grace from the Reformed perspective, "The covenant of grace is a compact or agreement between God and the elect sinner; God on his part declaring his free good-will concerning eternal salvation, and every thing relative thereto, freely to be given to those in covenant, by, and for the mediator Christ; and man on his part consenting to that good-will by a sincere faith." Witsius, *The Economy of the Covenants*, 1:165. Charles Hodge notes, "There are in fact two covenants relating to the salvation of fallen man, the one between God and Christ, the other between God and his people. These covenants differ not only in their parties, but also in their promises and conditions. Both are so clearly presented in the Bible that they should not be confounded. The latter, the covenant of grace, is founded on the former, the covenant of redemption." Charles Hodge, *Systematic Theology*, 3 vols. (Peabody, MA: Hendrickson Publishers, Inc., 2008), 2:357-58. Also, see Bavinck, *Reformed Dogmatics*, 3:212-12; Berkhof, *Systematic Theology*, 273-83. Gill's concept of the covenant of grace is also far from the general Baptist understanding whose concept is rather similar to the Reformed, "The first *Covenant* being broken by Man's Disobedience, and by his Sin, he was excluded from the Favour of God, and *Eternal Life*; in which deplorable condition of his, God being pleased out of his *Free-Grace*, and Love to faln Man, (in order to his recovery out of this sinful and *deplorable* Estate) hath *freely* offered him a Second, or a New Covenant of Grace, (which New Covenant of Grace is Jesus Christ) in remission of Sins, through Faith in his Blood,

Gill's theological direction in the *Divinity*, from eternal and immanent acts of God to temporal and economic works of God, rests on the sophisticated location of both council and covenant in his system. In other words, first, God's sublime scheme of men's redemption within the three divine persons from eternity is revealed by the everlasting council.[8] This council, which is an integration of all the attributes of the triune God, decrees, purpose, and wisdom, makes it ready for the three divine persons to settle or fix in the covenant of grace that is contrived in the council.

Secondly, the everlasting covenant of grace pertains more to the economic concerns of the three divine persons than the council, although these two acts of God happen in eternity.[9] This covenant, based on the

---

which God hath promised to give to all them that do obey and submit to the conditions of this Covenant, which Covenant of Grace, and Eternal Salvation annexed to it, is freely and fully offered unto all Men, upon the terms of the Gospel, *viz.* Repentance, and Faith." Thomas Monck et al., "An Orthodox Creed," *SWJT* 48, no. 2 (Spring 2006): 152. Italics original. Gill is not in the same line even with the Particular Baptist confession, "Moreover Man having brought himself under the curse of the Law by his fall, it pleased the Lord to make a Covenant of Grace wherein he freely offereth unto Sinners, Life and Salvation by Jesus Christ, requiring of them Faith in him, that they may be saved." William L. Lumpkin, *Baptist Confessions of Faith*, Second Revised Edition, rev. Bill J. Leonard (Valley Forge, PA: Judson Press, 2011), 246. Also, see Nehemiah Coxe and John Owen, *Covenant Theology: From Adam to Christ*, ed. Ronald D. Miller, James M. Renihan, and Francisco Orozco (Palmdale, CA: Reformed Baptist Academic Press, 2005), 33-41. Gill might be influenced by the covenant theology of Benjamin Keach who was Gill's predecessor of a church at Horsley-down, Southwark in London with regard to "one covenant of grace made in eternity." See Scheiderer, "John Gill and the Continuing Baptist Affirmation of the Eternal Covenant," 66. Keach in his work *the everlasting covenant* plainly articulates, "I have endeavoured to shew that the distinction some men make between the covenant of redemption and the covenant of grace is without ground, being but one and the same covenant, and that the covenant of grace comprehendeth that between God and Christ for us as mediator about our redemption, which was as full of grace in the first making of it as in the revelation and application thereof, according to what was promised thereupon. Its rise and constitution was from eternity, though the revelation and publication was in time." Benjamin Keach, *The Everlasting Covenant: A Sweet Cordial for a Drooping Soul*, ed. Quinn R. Mosier (Kansas City, MO: Baptist Heritage Press, 2022), ii. For further account for Keach's covenant theology, see Samuel D. Renihan, *From Shadow to Substance: The Federal Theology of the English Particular Baptists (1642-1704)*, Centre for Baptist History and Heritage Studies (Oxford: Regent's Park College, 2018), 299-319.

8. The council deals mainly with the immanent oriented formulation of who God is. God's knowledge, understanding, three persons' equivalence, etc., so as to prepare for the discussion of the covenant of grace in relation to the creation. See Gill, *Divinity: Book II*, ch 6.

9. The covenant of grace primarily deals with the economic oriented formulation of what God does. What is the meaning of 'making a covenant' in the Scripture in terms of the covenant of grace? What is the function of each divine person in the covenant and how does it affect the men's redemption? See Gill, *Divinity: Book II*, chs 7-14. These

everlasting council, embraces two realms of time and eternity to manifest the ultimate glory of God through men's redemption. Therefore, Gill's two-fold *pactum* functions as a nucleus of all the theological themes and doctrines with regard to the redemptive history in his system.

The Everlasting Council

Gill conceptualizes the everlasting council of God as "held between the three divine persons, Father, Son, and Spirit, concerning the affair of man's salvation before the world was."[10] Gill delineates the feature of this council, as aforementioned, by putting more focus on the internal business of God himself, who is perfect in all aspects of men's redemption. The substantive descriptions of the council, therefore, pertain to who the author of salvation is, i.e., the Father, Son, Spirit, and to what the manner of the redemption through the covenant of grace is.

Gill's First Concern of the Council

In relation to this, Gill's first concern of the council comes with a question: "In what sense counsel, consultation and deliberation, can be ascribed to God, to the divine persons (?)"[11] Comparing God's perfect knowledge that needs no consultation among the divine persons to man's incomplete one, Gill confirms four elements concerning the God who saves: (1) the council does not display the lack of knowledge in God for men's redemption because God is perfect in all knowledge; (2) the purpose of the council is not to gain more knowledge as man does; (3) the council does not suppose any inequality between the three divine persons; and (4) the council occurs "as quick as thought," which means "it is no other than his thought."[12]

---

questions are related to the function of the covenant of grace that includes the covenant of works and the typical Reformed meaning of the covenant of grace. More will be handled in the section of the properties of the covenant of grace.

10. Gill, *Divinity: Book II*, 45.

11. Gill, *Divinity: Bool II*, 45.

12. Gill, *Divinity: Book II*, 45. Explaining the meaning of Proverbs 11:14 regarding safety in making a decision with many counselors, says Gill, "because what one may miss another may hit upon; and, if they agree in their advice, it may be the more depended upon; and, if not, yet their different sentiments being compared together, and the reasons of them, a person may the better judge which is best to follow, and what is fit to be done . . . in the large capacity or endowments of a counsellor; in one that is abundantly qualified for a counsellor; whose abilities are not to be questioned; in the advice of such an one a man may safely confide; and who that answers to this

God's knowledge of the three divine persons is perfect, so the council of God happens and is completed in the twinkle of an eye, which causes no conflicts of opinion. Then, what is the reason or justification for ascribing this council to God in the name of consultation or deliberation? Gill answers in a clear articulation:

> When consultation about the salvation of man is ascribed to God, it is intended to express the importance of it; not things trifling, but those of importance, are what men consult about and deliberate upon; such is the work of men's salvation of the greatest moment, not only to men, to their comfort and happiness here and hereafter, but to the glory of God; the glory of all whose perfections is greatly displayed in it, being so wisely contrived as it is for that purpose; wherefore it is not put upon any footing; nor into any hands, but into the hands of the Son of God.[13]

Gill is fully aware that consulting human redemption in the council of God is by no means negligible; rather, for Gill, without exaggeration, it is one of the most important works of God to deal with human redemption.

---

character as Jesus Christ, the wonderful Counsellor? in whose counsel we may rest with the greatest safety." Gill, *An Exposition of the Old Testament*, 4:405. Many counselors do not compete with the one absolute and wonderful Counselor. It is a matter of quality. The obvious comparison between God and man in terms of the counsel leads Gill to magnify Christ as the *Wonderful Counselor* in Isaiah 9:6, who is with the Father and the Spirit regarding men's redemption: "This title belongs to Christ, as concerned with his Father, and the blessed Spirit, in the works of nature, providence, and grace. God stands in no need of counsel, nor does it properly fall on him, though it is sometimes ascribed to him, speaking after the manner of men. Creatures are not of his council, but Christ is; he was privy to all his thoughts, purposes, and decrees; he was consulted in creation, and in the works of providence, and in the great affair of redemption and salvation." Gill, *An Exposition of the Old Testament*, 5:54-55. Gill's last point is impressive. The council of God happens "as quick as thought" and the council is "his thought," from which Gill's understanding of time and eternity is again confirmed. To God who is infinite and who has eternality and omnipresence as his attributes, some sorts of theological concepts and notions in the matter of nomenclature, e.g., decrees, election, *ordo salutis*, justification, council, covenant etc., lie simple before God as he is simple. Dividing, diverging, analyzing, and all kinds of breaking down concepts into pieces are from man's perspective, man's job, which needs time with effort. While showing the features of God's council occurring beyond man's realm, Gill points out the limit of man's work in facing an issue even if sages put heads together: "When they have a matter of difficulty before them, do not suddenly and at once determine; but take time and consider it in every point of view, that they may fix on the wisest and most rational method of acting; consultations on an affair have been sometimes held many days successively." Gill, *Divinity: Book II*, 45.

13. Gill, *Divinity: Book II*, 45.

First, it pertains directly to the glory of God.[14] Formulating men's salvation is for the comfort and happiness of men; however, it ultimately manifests the glory of God.[15] Secondly, due to the significance of men's salvation

---

14. In the vision of the glorious new Jerusalem in Revelation 21-22, Gill pictures glorious things in Christ's spiritual and personal reign. A large conversion, distinctness of the light of the gospel, and the great purity of gospel concerning worship and ordinances in the spiritual reign of Christ in heaven and in the heart of believers, "will be done in the personal reign of Christ" in the new Jerusalem. Enjoying the personal appearance of the glorious one who is Christ, God's people dwell with him. Gill sees redemption realized in the glorious new Jerusalem by God's indwelling with his people: "This will issue in the ultimate glory; when the saints shall be forever with the Lord; shall see him as he is; enjoy uninterrupted communion with Father, Son, and Spirit; have the company of angels, and be in possession of those *things which eye hath not seen, nor ear heard, nor has it entered into the heart of man to conceive of*." John Gill, "Sermon IV: The Glory of the Church in the Latter Day," in *A Collection of Sermons and Tracks*, 3 vols. (London: George Keith, 1773), 1:61, 64, 69. Italics original.

15. Frame attempts to approach the glory of God from the perspective of God: "Glory is God's visible presence among people . . . . God's glory was in the cloud that led Israel through the wilderness (Ex. 16:6-10). It shone on Mount Sinai (24:16), and then it came and dwelled in the midst of Israel, in the tabernacle, and later in the temple (29:43; 40:34). This indwelling presence of God was called the *shekinah*, the Hebrew word meaning 'settle down, abide, dwell.' So in the glory, God dwelled as Lord among his people. You remember God's lordship attribute of covenantal presence. His glory is a form of that presence. In the NT, Jesus is God tabernacling with his people (John 1:14). He is our *shekinah*." Frame, *Systematic Theology*, 1009. Also, see Frame, *The Doctrine of God*, 592-95. Interesting is that Frame's dwelling concept of God's glory from Exodus to John is closely connected to the course of salvation of God's people as Gill mentions. In the exposition of Ps 21:5, Gill accounts for the meaning: "His glory is great in the salvation of his people by him; it was his glory as Mediator to be appointed to be the Lord's salvation to them; and it being effected by him declares the glory and greatness of his person; and the nature of it is such as cannot fail of bringing glory to him; and such is the sense his people have of it, that it obliges them to ascribe the glory of it alone to him." Gill, *An Exposition of the Old Testament*, 3:613. Gentry also relates Exodus 33-34 and John 1 to the glory of God. Though Gentry's interpretation of the glory is a little different from Frame's, he emphasizes that the trinitarian intimate relationship of the divine persons in love shines on the creation in the glory of God, which "can be described under two categories: the *name* of Yahweh and the *way* of Yahweh." Peter J. Gentry, "'The Glory of God'--The Character of God's Being and Way in the Word: Some Reflections on a Key Biblical Theology Theme," *SBJT* 20, no. 1 (2016): 149-161. God's self-revelation by name and the way of his work are related to the glory of God, which is revealed by the redemptive history. Bruce Baker's proposed definition of the glory of God, after working on the biblical and theological evidence, helps understand the relation between men's redemption and the glory of God: "The glory of God is his revelation of his own perfections, both eternally within the Godhead and temporally in all creation." Bruce A. Baker, "A Biblical and Theological Examination of the Glory of God," *JMAT* 22, no. 1 (Spring 2018): 24. The glory of God is revealed in his eternal, perfect Godhead; at the same time, this eternal glory shines in the creation as well, "The heavens declare the glory of God" (Ps 19:1). However, by committing a sin men fall short of the glory of God (Rom 3:23), the glory that they had in the creation before

in relation to the glory of God, God's method to fulfill the lofty task is to choose Christ, the Son of God, to be the redeemer who is "the wisdom of God."[16] The best manifestation of the wisdom of God in Christ is revealed in the gospel, which

> may be called all wisdom and prudence, because it is the wisdom of God; it is the produce of his wisdom, and a display of it; *the doctrines it contains* are full of wisdom, and are the means of communicating it to men, and of making them wise unto salvation; and it may be so called, to set forth the excellency and perfection of it, as greatly transcending all human wisdom; and in this the grace of God has much abounded, for the Gospel is a declaration of the free grace of God, in the salvation of sinners by Christ.[17]

---

the fall. God's plan to restore all things new in the new Jerusalem (new creation) had already begun right after the fall in Genesis 3:15 through covenantal promises to the sacrificial work of Christ. God's glory is revealed in the comprehensive way including both the fallen and the redeemed humanity in the redemptive work of Christ as the Saviour and King. While explaining the restoration of all things in Revelation 21 in the concept of "from glory to glory," Thiselton elucidates, "Glory . . . denotes what is weighty or impressive. In one sense, all glory belongs to God: 'My glory I give to no other' (Isa. 42:8). Further, Christ is 'the reflection of God's glory' . . . . The glory of God is seen 'in the face of Jesus Christ' (2 Cor. 4:6). As the Gospel of John stresses, what makes God so 'impressive' is not only his sovereign majesty, but also his humility in the incarnation and the cross . . . As Stauffer commented, 'John conceived of Christ's passion as the last and decisive service to the glory of God . . . . God Friday itself [is] the glorifying of the Son' (John 12:23). This verse reads, 'The hour has come for the Son of Man to be glorified.' In heaven this glory is seen from the very first." Thiselton, *Systematic Theology*, 383.

16. 1 Corinthians 1:30; Gill, *Divinity: Book II*, 45. Also, based on Ephesians 1:7, Gill states, "Redemption supposes captivity and slavery, and is a deliverance out of it; God's elect by nature are in bondage to sin, Satan, and the law; through the grace of Christ, they are redeemed from all iniquity; ransomed out of the hands of him that is stronger than they; and are freed from the law, its bondage, curse, and condemnation, and from every other enemy: and this benefit Christ is the author of; he was called to be the Redeemer of his people from all eternity." Gill, *An Exposition of the New Testament*, 3:62.

17. Gill, *An Exposition of the New Testament*, 3:63. Italics added. The doctrines the gospel contains are the "manifold wisdom of God" (Eph 3:10; NASB, 1995). Paul writes that this "multi-faceted wisdom" is "according to his eternal purpose accomplished in Christ Jesus our Lord," (Eph 3:11), which, according to Gill, is displayed in "election," "redemption," "justification," and in "pardon of sin." For more explanation, see Gill, *An Exposition of the New Testament*, 3:81. In terms of the wisdom's function as the communicator in the gospel of Jesus Christ, Treier notes, "the Gospel of John arguably presents him [Jesus] as Wisdom incarnate, and Matthew's Gospel seems to present Jesus as not only teaching but also somehow embodying wisdom. This extends the OT emphasis on wisdom (to whatever extent personified) as God's initiative of communication to

The Covenant of Redemption According to John Gill

The last point of Gill's first concern of the council is that the three divine persons reveal their "unanimity" with regard to this crucial decision of human salvation.[18] In other words, the Father, Son, and Spirit who share the same essence or nature in one Godhead always exist in the same mind. So, when "the Father signified his mind that his Son should be sent to be the Saviour of men . . . 'Whom shall I send, and who will go for us?' the Son, knowing his Father's will, and assenting to it, declared his agreement with it, 'Here am I, send me.'"[19] The Spirit also is not excluded from the decision to

---

humanity. The Christological implications are complex and the problems knotty. Yet wisdom apparently figures on the divine rather than the human side of the divide between Creator and creature, the Worshipped and the not worshipped." Daniel J. Treier, "Wisdom," in *Dictionary for Theological Interpretation of the Bible*, 845.

18. Gill, *Divinity: Book II*, 45. One might have a question regarding the expressions "council" and "unanimity," asking, "Did the three divine persons take a vote?", which is quite reasonable. When it comes to the term "vote," it basically presupposes that there are different opinions with a proposed agenda. Thus, those who are concerned with the agenda vote to make a better decision that is not determined yet before the vote. Disagreements of an agenda from different wills go through adjustment expecting a better idea to satisfy all participants regarding the agenda. However, Gill's term "unanimity" in the divine persons delivers a different nuance compared to the human level of decision by voting. It is another expression in emphasis of "they are one in nature," "they agree in one" in Gill's word. It is Gill's choice and expression to convey the one will of God in three divine persons regarding the salvation of men from eternity: i.e., this unanimity signifying God's one will about men's redemption is shown by acts of the three divine persons in translating from what belongs to eternity to the temporal.

19. Gill, *Divinity: Book II*, 45-46. Expositing Isaiah 6:8, Gill considers the Father's voice, "whom shall I send?" as "spoken after the manner of men" because "the Lord knew whom to send, and whom he would send; and could easily qualify any one he pleased . . . for who of all the creatures is the Lord's counsellor? but to the Son and Spirit." Gill, *An Exposition of the Old Testament*, 5:37. The discourse in Isaiah 6:8, as Gill mentioned, must be following "after the manner of men" because the Father and the Son knows everything in God's plan: "everything is done as it was purposed, and at the time it should, and which is known to God; particularly the time of Christ's first coming into the world, was agreed and fixed upon between the Father and the Son, called the fulness of time, (Gal. iv. 4.) and was known to them both, and made known in the word." Gill, "Sermon II: The Watchman's Answer to the Question, What of the Night?," in *A Collection of Sermons and Tracts*, 1:19. The concept of "agreement on sending" among the three divine persons not only shows the unanimity in the will of the three persons in one nature, but it also presupposes there are three distinct persons in the Godhead: "The Father's *sending* of the Son and the Holy Spirit makes it possible and necessary to discern distinctions within the life of the one God. . . . They [names of the three persons] are self-interpretations because Jesus spoke of the one who *sent* him as Father, and of himself, the *sent* one, as the Son." Sanders, *The Triune God*, 121-22. Italics added. The distinction between the three persons of one God is, for Gill, important as he later will question pertaining to the council, "who should be the Saviour, or be the author of this salvation . . . this was the business of this great council." Gill, *Divinity: Book II*, 48.

send the Son to join with the Father. Gill brings Isaiah 48:16b as the direct biblical support for the Spirit's approval of the agreement between the Father and the Son, "before the time that it was, there was I and now the Lord God and his Spirit hath sent me."[20] The participation of the Father, Son, Spirit, and all three persons in orchestrating men's redemption is meaningful in a significant manner, so Gill later treats the role of each person in both the council and covenant in detail.

---

20. Gill, *Divinity: Book II*, 46; Gill, *An Exposition of the Old Testament*, 5:281. There is a translation issue of Isaiah 48:16b ("פ וְעַתָּ֞ה אֲדֹנָ֧י יְהוִ֛ה שְׁלָחַ֖נִי וְרוּחֽוֹ", BHS) from Hebrew to English because Gill's translation ("the Lord God and his Spirit hath sent me") is not in line with the typical and conventional one ("the Lord God has sent me and his Spirit"). The issue is whether the subject is "the Lord God" in singular or "the Lord God and his Spirit" in plural, and grammatically the verb in parsing ("שלח") indicates that its subject is the third person, masculine, and "singular." Also, the usage of *vav* conjunction ("ו") between "me" and "his Spirit" reinforces the relation of both, and it seems to support the conventional ("singular") translation. Many of other English translations follow the "singular" subject including the Septuagint ("καὶ νῦν κύριος Κύριος ἀπέστειλέν με καὶ τὸ πνεῦμα αὐτοῦ", in spite of the possibility of using τὸ πνεῦμα as nominative, because the neuter takes the same article for both nominative and accusative, the conjunction καὶ strongly connects με and τὸ πνεῦμα αὐτοῦ as accusative): "And now the Lord God has sent Me, and His Spirit" (NASB); "And now the Sovereign Lord has sent me, endowed with his Spirit" (NIV); "And now the Lord God has sent me, and his Spirit" (ESV); "And now the Lord God has sent me and his Spirit" (CSB); "And now the Lord GOD has sent me and his Spirit" (RSV). Uniquely, however, the King James and the New King James Version translate it as "plural": "And now the Lord God, and his Spirit, hath sent me" and "And now the Lord God and His Spirit *have* sent Me" respectively (Italics added). Basically, the issue discussed above regarding Isaiah 48:16b has not been a significant concern of the OT scholars because their interest was about "who is the first person who suddenly occurred in the context as speaker?" while assuming the "singular" subject as granted. See J. Alec Motyer, *Isaiah: An Introduction and Commentery*, Tyndale Old Testament Commentaries, vol. 20 (Downers Grove: IVP, 1999), 343; Gary V. Smith, *Isaiah 40-66*, The New American Commentary, vol. 15B (Nashville: B&H, 2009), 329; Shalom M. Paul, *Isaiah 40-66: Translation and Commentary* (Grand Rapids: Eerdmans, 2012), 316-17. Interestingly, among the early church Fathers, Origen directly asked the very question and answered it: "Did the Father and the Holy Spirit send Jesus, or did the Father send both Christ and the Spirit? The latter is correct. For, because the Savior was sent, afterwards the Holy Spirit was sent also, that the prediction of the prophet might be fulfilled." Origen, *Against Celsus* 1.46; Mark W. Elliott, ed., *Isaiah 40-66*, Ancient Christian Commentary on Scripture, Old Testament XI (Downers Grove: IVP, 2007), 104. While Gill sticks to his translation as "plural" subject, he also opens the possibility of "singular" translation emphasizing the order of being sent: "it may be rendered, *and now the Lord God hath sent me and his Spirit*: both were sent of God, and in this order; first, Christ, to be the Redeemer and Saviour; and then the Spirit, to be the Convincer and Comforter; see John 14:26 and 15:26 and 16:7, 8." Gill, *An Exposition of the Old Testament*, 5:281. Italics original.

Gill's Second Concern of the Council

Gill's second concern of the everlasting council is to prove the existence of the council among the three divine persons regarding men's redemption. The substructure of Gill's second concern is composed of two main conceptions: (1) the purpose of God with the creation and redemption of man and (2) the gospel of God with Zechariah 6:13.[21]

First, the existence of the council is proved by the purpose of God. The purpose of God's planning for men's salvation requires "the highest wisdom" with "perfect faithfulness," which is "the basis and foundation of the council."[22] Both the wisdom and the faithfulness for the overall redemption of men, according to Gill, are richly demonstrated in Isaiah 25:1b,

> the decrees and purposes of God, which are from eternity, are all truly and faithfully performed; this is an amplification of the wonderful things which are done according to the counsel of the divine will; not only the choice of men to salvation, the redemption of them by Christ, and their effectual vocation; but the calling of the Jews and Gentiles, in particular, in the latter day, and all things relating to the church to the end of time; which, as they were fixed in the eternal purpose of God, they are punctually and exactly brought about in time; these are the true and faithful sayings of God.[23]

This redemptive plan in the council with the highest wisdom and perfect faithfulness is "according to his eternal purpose accomplished in Christ Jesus our Lord."[24] What is not to be ignored with regard to the purpose is that the purpose of God stems not only from the Father and the Son but also from the Spirit. The Holy Spirit penetrates deep into the essence of God as

---

21. As proof, Gill originally unfolds the elements of the substructure in order: the purpose of God, the gospel of God, the creation and redemption, Zechariah 6:13. The frame of the "two main conceptions" in formation of the substructure, however, conveys better understanding of Gill's second concern of the council as he continues relating each element according to its content.

22. Gill, *Divinity: Book II*, 46; Isaiah 25:1.

23. Gill, *An Exposition to the Old Testament*, 5:139.

24. Ephesians 3:11. Gill articulates an inseparable relation of the council and salvation: "The whole of salvation, in which is displayed the great wisdom of God, is according to a purpose of his; the scheme of it is fixed in the council of peace." Gill continues, "his purpose concerning the salvation of men must be eternal, since a council of peace was held, a covenant of peace was made, a promise of life was given, persons were fixed upon to be saved, a Saviour [Jesus Christ] was appointed for them, and grace, and the blessings of it were put into his hands before the world began." Gill, *An Exposition of the New Testament*, 3:81.

the apostle Paul affirms: "Now God has revealed these things to us by the Spirit, since the Spirit searches everything, even the depths of God. For who knows a person's thoughts except his spirit within him? In the same way, no one knows the thoughts of God except the Spirit of God."[25]

To prove the existence of the council in the purpose of God regarding men's redemption is inextricably linked to the "formation of man," i.e., creation.[26] Gill uniquely takes the words of God, "Let us make man in our image," to the eternal council: "It is not necessary to understand the words as spoken the moment, or immediately before the creation of man, but as spoken in eternity, in council between the divine Persons."[27] Because the

---

25. 1 Corinthians 2:10-11; Gill, *Divinity: Book II*, 46. Concerning the meaning of "the depths" of God, Gill explains, "for the *deep things of God* intend . . . the mysterious doctrines of the Gospel, the fellowship of the mystery which was hid in God, his wise counsels of old concerning man's salvation, the scheme of things drawn m [in] his eternal mind, and revealed in the word." Gill, *An Exposition of the New Testament*, 2:610. Italics original. The Spirit is the perfect person to assimilate "the mysterious doctrines and the mystery hidden in God" to and in himself because the Spirit himself is the very mystery. "He simply is when nothing else is." With the Father and the Son (Word), the Spirit *is*. Expositing Genesis 1:2, Malcolm Yarnell makes two concluding ideas regarding the Spirit's being God in mystery: "the Spirit remains mysterious from the perspective of positive definition in Gen 1:2, due to the lack of a positive analogy from creation . . . . the mystery of the Spirit does not extend to the divine identity of the Spirit . . . . He is substantively and personally the Spirit *of God*." See Malcolm B. Yarnell III, *Who Is the Holy Spirit: Biblical Insights into His Divine Person*, Hobbs College Library (Nashville: B&H, 2019), 6-9. Italics original. Then, the answer to the next question, "How does the Spirit know the 'counsels of old concerning man's salvation' in God's eternal mind?" is clear. It is because the Spirit is "within him." As Gill asserts, "the Son was not only *privy to this purpose or counsel*, and agreed to it;" but the Spirit also "is *privy to divine knowledge* and therefore *is God himself*" because "only a person knows his or her own inmost thoughts." See Gill, *Divinity: Book II*, 46; Robert A. Peterson, *Salvation Applied by the Spirit: Union with Christ* (Wheaton: Crossway, 2015), 303.

26. Gill, *Divinity: Book II*, 46.

27. Gill, *Divinity: Book II*, 46. In the exposition of Genesis 1:26, Gill avers, "A consultation is held among the divine Persons about the formation of him; not because of any difficulty attending it, but as expressive of his honour and dignity; it being proposed he should be made not in the likeness of any of the creatures already made, but as near as could be in the likeness and image of God." Gill, *An Exposition of the Old Testament*, 1:10. Emphasizing the importance of the creation of man, Cornelis Van Dam states, "*prior to his creation, God took counsel with Himself.* Instead of simply speaking the command, such as 'let there be,' we now read, 'God said, 'Let Us make man" (1:26). This is an astounding revelation from God Himself given to us in clear historical prose. *He takes counsel with Himself; He deliberates with Himself as He considers His next creative and climactic work.* The fullness of what the phrase 'let Us make' can imply only becomes evident in the New Testament revelation of the Holy Trinity--Father, Son, and Spirit." Cornelis Van Dam, *In the Beginning: Listening to Genesis 1 and 2* (Grand Rapids: Reformation Heritage Books, 2021), 210-11. Italics added. Also, John Pester helps us understand this relation of Genesis 1:26 to the eternal purpose in the council

expression "God said" (Gen 1:26) itself has the power to determine whatever comes to God's mind regardless of the realm of past, present, and future, according to Gill, the object to which God said is already fixed.[28] It is according to the will of God. Gill states,

> *God had determined on this in the decree of election*; for as in the decree of the end, he chose some of the creatures his power could make, to be happy with him, for his own glory; so in the decree of the means, he resolved on the creation of them; as has been before observed; however, be it, that this consultation was immediately before the creation of man, as all the three Persons were concerned in that, and in his creation; it may be reasonably argued, that if there was a consultation of the divine Persons

---

by investigating the triune God's eternal purpose for redemption and accomplishment of the Son's becoming flesh in incarnation: "The revelation of the Triune God in Genesis 1:26 and 27 is intrinsically related to the accomplishment of His eternal purpose because His eternal purpose is not limited to the creation of just physical things, including the heavens, the earth, and even man. The fulfillment of God's eternal purpose requires a new creation that is the issue of God's divine life and nature being dispensed into human vessels bearing His likeness for the enlargement of His image." John Pester, "And God Said, Let Us Make . . . And Let Them"–The Body of Christ as the Corporate Manifestation of the Triune God in the Flesh," *Affirmation & Critique* 18, no. 2 (Fall 2013): 17. Another significant issue must be brought into the question: "How is the plural usage to be understood?" John Goldingay articulates, "While the God who speaks is the trinitarian God, engaged in this act of making as Father, Son, and Spirit, and he might have had a smile on his face in inspiring Genesis to use this plural form, the author of Genesis and the people listening to the creation story did not know this fact about God's creating humanity, . . . The plural then underlines the authority of the one who speaks; it draws attention to the difference and the boundary between God and humanity even while making a point about humanity being made like God." John Goldingay, *Genesis*, Baker Commentary on the Old Testament: Pentateuch (Grand Rapids: Baker, 2020), 35. Thus, this plural does not indicate angels or heavenly entities because God clearly said, "Let us make the human being in our image and likeness." And "certainly God did not create humans in the image and likeness of angels and demons," says Rebecca Rine. She, borrowing Theodoret's idea, makes a final comment, "the contrast of singular 'God' and plural 'us' as well as singular 'image' and plural 'our' points to both 'the identity of substance' and the 'numerical distinction of persons' of the Trinity." C. Rebecca Rine, "Interpretations of Genesis 1-2 among the Nicene and Post-Nicene Fathers," in *Since the Beginning: Interpreting Genesis 1 and 2 through the Ages*, ed. Kyle R. Greenwood (Grand Rapids: Baker, 2018), 135-36.

28. In other words, the phrase "God said" implies God's invariable will manifested in time, i.e., what is determined in eternity due to the character of the verb אָמַר ("say, promise, declare, intend"), which conveys "to think with a purpose and planning." See אָמַר in James Swanson, *A Dictionary of Biblical Languages: Hebrew (Old Testament)*, Electronic ed. (Oak Harbor: Logos Research Systems, 1997).

about the making of man at first, then much more about the redemption and salvation of him.[29]

Secondly, the existence of the council is also proved by the gospel, that is, "an exhibition and declaration of the scheme of salvation, being called the counsel of God."[30] When Gill calls "the counsel of God" with respect to the gospel, based on Acts 20:27, it denotes not the "decrees of God, latent in his own breast" in secret but "his revealed will in the Gospel, concerning the salvation of men by Jesus Christ, even the whole of the Gospel, every truth and doctrine of it, necessary to salvation, and to the peace, joy, and comfort of the saints."[31] Thus, the gospel is "a transcript of the council of peace and covenant of grace, which were from everlasting" and the expression of the apostles through which "eternal transaction between God and Christ" is seen.[32]

---

29. Gill, *Divinity: Book II*, 46. Italics added. It may not be reasonable to directly articulate the relation of making of man to the redemption and salvation of man in the timeline from the human perspective because the conceptions of sin and fall are lacking in the process between the creation and redemption. So much emphasis on the sovereignty and decrees of God sometimes appears to miss a logical process that must exist in order to make sense in the viewpoint of man. However, Gill does not neglect what should happen in redemptive history centered in the incarnate Christ as will be dealt with in a later chapter in this volume. What is in God's mind is manifested and realized in the person and work of Jesus Christ by the cooperating work and help of the Holy Spirit. The formation of man in the eternal council, and the speaking of God as revelation in a written language are the relation of God's plan to the "human agency." With regard to this discussion, Vern Poythress notes two kinds of truths as a principle in understanding basic biblical doctrines, "So we may say that there are two kinds of truth. There are truths that are already true, within the plan of God, but are not yet known to human beings on the earth. Then there are truths that have become accessible to us on earth because God has brought about the situation specified by particular truths that express his plan. The distinction between the two kinds of truth arises because of the limits of human knowledge, not because of something innate in the quality of truth." Vern S. Poythress, *Truth, Theology, and Perspective: An Approach to Understanding Biblical Doctrine* (Wheaton: Crossway, 2022), 47.

30. Gill, *Divinity: Book II*, 46.

31. Gill, *An Exposition of the New Testament*, 2:340. Scholars agree with the meaning of πᾶσαν τὴν βοθλὴω τοῦ θεοῦ ("the whole plan of God") that it denotes the will, design, and purpose of God as revealed in the gospel for man's salvation. See Albert Barnes, *Notes on the New Testament: Acts*, ed. Robert Frew (London: Blackie & Son, 1884-85), 295; David G. Peterson, *The Acts of the Apostles*, The Pillar New Testament Commentary (Grand Rapids: Eerdmans, 2009), 567-68; Patrick Schreiner, *Acts*, Christian Standard Commentary (Nashville: Holman, 2021), 551.

32. Gill, *An Exposition of the New Testament*, 2:609; Gill, *Divinity: Book II*, 46. It is significant for Gill to capture such a relationship between the everlasting council and the gospel, i.e., the reality and "a transcript." The concept of the *pactum* has generally been considered as having no evidence rooted in Scripture. However, Gill finds that the overall story of Scripture goes toward the salvation of man through the gospel in

With regard to the counsel of God, Gill's former position takes it for granted that the concept of the counsel revealed in the gospel is deeply related to Zechariah 6:13's "counsel of peace." Gill links his understanding of the counsel of peace in 6:13 to the Jew and Gentile reconciliation in Zechariah 6:15, which signifies "the 'counsel of peace,' may be meant *the gospel*, called the counsel of God, and the gospel of peace, ... , has been among *Jews and Gentiles*, preached to them, ... , making peace between them, and *reconciling* them together."[33]

However, Gill later alters his position, interpreting Zechariah 6:13 in line with other covenant theologians, and accepts that the counsel of peace is the "council concerning the peace and reconciliation in eternity, between

---

Jesus Christ. Moreover, investigating each biblical passage concerning the covenantal redemptive work of the Father, Son, and Spirit, who is the *eternal* triune God, drives Gill to proceed to a connection between eternity and time in terms of salvation. In this regard, focusing on Jesus Christ the incarnate, the second person of the Trinity, the central locus of salvation, the only place where eternity and time meet, highlights the gospel that "concerns 'salvation,' the comprehensive reordering of God's relation to humankind." John Webster, "Gospel," in *Dictionary for Theological Interpretation of the Bible*, 263. Revealing to humanity what is in mind and the plan of God in the eternal council, takes the gospel of and through Jesus Christ as a unique and mysterious method to manifest the salvation of the triune God. Frame provides a Christ's centered definition of the gospel: "The good news that a child would be born to redeem mankind is the same gospel by which we today may be saved from God's wrath. As *Adam and Eve looked forward* to that child, *we look back* upon him, Jesus Christ, who died for our sin, rose again, and ever lives to intercede for us." Frame, *Systematic Theology*, 66. Italics added. God's wisdom and method, Jesus Christ, for the redemption of humanity is not hindered by man's episteme of time. Jesus Christ is beyond the matter of both Adam's looking forward and the contemporary's looking back. The bigger issue is that man is allowed to be able to see Jesus Christ the second person of the Trinity as God-Man, who is privy to every deep knowledge in the eternal council of the triune God, and moreover, who is the true Mediator between eternity and time. That is reason why the gospel in relation to the eternal council is important. Jesus Christ is the gospel of God.

33. Gill, *Divinity: Book II*, 46. Italics added. The reason why Gill infers such a conclusion lies in his interpretation of Zechariah 6:13, especially on the section, "and the counsel of peace shall be between them both." Gill makes two points: (1) Although Gill does not consider Joshua and Zerubbabel as the "both" who shall make the counsel of peace, his former understanding follows that the counsel of peace shall be made by Christ's two offices, i.e., priestly, and kingly; thus, (2) the counsel of peace cannot be the council of peace between the Father and the Son. In addition, the council of peace between the Father and the Son "was past in eternity"; the counsel of peace between "the priestly and kingly offices of Christ" has a future aspect. Thus, the counsel of peace in 6:13 is "better the Gospel of peace, called the whole counsel of God, which, in consequence of Christ being a Priest on his throne, was preached to both Jews and Gentiles; which brought the glad tidings of peace and salvation by Christ to both, and was the means of making peace between them both." Gill, *An Exposition of the Old Testament*, 6:709.

Jehovah and the Branch, between the Father and the Son."[34] Nevertheless,

34. Gill, *Divinity*, Book II, 46. First, this is the reason why both "counsel of God" and "council of God" might appear to be confused. In Gill's term, the counsel of God is the revealed will of God in the gospel. Thus, Gill first connected the counsel of peace in Zech 6:13 to the revealed gospel in the reconciliation between Jews and Gentiles. Later, however, Gill realized that the counsel of peace in Zech 6:13 pertains to the eternal council of God. The key to identify the difference between the counsel and council lied in the interpretation of the counsel of peace in Zech 6:13. Secondly, why do the covenant theologians strongly assert that the "both" in Zechariah 6:13 are Jehovah and the Branch? The biblical warrant of some of the *pactum* theologians does not appear to be cogent enough. See Gillespie, *The Ark of the Covenant Opened*, 6-7; Willard, *The Doctrine of the Covenant of Redemption*, 9-19; also, see a simple statement of Witsius concerning 6:13, "The counsel of peace, which is between the man whose name is the Branch, and between Jehovah, whose temple he shall build, and on whose throne he shall sit." Witsius, *The Economy of the Covenants*, 168-69. The key issue of this passage (Zech 6:9-15) focuses on two questions: (1) who is the Branch? (2) who is the other party who shall make the counsel of peace with the Branch? After examining the whole structure of Zechariah compared to the similar biblical covenantal context, e.g., Davidic promise, Fesko resolves the raised issues. First, the context of Zechariah 3:9-13b sees, according to Fesko, "the crowned high priest, Joshua, as a type of the Messiah, the one who will eventually build the temple of the Lord." Fesko, *The Trinity and the Covenant of Redemption*, 65-66. Petterson also adds, "In the context of this symbolic action, the sense may be that the Shoot will be a legitimate descendant of David, unlike Joshua, who simply represents the Shoot." Anthony R. Petterson, *Behold Your King: The Hope for the House of David in the Book of Zechariah*, Library of Hebrew Bible/Old Testament Studies 513 (New York: T&T Clark, 2009), 108. In this context, therefore, there is no room for Joshua and Zerubbabel to make the counsel of peace. Both kingly and priestly offices belong to the Branch the coming Messiah [regarding the relationship between the Branch, Royal figure, and priest in Zech 6:13b, see Wolter H. Rose, *Zemah and Zerubbabel: Messianic Expectations in the Early Postexilic Period*, Journal for the Study of the Old Testament Supplement Series 304 (England: Sheffield Academic Press, 2000), 59-68]. Jauhiainen also supports there comes only with one person in Zechariah 3:12-13, the Branch: "the fact that vv. 12-13 first mention Zemah and then go on to tell what he will do (. . . ; a total of five third masculine singular imperfective verbs whose subject is Zemah) would lead one to think that the immediately following verb in the same form also has Zemah as its subject." Marko Jauhiainen, "Turban and Crown Lost and Regained: Ezekiel 21:29-32 and Zechariah's Zemah," *Journal of Biblical Literature* 127, no. 3 (2008): 509; also, see George L. Klein who denotes, "We have already seen that one cannot defend the view that both Zerubbabel and Joshua are present and are both addressed by v. 12. Zechariah predicted a concord between the priestly and royal offices, and both are offices that the Branch will hold" in *Zechariah*, The New American Commentary, vol. 21B (Nashville: B&H, 2008), 204. Fesko's answer to the second question is hinted by the repeated expressions in Zechariah 6:13: "the temple of the Lord," and "his throne." Fesko finds the other party of the counsel Yahweh, and provides his understanding of Zechariah 3:12-13, although the logical process of determining Yahweh as the other party seems to slightly be forced or not smooth (in other words, Fesko's two support evidence seems to focus on the "temple" and "throne," not on Yahweh himself): "It is the Branch who shall build the temple of the Lord and shall bear royal honor, and shall sit and rule by Yahweh's throne. And the Branch shall be a priest by Yahweh's throne, and the counsel of peace shall be between them both, Yahweh and

even the altered position is not fully satisfactory to Gill because the everlasting council is always between the three divine persons, not just the Father and the Son.

Gill's Third Concern of the Council

Gill's third and last concern of the everlasting council turns toward the participants of the council. For Gill, this topic is crucial, and the council solely belongs to the Father, Son, and Spirit, neither angels nor men.[35] It is because, as will be handled in detail later in this chapter, the basic condition of the *pactum* is concerned with the ability to perform or meet with what is covenanted between the parties; in other words, the *pactum* requires responsibility on which the glory of God and the redemption of men rely. More words regarding the tasks of each participant will be delineated in a concrete manner.[36]

In sum, the everlasting council of the three divine persons is the unique method in Gill's *pactum* for the entire system of theology. In preparation for the everlasting covenant of grace, the justification of the eternal council's existence not only reveals that God himself is the true counselor and the perfect wisdom of the whole plan of salvation of the world but also makes the covenant of grace ready for jumping into economic redemptive history.

Now, the second phase of Gill's twofold definition of the *pactum*, the everlasting covenant of grace, unfolds.

---

the Branch." Fesko, *The Trinity and the Covenant of Redemption*, 72; also, see Petterson, *Behold Your King*, 110-11; E. B. Pusey, *Notes on the Old Testament: The Minor Prophtes: Micah to Malachi*, vol. 2 (New York: Funk and Wagnalls, 1885; reprint, Grand Rapids: Baker Book House, 1983), 376. For more detailed explanations, go to Fesko's section on Zechariah 6:13 in entirety, which takes the first place among exegetical passages as the biblical foundations of his argument for the *pactum*.

35. Gill, *Divinity: Book II*, 47.

36. As aforementioned, the everlasting council makes a distinction from the everlasting covenant of grace. The former intends more about God's immanent and inner attributes of each divine person in the Godhead for the redemption of men than the latter. Thus, in the third concern, Gill attempts to disclose how each person is perfect in the utmost *wisdom* to reveal the glory of God by redemption of men. The perfect wisdom, understanding, knowledge, and plan of God the Father, Son, and the Holy Spirit makes harmony in preparation for the settlement or adjustment in the covenant of grace regarding what happens in the redemptive history.

The Everlasting Covenant of Grace

At the beginning of this section, Gill's "twofold definition" of the *pactum*, a characteristic of the eternal covenant of grace, was described in an emphatic statement that the eternal covenant of grace concerns the economic aspect more than the eternal council. A significant reason to do so is deeply associated with the term "covenant," which is common in Scripture. Though recognizing various types and usages of covenant in the biblical narrative, Gill acknowledges that the concept of covenant solely belongs to God, who exists among the three divine persons. For Gill, therefore, the covenant is an authoritative mark of God carrying the weight of the triune God's divinity despite its deep connection to the economic administration.[37]

Nevertheless, the concept of covenant in Gill's theological system runs the whole Scripture from Genesis to Revelation and thus envisions the comprehensive picture of salvation history. In particular, the everlasting covenant of grace makes it possible that the concept of covenant takes control of overall temporal redemptive history in Scripture. To prove the point, Gill begins with the etymology of covenant in its usage of a couple of specified contexts, which will help draw a picture of God's grand framework of two administrations regarding men's redemption in time. Secondly, Gill's interest goes toward the sense of usage of the term "covenant" in Scripture and shows how this "sense" of covenant is related to the meaning of covenant of grace manifested in diverse expressions in Scripture. Third and lastly, Gill is carefully concerned with the contracting parties: the Father, Son, and Spirit, especially the relationship between person, nature, and will.

---

37. The fundamental ground of the chapter seven concerning the everlasting covenant of grace in Gill's *Divinity* is based on God's omni-series of the attributes, e.g., omnipotence, omniscience, omnipresence. God who can do anything in his good will is covenantal God in the Father, Son, and Spirit. God's reign in his sovereignty, power, and love always maintains the perfection and completion in the three divine persons' covenantal mystery being one. Gill's remark, "No man covenants with himself," signifies each perfect person and also distinct persons of the triune God makes everlasting harmony in their "federal transactions" with each other. Do the divine persons in eternity need such covenantal transactions? Then, what is the purpose and reason of that? If they need to do something with a "purpose" or "reason," does that itself not denote some kind of lacking to be perfect? In short, why covenant in eternity and in the triune God? Therefore, examining and comparing the related biblical passages as best as he could in the whole Scripture with the covenant concept in the redemptive history, Gill begins the everlasting covenant of grace with the "etymology and signification of the words used for 'covenant', in the writings of the Old and New Testament." Gill, *Divinity: Book II*, 49, 52.

Gill's First Task of the Covenant

Gill defines the covenant of grace as "a compact or agreement made from all eternity among the divine Persons, more especially between the Father and the Son, concerning the salvation of the elect."[38] For a better understanding of the covenant of grace in eternity and its influence and function in temporal redemptive history, Gill investigates, as the first task, the etymology of בְּרִית ("covenant") in OT. While looking into the various meanings of its usage, Gill pays special attention to the meaning, "select and choose" of בְּרִית, which underlies all other roots.[39] This implies each party's own will is

---

38. Gill, *Divinity: Book II*, 49. A seventeenth-century puritan and pastor-theologian also gives a similar definition, "the covenant of Grace, was made with Jesus Christ (not merely as God, but as to be incarnate, or designed to be Mediator) as a second Adam, and with *a Gospel seed in him*, promising all spiritual blessings, even eternal life and salvation upon the condition or consideration of his undergoing the curse, and yielding perfect obedience to the Law on their behalf." See "To the Reader" in Samuel Petto, *The Difference between the Old and New Covenant Stated and Explained* (London, 1674), no page number given. Italics added. For Petto, the *pactum* is made with Christ and with "a Gospel seed" in Christ, which is an interesting description compared to Gill's. Gill states, "The covenant of grace made between God and Christ, and with *the elect* in him . . ." Gill, *Divinity: Book II*, 51. Italics added. In the *pactum* mentioning the beneficiary, Petto's "a Gospel seed in Christ" and Gill's "the elect in Christ" appear to have a correlation or to provide a clue to figure out what Gill's understanding of the elect is. A greater detailed discussion will be in the chapter five of this volume regarding the concept of election in eternity and time. For further information about Samuel Petto's life and theology, see Michael G. Brown, "Samuel Petto (c. 1624-1711): A Portrait a Puritan Pastor Theologian," *PRJ* 2, no. 1 (2010): 75-91, especially, for Petto's covenant theology, see the pages 88-89.

39. Gill, *Divinity: Book II*, 50. The relation of covenant to election or "select and choose" is not unfamiliar to OT scholars. Eichrodt regards the association of the covenant and election as the underlying ideas forming the distinctive history of the Israelites. See Walther Eichrodt, *Theology of the Old Testament*, trans. J. A. Baker, The Old Testament Library, 2 vols. (Philadelphia: The Westminster Press, 1961), 1:36-69, esp. 42n3. Ernest Wright agrees, "The doctrine of election found its most concrete expression in the Old Testament language of the covenant." After explaining the covenantal social life of the Israelites in regard to the concept of election, which defines the special relation of Israel to God, Wright also states, ". . . covenant is no longer a legal compact between human beings, but a device for explaining the meaning and nature of Israel's election." G. Ernest Wright, *The Old Testament against its Environment*, Studies in Biblical Theology (London: SCM, 1950), 54, 55, also 55n17. In overture of his book *The Covenant Formula*, Rendtorff explains how covenant and election are related to each other in interpretation of Nehemiah 9:6-8: "Bund und Erwählung ercheinen als zwei ganz verschiedene Gegenstände, so dass zwischen den Untersuchungen über das eine oder das andere Thema kaum Verbindungen bestehen." From the example of the covenant formula with regard to "establishment" in Genesis 17:7, continues Rendtorff, "Das gleiche gilt für das Wort בחר erwählen, das im Deuteronomium mit der Bundersformel eine enge Verbindung eingegangen ist. In Dtn 7,6 und 14,2 heisst es fast gleichlautend: Denn du bist ein heiliges Volk für Jhwh, deinen Gott, (und) dich hat Jhwh (dein Gott)

decisive in a covenant, which denotes they are ready to meet with whatever comes as a result of the covenantal terms and conditions and to be able to take responsibility for the result.[40] Thus, the meaning of "select and choose" perfectly fits the working of the everlasting covenant of grace by the three divine persons.

בְּרִית is mostly translated into διαθήκη in NT.[41] For Gill, the significance of using διαθήκη (or διατίθεμαι) comes in large with two English

---

erwählt, ihm zum Eigentumsvolk zu sein von allen Völkern, die auf der Erde sind. Hier sind also Bundersformel und Erwählungsaussage nicht voneinander zu trennen." Rolf Rendtorff, Die „Bundesformel": eine exegetisch-theologische Untersuchung, Stuttgarter Bibelstudien 160 (Stuttgart: Verlag Katholisches Bibelwerk, 1995), 10, 11. Among the "various meanings" from different roots of covenant given by Gill, the meaning of "to cut in pieces and divide" signifies something related to the eternal covenant of grace. Two instances of this case happen in Scripture: Genesis 15:17 and Jeremiah 34:18. In circumstance of making a covenant with Abram, God's land promise is affirmed with "mysterious terms" in Genesis 15:17, "When the sun had set and it was dark, a smoking fire pot and a flaming torch appeared and passed between the divided animals." Bruce Waltke elucidates the circumstance, "According to extant ancient Near Eastern texts, passing between the slain animals is a ritual that invokes a curse on the participants if they break the covenant. To walk between the carcasses is to submit oneself to the fate of the slaughtered animals as a penalty for covenant breaking." Bruce K. Waltke, An Old Testament Theology: An Exegetical, Canonical, and Thematic Approach (Grand Rapids: Zondervan, 2007), 319. Delbert Hillers depicts an image of cutting a covenant, "The most widely attested form of swearing to a covenant, however, involved cutting up an animal. The man taking the oath is identified with the slaughtered animal . . . . Among the Israelites it seems that a common way of identifying the parties to a covenant with the victim was to cut up the animal and pass between the parts." Hillers, Covenant: The History of a Biblical Idea, 40-41. William Dumbrell also adds a point by emphasizing God's gracious protection of Israel, "the divine passage through the pieces (v. 17) is not imprecation but a theophanic assurance of Yahweh's protection in terms somewhat reminiscent of the later 'pillar of cloud' wilderness guidance . . . . the details present a daring anthropomorphism whereby God involves himself in an obligation dramatized by an acted oath of self-commitment (cf. Heb. 6:13). In any case, no undertaking is exacted from Abram; God alone is bound. From this point onwards the covenant with Abraham becomes critical to our biblical understanding of Israel." William J. Dumbrell, Covenant and Creation: An Old Testament Covenant Theology, Revised and Enlarged Edition (Nashville: Thomas Nelson, 1984; reprint, Milton Keynes, England: Paternoster, 2013), 85, 86. As Gill mentions, the meaning of "select and choose" as root of covenant is permeated into other roots. God's choice to pass through the divided animals by himself, while Abram is in a "deep sleep" (Gen 15:12), connotes that from initiation to completion, the covenantal promise solely relies on God himself. In other words, God alone is responsible for giving a covenantal promise to Abram. It was God's choice and determination to impose obligation upon himself in case of failure of the covenant promise. Later, this covenant is confirmed to Abraham in Genesis 17:7-8 in the name of "everlasting covenant."

40. Gill, Divinity: Book II, 50.

41. διαθήκη implies several senses of the meaning: (1) *disposition* of property by will; (2) *testament* or *will*; (3) mystic *deposits* on which the common weal depended;

words in meaning: "to dispose or to appoint" and "testament or will." First, Gill sees a covenantal method of disposition in the kingdom movement of Luke 22:29, "where the Father is said to appoint, or dispose of, by covenant, a kingdom to his Son, as he also is said to appoint, or dispose by covenant, a kingdom to his people."[42] In other words, the kingdom is allowed for God's people to enter, which indicates that redemptive history is in progress by embracing both Jews and Gentiles in Christ.[43] The point is that all kingdom

---

and (4) *compact, covenant*. See Henry George Liddel and Robert Scott, comp., *A Greek-English Lexicon* (Oxford: Clarendon Press, 1996), 394-95.

42. Gill, *Divinity: Book II*, 50. Interestingly, the direct covenantal remark is not found in his exposition of Luke 22:29. Rather, he focuses on the kingdom itself: its spiritual character and relationship with the gospel. See Gill, *An Exposition of the New Testament*, 1:707. Regarding the usage and meaning of διατίθεμαι used in Luke 22:29, scholars have slightly different points of view. Howard Marshall, listing a couple of possible meanings of διατίθεμαι, e.g., "to issue a decree," "to make a covenant," "to assign, confer," and "to bequeath," states, "It is not clear whether the idea of a covenant is contained in διατίθεμαι; elsewhere this is made clear by the use of δισθήκην with the verb. Here, however, διαθήκη is present in the context (22:20), and the thought may be present for Greek readers." I. Howard Marshall, *The Gospel of Luke: A Commentary on the Greek Text*, NIGTC (Exeter, England: Paternoster Press, 1978), 816. Leon Morris, however, explaining the context of Luke 22:28-30, stresses the covenant way of thought, "Jesus speaks of all this in the language of covenant. The verbs *assign* and *assigned* both render forms of *diatithemai*, the useful biblical word for the making of a covenant. The glorious future of which Jesus speaks is as sure as the covenant of God." Leon Morris, *Luke: An Introduction and Commentary*, TNTC, vol. 3 (Downers Grove: IVP, 1988), 327. Italics original. Philip Ryken also remarks, "when Jesus spoke about 'assigning' these things to his disciples, he used the biblical verb for making a covenant (*diatithomai*). These were solemn promises, which Jesus was swearing by oath. He wanted to give his friends what he had received from his Father: an everlasting kingdom." Philip Graham Ryken, *Luke*, Reformed Expository Commentary, vol. 2 (Phillipsburg, NJ: P&R, 2009), 483.

43. Acts 3:25 using both terms διαθήκη and διατίθεμαι and reflecting what Gill meant in Luke 22:29, reads, ὑμεῖς ἐστε οἱ υἱοὶ τῶν προφητῶν καὶ τῆς διαθήκης ἧς διέθετο ὁ θεὸς πρὸς τοὺς πατέρας ὑμῶν λέγων πρὸς Ἀβραάμ· καὶ ἐν τῷ σπέρματί σου [ἐν]ευλογηθήσονται πᾶσαι αἱ πατριαὶ τῆς γῆς ("You are the sons of the prophets and of the covenant that God made with your ancestors, saying to Abraham, 'And all the families of the earth will be blessed through your offspring"). Italics original. Gill expounds, "Of Abraham, Isaac, and Jacob, who are called prophets, Psal. 105:15 being lineally and naturally descended from them; to them belonged the prophcies of the Old Testament concerning the Messiah, and the promises of him; they were heirs of them." Though the title of 'children of the covenant' belongs only to the Jews; and the law, covenant, and promises also belong to them, true meaning of the 'children of the covenant' is manifested in the saying to Abraham in Genesis 22:18, according to Gill, "meaning the Messiah, that sprung from him, and is called the son of Abraham; in whom, not only all Abraham's spiritual seed among the Jews, or the elect of God in that nation, and who were truly the children of Abraham, and of the promise, but even all the chosen of God among the Gentiles, in every nation, and of every kindred and family among them, are blessed in Christ, with all spiritual blessings; with peace, pardon, righteousness, redemption, and salvation." Gill, *An Exposition of the New Testament*, 2:169-70. More in detail concerning this topic

related events and their consequences from God to man, e.g., pardon of sin, righteousness, redemption, and salvation, are by and through covenant.

Secondly, διαθήκη is also used for the meaning of testament or will. As aforementioned, the big picture of "God's grand framework" for men's redemption stems from the word διαθήκη, which "signifies both covenant and testament."[44] Simply put, "The covenant of grace, as administered under the Gospel dispensation, is a testament or will."[45] According to Gill, the temporal covenantal realm in time consists of two administrations of the covenant of grace: namely, the Old and New Testaments or the Old and New Covenants. The covenant of grace manifested by the "two administrations" in time is centered on Jesus Christ. Based on Acts 4:12, regardless of the Old and New, which reads, "There is salvation in no one else, for there is no other name under heaven given to people by which we must be saved," Gill claims, "For though the covenant is but one, there are different administrations of it; particularly two, one before the coming of Christ, and the other after it."[46] With regard to the grand framework of the two administrations in God's eternal scheme, Gill elucidates,

> The covenant of grace, is properly a covenant to Christ, and a testament or will to his people: it is his and their father's will, concerning giving them both grace and glory; it consists of many gifts and legacies; in it Christ is made heir of all things, and his people are made joint heirs with him; they are given to him as his portion; and they have all things pertaining to life and godliness bequeathed to them, even all spiritual blessings; the witness of it are Father, Son, and Spirit; and the seals of it are the blood of Christ, and the grace of the Spirit; and this is registered in the Scriptures by holy men as notaries; and is unalterable and immutable.[47]

The everlasting covenant of grace, therefore, embraces two realms of time and eternity in Christ. Moreover, this covenant is more concerned

---

of the son of Abraham will be written in chapter five later.

44. Gill, *Divinity: Book II*, 50.

45. Gill, *An Exposition of the New Testament*, 3:438.

46. Gill, *Divinity: Book IV*, 175. In the same context, regarding the old and new dispensations, Gill adds, "the two administrations of the same covenant, are allegorically represented by two women, Hagar and Sarah, the bondwomen and the free (Gal. 4:22-26), which fitly describe the nature and difference of them." For the general covenantal picture of Hagar and Sarah comparison, see Horton, *Introducing Covenant Theology*, 35-50.

47. Gill, *An Exposition of the New Testament*, 3:438.

The Covenant of Redemption According to John Gill

with the economic aspect of men's redemption than the everlasting council, which makes Jesus Christ sit at the center of both realms.

Gill's Second Task of the Covenant

Gill's second task for a better understanding of the everlasting covenant of grace is to demonstrate that a covenant is the covenant of God. Gill means, at least, "a covenant, when ascribed to God, is often nothing more than a mere promise."[48] In other words, when God makes a covenant with men, it cannot essentially embody the same shape as the covenant between the divine persons. Due to the ontological difference between God and man in power, integrity, and responsibility, "the covenant of grace, with respect to the elect, is nothing else but a free promise of eternal life and salvation by Jesus Christ, which includes all other promises of blessings of grade in it."[49] Then, what pacts or agreements could be the covenant in the real sense, not just a promise? Gill answers, "The (everlasting) covenant of grace made between God and Christ, and with the elect in him, as their Head and Representative, is *a proper covenant*, consisting of stipulation and restipulation."[50] Namely, a proper covenant is a covenant between the Father, Son, and Holy Spirit in the Godhead, "which is to be entered into of free choice on both sides," with "inclination of will to yield the obedience required," and "power to perform it."[51] In the genuine sense, therefore, the everlasting covenant

---

48. Gill, *Divinity*: Book II, 50.
49. Gill, *Divinity*: Book II, 51.
50. Gill, *Divinity*: Book II, 51. Italics added.
51. Gill, *Divinity*: Book II, 51. To put it another way, the everlasting covenant of grace among the divine persons is, strictly speaking, qualified only to be called a covenant, according to Gill, because of the "power to perform it." In the same manner, Tobias Crisp notes, "if the covenant stands upon any conditions to be performed on man's part, it cannot be an '*everlasting covenant*,' except man was so confirmed in righteousness, that he should never fail in that which is his part . . . . man hath no tie upon him to perform any thing whatsoever in the covenant, as a condition that must be observed on his part; let the covenant itself be judge in this case: it plainly shews where all the tie lies, and as plainly shews, that the whole performance of the covenant lies only upon God himself; and that there is not one bond, or obligation, upon man to the fulfilling of the covenant, or partaking of the benefits of it." Tobias Crisp and John Gill, *Christ Alone Exalted: The Complete Works of Tobias Crisp*, 2 vols. (London: John Bennett, 1832), 1:87. Gill and Crisp agree with the concept of everlasting covenant. Why is a proper concept of a covenant only applied to the 'covenant' between the divine persons as 'the everlasting covenant'? A covenant between men may be called a covenant, or mutual pacts and agreements as Gill mentions. However, the prototype of the human covenant lies in the everlasting covenant among the divine persons, which features the never-failed or broken pact or promise. For Gill, all biblical covenants,

of grace among the three divine persons is the formal covenant of "mutual engagements"; i.e., "each party enters into, stipulate and restipulate about" the covenantal conditions as equivalent counterparts with the same power and authority.[52]

---

being derived from the everlasting covenant, reflect who the covenantal God is and at last show one of the original covenant party, the second person of the Trinity, becomes flesh as the new covenant.

52. Gill, *Divinity: Book II*, 51. In relation to this context, a fundamental question is raised by the comparison between the everlasting covenant of grace and the biblical covenants, i.e., the *pactum*'s being the archetype of a covenant and its reflection of the biblical covenants. The opponents ask, "Is there such a concept of a covenant called a kind of 'archetype' covenant in Scripture? In other words, where is biblical evidence for arguing for the existence of the everlasting covenant of grace between the Father and Son?" In the first chapter of this volume, a strong opponent of the concept of the *pactum*, O. Palmer Robertson, argues against the concept due to its "newness" and the lack of biblical evidence, asserting, "Scripture simply does not say much on the pre-creation shape of the decrees of God." See the note 37 in chapter one. The same situation happened in the eighteenth century. Denying the existence of the *pactum*, John Wesley avers, "I have heard of another (covenant) which I understand not. I have heard, 'that God the Father made a Covenant with his Son, before the world began, wherein the Son agreed so suffer such and such Things, and the Father to give him such and such Souls for a Recompence: That in Consequence of this, those Souls must be saved, and those only, so that all others must be damned.' I beseech you where is this written? in what Part of Scripture, is this Covenant to be found?" John Wesley, *Predestination Calmly Considered* (London: Printed by Henry Cock, 1755), 44-45. In opposition to Wesley's *Predestination Calmly Considered*, Gill firmly vouches for the *pactum*, "Now not to inform or instruct Mr *Wesley*, but for the sake of such who are willing to be informed and instructed, read *Psal.* 40:6-8. *Isa.* 49:1-6. and chap. 53:10-12. *Psal.* 89:3, 4, 28-36. in which will appear plain traces and footnotes of a covenant, or agreement, of a stipulation and restipulation, between the Father and the Son; in which the Father proposes a work to his Son, and calls him to it, even the redemption of his people; to which the Son agrees, and says, *Lo I come to do thy will, O my God!* and for a recompence of his being an offering for sin, and pouring out his soul unto death; it is promised he should see his seed and prolong his days, and have a portion divided him with the great, and a spoil with the strong. And that there was such a covenant subsisting before the world began is clear; for could there be a Mediator set up from everlasting, as there was, and a promise of life before the world began made to Christ and put into his hand, and all spiritual blessings provided, and all grace given to his people in him, before the foundation of the world; and yet no covenant in being? See *Prov.* 8:23. *Tit.* 1:2. 2 *Tim.* 1:1, 9. *Eph.* 1:3." Gill, "The Doctrine of Predestination: Stated, and Set in the Scripture Light," in *A Collection of Sermons and Tracks*, 3:271-72. Italics original. Gill's explanation is good enough to show the existence of the *pactum* with more supportive words coming next in his essay; however, the key thought comes with the Hoeksema's question as aforementioned above in chapter one, "the supportive passages of the *pactum* need to be identified whether they belong to the *pactum* or the 'covenant with Christ in the human nature.'" Do Gill's supportive passages for the *pactum* fit the definition of the *pactum*, i.e., is it legitimate to claim that those biblical passages happen in eternity between the Father and the Son? For example, one of the supportive passages Ps 89:3-4 read, "The Lord said, 'I have made a covenant with my chosen one; I have sworn an oath

This everlasting covenant of grace featuring the "power to perform it" is called in Scripture by diverse expressions or epithets: the covenant of life, the covenant of peace, the covenant of grace, and the covenant of redemption.[53] All these covenants that include specific terms in origin, e.g., life, peace, grace, and redemption, applied only to God, help better understand that a covenant is the covenant of God. Regarding the covenant of life, based on Malachi 2:5; Titus 1:2; 2 Timothy 1:1; and Psalm 21:4, Gill underlines the "everlastingness" of life in God's covenantal promise compared to the "temporariness" of human covenantal promises of life. God's covenant in Malachi 2:5 is

> not with Aaron, nor with Phinehas; nor is it to be understood of a covenant, promising temporal life and outward prosperity to either of them ... but of the covenant made with Christ from everlasting, called a *covenant of life*, because it was made with Christ the Word of life, who was with the Father from all eternity, and in time was made manifest in the flesh; and was made in behalf of persons ordained to eternal life, and in which that was promised and given to them in him; and in which it

---

to David my servant: I will establish your offspring forever and build up your throne for all generations.'" Is not this covenant made with God's chosen one David? Can this covenant with David be called the everlasting covenant of grace? Here is Gill's comment on the question: The covenant is "not (made) with Abraham ... , but with David, as in the following cause; not David, literally understood, though he was chosen of the Lord to be his servant, and a covenant was made with him, and a promise made to him of the perpetuity of his throne and kingdom in his family, Psal. 78:70; 2 Sam. 7:16 but mystical David, the Messiah, David's son and antitype; after, on this account, called David in Scripture, ... , and who is the Lord's *chosen* One, fore-ordained to be the Redeemer, of lost sinners, chosen to be the Mediator between God and them, to be the head of the church, and Saviour of the body." Gill, *An Exposition of the Old Testament*, 4:75. Also, see Gill's words in a sermon in *Great Eastcheap* in 1756, " ... God has made with Christ, with *David*, his chosen, an everlasting covenant; that Christ is set up from everlasting as mediator of it ... " Gill, "Sermon VIII: The Agreement of the Old and the New Testament," in *A Collection of Sermons and Tracts*, 1:129. Gill considers David with whom God made a covenant as the mystical David; namely, the Messiah, David's Son and Antitype. Thus, this covenant made with David is the everlasting covenant of grace made with Christ the second person of the Godhead in eternity. Also, Keach drawing Psalm 89 denotes, "For none can doubt, but David was a type of Christ." Especially, by focusing on 89:20, 28-29 he observes, "Now this, they confess, chiefly respecteth Christ, of whom David was a figure, and also referreth to that which they call the covenant of redemption." Keach, *The Everlasting Covenant*, 23. From the grand perspective of the biblical and theological framework of Scripture, therefore, does Gill provide a resolution for both the Robertson's concern and Hoeksema's question regarding the *pactum*'s biblical evidence.

53. Gill, *Divinity: Book II*, 51-52.

was agreed that he should become man, and lay down his life as such, that they might enjoy it.[54]

This everlasting federal transaction, that is, the eternal covenant is also literally called a covenant of "grace," which "entirely flows from, and has its foundation in the grace of God."[55] For Gill, the emphasis on the word "grace" of God is never exhausted with overstatements, especially in terms of the covenant of grace. At a sermon in the *Great-Eastcheap* evening lecture, which he regularly provided on Wednesdays as a preacher for over two decades, Gill deals with the significance of the doctrine of grace expositing the last part of 1 Timothy 6:3:

> By *the doctrine of grace*, I mean that system of evangelical truths which is commonly called Calvinistical; as, **that** God has from all eternity loved some of the human race, and has chosen them unto everlasting salvation, by Jesus Christ; **that** he has made a covenant of grace with his Son on the behalf of the chosen ones, which is absolute and unconditional; **that** Christ in the fulness of time assumed human nature, suffered and died, to redeem a special and peculiar people to himself; **that** by bearing their sins, and all punishment due unto them, he has made full satisfaction to the justice of God; **that** a sinner's justification before God is only by the righteousness of Christ imputed to him, without any consideration of works done by him; **that** pardon

---

54. Gill, *An Exposition of the Old Testament*, 6:760.

55. Gill, *Divinity: Book II*, 52. In terms of the "covenant of peace," see the explanation concerning the everlasting council above in which Gill discusses the covenant of peace of Zechariah 6:13, that is, the council of peace. Prior to Gill, Robert Towne (1592-1664), who emphasized the free grace of God, also captured the concept of the covenant of peace while making a sharp distinction between the Law and Gospel, "Neither did the Law instrumentally convert and turn the heart to God: for Christ is the way to the Father; his blood and cross slayeth the enmity that is between divine justice and the sinner, and removeth all lets whatever did hinder or separate, and so openeth a free way for access, Heb. 10.19, 20. and his righteousness is the Melius terminus, bond or mean of union between God and the soul, bringing them into a sure and *everlasting covenant of peace*: he is first King of righteousness, and after that King of Salem, that is, of peace Heb. 7.2. Now Christ, his death and resurrection, with the fruits and benefits thereof, are the subject and peculiar treasures of the Gospel." Robert Towne, *A Re-Assertion of Grace, Or, Vindiciae Evangelii: A Vindication of the Gospel-truths, from the unjust censure and undue aspersions of Antinomians* (London, 1654), 104. Italics added. Thomas Collier (1615-1691) also had an eternal covenant of peace, "God was ever reconciled to his elect in his Son from all eternity, for he loved them in his Son, *Ephe.* 1.4. . . . the Gospel of Christ is called the *Gospel of peace, Ephes.* 6.15. and the *glad tidings of peace, Esay* 57.7. the Covenant of the Gospel is a *Covenant of peace, Esay* 54.10. Ezek. 37.26." Thomas Collier, *The Exaltation of Christ In the dayes of the Gospel: as the alone High-Priest, Prophet, and King of Saints* (London, 1641), 32, 34. Italics original.

of sin is only through the blood of Christ, and for his sake, according to the riches of his grace; **that** God sees no sin in his justified and pardoned ones, so as to condemn them for it; **that** regeneration and conversion are by the powerful and efficacious grace of God; and **that** those who are effectually called by grace, shall persevere to the end, and be eternally saved.[56]

Several "that" clauses above clearly demonstrate the whole redemptive process in order, including both eternity and time. The everlasting covenant of grace is the center of the whole process of salvation, which means the covenant of grace is connected with both realms, i.e., eternity and time, and functions as a leading concept in the basis of the person and work of Jesus Christ. Each concept of the process, i.e., election, incarnation, Christ's justifying work in bearing sins by imputation, pardon of sin, regeneration, and conversion, and finally, perseverance to the end, pertains to the role of the covenant of grace. In other words, every element of the gospel of grace is a part of the covenant of grace, which occupies the central locus of the biblical and theological metanarrative in Scripture.

With regard to the relation of the covenant of redemption to the covenant of grace, Gill, following Benjamin Keach's concept of the covenant of grace, maintains "one covenant of grace."[57] Gill clearly recognizes the typical distinction between the covenant of redemption and the covenant of grace among the Reformed federal theologians and rejects the idea:

> the covenant of redemption, they say, was made with Christ in eternity; the covenant of grace with the elect, or with believers, in time: but this is very wrongly said; there is but one covenant of grace, and not two . . . What is called a covenant of redemption, is a covenant of grace . . . wherefore there can be no foundation for such a distinction between a covenant of redemption in eternity and a covenant of grace in time.[58]

---

56. Gill, "Sermon I: The Doctrine of Grace cleared from the Charge of Licentiousness," in *A Collection of Sermons and Tracks*, 1:2. Emphasis in bold added.

57. Gill, *Divinity: Book II*, 52. See note 7 above.

58. Gill, *Divinity: Book II*, 52. Keach, though he was a Baptist, not a Reformed, used to be among the federal theologians in defense of the typical distinction: "I must confess, I have formerly been inclined to believe the covenant, or holy compact between the Father and the Son, was distinct from the covenant of grace. But upon farther search, by means of some great errours sprang up among us, arising, as I conceive, from that notion, I cannot see that they are two distinct covenants, but both one and the same glorious covenant of grace, only consisting of two parts, or branches." Keach, *The Everlasting Covenant*, 11. Keach's notion of the two parts or branches of the one covenant of grace is described as "two subjects of the same covenant" in Petto's words. "Indeed," says Petto, "the same Covenant of grace, may be distinguished, *as it is made with Jesus*

Here is the significance of the one covenant of grace. This idea in Gill's covenantal system reinforces the status of the *pactum* (council and covenant) that plays the central role in the whole system by embracing all theological doctrines in both realms through the biblical redemptive history to fulfill its goal, God's glory, i.e., men's redemption. In particular, Gill's two administrations of the one covenant of grace in Scripture reveal how each step of the redemptive narrative proceeds under the control of the *pactum*.

Gill's Third Task of the Covenant

Gill's third and last task is to have a better understanding of the everlasting covenant of grace that pertains to the contracting parties, the Father, Son, and Holy Spirit.[59] Before analyzing each party's job in greater detail, Gill discusses an important predictable issue regarding the divine legal subjects of the *pactum*.[60] With the famous and provoking statement, "This is mythology," a critical inquiry made by Karl Barth hits the mark, "The question is necessarily and seriously raised of a will of God the Father which originally and basically is different from the will of God the Son."[61] Barth's remark

---

Christ, and, *as with us*, yet not to intimate two distinct and compleat Covenants, but two Subjects of the same Covenant. *As with Jesus Christ*, it had its constitution from eternity, before we had a being, *as with us*, it hath its application in time after we exist." Petto, *The Difference between the Old and New Covenant*, 20-21. This eternity and time aspect of God's covenant is not to be separated because the God who controls both realms is the God of the covenant. Simply, this also is the exact work of the Holy Spirit, the covenantal God, says Gill, "as the Spirit freely bestows his grace, and the gifts of it in time, so he freely engaged to do it in the covenant in eternity." Gill, *Divinity: Book II*, 53.

59. Gill, *Divinity: Book II*, 52-54.

60. In this regard, for Gill, it has been taken for granted that the Holy Spirit is not to be barred from participating in the *pactum* as a legal member. It is because "he is certainly promised in it [the covenant] both to Head and members; and in consequence of it, is sent down into the hearts of God's covenant ones, to make application of the blessings, promises, and grace of the covenant to them, and to work a work of grace in them; all which must be by agreement, and with his consent." Gill, *Divinity: Book II*, 52.

61. Barth, *CD*, IV/1: 65. In pointing out the difference of the will between the Father and the Son (the discuss should be also applied to the Spirit) in the *pactum*, Barth presupposes that "God is one God." This thought leads him to state regarding the subject of the *pactum*: "If He is thought of as the supreme and finally the only subject, He is the one subject. And if, in relation to that which He obviously does amongst us, we speak of His eternal resolves or decrees, even if we describe them as a contract, then we do not regard the divine persons of the Father and the Son as partners in this contract, but the one God – Father, Son and Holy Spirit – as the one partner, and the reality of man as distinct from God as the other." Barth, *CD*, IV/1: 65. The concept of one God is also crucial in understanding of the *pactum* because there is only one redemptive history under one God's control and only one way of salvation in the great

is based on a huge claim that God's will is one because God is one, which is one of the most fundamental ideas in terms of God's ontology. Thus, for Barth, the seemingly absurd notion that differentiates the "will of God the Father" from the "will of God the Son" in the *pactum* is beyond imagination. It is correct to say that God's will is one because God is one. Therefore, one is not allowed to use such expressions as "the will of God the Father" and "the will of God the Son" separately. There is only one will of God. However, as already shown in the expressions "God the Father" and "God the Son" (and surely, "God the Spirit"), God is three as well as God is one.[62]

Gill is in the same line with the traditional orthodox viewpoint regarding who God is. Barth points out that God's will is one because God is one, namely, God is one nature. At the same time, however, Gill does not ignore God as three persons. God's will in one nature cannot be covenantal by itself because "no man covenants with himself," as Gill said.[63] Instead, under the one will of a God of one essence, the three divine persons who "[are] not distinct from essence or existence" of God perform the covenantal "acts." In other words, according to Gill,

> As they are distinct Persons, so they have distinct acts of will; for though their nature and essence is but one, which is common to them all, and so their will but one; yet there are distinct acts of

---

plan of one covenantal God. Frame lists a couple of senses in relation to God's unity, namely, the concept of one God: i.e., simplicity, unity of the persons within the Trinity, uniqueness of God's nature, and God's numerical oneness. Especially, God's numerical oneness means that "there is only one being with that unique nature." Frame, *Systematic Theology*, 423. However, "Though," says Frame, "God is numerically one and simple, he has many attributes, as we have seen, thinks a vast number of thoughts, and performs innumerable actions. His attributes are one, but a oneness that can be characterized in many ways. His thoughts are one, but they are thoughts about innumerable objects. His actions are one, but they have vast numbers of effects in the world." Frame, *Systematic Theology*, 433. Two propositions representing the triune God, i.e., "God is one," and "God is three," are concerned with the fundamental doctrine of who God is. Interestingly, the doctrine of the *pactum* is the very locus to reveal who God is as the triune personal God according to Gill. As aforementioned in the beginning of this chapter, all things that pertain to the person and act of the triune God in eternity and time, are necessarily proclaiming the pure act of God of salvation in the divine three persons.

62. See the note 62 above. The "three" means three "persons." Then, what is the relation of the person of God to the essence or nature of God? Do these two exist as different two "things"? Sheri Katz, borrowing Augustine's idea, mentions, "personhood is not distinct from essence or existence. 'Still, we say three persons of the same essence or three persons from the same essence: however, we do not say three persons from the same essence, as if essence were one thing and person another thing.'" Sheri Katz, "Person," in *Augustine through the Ages: An Encyclopedia*, ed. Allan D. Fitzgerald, O.S.A. (Grand Rapids: Eerdmans, 1999), 648.

63. Gill, *Divinity: Book II*, 52.

this will, put forth by and peculiar to each distinct Person: thus their nature being the same, their understanding must be the same; and yet there are distinct acts of the divine, understanding, peculiar to each Person; the Father knows the Son, and the Son knows the Father, and they have a distinct knowledge and understanding of one another, and the Spirit knows them both, and they know him. And as their nature and essence, so their affections are the same; and yet there are distinct acts of them, peculiar to each Person.[64]

64. Gill, *Divinity: Book II*, 53. Another related essential question is, "Can the acts of the persons be called covenantal in the sense of making a covenant?" "Is not act just an act or performance according to the will of nature?" In discussing regarding the relation of the Trinity to creation, Webster explains God's essence and persons, "The triune God is one simple indivisible essence in an irreducible threefold personal modification. That is, God's unity is characterized by modes of being in each of which the entire divine essence subsists in a particular way; this simultaneous, eternal existence in these three modes *is* the one divine essence. Accordingly, the persons of the godhead are not distinguished from the divine essence *realiter*; there are not three eternals, or three incomprehensibles, or three uncreated, or three almighties, or three gods. This is not to reduce the persons back into some anterior unity . . . , but simply to state that the persons are inseparable from the essence, and the essence inseparable from its threefold personal modification. *Pater et filius et spiritus sanctus unus deus est*: the singular verb is decisive." John Webster, "Trinity and Creation," *International Journal of Systematic Theology* 12, no. 1 (January 2010): 8. Italics original. Thus, the person's act is inseparable from the essence. The principle of God's essence and persons handled in the relation of the Trinity to creation, is also applied to the relation of the Trinity to salvation because, according to Gill, both the creation of man and the redemption and salvation of man do not belong to the different category. Gill, dealing with Genesis 1:26 in the everlasting council, already mentioned, "it may be reasonably argued, that if there was a consultation of the divine Persons about the making of man at first, then much more about the redemption and salvation of him." Gill, *Divinity: Book II*, 46. Interesting is that Barth in the volume three of his *Church Dogmatics* acknowledged "covenant as the internal basis of creation," says McDowell, and cites Barth in his volume three, "'The inner basis of the covenant is simply the free love of God, or more precisely the eternal covenant which God has decreed in Himself as the covenant of the Father with the Son as the Lord and Bearer of human nature, and to that extent the Representative of all creation.' Leaving aside for the moment the fact that this statement strongly suggests that Barth appears to embrace a position that he will later criticize in volume 4, namely, the covenant of redemption, it is important to see at this stage that Barth is working out the claim that while the doctrine of creation has historical precedence, the doctrine of the covenant has material precedence." Mark I. McDowell, "Covenant Theology in Barth and the Torrances," in *Covenant Theology: Biblical, Theological, and Historical Perspectives*, 407. Back to the issue of God's essence and persons, Thomas Aquinas's concept of notional acts also supports the understanding of the relationship between the divine persons and acts. Nicholas Lombardo, while investigating a single eternal act of the divine persons, notes, "the Divine Persons are identical with their personal relations . . . . Yet the Divine Persons do not just relate to each other. They also actively communicate or receive their deity. They can therefore also be understood through the category of act." In dealing with the notional acts of the divine persons in Aquinas, Lombardo continues

For Gill, therefore, in the grand picture of the everlasting covenant of grace, each person of the triune God acts in eternity for the temporal manifestation of men's redemption. Gill's articulation, "distinct acts of will" of one God in the three divine persons pictures and reveals who God is in a covenantal framework. In the covenant of grace, there are three acts of the divine will, "peculiar to each Person; and which appear in their covenanting with each other, and are necessary to it."[65] In the divine Godhead, there are not two (or three) legal subjects who need to settle a disagreement or difference of will because there is only one will in God; rather, there exist three distinct acts of the one will by the three divine persons who are never distinct from the Godhead. Therefore, one can conclude that the distinct acts of the three divine persons are covenantal, which denotes that the everlasting covenant of grace exists in the three divine persons and that this does not betray the will of the one Godhead.

In sum, for Gill, the everlasting covenant of grace embraces two realms, i.e., eternity and time, which only the divine Trinity can recognize and minister in his unique power for the purpose of men's redemption, ultimately leading to the glory of God. The concept of covenant stems from the covenant of grace between the three divine persons as an archetype and belongs to the triune God only, who is, in a real sense, able to stipulate and restipulate perfectly in the absolute power to perform the conditions of the

---

to assert in citing Aquinas, "Speaking of the Father, Aquinas explains, 'Just as God's act of understanding is God himself understanding, so the Father's act of begetting is the begetting Father himself, although the modes of signifying are different.' The same applies to the other Divine Persons. Just as the Father is an act, the Son and the Spirit are acts, too. The Son is the act of proceeding from the Father, and the Holy Spirit is the act of proceeding from the Father and the Son. The reason for this identity between Person and action is, ultimately, divine simplicity. If there were a real distinction between Person and action in God, then action would be an accident, and divine simplicity rules out there being any accident in God." Nicholas E. Lombardo, OP, "Divine Persons and Notional Acts in the Trinitarian Theology of Thomas Aquinas," *Theological Studies* 82, no. 4 (December 2021): 605, 614.

65. Gill, *Divinity: Book II*, 53. Webster also notes that there are no forced acts in God's inner activities between the three divine persons: "there is no Father 'behind' the generation of the Son, no Father and Son 'behind' the breathing of the Spirit (relations of origin are eternal, not sequential). In this sense, therefore, God's immanent activities are 'necessary', not by external compulsion but by absolute or natural necessity: these activities are what it is for God to be God." Webster, "Trinity and Creation," 10-11. Simply put, each person's act in the immanent activities of the Godhead exists as who God is. It is "necessary" not "compulsory." In Gill's words, "These contracting Parties entered into covenant freely and voluntarily, of their own choice, as all covenantors do, or should." Each person exists as who he is in the covenantal act in eternity with deep connection with the essence of God. Respective act of each person is who God is. That is, in Webster's words, "what it is for God to be God." See Gill, *Divinity: Book II*, 53.

covenant. The fundamental question regarding the number of will and legal subjects raised by Karl Barth is resolved by the distinct acts of the three divine persons who are linked inextricably to the Godhead.

Summary

The first section of this chapter deals with Gill's twofold definition of the *pactum*: the everlasting council and the everlasting covenant of grace of the three divine persons. Both council and covenant in the eternal transaction between the Father, Son, and Holy Spirit function as "advising, consulting, contriving," and "adjusting, settling, fixing," respectively, regarding men's salvation. The everlasting council pertains more to who the saving God is than the covenant. Thus, Gill first examines God himself, especially his perfect knowledge, wisdom, and power to save his people through the creation and redemption in the gospel of peace in Christ, which proves the existence of the everlasting council.

The everlasting covenant of grace adjusts and settles the redemptive scheme based on the council. Investigating the etymology of the term "covenant" helps make sense of the existence of the concept of the covenant of grace by providing its major sense, "choose or select." Another meaning of the covenant, i.e., "testament," becomes the root in the making of two administrations of the Bible: the old covenant and the new covenant. The covenant of grace that requires parties as legal subjects manifests one will of God because God is one. However, the mystery of "who God is" also exists as three divine persons make the "covenant" of grace "the" covenant through the divine covenantal actions of the three divine persons who are never distinct from the Godhead.

As a significant requisite or condition for both council and covenant, Gill underlines the contracting parties of the *pactum*: Father, Son, and Spirit, which discussion Gill saved for later in detail. The second section of this chapter, therefore, deals with the concrete role and function of each contracting party of the Godhead in the covenant of grace.

OPERATIONS OF THE THREE DIVINE PERSONS

The Father, Son, and Holy Spirit are the three divine persons of the Trinity. These three divine persons always work together not only in the internal activity but also in the external business. Three divine acts move in purpose because an act entails an aim. No one is allowed to access or know the deep things of God in eternity without God's self-movement on purpose to reveal himself. Thus, creation reacts only to the act of God. No one is allowed to apprehend or perceive what kinds of actions and various movements God enjoys in eternity as well. However, at least one act of God is clearly seen in the whole Bible: God moves, making himself engaged in something other than God himself and acting on purpose. This "one act" is to save man, and the Bible demonstrates that this "act" of God unfolds as a covenantal way of saving man.

Gill allocates seven chapters in Book II of his *Divinity* to expand each party's work in the covenant of grace. Each person's unique task is organically associated with one another: the Father is the proposer, the Son is the assenter, and the Holy Spirit is the approbator of the covenant. These three actions of "proposing," "assenting," and "approbating" make no sense without an interlocutor's proper response by performing an action. Thus, rather than just listing each person, as Gill unfolds in his chapters, to describe a peculiar job in the covenant respectively, this section following Gill's biblical and theological evidence pays special attention to the major incidents, e.g., incarnation, sufferings, and death of Jesus Christ while considering how the three divine persons mutually engage in the incidents.

Proposal – Assent – Approbation

The *pactum* is the very locus where the mysterious and harmonious acts of the three divine persons are revealed for men's redemption. In what sense could it be asserted as "harmonious acts" and how three divine persons' works concern one another "mysteriously" in the *pactum*? Gill elaborately demonstrates that the Father's proposal, the Son's assent, and the Spirit's approbation, these three ideas reach the sublime harmony and the full balance of the everlasting covenant of grace.

Proposal

Everything that has a concept and exists with a feature of the concept begins with God the Father. Thus, the Father conceives and plans man's peace with God through reconciliation in the council and proposes and settles it in the covenant, all of which are concepts from the Father.[66] All things, e.g., ideas, substances, notions, and materials, are derived from God the Father. Based on 2 Corinthians 5:18, Gill notes, "'All things are of God,' that is, of God the Father; they are of him originally, they begin with him; all things in

---

66. Gill, *Divinity: Book II*, 54-55.

creation; he has made the world, and created all things by his Son; and so all things in the salvation of men, 'who hath reconciled us to himself by Jesus Christ.'[67] Especially with regard to men's redemption, the Father creates the concept of reconciliation.[68] Then, he proposes it to the other two divine persons in the council because it can be solely accomplished by the three divine persons as a covenantal work that includes a grand picture of the whole restoration of the entire universe in creation, particularly the man.[69]

---

67. Gill, *Divinity: Book II*, 54. 2 Corinthians 5:18-19 reads, "Everything is from God, who has reconciled us to himself through Christ and has given us the ministry of reconciliation. That is, in Christ, God was reconciling the world to himself, not counting their trespasses against them, and he has committed the message of reconciliation to us." Gill recognizes that Paul makes a relation between the origin of all things and the idea of reconciliation, which means the origin of men's redemption also begins with God the Father. The concept "reconciliation" comes from God the Father. Only the Father with the other two persons creates in action. The "new creation" in 2 Corinthians 5:17 has something to do with the concept "reconciliation," which is "exclusively God's work." "He continues in this mode by asserting that humans have done nothing to reconcile God; God has instead acted to reconcile them. Reconciliation therefore begins with God who acts unilaterally." David E. Garland, *2 Corinthians*, Christian Standard Commentary (Nashville: Holman, 2021), 323. Gill also comments, "All things in redemption are of him; he drew the plan of it ... The work of reconciliation, or making atonement for sin, is ascribed to the father; not that he is the author of it, for it is properly Christ's work; but because he took the first step towards it; he formed the scheme of it; he set forth his son in his purposes and decrees to be the propitiary sacrifice; he assigned him this work in council and covenant." Gill, *An Exposition of the New Testament*, 2:790.

68. The term reconciliation ("καταλλαγή") basically has a meaning of "to exchange, to give in exchange, to make otherwise, and purchase-money" concerning the related word group, such as ἀλλάσσω, ἀντάλλαγμα, and especially to καταλλάσσω. See Rostock Friedrich Büchsel, "ἀλλάσσω, ἀντάλλαγμα, ἀπ-, δι-, καταλλάσσω, καταλλαγή, ἀποκατ-, μεταλλάσσω," TDNT, 1:251-59. In this respect, Murray Harris explains, "Metaphorically it denoted the exchange or substitution of peace for war, of love for anger, or of friendship for enmity." And he continues to list four essential elements, recognizing reconciliation as "a transformation of relations ... in the sense that friendly relations now replace former hostility," in Paul's concept of καταλλαγή: (1) God (the Father) is both the initiator and goal of reconciliation; (2) Christ was God's agent in achieving reconciliation; (3) Human beings and the whole created universe are the objects and principal beneficiaries of God's reconciling action; and (4) Reconciliation is an accomplished fact on God's side, yet it must be embraced on the human side. See Murray J. Harris, *The Second Epistle to the Corinthians: A Commentary on the Greek Text*, NIGTC (Grand Rapids: Eerdmans, 2005), 435-39.

69. The Father's plan of reconciling man to himself is shared with the Son and Spirit immediately in eternity. Practically, the redemptive work of the plan is proposed to the Son; however, the Father does not propose to the Son without consideration of the act and help of the Holy Spirit. The Spirit of God is the true resource of the work of the Son. In addition, according to Gill, it was already discussed that the Lord God and his Spirit together sent the Son in Isaiah 48:16. In this regard, the Spirit also participates in the covenant as one of the senders.

Assent

The proposal of the Father becomes nothing without the assent of the Son. Christ's actual performance on the conditions in the covenant proves that he fully and freely agrees with the Father's proposal.[70] Greatly concerned with the covenant of grace, says Gill, Christ "is said to be the Covenant itself" based on Isaiah 42:6 and 49:8, " . . . and I will appoint you to be a covenant for the people . . . "[71]

Being a covenantee in the covenant of grace and doing all necessary works as the representative head of his people is both Christ's will and God's will through practical actions.[72] What is proposed by the Father, according to Gill, is all accepted and accomplished by the Son: (1) taking the care and charge of all his elect; (2) assuming human nature; (3) obeying the law; (4) suffering death; and (5) making himself an offering.[73] Christ's assent to the Father's proposal becomes the very certain proof of the existence of the covenant of grace because of Christ's assumption of human nature and his suffering and death in the visibility of the temporal realm.

---

70. Gill does not provide Christ's actual performance in time as an immediate proof of Christ's role in the covenant of grace. For Gill, the proposal and assent formula between the divine persons, especially the Father and the Son is fully expressed in Ps 40:6-8 in relation to Heb 10:5-10. These two are one of the most important passages to Gill in terms of Christ's assuming human nature, which will be handled in the part of the incarnation.

71. Gill, *Divinity: Book II*, 61. That Christ is said to be the Covenant itself denotes Christ will take all the tasks and responsibilities for redemption instead of his chosen people, which is "the great condition of the covenant, and he himself is the great blessing of it." Due to Christ's consent to the Father's proposal in the covenant, "all the blessings of it are the sure mercies of him, who is David, and David's Son . . . and the covenant people are blessed with all spiritual blessings in him, as their covenant head." Gill, *Divinity: Book II*, 61. Gill also notes in his comment on Isaiah 42:6, "Christ is a covenantee, a party concerned in the covenant of grace; the representative of his people in it; the surety, Mediator, messenger, and ratifier of it; the great blessing in it, the sum and substance of it; all the blessings and promises of it are in him, and as such be is *given*; it is of God's free grace that he was appointed and intrusted with all this in eternity, and was sent in time to confirm and secure it for *the people*." Gill, *An Exposition of the Old Testament*, 5:240; also, see 5:287. Italics original. A crucial truth of Christ's being the covenant as Gill already noted in the commentary above, comes with the concept of the representative. Christ is the representative head of his people in the covenant; "he is the Mediator, Surety, Testator, and Messenger of it." All these parts Christ takes in the covenant will be fully dealt with later in chapter five.

72. The "will" issue has already discussed above. The agreement of Christ is manifested by his fulfilling actions of the covenantal conditions, which is the different actions of the Father, but in the end, all are coming from the same will of the Godhead.

73. The list is what the Father proposes in the covenant for men's redemption. For the greater details of each element, see Gill, *Divinity: Book II*, 55-57.

Approbation

The Father's proposal and the Son's assent presuppose the Holy Spirit's approbation. The Spirit is "not a mere bystander, spectator, and witness of this solemn transaction, compact, and agreement, between the Father and the Son," but an indispensable party without whose approbation no covenant is validated in God.[74] As the men's redemption in God's plan includes the final consummation of humanity and of the entire creation, the Spirit's main work in the sanctification is required for the purpose of the whole salvation, which "makes meet for the enjoyment of complete and eternal salvation."[75]

Particularly, Gill relates 2 Thessalonians 2:13 and 1 Peter 1:2 to the sanctification of the Spirit, which demonstrates that the Spirit is closely engaged to the whole scheme of salvation in the covenant:

> from the beginning God has chosen you for salvation through sanctification by the Spirit and through belief in the truth; (chosen) according to the foreknowledge of God the Father, through the sanctifying work of the Spirit, to be obedient and to be sprinkled with the blood of Jesus Christ.[76]

---

74. Gill, *Divinity: Book II*, 79.
75. Gill, *Divinity: Book II*, 79.
76. "By *sanctification*," explains Gill, "is meant, not any thing external, as reformation of life, obedience to the law, or outward submission to Gospel ordinances; but internal holiness, which lies in a principle of spiritual life in the soul, and in a principle of spiritual light in the understanding; in a flexion of the will to the will of God, and the way of salvation by Christ; in a settlement of the affections on divine and spiritual things, and in an implantation of all grace in the heart; and is called the sanctification of *the spirit*." Gill, *An Exposition of the New Testament*, 3:261. Italics original. For Gill, the salvation by Jesus Christ, i.e., through belief in the truth, mostly accompanies the sanctification by the Spirit; namely, as the apostle affirms with respect to salvation of the chosen, "God ('the Father') has chosen you for salvation through sanctification by 'the Spirit' and through belief in the truth ('the Son')." In another place, Gill confirms the apostle's concept of redemption in 2 Thess 2:13, "It is certain that these persons were chosen not merely to external means and outward blessings and privileges, but to grace here, and glory hereafter; for they were *elect according to the foreknowledge of God the Father, through sanctification of the Spirit, unto obedience, and sprinkling of the blood of Jesus*; and in consequence of this were *begotten again to a lively hope of an inheritance, incorruptible, and undefiled, and that fadeth not away, reserved in heaven*, and were *kept by the power of God through faith unto salvation*." Gill, *The Cause of God and Truth*, 111. Also, see the pages 130–31, 160. The sanctification of the Spirit happens also by embracing both realms, i.e., eternity and time, in his work for the chosen because "God's appointment of men to salvation, that is, to eternal glory, is not without respect to any good thing done by them, but with respect to their faith, repentance, and perseverance; for God chooses to salvation through sanctification of the Spirit, and belief of the truth; though not with respect to these, as causes of his decree, but as means unto the end... so that their everlasting fate is not determined without respect to any good done by

These two verses, by themselves, convey enough for the Spirit to collaborate on the covenant of grace with the Father and the Son. Holiness leads redemption into completion.

The Father's proposal, the Son's assent, and the Spirit's approbation make several stages of the everlasting council and covenant of grace possible to happen regarding men's redemption from eternity to time. Among the important incidents, two loci take center stages where the biblical, theological, and historical significance of the everlasting council and covenant of grace is perfectly revealed through the threefold cooperative action of the Father, Son, and the Holy Spirit: the incarnation and the sufferings and death of Christ. The last part of this section focuses on these two issues.

Incarnation

As aforementioned, the Father's first and primary proposal to the Son is "to take the care and charge of the chosen ones," which, according to Gill, is based on John 6:39 and Isaiah 49:5-6. Two expressions from these verses cover the first proposal: "should lose nothing" and "raising up the tribes of Jacob."[77]

For the purpose of the restoration and protection of the chosen, Gill's first concern pertains to the incarnation of Jesus Christ. Assuming human nature in the second person of the Trinity comes as the significant proposal of the Father in necessity to the Son in order for the first proposal to be secured, which is "a most extraordinary and amazing affair," says Gill, who continues regarding the incarnation,

> The whole gospel is a mystery; the various doctrines of it are the mysteries of the kingdom; the knowledge of which is given to some, and not to others; it is the mystery of godliness, and, without controversy, great; and this stands the first and principal article of it; "God manifest in the flesh" (1 Tim. 3:16). This is the basis of the Christian religion; a fundamental article of it; and without the belief of it no man can be a Christian; "Every spirit that confesseth that Jesus Christ is come in the flesh, is of God;" born of God, and belongs to him, and is on the side of God and truth; "And every spirit that confesseth not that Jesus Christ is come in the flesh, is not of God" (1 John 4:2, 3).[78]

---

them, nor without any reason on the part of God, though without conditions on their parts." Gill, *The Cause of God and Truth*, 281-2.

77. Gill, *Divinity: Book II*, 55.

78. Gill, *Divinity: Book V*, 8. Agreeing with Gill, Bavinck adds in emphasizing the

As Gill clarifies, the incarnation, though mysterious, is the kernel of the Christian basics for Christianity to be as it is.[79] It is utterly natural, therefore, for the three divine persons of the Godhead to take part in the critical and serious act of the incarnation by and through the *pactum*.[80]

According to Gill, the key biblical evidence for the Father's proposal and the Son's assent concerning the incarnation is clearly expressed in Psalm 40:6-8, which reads:

> You do not delight in sacrifice and offering; you open my ears to listen. You do not ask for a whole burnt offering or a sin offering. Then I said, "See, I have come; in the scroll it is written about me. I delight to do your will, my God, and your instruction is deep within me."

First, one thing is clear that: "You" is God (the Father) in context. Then, who is the speaker? Who is the "I" who has come? Who is the "I" about whom the scroll writes? Who is the "I" who delights to do the will of God? Gill goes to Hebrews 10:5-10 and cites Psalm 40:6-8 to disclose the identity of the speaker:

---

pactum's relation to the incarnation, "It is 'the mystery of godliness' (1 Tim. 3:16). From this mystery all Christology has to proceed. If, however, Christ is the incarnate Word, then the incarnation is the central fact of the entire history of the world; then, too, it must have been prepared from before the ages and have its effects throughout eternity." Bavinck, *Reformed Dogmatics*, 3:274. Also, Bavinck denotes the incarnation is prepared for the temporal effects from the everlasting covenant of grace in eternity, asserting, "Not just after the fall, not even first at the creation, but in eternity the foundations of the covenant of grace were laid. And the incarnation is not an incidental decree that emerged later: it was decided and determined from eternity. There was no time when the Son did not exist; there was also no time when the Son did not know he would assume and when he was not prepared to assume the human nature from the fallen race of Adam. The incarnation was prepared from eternity." Bavinck, *Reformed Dogmatics*, 3:276-77.

79. Bird, citing Karl Barth's divinity-centered expression from the christological standpoint of incarnation, notes on the mysterious incarnation, "Karl Barth's christological approach assumes the divinity of Jesus and follows his movement from eternity to temporality in the incarnation . . . . The incarnation is a mystery that 'can be contemplated, acknowledged, worshiped and confessed as such, but it cannot be solved, or transformed into a non-mystery.'" Michael F. Bird, *Evangelical Theology: A Biblical and Systematic Introduction*, Second Edition (Grand Rapids: Zondervan, 2020), 404.

80. Gill delineates how all the three persons get involved with the incarnation: (1) "The Father prepared a body for the Son in his purpose, and proposed it to him in council and covenant to assume it"; (2) "The Son having agreed to it, being sent, came in the flesh, by the assumption of it"; and (3) "The Holy Ghost had a very great concern in this affair; for that which was conceived in the Virgin was of 'the Holy Ghost' (Matthew 1:20)." See Gill, *Divinity: Book V*, 13.

The Covenant of Redemption According to John Gill   101

Therefore, as he was coming into the world, he said: *You did not desire sacrifice and offering, but you prepared a body for me. You did not delight in whole burnt offerings and sin offerings. Then I said, "See–it is written about me in the scroll–I have come to do your will, God."* After he says above, *You did not desire or delight in sacrifices and offerings, whole burnt offerings and sin offerings* (which are offered according to the law), he then says, *See, I have come to do your will.* He takes away the first to establish the second. By this will, we have been sanctified through the offering of the body of Jesus Christ once for all time.[81]

---

81. Emphasis original. An interesting point is that a difference is found between Psalm 40:6-8 and Hebrews 10:5-10 in terms of the citation of the author of Hebrews. In the Hebrew Masoretic text there is no expression of "you prepared a body for me." The author of Hebrews writes about "a body" whereas the Hebrew text writes, "you open my ears to listen." Gill certainly does not miss the point in difference. In the exposition of Psalm 40:6, he articulates, "though the phrase rather signifies the formation and excavation of the ear; or the preparing and fitting it for its use; that is, to hearken to the will of his heavenly Father, to become man, offer himself a sacrifice, and suffer and die in the room of his people; to which he became obedient, taking upon him a form of a servant, when found in fashion as a man; and was obedient unto death, even the death of the cross; see Isa. 1:4-6. In Heb. 10:5, the words are rendered as by the Septuagint, *but a body hast thou prepared me*; . . . a part of the body being put for the whole; and which, indeed, is supposed: for unless a body had been prepared for him, his ears could not have been opened; and it was in the body, in human nature, that he was the obedient servant; and this is to be understood, not only of a preparation of this body, in the purposes, counsel, and covenant of God; but chiefly of the formation of it in the womb of the virgin, where it was curiously wrought and prepared by the Holy Ghost, that he might have something to offer, and in it become, as he did, an offering and a sacrifice to God, of a sweet-smelling savour." Gill, *An Exposition of the Old Testament*, 3:696. Italics original; also, see Gill, *Divinity: Book II*, 62. Grant Osborne also comments on the body concept in the Septuagint (LXX), "The actual Masoretic Text (the Hebrew Old Testament) has 'you have given me an open ear,' but the author used the *Septuagint* for the emphasis on the 'body,' thus a reference to the incarnation of Christ. He and the other New Testament writers considered the Septuagint not more inspired than the Hebrew but a Spirit-led paraphrase interpreting the Hebrew text and adding nuances God was approving, here extending the ear to encompass the whole body." Grant R. Osborne with George H. Guthrie, *Hebrews: Verse by Verse*, Osborne New Testament Commentaries (Bellingham, WA: Lexham, 2021), 199. Emphasis original. Cf. Isaiah 39:7 in BHS reads, "זֶבַח וּמִנְחָה לֹא־חָפַצְתָּ אָזְנַיִם כָּרִיתָ לִּי עוֹלָה וַחֲטָאָה לֹא שָׁאָלְתָּ׃" whereas LXX translates it as "θυσίαν καὶ προσφορὰν οὐκ ἠθέλησας σῶμα δὲ κατηρτίσω μοι ὁλοκαύτωμα καὶ περὶ ἁμαρτίας οὐκ ᾔτησας." The LXX is from Randall Tan, David A. DeSilva, and Isaiah Hoogendyk, eds., *The Lexham Greek-English Interlinear Septuagint: H. B. Swete Edition*, vol. 2 (Bellingham, WA: Lexham, 2012), 264. Donald Hagner also senses the difference but from a little different viewpoint, "The LXX translator apparently understood an allusion to the creation of Adam in the words 'ears you have dug for me,' for in the sculpting of a body from clay, ears must be dug out. Thus he translated the expression from Hebrew idiom into language that would more readily be understood in the Hellenistic world: *a body you prepared for me*." Donald A. Hagner, *Hebrews*, NIBC (Peabody, MA:

From the comparison between Psalm 40 and Hebrews 10, Gill identifies the "I" as Jesus Christ, the Son of God who has come in a human body ("you prepared a body for me") following the interpretation of the author of Hebrews 10: "though it [Psalm 40:6-8] might be wrote [sic] by David, it was not written concerning himself, or on his own account, but of another."[82] The Father "prepared a body" for his Son in the eternal plan, and the Son exactly knew the will of the Father.

Another explicit articulation regarding the proposal and assent between the Father and the Son is more fully expressed in the Son's words, "See, I have come to do your will." Gill interprets and summarizes what the phrase means: "to assume human nature, to lay down his life in it, to suffer death, make atonement for the sins of his people, and obtain their redemption and salvation."[83] Gill's abstract of the phrase "I have come to do your will" is significant in terms of the work of the Holy Spirit. Christ's performance in time to fulfill the proposal of the Father connotes not only the assent of the Son to the proposal but also the approbation of the Holy Spirit to both the proposal and the assent. It is because no performance of Christ is feasible without the involvement of the Holy Spirit.

Likewise, the incarnation of the Son is not possible without the power of the Holy Spirit. Gill brings Matthew 1:18, 20 as proof of the Spirit's approbation in the covenant of grace, which reads: " . . . it was discovered

---

Hendrickson, 1990), 154. Emphasis original.

82. Gill continues, while working on the psalm 40 itself and its title, that it is "not concerning David himself, but concerning his antitype and son, who is called by his name, Ezek. 37:24, 25; Hos. 3:5 and that it is to be interpreted of him is evident from the application of ver. 6, 7, 8, unto him by the apostle in Heb. 10:5-9 and the whole of it is applicable to him." Gill, *An Exposition of the Old Testament*, 3:694.

83. Gill, *Divinity: Book II*, 62. Already knowing the limit of the legal sacrifice system, Christ knew what the Father acted in "preparing a body" in eternity. A body prepared was not made with no purpose. Christ had to come in "a body." The purpose of Christ's coming in a body is explained by Gill in an excellent descriptive words, "The end of his coming is next expressed by him, *to do thy will, O God*; which, when he came, he set about with the utmost delight, diligence, and faithfulness, in preaching the Gospel, performing miracles, doing good to the bodies and souls of men, and in finishing the great work of men's redemption, which was the main part of his father's will he came to do; and which he did, by fulfilling the law in its precept and penalty; by offering himself a sacrifice to God; by suffering death, the death of the cross; by destroying all his and our enemies, and so working out everlasting salvation." Gill, *An Exposition of the New Testament*, 3:445. Italics original. By focusing on the expression, ἥκω ("I have come"), Grant also signifies the meaning of incarnation, "The perfect tense 'I have come' (*eko*) in verse 7 looks at his life of obedience as a single complete whole and shows he was always characterized by his faithful reflection of his Father's will. In the incarnation and life of obedience of Christ, the old covenant system ended and the new order was inaugurated to replace it." Osborne, *Hebrews*, 200-01.

before they came together that she was pregnant from the Holy Spirit"; " . . . because what has been conceived in her is from the Holy Spirit." The Holy Spirit agreed and approbated the necessity. In other words, the Spirit knew what must happen in time for Christ to be born of a virgin as the Savior and also "seeing it was necessary that the Saviour of men should suffer and die for them, to satisfy law and justice."[84] In order for all these to happen, the Spirit's power comes first upon the conception of the incarnation of the Son, which happens that "the human nature of Christ might be clear of original pollution" and "so being the immediate produce of the Holy Ghost and without sin."[85] This is an initiating point of the Spirit's work. All of Christ's onward covenantal works in the redemptive history are deeply linked to empowering of the Spirit upon Christ.[86] The Spirit is not just the Spirit of God but the Spirit of Christ as well (Rom 8:9).

Sufferings and Death

The application of the covenantal conditions and agreements by the three divine persons in the everlasting council and covenant of grace unfolds in time slowly but strongly before the Bible reader's very eyes in a marvelous and unique fashion: humiliation. Christ's humiliation is not just his own; the Father proposed it, and the Spirit approbated it. The divine three persons are mutually interrelated to the incarnate Christ's humiliation.

Gill articulates, "Christ's state of humiliation began at his incarnation and was continued through the whole of his life unto death."[87] He demonstrates Christ's whole humiliation based on Philippians 2.7-8, "Instead he emptied himself by assuming the form of a servant, taking on the likeness of humanity. And when he had come as a man, he humbled himself by becoming obedient to the point of death–even to death on a cross."[88] From

---

84. Gill, *Divinity: Book II*, 79.

85. Gill, *An Exposition of the New Testament*, 1:7. Gill points out that "the human nature assumed, should be holy and pure from sin, that it might be offered up without spot to God; and be a sacrifice to take away sin, which it could not be, if sinful." Gill, *Divinity: Book II*, 49.

86. Dealing with the Holy Spirit as companion of Christ, Yarnell observes, "with the annunciation of the incarnation of the Son of God, there was a magnificent burst of spiritual activity . . . . The work of the Spirit in relation to the Son was not, however, limited to the incarnation: 'From womb to tomb to throne, the Spirit was the constant companion of the Son.' The Spirit was explicitly evident during the life of Jesus Christ, especially in his incarnation, baptism, ministry, and resurrection." Malcolm B. Yarnell III, "The Person and Work of the Holy Spirit," in *A Theology for the Church*, 489.

87. Gill, *Divinity: Book V*, 19.

88. By appealing Phil 2:7-8 explains Gill, "he voluntarily subjected himself (to the

this passage, Gill, making several points of humiliation, highlights Christ's low estate "which the apostle illustrates and confirms by placing it in contrast with his glorious estate previous to it."[89] To put it another way, Gill

---

assumption of human nature) . . . this was Christ's own act and deed, he willingly assented to it, to lay aside as it were his glory for a while, to have it veiled and hid, and be reckoned any thing, a mere man, yea, to have a devil, and not be God: O wondrous humility! astonishing condescension!" Regarding Christ's humbleness even to the death of the cross, "which was both painful and shameful," continues Gill, "it was accursed one, and shewed that he bore the curse of the law, and was made a curse for us: this was a punishment usually inflicted on servants, and is called a servile punishment; and such was the form which he took, when he was found in fashion as a man: this is now the great instance of humility the apostle gives, as a pattern of it to the saints, and it is a matchless and unparalleled one." Gill, *An Exposition to the New Testament*, 3:133-34. G. Walter Hansen in his exposition of Phil 2:7-8 provides three interpretations with "emptied himself": (1) The kenotic theory; (2) The incarnation view; (3) The Servant of the Lord portrait. From the second position, he makes a helpful comment, "*The form of God* is the glory of God: the glorious splendor of the highest position, the power displayed in the creation of the universe, and the sovereignty expressed in his universal rule over all hi creation. *The form of a slave* is the exact opposite of glory: a slave does not have a high position; he is powerless; he has no rights. He has no glory: no honor; only shame." Also, from the third position and the expressions of "humbled himself," "even death on a cross," Hansen connects Phil 2:7-8 to Isaiah 53, "The Philippian readers were probably first reminded of the humiliation of slaves in their own contemporary Roman context when they heard the hymn about the humiliation and death of a slave. But their understanding of the suffering of Christ depicted by the hymn would have been deepened by hearing the song of the suffering of the 'man of sorrows' in Isaiah 53." G. Walter Hansen, *The Letter to the Philippians*, The Pillar New Testament Commentary (Grand Rapids: Eerdmans, 2009), 146-59, esp. 148, 150. In Isaiah 53, the suffering servant is "despised by others (49:7). He subjects himself to bodily harm and humiliation, . . . The servant's appearance is disfigured and causes people to shudder (52:14)." Regarding the point of "man of sorrows ("מַכְאֹבוֹת")," "The Hebrew word מַכְאֹב," explains Duby, "can signify both corporeal and mental pain. It is the common lot of the human race laboring in vain under the sun (Eccles. 2:23). It is what evokes God's deliverance of his people from the oppression of Egypt (Exod. 3:7-8). It is what David feels because of God's opposition to David's sin and because of the hatred of his enemies (Ps. 38:18 MT; cf. 69:27 MT). It is the state of Israel and Judah after their destruction . . . Given that the servant in Isaiah 53 experiences things like bodily disfigurement and abandonment, his sorrow is evidently both corporeal and mental." Steven J. Duby, *Jesus and the God of Classical Theism: Biblical Christology in Light of the Doctrine of God* (Grand Rapids: Baker, 2022), 316.

89. Gill, *Divinity: Book V*, 19. Gill makes two points of Christ's humiliation in large. First, the incarnation itself is one of the most humiliating elements with respect to Christ's "conception and birth," passing through all the states of "infancy, childhood, and youth, as other men do," being "harassed with the temptations of Satan, being "appeared in the reproaches, indignities, and persecutions" and "even contradiction of sinners against himself, and finally "emptied" and "humbled" himself. Secondly, the incarnation entails subjection to the law of God, which includes two things: "made of a woman" and "made under the law" as stated in Gal 4:4. Subjection to the law accompanies being "made under the judicial, or civil law of the Jews and being made under

underlines a stark difference between divinity and humanity, namely, how disgraceful and difficult it is for Christ, the Son of God, to endure and assume the sinful human nature, to suffer, and even to die. The more Christ's humiliation is deep and profound, the greater the sharp ontological difference between divinity and humanity, between eternity and time, is clearly revealed.

Gill emphasizes Christ's being a servant according to the will of the Father. As Isaiah 53 denotes, being a servant, which is the key concept of Philippians 2:7-8, is being obedient "to the work and office of a servant; and said unto him, in the everlasting council and covenant of grace and peace" by the Father.[90] The Father's "choosing, appointing, calling, sending,

---

the ceremonial law. See Gill, *Divinity: Book V*, 19-26. For the full explanation of "born of a woman" and "born under the law," see Gill, *An Exposition to the New Testament*, 3:27-28.

90. Gill, *Divinity: Book V*, 26. Isaiah 49:3 reads, "He said to me, 'You are my servant, Israel, in whom I will be glorified.'" Gill explains that Israel is "a name of Christ, and which properly belongs to him, being the antitype of Jacob or Israel; the Head and representative of the whole Israel of God." Christ "appeared in the form of servant, and came not to be ministered unto, but to minister, and give his life a ransom for many; thereby to obtain redemption, which was the great work and service he was appointed to; which he readily undertook, and willingly and cheerfully engaged in, and diligently and faithfully performed; to whom justly belong the characters of an obedient, diligent, prudent, and faithful servant; in answering which he shewed his regard to his father's will, his love to his people, and his great humility and condescension." Gill, *An Exposition to the Old Testament*, 5:284. Another important issue comes with that "being obedient to the work and office of a servant" requires substantive and substitutive sufferings; one of the most visual and direct expressions regarding sufferings is "the cup" ordered by the Father "in the everlasting covenant." Gill, *Divinity, Book II*, 57. Citing John 18:11, Gill calls Christ's sufferings "the cup," which reads, "At that, Jesus said to Peter, 'Put your sword away! Am I not to drink the cup the Father has given me?'" What does the cup mean? Gill answers, "by the cup is meant, the wrath of God, and punishment due to sin, endured by Christ in his sufferings, and is said to be *given* him by his father." Gill, *An Exposition to the New Testament*, 2:96. Morris agrees with Gill, "In the Old Testament 'cup' often has associations of suffering and of the wrath of God (Ps. 75:8; Isa. 51:17, 22; Jer. 25:15; Ezek. 23:31-33, etc.; cf. Rev. 14:10; 16:19)." Leon Morris, *The Gospel according to John*, NICNT, Revised Edition (Grand Rapids: Eerdmans, 1995), 660-61. Boice extends the meaning of cup into two: "One is the cup of salvation. It is mentioned in Psalm 116:13 . . . . The other cup is the cup of God's wrath or tribulation, which is referred to here. Earlier Jesus has prayed that this cup might pass from him (Matt. 26:39). David had spoken of it, saying, 'Upon the wicked he shall rain snares, fire and brimstone, and an horrible tempest; this shall be the portion of their cup' (Ps. 11:6). Two cups: the cup of salvation and the cup of God's wrath! Every person who has ever lived shall drink from one of them. But those who drink of the cup of salvation by God's grace will drink of it only because Jesus drank the cup of God's wrath in their place." James Montgomery Boice, *The Gospel of John: An Expositional Commentary: John 18:1-21:25*, vol. 5 (Grand Rapids: Zondervan, 1979), 44-45. Also, see Karen H. Jobes, *John: Through Old Testament Eyes* (Grand Rapids: Kregel, 2021), 267.

bringing forth, and supporting" make the Son fulfill his work and office, "especially in the estate of humiliation."[91] The Son's humiliating work and office, says Gill, includes the obedience both to men and to God, which is the peculiar way to accomplish the servant job as the Mediator between God and men.[92]

The final course of Christ's sufferings of humiliation ends in death on the cross.[93] "The cross is put for the whole of his sufferings and death," says Gill. The cross also manifests both the most painful punishment and shameful dishonor.[94] Regarding the humiliating death of Christ on the cross in relation to the works of the three divine persons, Gill directs 1 Peter 3:18, "For

91. Gill, *An Exposition to the Old Testament*, 5:284.

92. Gill, *Divinity: Book V*, 27; Gill, *An Exposition to the Old Testament*, 5:284. From incarnation, "Christ's whole life was a life of sufferings," says Gill. Though things like Satan's temptations, men's reproaches and persecutions were surely sufferings, Gill also focuses on what Christ endured as "preparatory to his death": (1) the conspiracy of Jewish leaders to kill Jesus; (2) betrayal of Judas Iscariot; (3) men's rude and inhumane treatment. See Gill, *Divinity: Book V*, 30-32.

93. Robert Howell, a nineteenth-century Baptist theologian, begins with the covenant of redemption dealing with the cross of Christ, "In the cross, you behold a practical development of his infinitely gracious *designs* towards miserable and lost sinners; designs which occupied his thoughts, and entered into his counsels, long ere the heavens were spread out above us . . . And can it be that God's purposes of mercy towards the children of men, through the cross of our Lord Jesus Christ, were cherished by him *from eternity? Did he even then, design to redeem you from sin, by this strange instrumentality?* . . . His purposes are made apparent by all that is revealed to us in relation *to the Covenant of Redemption*. When he sent forth his Son into the world, he announced him as 'The Messenger of the Covenant,' 'The blood of the cross,' he designates as 'The blood of the Covenant,' and 'The blood of the everlasting Covenant.' Referring to 'the mystery of redemption,' an apostle declares it to have been 'according to the eternal purpose which he purposed in Christ Jesus our Lord'" Robert Boyte C. Howell, *The Cross* (Charleston, SC: Southern Baptist Publication Society, 1854), 2, 5-6. Italics original.

94. "This kind of death was a shameful one; hence Christ is said to endure the cross, and despise the sham . . . ; and it was also a painful and cruel one, . . . ; to have the whole body stretched to the uttermost; the hands and feet, those sensible parts of it, pierced; and to have the weight of the body depending on them! it was so cruel, that the most humane among the Romans, wished to have it disused, even to servants." Gill, *Divinity: Book V*, 32. Expositing the relation of peace and the blood of his cross in Colossians 1:20, Gill adds, "this peace he has made by his *blood*, that is, by the shedding of it, by his death as a sacrifice, which he underwent on the *cross*; partly to denote the shame, and chiefly to signify the curse he endured in the room of his people." Gill, *An Exposition of the New Testament*, 3:175-76. "Crucifixion seems to have been invented by 'barbarians' on the edge of the known world and taken over from them by both Greeks and Romans. It is probably the most cruel method of execution ever practiced, for it deliberately delayed death until maximum torture had been inflicted. The victim could suffer for days before dying." John Stott, *The Cross of Christ*, Stott Centennial Edition (Downers Grove: IVP, 2021), 29.

Christ also suffered for sins once for all, the righteous for the unrighteous, that he might bring you to God. He was put to death in the flesh but made alive by the Spirit."[95] Among many other biblical passages that proclaim the suffering death of Christ, Gill's choice of 1 Peter 3:18 denotes a critical signification. 1 Peter 3:18 includes three essential components to reveal the *pactum*'s pattern regarding the participation of the three divine persons in redemption: (1) Christ's substitute suffering and death in the flesh; (2) the Father's acceptance of Christ's sacrifice meeting qualification; (3) the Spirit's raising the Son from the dead.[96]

Particularly, the works of the Holy Spirit make the eternal scheme and conditions of the everlasting covenant of grace complete in perfection, especially of Christ's death and resurrection.[97] Gill affirms the Spirit's involvement in each and every stage of Christ's role in the *pactum*: "'the sufferings of Christ, and the glory that should follow'; as well as was assisting to the human nature of Christ, in the sacrifice of himself; since it was 'through the eternal Spirit,' he offered up himself without spot to God (1 Peter 1:11; Heb 9:14)."[98] Why is the Spirit concerned with being "complete in perfection"?

95. Gill, *Divinity: Book II*, 62.

96. 1 Peter 3:18 reveals the fundamental roles of three divine persons to fulfill the conditions of the *pactum*. First, the sufferings and death of Christ aim completely for others, states Gill, "Not his own, for he committed none, but for the sins of his people; in order to obtain the remission of them; to make reconciliation for them." Secondly, Christ death and sacrifice, originally planned by the Father in eternity and agreed by the Son, are qualified enough to be accepted by God the Father. What, then, would be the outcome of the acceptance by the Father? Those who "were far off from him [the Father] . . . might have freedom of access, with boldness, unto God, through his precious blood, and the vail of his flesh; and that he might offer them to God." The Father only accepts the Son's voluntary and obedient sacrifice in Christ's perfection, which is the Father's unique scheme in the *pactum*. Thirdly and finally, the Holy Spirit performs what is promised in the *pactum*, "(Christ) raised from the dead by his divine nature, the spirit of holiness, the eternal Spirit, by which he offered up himself, and by virtue of which, as he had power to lay down his life, so he had power to take it up again." See Gill, *An Exposition to the New Testament*, 3:562-63. Dennis Edwards stressing the redemptive work of Christ notes, "The verse reads like a creedal statement, an affirmation of the suffering, crucifixion, and resurrection of Christ." Theologians might easily think of the redemption as the Christ's sole work. However, the three words of Edwards' "suffering, crucifixion, resurrection" cannot happen without the other two divine persons. The importance of the doctrine of the *pactum* to Gill is that all Christian essential doctrines centered in the three persons are derived from the everlasting covenant of the three divine persons in eternity: i.e., the *pactum*.

97. Sure, Gill does not neglect that the Father also is concerned with the resurrection of the Son based on Ephesians 1:17-20 and 1 Peter 1:3. Gill, *Divinity: Book V*, 43.

98. Gill, *Divinity: Book II*, 79. Gill considers the glory as "his resurrection from the dead, his ascension to heaven, his session at the right hand of God, and having all power, authority, and judgment committed to him." Gill, *An Exposition to the New Testament*,

Gill regards the Spirit as a guarantor of the whole process of Christ's ministry proposed by the Father according to the covenant of grace. The invisible, eternal, redemptive plan of God the Trinity comes to the visible substance in time by the Spirit's full application of the plan. Gill states,

> As it was highly proper, that as Christ should be delivered to death for the offences of men, so that he should rise again for their justification; or otherwise, the whole affair of salvation would have miscarried; hence the Father in covenant enjoined his Son, as to lay down his life, so to take it up again; and which he did, and in which the Spirit was concerned; and which showed his approbation of this closing part of the scheme of salvation by Christ.[99]

Summary

The second section of this chapter has focused on the operations of the three divine persons in the everlasting covenant of grace. Each person takes a unique role in order for the redemptive purpose to be completed in perfection. The Father, who is the origin of all existence, proposes the redemption of men through the concept of reconciliation. The Son assents to the Father's proposal and executes the conditions of the covenant voluntarily. The Holy Spirit approbates the Father's proposal and the Son's assent by getting involved in the covenantal applications while maintaining the whole consummation process of each stage of Christ's performances.

3:534. Garrett supports that the Holy Spirit relates to Jesus' life and ministry as well as to the death and resurrection of Jesus by appealing to Hebrews 9:14 and Romans 1:4: e.g., the virginal conception, Baptism, wilderness temptations, and so forth. Garrett, *Systematic Theology*, 2:147, 154. Beeke and Smalley also adds, "If the Spirit led Christ in the path of obedience into the wilderness, then we could expect that the Spirit also led Christ in his obedience unto death on the cross." Joel R. Beeke and Paul M. Smalley, *Reformed Systematic Theology*, vol. 3: Spirit and Salvation (Wheaton: Crossway, 2021), 123. Interestingly, as Yarnell affirmed in the note 86 above, the Synoptic Gospels do not clearly and directly mention the Holy Spirit's participation in the death of Christ. The Spirit gets involved with Christ's "incarnation, baptism, ministry, and resurrection."; also, see Adam Harwood, *Christian Theology: Biblical, Historical, and Systematic* (Bellingham, WA: Lexham, 2022), 495-98. Though the reason why the Synoptic Gospels are not related to the Son's death is the question unanswerable, as long as the Spirit's involvement with Christ's whole life and ministry through his resurrection, one thing is certain as Thiselton claims, "The Holy Spirit never works on his own, but always in cooperation with the Father and with Jesus. Paul, John, and the Church Fathers make this clear." Thiselton, *Systematic Theology*, 273.

99. Gill, *Divinity: Book II*, 79.

The Covenant of Redemption According to John Gill

The two most obvious scenes of the *pactum*'s manifestation with the three divine persons are revealed in Christ's incarnation, sufferings, and death. Based on two key biblical passages, Psalm 40:6-8 and Hebrews 10:5-10, Gill explains Christ's incarnation that a body is prepared for the Son to be sent by the Father. The old law, including worship and obedience, is no longer working in men's economy as the Son assents and comes to do the will of the Father with the help and power of the Holy Spirit. The humiliation of the Son already began with the incarnation, according to Gill, reaching the sufferings and death of Christ. Gill brings Isaiah 53 and Philippians 2:7-8 to emphasize that the sufferings and death of Christ are not just his own humiliation but also the humiliation of the Father and the Spirit. However, these are all part of the process of fulfillment of the everlasting covenant of grace, and it is completed through Christ's resurrection and ascension by the power of the Holy Spirit and the Father's raising the Son from the dead.

For Gill, the *pactum* is the mysterious and harmonious work of the three divine persons in eternity. Though it appears like a secret agreement only between the Father and the Son, the Holy Spirit is always presupposed in the covenant no matter what is conditioned between the Father and the Son, as Gill demonstrates in 2 Thessalonians 2:13 and 1 Peter 1:2. It is because God reveals things to his people by the Spirit and "the Spirit searches everything even the depths of God" (1 Cor 2:10).

Finally, this chapter arrives at the third and last section of the everlasting council and the covenant of grace according to Gill, i.e., the properties of the *pactum*.

PROPERTIES OF THE PACTUM

That the *pactum* takes the central locus in Gill's systematic theology has been supported by exploring God's whole plan revealed in the redemptive history through the concept of covenant. Not only the notion of one God but also the three divine persons of the one God mysteriously balance in working on humanity's redemption. Due to the main concept of the term "covenant," the Father's scheme, the Son's obedience, and the Spirit's witness in application call for the everlasting covenant of grace to be shaped based on the idea of election.

In Gill's theology, it is crucial to examine the *pactum* through which the attributes of God in the three divine persons are richly revealed, laying stress on the incarnate Christ, who is the elect of the Father. In this regard, the "properties of the *pactum*" confirms the features and attributes of God already observed with regard to the everlasting council and the covenant of grace. Gill provides and lists seven properties of the *pactum* in *Divinity*, which displays God's attributes in reflection of the *pactum*.[100] Considering its significance and avoiding overlapping, this section briefly points out three important properties: the covenant's eternity, free grace, and unconditionality.

Eternal Covenant

The first and foremost feature of the covenant is that it is an eternal covenant. Eternity, one of the most important attributes of God, comes as the origin and source of every existence regardless of when and where the entity happens. Gill states what comes from the eternal covenant-making for divine sublimity and nobility indicates how God's essential attributes are most indispensable to save sinful men: "It [covenant of grace] was made in eternity, and commenced and bears date from eternity. The spring of it is the mercy, grace, and love of God."[101] The mercy, grace, and love of God flowed from the eternal covenant established in Christ, the entire Christianity as a whole.[102] Thus, for Gill, the eternal covenant makes the foundation of Christian theology, tradition, and redemptive history.

Secondly, the covenant of grace is the work of the eternal Father, eternal Son, and eternal Spirit solely because it is an eternal covenant. Also, since the fundamental element of the covenant is election, according to Gill, and the Father's election with his proposal is the Son himself, Christ, God's chosen people, i.e., the elect, is always found in Christ: "the covenant is

---

100. Gill indicates that the properties of the covenant of grace "may serve to lead more fully and clearly into the nature, use, and excellency" of the *pactum*. Here are the seven features: (1) it is an eternal covenant; (2) the covenant of grace is entirely free, of free grace; (3) the covenant is absolute and unconditional; (4) the covenant of grace is perfect and complete; (5) the covenant is holy; (6) it is a sure covenant, firm and immoveable; and finally (7) it is called an everlasting covenant. See Gill, *Divinity: Book II*, 81-85.

101. Gill, *Divinity: Book II*, 81.

102. Pertaining to God's eternal promises in his covenantal mercy, love and grace, Gill explains while expositing Ps 89:2, "this [the perpetuity of the mercy of God] may be said to be done, when saints are rooted and grounded in the love, grace, and mercy of God, and are built up in Christ, and established in him, in whom this mercy is displayed; and the church of God in general, which is a monument of mercy, and which, though it may decay and fall into ruins, shall be raised up again, and rebuilt, and the head-stone brought in with acclamations of God's grace unto it." Gill, *An Exposition to the Old Testament*, 4:75.

made with Christ, God's elect, and with men chosen in him, and who were chosen in him to be holy and happy, before the foundation of the world."[103]

Thirdly, all the blessings and promises of the covenant in relation to eternal life prove the covenant's antiquity.[104] Christ, being the center of all the blessings and promises, leads the elect to the blessings in him as "they were chosen in him before the foundation of the world, and are the 'grace' given to them in him, 'before the world began.'" Thus, the elect with the blessings certainly existed in Christ before the foundation of the world, "not having an actual being, yet a representative one in him their Head," because "all the promises of the covenant are, being put into his [Christ's] hands so early" in eternity.[105]

---

103. Gill, *Divinity: Book II*, 82. As aforementioned somewhere of this chapter, the doctrine of election will be greatly dealt with in the chapter five while working on Gill's relation of Christology to the *pactum*.

104. Gill, *Divinity: Book II*, 82.

105. Gill's primary proof passage for the covenant's antiquity in granting the spiritual blessings to the elect by the divine choice, comes from Ephesians 1:4. Regarding the expression "before the foundation of the world," expounds Gill, "that it was so early, is certain, from the love of God to his people, which this is the effect of, and which is an everlasting love; and from the covenant which was made with Christ from everlasting, on account of these chosen ones, when Christ was set up as the head and representative of them; and from the provision of all spiritual blessings for them in it, which proceeds according to this choice; and from the preparation of a kingdom for them from the foundation of the world; and from the nature of God's decrees, which are eternal; for no new will, or act of will, can arise in God, or any decree be made by him, which was not from eternity: God's foreknowledge is eternal, and so is his decree, and is no other than himself decreeing." Gill, *An Exposition of the New Testament*, 3:61. In God's work, there is no new will, no new act of will in eternity. Magee and Arthurs also state, "God's plans for Paul's readers were rooted in eternity past. Nothing had happened by accident or as a last-minute response to the world's desperate situation. With the wording 'before the foundation of the world' modifying 'he chose us,' Paul affirmed that on a personal level God had desired and planned for the readers' welfare all along." Gregory S. Magee and Jeffrey D. Arthurs, *Ephesians: A Commentary for Biblical Preaching and Teaching*, Kerux Commentaries (Grand Rapids: Kregel, 2021), 53. Allen associating God's exercise of the divine will with his divine choice and selection denotes the expression "before the foundation of the world" implies "precedence and eternal depth." Michael Allen, *Ephesians* (Grand Rapids: Brazos, 2020), 13. More detailed explanation of the expression does Hoehner provide. According to Hoehner, πρὸ καταβολῆς κόσμου ("before the foundation of the world") basically means "to throw down," e.g., throwing down "seed in the ground," throwing down "seed in a female," or throwing down stones "for the foundation or the starting point of a building." A significant point Hoehner makes comes with the proposition πρὸ ("before"), which happens in three times in the NT (John 17:24; Eph 1:4; and 1 Pet 1:20). From the contexts of the usage of πρὸ, Hoehner presents its idea, "an action occurred before the foundation or creation of the world," which is different from the usage of the similar preposition ἀπό ("from"), casting the meaning of "something has been in process from the beginning of the world." Thus, according to Hoehner, Eph 1:4 signifies, "God chose the believer before the world was

Covenant of Free Grace

The second major feature of Gill's covenant is it is of free grace. "Grace," says Gill, "is the moving cause of it [covenant of grace]; God was not induced to make it from any motive and condition in men."[106] For Gill, grace is the very core framework that underlies and composes his systematic theology through the covenant of grace.[107] Thus, grace is also concerned primarily with the three divine persons with regard to the covenant of grace as it is one of God's critical attributes: "The Father, of his own grace and goodwill to men, proposed the terms of the covenant to his Son; and the Son of God, from his great love he bore to the same persons, voluntarily agreed unto

---

even created, that is, in eternity past." Harold W. Hoehner, *Ephesians: An Exegetical Commentary* (Grand Rapids: Baker, 2002), 177-78. Merkle also comments on the time of election pertaining to God's sovereignty, "God's choice in election occurred before time and creation. God's timing emphasizes that this choice was based on God's sovereign purpose and not human merit." And then, he concludes with Romans 9 on God's selecting Jacob over Esau, "'though [the twins] were not yet born and had done nothing either good or bad–in order that God's purpose of election might continue, not because of works but because of him who calls' (Rom. 9:11)." Benjamin L. Merkle, *United to Christ, Walking in the Spirit: A Theology of Ephesians*, New Testament Theology (Wheaton: Crossway, 2022), 23-24.

106. Gill, *Divinity: Book II*, 82. Bruce Demarest brings Anselm's famous inquiry into his conversation regarding Christ's death and human merits to stress God's free grace. Anselm in *Cur Deus Homo* ("Why God Became Man") raised a question, "For what reason and on the basis of what necessity did God become a man [i.e., a human being] and by His death restore life to the world (as we believe and confess), seeing that He could have accomplished this restoration either by means of some other person (whether angelic or human) or else by merely willing it?" After giving three possible responses to this question: *absolute necessity, hypothetical necessity, and consequent absolute necessity*, Demarest, unwilling to use the terms like "necessity" and "absolute necessity" because "these may imply that there is a principal or power higher than God that determines occurrences," avers, "It was not necessary for the divine Judge, after pronouncing the just sentence against sin, to move from behind the bench and take upon himself the penalty of the accused. God's decision to save was a free movement of love and grace. If the creation of the cosmos was a free act of love, how much more was Christ's provision on the cross for the re-creation of sinners an unmerited expression of sheer grace." See St. Anselm, *Complete Philosophical and Theological Treatises of Anselm of Canterbury*, trans. Jasper Hopkins and Herbert Richardson (Minneapolis, MN: Arthur J. Banning Press, 2000), 300; Bruce Demarest, *The Cross and Salvation*, Foundations of Evangelical Theology (Wheaton: Crossway, 2006), 187-89.

107. "Perhaps, no man, since the days of St *Austin*, has written so largely, in defence of *the system of* GRACE: and, certainly, no man has treated that momentous subject, in all its branches, more closely, judiciously, and successfully." John Gill, "A Summary of the Life, Writings, and Character, of the late Reverend and Learned John Gill, D.D.," in *A Collection of Sermons and Tracts*, 1:xxxiii-xxxiv.

them; and the same love in the blessed Spirit, engaged him to undertake what he did in it."[108]

Moreover, the free grace of the covenant in the love of the three divine persons correlates deeply with the whole process of men's redemption. God's act of election, adoption, justifying righteousness, pardon of sin, and all other blessings are from the grace of God, which implicitly indicates that any mental, intellectual, and physical works of men are excluded.[109] For Gill, men's redemption through the whole process in the covenant reveals the glory of God, as aforementioned. Thus, the final station of the covenant of grace arrives at the glory of the grace of God,

> as God has made all things for himself, for his own glory, in nature and providence; so all things in grace, and particularly the covenant of grace, is made and stored with all the blessings of it, to the glory of his grace, (Eph. 1:3-6) and therefore with great propriety may, on all accounts, be called the covenant of grace.[110]

---

108. Gill, *Divinity: Book II*, 82.

109. This feature of grace in Gill's covenant is in line with Gill's understanding of grace. Each process of men's redemption from election through pardon of sin to every blessing, requires of experiencing God's grace. It deserves to quote Gill's concept of grace in whole, though long, to help understand how the covenant of "grace" relates to all the process of men's redemption throughout the Scripture: "By *the doctrine of grace*, I mean that system of evangelical truths which is commonly called Calvinistical; as, that God has from all eternity loved some of the human race, and has chosen them unto everlasting salvation, by Jesus Christ; that he has made a covenant of grace with his Son on the behalf of chosen ones, which is absolute and unconditional; that Christ in the fullness of time assumed human nature, suffered and died, to redeem a special and peculiar people to himself; that by bearing their sins, and all punishment due unto them, he has made full satisfaction to the justice of God; that a sinner's justification before God is only by the righteousness of Christ imputed to him, without any consideration of works done by him; that pardon of sin is only through the blood of Christ, and for his sake, according to the riches of his grace, that God sees no sin in his justified and pardoned ones, so as to condemn them for it; that regeneration and conversion are by the powerful and efficacious grace of God; and that those who are effectually called by grace, shall persevere to the end, and be eternally saved." Gill, "Sermon I: The Doctrine of Grace Cleared from the Charge of Licentiousness," in *A Collection of Sermons and Tracks*, 1:2.

110. Gill, *Divinity: Book II*, 83. Gill goes further in terms of "the glory of the grace of God" in Ephesians 1:6, "the glory of the grace of God appears herein [adoption as sons in the previous verse]; the glory of God is the supreme end of all he does; and the glory of his grace, and not his power, or other perfections of his, and the manifestative glory of that is here intended; yea, the *praise* of that glory: and this end is answered, when the children of God ascribe their adoption to the free grace of God; and when they admire it, and are thankful for it, and walk worthy of the relation they are brought into." Gill, *An Exposition of the New Testament*, 3:62.

Covenant of Unconditionality

The third and final feature of Gill's covenant selected by this section is it is absolute and unconditional. Both absoluteness and unconditionality utterly rely on the parties of the covenant who are able to meet the covenantal conditions and maintain its status to the full completion. In this regard, for Gill, every covenant made with men by God is conditional; in other words, not only the covenant made with Adam, which is called the covenant of works, but even the covenant made with Abraham as well, which is commonly considered to be an unconditional covenant, and often referred to by Reformed thinkers as the covenant of grace.[111]

Such an absolute and unconditional feature of the covenant of grace, therefore, never tolerates ascribing any conditions of the covenant to men, especially in terms of faith and repentance, according to Gill. It is because the official determination and finalization of men's redemption by fulfilling the conditions of the covenant must be completed by the responsible persons who can perform all the conditions in perfection to the end. Gill explains why:

> If these were conditions of the covenant, to be performed by men in their own strength, in order to be admitted into it and receive the benefits of it; they would be as hard, and as difficult to be performed, as the condition of the covenant of works, perfect obedience; since faith requires, to the production of it, almighty power, even such as was put forth in raising Christ from the dead, (Eph. 1:19, 20) and though God may give men means, and time, and space of repentance, yet if he does not give them grace to repent, they never will.[112]

---

111. Gill, *Divinity: Book II*, 83. The Westminster Confession chapter 7 reads, "... II. The first covenant made with man was a covenant of works, wherein life was promised to Adam and in him to his posterity, upon condition of perfect and personal obedience. III. Man by his fall having made himself incapable of life by that covenant, the Lord was pleased to make a second, commonly called the Covenant of Grace ... " Westminster Assembly, *The Westminster Confession of Faith: Edinburgh Edition* (Philadelphia: William S. Young, 1851), 45-46; also, see R. C. Sproul, *The Promises of God: Discovering the One who keeps his Word* (Colorado Springs, CO: David C Cook, 2013), chapter six, no page numbers given, "Every covenant that God made with people after the fall is incorporated under the general heading 'the covenant of grace.'" As already dealt with in the first section of this chapter, Gill's basic concept and structure of covenant theology is different from the traditional Reformed covenantal idea. For Gill, there is one and only covenant of grace between the three divine persons. For this reason of the covenantal parties who are eternal, Gill's covenant of grace is the covenant of redemption according to the Reformed definition, which happens in eternity.

112. Gill, *Divinity: Book II*, 83. The relation of the covenant's unconditionality to

The Covenant of Redemption According to John Gill

With respect to God's sole work in the covenant without conditions, Gill emphasizes God's firm will by the many covenantal descriptions found in Scripture: e.g., Jeremiah 31:33-34, 32:38, 40; Ezekiel 36:25-27.[113]

The determined will of God for men's redemption by and through the work of Christ in the power of the Holy Spirit in the everlasting council and the covenant of grace is fully expressed in Romans 5:6, 8, which reads, "... while we were still helpless ... Christ died for the ungodly ... God proves his own love for us in that while we were still sinners, Christ died for us."[114] The perfect and holy covenantal will of God the Father, Son, and Holy Spirit is purposed by preparing a body for the Son, executed by obeying the Father in sufferings and death and approbated by following the Father's proposal in empowering the Son to perform what must be done for the elect.

Summary

This short but essential section of the chapter has briefly dealt with the properties of the covenant of grace. The covenant in Gill's mind has several features: it is the holy, perfect, immovable, and everlasting covenant. Above all things, however, this covenant is eternal. By relating to the attributes of God, eternity reveals the three divine persons' mercy, grace, and love through the covenant of grace to creation in time.

---

faith and repentance is similar to the relation of regeneration to conversion: i.e., whether God's work or man's work. While stressing God's sovereignty on men's redemption, Gill does not ignore and neglect man's part, which all of them are under God's blessings of grace. "Regeneration," says Gill, "is the sole act of God; conversion consists both of God's act upon men, in turning them, and of acts done by men under the influence of converting grace; they turn, being turned. Regeneration is the motion of God towards and upon the heart of a sinner; conversion is the motion of a sinner towards God, as one (Charnock) expresses it." Gill, *Divinity: Book VI*, 171.

113. "I will put my teaching within them ... I will be their God, and they will be my people ... They will all know me ... I will forgive their iniquity ..." "I will also sprinkle clean water on you ... I will cleanse you from all your impurities ... I will give you a new heart ... I will remove your heart of stone ... I will place my Spirit within you ..."

114. Gill, *Divinity: Book II*, 84. Gill clearly and delicately explains what the apostle tried to convey in Romans 5:6 and 8, "that before conversion is particularly mentioned here, to illustrate the love of God to them, notwithstanding this their character and condition; and to shew that the love of God to them was very early; it anteceded their conversion; it was before the death of Christ for them; yea, it was from everlasting: and also to express the freeness of it, and to make it appear, that it did not arise from any loveliness in them; or from any love in them to him; nor from any works of righteousness done by them, but from his own sovereign will and pleasure." Gill, *An Exposition of the New Testament*, 2:451.

The covenant is also of free grace. The cause and motive of the covenant is solely from God the Trinity, who is eternal. The divine works of the Trinity derived from his free grace control every process of men's redemption: election, adoption, righteousness, pardon of sin, and embracing every other blessing that brings glory to God.

Finally, the covenant is absolute and unconditional. Differentiating his concept of the covenant from the typical Reformed understanding, Gill only accepts the covenant of grace between the three divine persons from eternity. Thus, any covenant made with men is not called the unconditional covenant of grace. The firm will of God to save his people comes only from the Father's proposal, the Son's assent, and the Spirit's approbation by the way of covenant.

CONCLUSION

Does the *pactum* take the central locus in Gill's systematic theology with special regard to men's salvation? This chapter has made three major points to confirm the essential status of the *pactum* in Gill's system.

First, Gill's unique twofold definition of the *pactum* has established the cornerstone to unfold how Gill's *pactum* functions in relation to other biblical and theological areas. The basic concepts of the everlasting council and the covenant of grace, which embrace both realms of eternity and time, have demonstrated that Gill's *pactum* should not be considered as an eternal-capturing only or an artificial fiction with no use for the virtual discussions based on the biblical and theological interpretation. Gill's *pactum* practically affects all theological issues regarding men's redemption from eternity to time *ad totum*.

Secondly, the specific role of each divine person of the Trinity in the *pactum* reveals that the whole redemptive history of the Bible pertains to the cooperative mutual work of the three divine persons, who are free from the temporal realm beyond man's limited comprehension in time. Gill's emphasis that there is nothing new in time has taken it for granted that there must be something other than Christ's ministry in the temporal realm for men's redemption to make sense with the doctrine of God the Trinity, especially with the three divine persons, not just the Son. Thus, the Father's proposal to prepare a body for the Son in eternity is based upon the scheme of the Father from the everlasting council and the covenant of grace. The Son's assent to the Father's proposal and the execution in obedience by assuming human nature through suffering and death to the resurrection and ascension proves that the redemption of men and women is not just one divine person's work, nor does it happen solely in the temporal area. Without grasping the *pactum*, according to Gill's systematic theology, no understanding of the redemptive history in its entirety is feasible. Lastly, the part that the Holy Spirit takes in the *pactum* is indispensable. Knowing everything regarding the Father's proposal and the Son's assent through the whole process of the council and the covenant of grace, which is "as quick as thought" in eternity, the Spirit approbates the agreement and supports all the ministries that are to be realized in Christ; e.g., incarnation, sufferings through temptations, death, and resurrection. Therefore, the Father, the Son, and the Holy Spirit all together participate in men's salvation by and through the most appropriate method, the *pactum*.

Thirdly and finally, Gill provides three features of the *pactum*: eternality, free grace, and unconditionality. Men's redemption begins with God's grace by and through which God elects the Son and his people in Christ. *Pactum*'s eternality explains the very beginning of men's redemption. The *pactum* embraces all the processes for salvation in logical order: election, adoption, justifying righteousness, pardon of sin, and all other blessings. Moreover, God's will in and through the *pactum* with unconditionality is realized in the works of the three divine persons.

For Gill, the *pactum* is the most fundamental and foundational framework for seeing the whole picture of the Scripture with special respect to men's redemption. The next chapter will examine Gill's concept of the doctrine of the Trinity, which will help us better understand the *pactum* from the perspective of the three divine persons in both eternity and time.

CHAPTER 4

The Doctrine of the Trinity According to John Gill

THIS VOLUME HAS ATTEMPTED to prove the thesis that John Gill's *pactum* plays a critical role, occupying a central locus in his systematic theology, with time and eternity carefully related to the various loci. First, it began with Gill's understanding of time and eternity functioning as a grand presupposition in Gill's whole theological system. The sharp distinction between time and eternity stems from God's eternality, one of his divine attributes, which makes it clear that God is the creator and time is a creation. Thus, one who delves into the concept of eternity, according to Gill, realizes that God is the ultimate object and goal of the investigation.

Secondly, it dealt with Gill's unique comprehension of the *pactum*. Different from the typical Reformed understanding of the distinction between the covenant of redemption and the covenant of grace, Gill, in line with Benjamin Keach, claims that there is only one covenant of grace. From eternity, there are two concepts of the *pactum*: the everlasting council and the everlasting covenant of grace. Furthermore, Gill's theological consideration regarding the council and the covenant demonstrates that the council pertains to the immanent covenantal acts and relations among the three divine persons, and the covenant concerns the economic acts and relations with the creation, respectively, though both happen in eternity.

Based on the theological flow above moving toward the function of Gill's *pactum* in *Divinity*, this chapter will explore the doctrine of the Trinity according to Gill. One might ask, in terms of Gill's internal theological system, "Why does the dissertation need to deal with the doctrine of the Trinity at this point? Is not the concept of the Trinity already handled implicitly and included in unfolding Gill's *pactum* in the previous chapter?"

The Doctrine of the Trinity According to John Gill

It is an important question. Even Gill himself discusses the doctrine of the Trinity before treating the *pactum* in *Divinity*.[1] Another reasonable question may be raised, with regard to the external circumstances in Gill's contemporary and the previous era, which will be answered from the historical and theological perspective below, that is, "Does the Trinity pertain to the *pactum* and to the central locus of the *pactum* directly in Gill's systematic theology?" In other words, "Is the doctrine of the Trinity helpful to prove or understand the thesis of the whole volume with respect to the *pactum* itself?" This second question is significant because it is directly related to the conceptual existence of the *pactum* itself.

With bearing these two critical questions in mind, first, this chapter will attempt to answer the two significant questions, i.e., why the Trinity? Then, it will examine the doctrine of the Trinity according to Gill: the unity of the divine essence, three in plurality, and finally, personal relations of the three divine persons, especially focusing on the distinction of the three persons in the unique ontological relations. In addition, in relation to the second question above, this chapter, while unfolding Gill's Trinity, will give special attention to the issue of eternal relational authority-submission (ERAS) or eternal functional subordination (EFS) of the Son to the Father and how it relates to the *pactum*.

RATIONALE

First, why the Trinity at this point? To put it concretely, why does this chapter deal with Gill's doctrine of the Trinity after examining Gill's *pactum*? It is because, in Gill's systematic theology, the *pactum*'s centrality with respect to the everlasting council is best revealed in the doctrine of the Trinity. On the other hand, the *pactum*'s centrality with regard to the everlasting covenant of grace is best understood in the doctrine of Jesus Christ, which, therefore, will be the subject of the next chapter.[2]

   1. See the theological order and structure of Gill's systematic theology in *Divinity*. The doctrine of the Trinity belongs to the nature and persons of God in Book I whereas the *pactum* to the acts and works of God in Book II.

   2. The order of chapters in this volume is structuralized to maximally disclose the centrality of the *pactum* following Gill's *Divinity*. As seen in Gill's whole system, the Trinity is dealt with before God's immanent acts whose focus is on the *pactum*. Namely, the peculiar formation of Gill's system in *Divinity* shows a big picture of the *pactum*'s central function in both realms, i.e., time and eternity: the attributes of God – the Trinity – everlasting council and covenant in *pactum* – Christology – final state. Especially, the positions of the Trinity and Christology right before and after the *pactum* in *Divinity* supports how Gill's soteriological mindset flows from the transcendent holy triune God to his creature putting the *pactum* as the essential, central, and connecting bridge

Another cause for the first question comes from the internal relationship between the Trinity and the *pactum*. When it comes to the biblical and theological doctrines in Christianity, the doctrine of the Trinity occupies the very unique and significant locus among all doctrines. "This is a doctrine of pure revelation," says Gill, with a premise that God is mysterious and hidden in relation to the creation.³ But God makes himself known to his creation as the Father, Son, and the Holy Spirit, three divine persons in one nature. This manifestation is pure revelation because the unique way of revelation of God in the Father, Son, and the Holy Spirit is the intrinsic characteristic of "I AM WHO I AM" in Christianity.⁴ Thus, God is mani-

---

in position between the Trinity and Christology. Thus, this chapter on Gill's understanding of the Trinity and the next chapter on Gill's Christology will play a significant role in proving that the *pactum* in Gill's systematic theology occupies the centrality regardless of the temporal and eternal realm.

3. Gill, *The Doctrine of the Trinity*, 4.

4. Basically, the expression I AM WHO I AM ("אֶהְיֶה אֲשֶׁר אֶהְיֶה") in Exodus 3:14 conveys two meanings, according to Ralph Hawkins: first, the name delivers "the timelessness of God, who not only existed in the past but also exists in the present, and will always exist in the future"; secondly, the name also signifies that "not only is Yahweh the God who was, is and always will be, but he is also the causative force behind everything else that ever was, is or will be." In this regard, Hawkins asserts, "The divine name is clearly intended to be viewed as expressing the complete distinctiveness of Yahweh." See Ralph K. Hawkins, *Discovering Exodus: Context, Interpretation, Reception* (Grand Rapids: Eerdmans, 2021), 52-53. Brevard Childs, emphasizing that "'I am who I am', does not mean 'It is not your concern'" explains "the formula is not simply an expression of indefiniteness, but emphasizes the actuality of God: 'I am who I am' means: 'I am there, wherever it may be . . . I am really there!'" Especially, recognizing the wordplay of the formula, which can be translated by 'I will be who I will be,' Childs notes that "the tenses of the formula indicate that more than a senseless tautology is intended, as if to say, I am who I am, a self-contained, incomprehensible being. . . . Rather God announces that his intentions will be revealed in his future acts, which he now refuses to explain." Brevard S. Childs, *The Book of Exodus: A Critical, Theological Commentary*, The Old Testament Library, paperback edition (Louisville: Westminster John Knox, 2004), 69, 76. Terence Fretheim suggests some translations for the name: e.g., I am who I am, I will be what (who) I will be, I will cause to be what I will cause to be, and finally, I will be who I am / I am who I will be. Then, he opines, "The last-noted seems to be the best option, in essence: I will be God for you. The force is not simply that God is or that God is present but that God will be faithfully God for them." Terence E. Fretheim, *Exodus*, Interpretation: A Bible Commentary for Teaching and Preaching (Louisville: Westminster John Knox, 1991), 63. Peter Enns adds, "The play on the verb 'to be' may also suggest God's unswerving existence with his people from the patriarchal period onward. This is supported fairly clearly by the pun with verse 12: 'I will be with you.' At least one of the reasons for using this name is to highlight God's continued existence with his people." Peter Enns, *Exodus*, The NIV Application Commentary (Grand Rapids: Zondervan, 2000), 103. God's revelation is only by himself with no other because God is the creator of the whole universe including time. Even though the being of God is transcendent and exists in mystery beyond man's capacity, even though the sinful

fested through a pure revelation, which makes it possible that God's eternal will, decree, and mind exist only pure and active.[5] Therefore, the internal acts and works of God in his perfect will and mind run active through a pure revelation of the Father, Son, and the Holy Spirit from eternity to time, from creator to creation.[6] Moreover, the essence or apex of God's internal acts and works in the Father, Son, and the Holy Spirit, according to Gill, lies in the *pactum* through which the genuine passion of the eternal triune God for humanity's redemption flows to the creation; precisely speaking, the elect in Christ.

Secondly, does the Trinity pertain to the *pactum* and to the *pactum*'s role as occupying the central locus directly in Gill's systematic theology? The second question is in quality like the first question in asking why the Trinity is important to the *pactum*: i.e., why does the *pactum*'s centrality in Gill's systematic theology require the doctrine of the Trinity? This inquiry does not relate to Gill's internal systematic order of theology only, as already answered in the first question; rather, it demands an explanation of the historical development of the doctrine of God or of specifically justification of the doctrine of the Trinity, at least during the sixteenth and seventeenth

---

humanity is not ready to receive or understand the way of his self-revelation, as Enns says, at least one thing is coming through loud and clear regarding God who says, "Certainly I will be with you (Exo 3:12)."

5. This does not necessarily mean that God's act of movement in manifestation of himself to creation through a pure revelation entails any development in himself or becoming other in change. "One could perhaps say that God is the unity of potentiality and actuality in the dynamism of an unceasing becoming, but God remains eternal being even as he freely relates to himself and to his creatures. Every possibility that will be realized in the world is already realized in the mind of God, but he unceasingly gives these possibilities concrete existence in the realm of temporality." Donald G. Bloesch, *God the Almighty: Power, Wisdom, Holiness, Love* (Downers Grove: IVP, 2006), 36.

6. Regarding the relation of revelation to the Trinity, Barth notes, "*God* reveals Himself. He reveals Himself *through Himself*. He reveals *Himself*. If we really want to understand revelation in terms of its subject, i.e., God, then the first thing we have to realise is that this subject, God, the Revealer, is identical with His act in revelation and also identical with its effect. It is from this fact, . . . , that we learn we must begin the doctrine of revelation with the doctrine of the triune God." Barth, *CD*, I/1: 296. Barth also recognizes that the triune God as a pure revelation is a pure act, which means the revealed God is his act. Such a concept of God as a pure act in a pure revelation of the Father, Son, and the Holy Spirit makes soteriological concepts that are divided by pieces simple and one in his being. In other words, the *pactum* as internal and immanent works in the true revelation in the Father, Son, and the Holy Spirit embraces both realms of time and eternity in Christ. Why in Christ? Fesko helps by bringing Christ's incarnation in the Gospel of John, "John's movement from 'in the beginning' to 'the Word became flesh and tabernacled among us' takes us from eternity into the middle of redemptive history." Fesko, *The Trinity and the Covenant of Redemption*, 165. Therefore, it is crucial for God to be in three persons: the Father, the Son, and the Holy Spirit.

centuries. This was the case in order for Gill to establish his theological system upon the *pactum* with regard to the Trinity. Simply speaking, without the confirmation of the doctrine of the Trinity, there is no room for the *pactum* to stand conceptually and theologically. Thus, the answer to the second question calls for a study of the theological context of Gill's contemporaries and those who lived before Gill, though briefly, unfolding the historical circumstances of the doctrine of the Trinity, especially focusing on the trinitarian controversy during the sixteenth and seventeenth centuries.

Socinianism

Gill's comprehensive awareness or cognition of many false and heretical ideas regarding the doctrine of the Trinity is clearly seen in an abstract form as he articulates the concept and scope of Unitarianism, which is enunciated below:

> *All*, professing Christians, are Unitarians *in a sense*, but not in the same sense. Some are Unitarians in opposition to a Trinity of Persons in one God. Others are Unitarians in perfect *consistence* with that doctrine. Those of the former sort stand ranked in very bad company; for a Deist, who rejects divine revelation in general, is a Unitarian. A Jew that rejects the writings of the New Testament, and Jesus of Nazareth as the Messiah, is a Unitarian. A Mahometan is a Unitarian who believes in one God, and in his prophet Mahomet. A Sabellian is a Unitarian, who denies a distinction of Persons in the Godhead. A Socinian is a Unitarian, who asserts that Christ did not exist before he was born of the virgin, and that he was God not by nature but by office. An Arian may be said, in a sense, to be a Unitarian, because he holds one supreme God, though rather he may be reckoned a Tritheist, since along with the *one* supreme God, he holds two subordinate ones. Those *only* are Unitarians, in a *true* and sound sense, who hold a Trinity of *distinct* Persons in *one* God; who is but *one* in his *essence*.[7]

---

7. Rippon, *A Brief Memoir*, 88-89. Italics original. What is the basic idea of Unitarianism? James Leo Garrett Jr. gives a kernel of the unitarian view, which "interprets Jesus of Nazareth in such a way that he does not belong within the nature and being of God and thus interprets God as unipersonal, or without internal differentiations." Garrett, *Systematic Theology*, 1:318. Malcolm Yarnell, in his note of systematic theology lecture, adds the Holy Spirit to this concept, "(Unitarianism) magnifies the Godhood of the Father at the expense of the Son and the Holy Spirit, thus making the Son and the Holy Spirit less than God." Yarnell also notes that some earlier theologians emphasized the monarchy of the Father so much that they "endangered the identity of Jesus with

The Doctrine of the Trinity According to John Gill

While recognizing the seriousness of the unitarian challenges in various forms above, i.e., deist, Jew, Mahometan, Sabellian, Socinian, and Arian, Gill, considering Christ's filiation as *"essential* to the defense of the Trinity," paid special attention to opposing the Socinianism that was widespread in England during the seventeenth and even early eighteenth centuries.[8] The

---

God and turned the Holy Spirit into a mere power, or they nullify any distinction between the Father, his Son, and the Holy Spirit." Then, he provides two branches of those early unitarian theologians; namely, dynamic monarchian theologians and modalistic monarchian theologians. For more explanations about the divine monarch, see Yarnell, *God the Trinity*, 126-29.

8. Rippon, *A Brief Memoir*, 87. Italics original. Deism whose doctrinal boundary is broad was based on the teaching of Herbert of Cherbury (1582-1648), the father of deism, in England. "Deists questioned major doctrines concerning the being and attributes of God, the necessity of a creed for salvation, miracles, and the inspiration of Scripture." Gerard Reedy, S.J., "Socinians, John Toland, and the Anglican Rationalists," *Harvard Theological Review* 70, no. 3-4 (July-October 1977): 286. For more about Deism in the seventeenth and early eighteenth century, see Thomas C. Pfizenmaier, *The Trinitarian Theology of Dr. Samuel Clarke (1675-1729): Context, Sources, and Controversy*, Studies in the History of Christian Thought (Leiden: Brill, 1997), 30-37. Concerning Mahometanism, see William Nicholls, *An Answer to an Heretical Book Called the Naked Gospel, which was condemned and ordered to be publicly burnt by the Convocation of the University of Oxford, Aug. 19, 1690* (London: Bishop's Head in St. Paul's Church-Yard, 1691), an answer to the preface, in which William was against an antitrinitarian work *The Naked Gospel* written by Arthur Bury (1624-1713) in 1690. Sabellianism, known as one of the earliest forms of Unitarianism in the third century, was also affecting the churches in England during seventeenth and early eighteenth century. Robert Oliver borrowing Rippon's explanation mentions that Gill's *A Treatise on the Doctrine of the Trinity* (1731) was published in the situation of "the spread of Sabellianism among some of the Baptist churches." He continues to briefly clarify Sabellianism, "Named after the third-century heretic Sabellius, this doctrinal perspective teaches that the Father, Son and Holy Spirit are not distinct persons, but rather separate roles that the one God has taken at different stages in the economy of salvation." Robert W. Oliver, "John Gill (1697-1771): His Life and Ministry," in *The Life and Thought of John Gill (1697-1771): A Tercentennial Appreciation*, ed. Michael A. G. Haykin, Studies in the History of Christian Thought (Leiden: Brill, 1997), 30-31. During the sixteenth and early seventeenth centuries, many who advocated Arianism in British were burnt to death. Maurice Wiles, giving a direct example, delivers the situation of the Arianism and persecution, "The last person to be burnt for his beliefs in Britain, Edward Wightman in 1612, is described as condemned for being an Arian." Wiles also gives an account of 'Antitrinitarians and new Arians' out of the movement of antitrinitarian heretical groups as origins of Arianism in the seventeenth century including the so-called 'Arian Controversy' raised mainly by Samuel Clarke's *Scripture-Doctrine of the Trinity* (1712). See Maurice Wiles, *Archetypal Heresy: Arianism through the Centuries* (Oxford: Clarendon, 1996), 62-63, 110-134. Regarding the assessment of Samuel Clarke's Arianism, there is an argument. First, the scholars such as K. R. Hagenbach, George Park Fisher, and William Shedd assert that Clarke reconstructed the Arian theology, i.e., "Clarke's work represented a revival of the Arian system, and holds the 'high Arian view.'" In contrast, Pfizenmaier argues that Clarke "was certainly no Arian as he expressly denied the two Arian tenets. The Son was not a creature, nor was there 'a time

trinitarian controversy in the late seventeenth century in England was inextricably linked to the issue of Christ's divine status in terms of the relation to the Father, which caused Gill to hold a pen even in coming to the end of his life to make a thorough investigation regarding the matter and to write *A Dissertation concerning the Eternal Sonship of Christ*.[9] Gill, seeing Socinianism occupying the central idea of the heretical unitarian concepts, begins the very first sentence of his defense with, "The eternal Sonship of Christ, or that he is the Son of God by eternal generation, or that he was the Son of God before he was the son of *Mary*, even from all eternity, which is denied by the Socinians, and others akin to them, was known by the saints under the Old Testament."[10] Gill unfolds, then, that the rest of the whole disserta-

---

when he was not.'" "Clarke's thought," continues Pfizenmaier, being influenced by the patristic and contemporary sources, "represents a re-emergence of the views of Origin, Eusebius of Caeserea, and, in a sense, of the Eastern tradition in general. Clarke was not an Arian, nor an Athanasian, but a Eusebian. His work must be understood and studied within the multi-faceted context of the Arian controversy which in many ways paralleled the trinitarian controversy of his own time." Pfizenmaier, *The Trinitarian Theology of Dr. Samuel Clarke*, 3, 137-141. For the details of the early Christian trinitarian controversy during the first four centuries, see William G. Rusch, ed. and trans., *The Trinitarian Controversy*, Sources of Early Christian Thought (Philadelphia: Fortress, 1980). With regard to the cultural and theological context in Gill's contemporary in relation to these unitarian concepts, see Steven Tshombe Godet, "The Trinitarian Theology of John Gill (1697-1771): Context, Sources, and Controversy" (PhD diss., The Southern Baptist Theological Seminary, 2015), chapter two. All resources above concerning deist through Arian verify that there were many groups of Unitarianism in various names in the seventeenth and early eighteenth centuries. Socinianism will be more deeply dealt with by next section.

9. Rippon, *A Brief Memoir*, 87.

10. John Gill, "A Dissertation concerning the Eternal Sonship of Christ," in *A Collection of Sermons and Tracks* (London: George Keith, 1773), 2:534. Italics original. Gill closely scrutinizes this controversy from the first century through the eleventh century and to the Reformation in the sixteenth century. In this research, Gill studies key figures of each century for and against the eternal generation of the Son. Emphasizing the church tradition and the importance of the historical orthodox theology handed down, Gill points out in the same writing that "the church of God has been in the possession of this doctrine of the eternal generation and Sonship of Christ, from the beginning of Christianity to the present age, almost *eighteen hundred years*; nor has there been any one man who professed to hold the doctrine of the Trinity, or of the three distinct divine persons in the unity of the divine essence, that ever opposed it, till the latter end of the *seventeenth century*." Thus, for almost eighteen hundred years, the eternal generation of the Son has been maintained as an orthodox doctrine. Gill plainly articulates the names who were against or rejected the doctrine: Simon Magus, Cerinthus, Ebion, Carpocrates, the Gnosticks, Valentinus, Theodotus the currier, Artemon, Beryllus of Bostra, Praxeus, Hermogenes, Noetius, Sabellius, the Samosatenians, Arians, Aetians, Eunomians, Photinians, the Priscillianists, Bonotians, Mahomet, Socinians, and Remonstrants. See Gill, "A Dissertation concerning the Eternal Sonship of Christ," in 2: 562, 564.

The Doctrine of the Trinity According to John Gill

tion is concerned with the two contrasting parties in Christian history: one is so-called the opponents of the doctrine of the Son's eternal generation whose followers "were much the same with our modern Socinians"; the other is the defenders of the eternal generation of the Son.[11]

Socinianism has been deeply related to Unitarianism, whose historical and religious background was provoked during the period of changes in cognitive upheaval.[12] A. J. Pollock draws a quick pedigree of the major unitarian figures: i.e., Sabellius in the third century, Michael Servetus and Faustus Socinus in the early and late sixteenth century, respectively, and Joseph Priestley in the eighteenth century.[13] Interestingly, it was not until the sixteenth century that Unitarianism reared its head again after Sabellius. Socinianism in the movement of Unitarianism took place in the social and cultural trends motivated by "the enlightened humanism of the Renaissance" and "the influence of Erasmus of Rotterdam."[14] McLachlan

11. Gill, "A Dissertation concerning the Eternal Sonship of Christ," 2:550.

12. In his book *Socinianism in Poland*, Stanislas Kot explains the relation of the antitrinitarian groups of Unitarianism to Socinianism, "the Unitarian movement which had been rising in Poland and Lithuania in the twenty-five years preceding Socinus' advent, producing numerous writers and a rich literature–mainly in Polish–comprised manifold trends.... This group [labelled by Catholic and Protestant as Sabellians, Samosatinians, Ebionites, and Arians] called themselves Christians or Brothers, whence the subsequent appellation 'Polish Brethren.'" The Polish Brethren and their doctrines with the work of Socinus were disseminated to the Western world and became widespread after dedicating their famous Racovian Catechism to the King James I, though it was rejected by the King as an insult. When the teachings of Unitarianism "swept from Poland in a tide, flowing through both Danzig and the Netherlands, carrying the doctrine to England," "it was called Socinianism by its detractors." See Stanislas Kot, *Socinianism in Poland: The Social and Political Ideas of the Polish Antitrinitarians in the Sixteenth and Seventeenth Centuries*, translated from the Polish by Earl Morse Wilbur (Boston: Starr King Press, 1957), xviii, xxii.

13. Algernon J. Pollock, *Unitarianism: The Negation of the Christian Faith* (London: Central Bible Truth Depot, 1951), 3-5. In this short pamphlet throughout, Pollock makes with seven propositions of Unitarianism's main thought: (1) unitarians teach there is only one God, the Father; (2) Unitarianism teaches that our Lord was only human; (3) Unitarianism denies the virgin birth of our Lord; (4) the unitarians make light of our Lord's miracles; (5) unitarians teach that our Lord's death was not sacrificial; (6) unitarians deny worship to the Son of God; and (7) Unitarianism exalts human reason above the Scripture. It is interesting that the teachings of Unitarianism are almost the same with the Socinian ones. Regarding the life of Joseph Priestley and how he became a Socinian, see Michael A. G. Haykin, "A Socinian and Calvinist Compared: Joseph Priestley and Andrew Fuller on the Propriety of Prayer to Christ," *Nederlands archief voor kerkgeschiedenis* 73, no. 2 (1993): 178-82.

14. H. John McLachlan, *Socinianism in Seventeenth-Century England* (London: Oxford University Press, 1951), 4-5. McLachlan explains more about the impact of Erasmus on the antitrinitarian movement, "His [Erasmus] edition of the text of the New Testament and his exegetical paraphrases and annotations helped to spread

describes the historical atmosphere of Socinianism's emergence in England: "Contemporaries in the sixteenth, seventeenth, and eighteenth centuries may, perhaps, be excused for their pronounced hostility to a religious system which they conceived to be anti-Christian and subversive of all moral and spiritual values."[15] In the midst of such a sweeping mood of challenge questioning the medieval religious ethos and social structure of the traditional Christian system, it was Michael Servetus (1511-1553), a Spaniard who made a deep impact on the concept of Unitarianism, which ultimately affected the development of Socinianism.[16]

The theology of Servetus was a historical product of the early sixteenth century and the social circumstances in Spain. Namely, the "intellectual climate" of the land drove young Servetus to be influenced by the humanistic idea.[17] The Reformation's influence on the thought process of Servetus

---

unorthodox opinions amongst Dutch Anabaptists, and later, Arminians, Polish Socinians, and English Latitudinarians handling of the Scripture to him." For more about Erasmus in Reformation, see W. R. Estep, *The Reformation: Luther, the Anabaptists*, Christian Classics (Nashville: Broadman Press, 1979), 20-25, 49-92. With regard to the Socinian's challenge to the doctrine of the Trinity in the social atmosphere, see Sarah Mortimer, *Reason and Religion in the English Revolution: The Challenge of Socinianism*, Cambridge Studies in Early Modern British History (Cambridge: Cambridge University Press, 2010), chapter six and seven.

15. McLachlan, *Socinianism in Seventeenth-Century England*, 1. An example of such a strong color of human-oriented culture is seen in the seventeenth century: "Central to at least one major strand in seventeenth-century English culture–the strand framed by Francis Bacon writing at the beginning and John Locke writing at the end of the century–was a massive effort to restore what Bacon called the 'commerce between the mind of man and the nature of things' to something like 'its perfect and original condition.'" William S. Babcock, "A Changing of the Christian God: The Doctrine of the Trinity in the Seventeenth Century," *Interpretations* 45, no. 2 (April 1991): 136.

16. Kot describes, "The movement's [Polish Brethren's Unitarian movement, later known as Socinianism] inspiration stemmed from Servetus, a Spanish exile residing in France, and communicated itself to certain Italians who had migrated across the Alps, namely Camillo Renato, Lelio Socini, Celio Secundo Curione, Bernardino Ochino, Matteo Gribaldi, Valentino Gentile, and Giorgio Blandrata." Kot, *Socinianism in Poland*, xx. Willliam Everts agrees that the writings of those Italians, including Servetus, "were the storehouse from which Socinus constructed his system." He continues and explains about their intellectual characteristics, "Their delight was to raise questions, to insinuate doubts, to tolerate indifference as to established truth. They laid a foundation, not as the Reformers did in the Bible, but in classical literature and the skeptical philosophy. The Bible was an after-thought with them." W. W. Everts, "The Rise and Spread of Socinianism," *Review and Expositor* 11, no. 4 (October 1914): 522-23.

17. "The Spain in which he [Servetus] grew up was influenced by the humanism of Cardinal Jimenez de Cisneros and Desiderius Erasmus, whose influence in Spain was boosted by Charles V's presence in the country beginning in 1522. Jimenez and Erasmus represented the hope of the purification of Christianity through the mechanisms of philosophy and translation. The way in which humanistic thought and method

The Doctrine of the Trinity According to John Gill

called on him to focus on the careful investigation of the Bible because "Servetus thought that authentic Christianity was dependent upon a return to the true teaching of the Bible and of the first Christians" with special regard to the doctrine of the hypostatic union and the doctrine of the Trinity.[18] However, he could find no evidence of such traditional language, e.g., the Trinity, and thus "concluded that the elaboration of this doctrine [the Trinity] was one of the marks of the fall of the church."[19] In his infamous work *On the Errors of the Trinity*, Servetus strenuously insists,

> The doctrine of the Trinity can be neither established by logic nor proved from Scripture, and is in fact inconceivable. There are many reasons against it. The Scriptures and the Fathers teach one God the Father, and Jesus Christ his Son; but scholastic philosophy has introduced terms which are not understood, and do not accord with Scripture. Jesus taught that he himself was the Son of God. Numerous heresies have sprung from this philosophy, and fruitless questions have arisen out of it. Worst of all, the doctrine of the Trinity incurs the ridicule of the Mohammedans and the Jews. It arose out of Greek philosophy rather than from the belief that Jesus Christ is the Son of God; and he will be with the Church only if it keeps his teaching.[20]

In other words, Servetus indicates that the doctrine of the Trinity is "a concoction influenced by Greek philosophy and developed to higher levels of speculation by medieval scholasticism."[21] Talha Fortaci offers a crucial and conclusive word on the theology of Servetus: "Examining the Christian thought of Servetus from his first to his last work reveals that one of his most fundamental assumptions is the doctrine that God is one and unique."[22]

---

affected Servetus in his early years, however, is unclear. Despite the fact that when Servetus was fourteen he began working for Juan de Quintana, who had strong humanistic tendencies, it seems that he began questioning traditional Christian doctrines while at the University of Toulouse, where he went to study law." Joao Chaves, "The Servetus Challenge: Eisegesis and the Problematic of Differing Chronologies of Ecclesiastical Corruption," *Journal of Reformed Theology* 10, no. 3 (2016): 199.

18. Chaves, "The Servetus Challenge," 203.

19. Roland H. Bainton, "Burned Heretic: Michael Servetus," *The Christian Century* 70, no. 43 (October 1953): 1230.

20. Michael Servetus, "On the Errors of the Trinity," in *The Two Treatises of Servetus on the Trinity*, trans. Earl Morse Wilbur, Harvard Theological Studies 16 (Cambridge: Harvard University Press, 1932), 3.

21. Chaves, "The Servetus Challenge," 205.

22. Talha Fortaci, "Trinity in the Theology of Michael Servetus," *Oksident* 4, no. 2 (2022): 177. For the biblical and theological meaning of 'God is one and unique,' see Yarnell, *God the Trinity*, 57-84. Catholics and Protestants were being nervous and

The social and cultural trend of the times and rich soil of Unitarian thought spread and enhanced by Italian theologians, including Servetus, a Spaniard, were good enough to give rise to another notorious Unitarian theologian, Faustus Socinus (1539-1604), the founder of Socinianism.[23] In a big picture of Socinianism, Alan Gomes, who sees the Socinian thought as "a reconstruction and reinvention of the entire Christian edifice," appraises Socinians, forming a striking contrast to the relationship between Reformers and Roman Catholics who at least share the essential doctrines of Christianity, as following:

> Socinianism, on the other hand, utterly rejects the ecumenical doctrines of the Trinity and the two natures in Christ, *creatio ex nihilo*, eternal conscious punishment for the lost, Christ's satisfaction for sin on the cross, original sin, the immortality of the soul, the orthodox doctrine of the intermediate state, and the traditional attributes of God, such as his omnipresence and his foreknowledge of future contingent events. We therefore must bear in mind that "the controversy with the Socinians is not a mere dispute about some particular doctrines, however

---

disturbed by the spread of Servetus' theology. Fortaci records that "Heinrich Bullinger, Johannes Oecolampadius, and Huldrych Zwingli organized a meeting about Servetus in which they discussed some matters such as Servetus' contradictory behavior in religious issues, his stubbornness, and the danger of the spread of his theological errors." More interesting comes with the relation of Servetus to Calvin. While they corresponded each other regarding theological issues, says Fortaci, "Calvin was enraged by Servetus' *sinful* theses and *arrogant* tone." Moreover, one of the most significant concerns Calvin had with Servetus was "Servetus' focus on the pre-Nicene Church Fathers [Tertullian and Irenaeus] because it posed a severe threat to the legitimacy of the Geneva Church. Additionally, the majority of Servetus' argumentations were biblical." See Fortaci, "Trinity in the Theology of Michael Servetus," 199-200. Italics original; also, see Chaves, "The Servetus Challenge," 206. Gregg Allison also denotes, "Michael Servetus's anti-Trinitarianism was so dangerous that much of Calvin's writing on the doctrine in his Institutes was a defense of the traditional formulation against Servetus's heretical view." Gregg R. Allison, *Historical Theology: An Introduction to Christian Doctrine* (Grand Rapids: Zondervan, 2011), 247. Sentenced as a heretic, Servetus was burnt to death in 1553 because "in that age all theologians were agreed that heresy was a crime." Everts, "The Rise and Spread of Socinianism," 528.

23. For the historical summary of the Socinus's life and background, see F. L. Cross, "Socinus," in *The Oxford Dictionary of the Christian Church* (Oxford: Oxford University Press, 1997); McLachlan, *Socinianism*, 9-17; Marian Hillar, "Laelius and Faustus Socinus, Founders of Socinianism: Their Lives and Theology," Part One and Two, *A Journal from the Radical Reformation: A Testimony to Biblical Unitarianism* 10, no. 2-3 (2001-2). Especially, regarding the relation of Socinus to the Polish Brethren, see Kot, *Socinianism in Poland*, xviii-xxii; Marian Hillar, "The Polish Socinians: Contribution to Freedom of Conscience and the American Constitution," *Dialogue and Universalism* 19, no. 3-5 (2009): 6-7.

important these may be, but really involves a contest for everything that is peculiar and important in the Christian system."[24]

This holistic rejection of Christianity by Socinianism is based on and begins with the critically heretical understanding of the doctrine of the Trinity and Christology. Gerard Reedy affirms in a nutshell what Socinians deeply held regarding Christian doctrines, "God is one person, not three; that Jesus is a messenger, minister, servant, creature, and son of God, but not God almighty and eternal; and that the Holy Spirit is the power of God, but not God himself."[25]

The theology of Faustus Socinus did not come out of a vacuum. Laelius Socinus, who is called "the patriarch of Socinianism," helped his nephew, Faustus, open the eyes to see and renovate the old system of Christianity.[26] McLachlan, observing that Laelius "travelled widely, studying in Wittenberg, visiting England and Poland, settling for a time in Zürich, always mentally on the move, seeking answers to his religious inquiries," describes him as,

> A man of reflective temperament and incisive views, he gave anxiety to Calvin and Bullinger by his continued questioning of the accepted doctrines of the Trinity, the atonement, justification, and the sacraments. Too cautious to commit himself outright, and lacking in positive, systematic ideas, when he died at the early age of thirty-seven, his papers came into the possession of his nephew, Fausto, and are thought to have suggested to the more famous heresiarch some lines of thought which he later incorporated into his system of doctrine.[27]

Inheriting Laelius's papers and not being satisfied with Reformed Protestantism, Faustus went to Poland, where he "aligned himself with an existing community of anti-Trinitarians and Anabaptists based at Rakow, known as the Polish Brethren."[28] At the end of the sixteenth century, Faus-

---

24. Alan W. Gomes, "Some Observations on the Theological Method of Faustus Socinus (1539-1604)," *WTJ* 70 (2008): 50, 51.

25. Reedy, "Socinian, John Toland, and the Anglican Rationalists," 285.

26. McLachlan, *Socinianism*, 7.

27. McLachlan, *Socinianism*, 7. Mortimer also states, "He [Faustus] also absorbed the familial tradition of religious heterodoxy. Several of his uncles had been in trouble with the Catholic Church, but one, Laelius (1525-1562), had gone all the way to Protestantism and beyond. Laelius knew the leading Reformers well, he was on friendly terms with Bullinger and Melanchthon, but he maintained serious doubts about the truth of some of their doctrines." Mortimer, *Reason and Religion in the England Revolution*, 14.

28. Mortimer, *Reason and Religion in the English Revolution*, 14. Even before Faustus's reaching to the land with the antitrinitarian and Unitarianism thought, those ideas

tus became recognized as an important person with authority among the Rakow Unitarians for "systematizing the doctrines of the Polish Brethren."[29] Unitarianism in Poland spread through the Netherlands and finally to England. The catalyst of the Unitarian spread over Europe, particularly to England, was the publication of the Racovian Catechism, with which other major writings of the Polish Brethren were printed in Rakow, "the centre of Socinianism."[30]

While other European countries, e.g., Spain, Italy, and Poland, had a rough time due to the trinitarian controversy, namely, the spread of Unitarianism with the major figures like Michael Servetus, Laelius and Faustus Socinus, England could not be an exception. Before moving into Gill's doctrine of the Trinity, the rest of this section deals with John Biddle (1615-1662), "the founder of Unitarianism in England."[31]

---

were not new in Poland. See Zbigniew Ogonowski, "Antitrinitarianism in Poland before Socinus: A Historical Outline," *Roczniki Filozoficzne* 70, no. 4 (2022): 87-142. Especially, Peter Giezek contributed to the historical early antitrinitarianism in Poland. His main argument comes with: "1. He declared that the Trinity did not exist, and that the word was a new invention. 2. He criticized the Athanasian Credo, and rejected it completely as a 'human invention.' 3. God the Father is the sole God, and there is no other. 4. Christ is inferior to his Father, he is his father's servant. 5. He stated that Logos was The Word, invisible, immortal, transformed at a given time into flesh in the Virgin's womb, and he called this Word the seed of the Incarnated Son. 6. He denied the coexistence of Jesus Christ and God the Father within divinity." Kot, *Socinianism in Poland*, xi-xii.

29. Hillar, "The Polish Socinians," 1.

30. Mortimer, *Reason and Religion in the English Revolution*, 1. The first generation of the Polish Brethren was not interested in propagating their religious thought to the world, focusing on "making its way and consolidating its teachings." However, the second generation who was affected by Faustus "felt strong enough for the propagation of principles to other lands" and began to publish their doctrinal abstracts. Racovian Catechism was one of the most popular works and even dedicated to the King of England, James I. Though it was rejected and burned by the King, such act of the King only was "contributing to popularize the catechism" in England. See Kot, *Socinianism in Poland*, xxi-xxii. For the historical development of Unitarianism, see Thomas Rees, *The Racovian Catechism: with Notes and Illustrations, translated from the Latin; to which is prefixed a sketch of the history of Unitarianism in Poland and the adjacent countries* (London: Longman, Hurst, Rees, Orme and Brown, 1818; repr., Lexington, KY: American Theological Library Association, 1962), historical instruction. The inflow of Unitarianism into England happened not only through the Catechism incident but by various routes as well: "English notables were being persuaded to Unitarianism by letters and tracts, or through the British merchants of the Moscow Eastern Company." Kot, *Socinianism in Poland*, xxii. For the more historical facts of the connection between Poland and England, see McLachlan, *Socinianism*, 25-29.

31. W. K. Jordan, "Sectarian Thought and Its Relation to the Development of Religious Toleration, 1640-1660; Part III: 'The Socinians,'" *Huntington Library Quarterly* 3, no. 4 (1940): 408. Jordan in the same page also provides the brief sum of Biddle's life. It is impressive to see his life imprisoned several times because of his insistence on the

Devoting himself to reading the Scripture and investigating ardently divine illumination, Biddle "perceiv'd the common Doctrine concerning the Holy Trinity was not well grounded in Revelation, much less in Reason."[32] Not only denying the divine personhood of the Son but also vigorously denouncing that the Holy Spirit shared the essence of the Godhead with the Father and the Son, Biddle insisted,

> As for my Opinion touching the Holy Spirit . . . I do place him, . . . in the third Rank, after God and Christ, . . . there is, I say, one principal Spirit among the Good Angels, called by the Name of the (a) Advocate; or (b) the Holy Spirit; or (c) the good Spirit of God; or (d) the Spirit of God; or (e) the Spirit, by way of eminence. This Opinion of mine is attested by the whole Tenour of the Scripture, which perpetually speaketh of him as differing from God, and inferior to him.[33]

In other words, he argued that "the Holy Ghost must be separated in both person and essence from God the Father. The Holy Ghost was God's messenger; it received instruction from God, and it spoke of God."[34] Biddle's biblical hermeneutics was derived from his two strong convictions: (1) being simple in reason, which indicates that "truth being in itself plain and simple, especially what is necessary and very useful, is easy to be apprehended by few words"; (2) no communal method in doing theology, that is,

---

heretical doctrine of God, though saved each time by "Cromwell's personal intervention," and eventually, his death in prison in 1662. For the detail of Biddle's life, see McLachlan, *Socinianism*, 163-217.

32. John Bidle, "A Short Account of the Life of John Bidle," in *The Apostolical and True Opinion concerning the Holy Trinity, Revived and Asserted: Partly by Twelve Arguments levied against the Traditional and False Opinion about the Godhead of the Holy Spirit. Partly by a Confession of Faith touching the Three Persons*, by John Bidle (1653; repr., London: s.n., 1691), 5. Bidle's propositions regarding the doctrine of the Trinity and Christology came with three abstract sentences, which provoked an issue: "1. I believe there is but one Infinite and Almighty Essence, called God. 2. I believe, that as there is but one Infinite and Almighty Essence, so there is but one Person in that Essence. 3. I believe that our Saviour Jesus Christ is truly God, by being truly, really and properly united to the only Person of the Infinite and Almighty Essence." "A Short Account of the Life of John Bidle," 5. In other words, Biddle denies the ontological eternal person of Christ, the Son of God because, according to him, Jesus Christ only becomes God by being united to the only person of the essence, that is, the Father.

33. John Bidle, "A Letter written to Sir H. V. a Member of the Honourable House of Commons," in *The Apostolical and True Opinion concerning the Holy Trinity, Revived and Asserted* (1653; repr., London: s.n., 1691), 12-13.

34. Mortimer, *Reason and Religion in the English Revolution*, 161.

"his theology was his own and not taken from any other sect or group.... he was the necessary first cause... not the monstrous terms of the school."[35]

Another crucial cause of Biddle's rejection of trinitarianism lay in the pattern of worshipping God. Seeing the English churches falling into idolatry by "giving the glory of God to another," i.e., including Jesus Christ and the Holy Spirit as the object of the worship, Biddle wanted to restore the simple worship, getting rid of such a "devotional legacy."[36]

These theological concepts of John Biddle were eventually on the same track as the anti-trinitarianism of the Socinians, though it is reckoned that Biddle's initial theology was not affected by Socinianism.[37] Reedy points out two common ideas of the Socinians from which Biddle's theology would not be free: (1) emphasizing reason and common sense in interpreting the Scripture; (2) rejecting a communal context of reading the Scripture.[38]

The so-called trinitarian controversy in the late seventeenth century, ultimately, was the concomitant result of the historical Unitarian movement sprouted by the Polish Brethren and flowered by the name of Socinianism in England.[39] Though its influence was "stamped out by bitter persecution

---

35. "A Short Account of the Life of John Bidle," 9; Mortimer, *Reason and Religion in the English Revolution*, 162.

36. Mortimer, *Reason and Religion in the English Revolution*, 161. Biddle asserts, "And that this practice of Worshipping the Holy Spirit as God, is such a Plant as God never set in his Word, ... they endeavour to delude both themselves and others with Personalities, Moods, Subsistence, and such like brain-sick Notions, that have neither sap nor sense in them, and were first hatched by the subtilty of Satan in the Heads of Platonists, to pervert the Worship of the True God." Biddle, "A Letter written to Sir H. V. a Member of the Honourable House of Commons," 14-15.

37. Mortimer, *Reason and Religion in the English Revolution*, 161. Regarding the relation of the Socinian thought to the theology of Biddle, Mortimer goes further by simply saying, "In July 1652, an English translation of the Racovian Catechism was also printed; the translator was almost certainly John Biddle." Mortimer, *Reason and Religion in the English Revolution*, 165.

38. "The Socinians," says Reedy, "claim that the scriptural doctrine of God is perfectly clear to one who inquires after it without prejudice, and that this doctrine is Unitarian. ... The unbiased reader, reliant simply on common sense, grace, and the text, is the ideal Socinian reader of Scripture." Secondly, Reedy inevitably could not help asserting that "the Socinian ideal for reading Scripture, then, is not at all in a communal or ecclesiastical context. The Socinian reader is a lonely reader, alone with his reason and the text. He especially rejects assistance from the later Fathers and Councils of the Church." Reedy, "Socinians, John Toland, and the Anglican Rationalists," 291. Reedy's two points perfectly fit to the hermeneutics and theological method of John Biddle. See note 35 above.

39. Such a fierce controversy in debate regarding the doctrine of the Trinity is proved by several letters and treatises handed down even to the present. For example, see the arguments between John Wallis and Stephen Nye: John Wallis, *The Doctrine of the Blessed Trinity Briefly Explained, In a Letter to a Friend* (London: Tho. Parkhurst,

on the part of the Jesuits," Unitarianism continued to exist even in the eighteenth century.⁴⁰

Summary

"Is the study of Gill's doctrine of the Trinity required to prove that Gill's *pactum* occupies the central locus in his theological system?" The second question at the beginning of this chapter has left the pages filled with the trinitarian controversies during the sixteenth and seventeenth centuries, particularly focusing on the historical and theological development of Unitarianism, which would be called later Socinianism in England. Due to the close relationship between the doctrine of the Trinity and the *pactum* in terms of the conceptual and theological existence of the *pactum*, this chapter has surveyed a historical development of Socinianism, which provides the ground or reason why Gill was so serious with regard to writing on the doctrine of the Trinity.

1690); Stephen Nye, *Doctor Wallis's Letter Touching the Doctrine of the Blessed Trinity Answer'd by his Friend* (London: s.n., 1691); Stephen Ney, *A Letter of Resolution concerning the Doctrines of the Trinity and the Incarnation* (London: s.n., 1691). For another Unitarian letter, see Anonymous, *The Unreasonableness of the Doctrine of the Trinity Briefly Demonstrated, In a Letter to a Friend* (London: s.n., 1692). William Nicholls wrote against Arthur Bury's *Naked Gospel* with a short history of Socinianism. See William Nicholls, *An Answer to an Heretical Book Called the Naked Gospel, which was condemned and ordered to be publickly burnt by the Convocation of the University of Oxford, Aug. 19. 1690* (London: Walter Kettilby, 1691). For later defence of the doctrine of the Trinity, see Edward Fowler, *A Second Defence of the Propositions, by which the Doctrine of the Holy Trinity is so Explained, according to the Ancient Fathers, as to speak it not contradictory to Natural Reason: in Answer to a Socinian Manuscript* (London: B. Aylmer, 1695); Francis Gregory, *The Doctrine of the Glorious Trinity, not Explained, but Asserted by Several Texts, as they are expounded by the ancient Fathers and later Divines* (London: Walter Kettilby, 1695); John Tillotson, *A Seasonable Vindication of the B. Trinity Being an Answer to this Question, Why do you believe the Doctrine of the Trinity?* (London: B. Aylmer, 1697); Edward Stillingfleet, *A Discourse in Vindication of the Doctrine of the Trinity: with An Answer to the Late Socinian Objections Against it from Scripture, Antiquity and Reason and a Preface concerning the different Explications of the Trinity, and the Tendency of the present Socinian Controversie* (London: Henry Mortlock, 1697).

40. Pollock, *Unitarianism*, 4. Pollock notes two Unitarian persons in the eighteenth century: Theophilus Lindsey and Joseph Priestley. Especially one might suppose a reasonable assumption that Gill wrote his *Dissertation concerning the Eternal Sonship of Christ* in his late days against Joseph Priestley (1733-1804) who "denied the miraculous birth of Jesus, and thought He [Jesus] was born in Nazareth with the same physical, mental and moral imperfections as other human beings . . . ." Priestley also, "regarded the doctrines of the Trinity and the Atonement as corruptions of primitive Christianity." Pollock, *Unitarianism*, 4.

The social and cultural ethos of the sixteenth century, both early and late, produced two major Unitarian theologians: Michael Servetus and Faustus Socinus, respectively. Particularly, Faustus's influence in leading the Polish Brethren to publish Unitarian documents ignited a Unitarian movement in England; ultimately, Socinianism in England could spread over the English churches with the works of John Biddle in the early seventeenth century. The intense trinitarian controversy that occurred in the late seventeenth century was the outcome of the historical accumulation of the Socinian movement.

With the historical circumstances of the sixteenth and seventeenth centuries in Europe, especially in England, regarding the doctrine of God the Trinity, Gill published *The Doctrine of the Trinity Stated and Vindicated* as one of his early works in 1731. Almost four decades later, Gill published the *Divinity* in 1767, which also includes the doctrine of the Trinity that becomes mature in vindicating the Trinity through maintaining the original framework of the contents. The rest of this chapter unfolds Gill's doctrine of the Trinity following his theological order.

THE DOCTRINE OF THE TRINITY ACCORDING TO JOHN GILL

In the first book of his *The Trinity*, Augustine begins with the words that advocate faith in which one could discuss who God is as the creator, not the words of reason: "My pen is on the watch against the sophistries of those who scorn the starting-point of faith, and allow themselves to be deceived through an unreasonable and misguided love of reason."[41] The object of theological study in Christianity comes first as the object of awe and faith because of the unique characteristics of the object: God, the creator, and the transcendent.[42] Following the same line of Augustine's method of studying

---

41. Saint Augustine, *The Trinity*, trans. Edmund Hill, O.P., ed. John E. Rotelle, O.S.A., The Works of Saint Augustine: A Translation for the 21st Century (Hyde Park, NY: New City Press, 1991), 1.1.1.

42. The vastness and fathomlessness of God's being transcendent creator is minutely explicated in the words of Gregory of Nazianzus in his oration on the doctrine of God. He clearly affirms what his oration points to: "the incomprehensibility of deity to the human mind and its totally unimaginable grandeur." While making sure that "no one has yet discovered or ever shall discover what God is in his nature and essence," Gregory 'the Theologian' depicts all the principles of how the nature in the world and universe move and exist in God's creation. The whole creation reflects the awe and wonder of the first light, i.e., God the creator. The Theologian explains, "so strongly do they bear the shape and imprint of God's beauty, that they become in their turn lights, able to give light to others by transmitting the stream that flows from the primal light

the Trinity, Gill begins his words on the Trinity with wonder, awe, humility, and faith:

> The Doctrine of a Trinity of persons in the unity of the divine essence is, without controversy, a great mystery of godliness. The ancient *Jews used* to call it the *sublime mystery*, and sometimes the *mystery of all mysteries*; which if a man did not endeavor to make him feel acquainted with, it would have been better for him if he had never been created: And sometimes they called it the *mystery of faith*; a phrase which the apostle uses in 1 Timothy 3:9. Where he makes it one part of the qualification of a deacon, to hold the mystery of the faith in a pure conscience.[43]

Though recognizing God's trinitarian being in the 'mystery of all mysteries' and acknowledging faith as the starting point of the work, Augustine exhorts his readers to seek and search for the incomprehensible while explaining the dynamic mechanism of seeking and understanding God.[44] Gill's 'mechanism of seeking and understanding' in searching for the Trinity depends on God's revelation in the Old and New Testaments.[45] Thus, based on this sole authority of the Scripture, Gill expands the doctrine of the Trinity in a threefold framework: (1) the unity of the divine essence and

---

of God." See St. Gregory of Nazianzus, *On God and Christ: The Five Theological Orations and Two Letters to Cledonius*, trans. Frederick Williams and Lionel Wickham, St Vladimir's Seminary Press Popular Patristics Series 23 (Crestwood, NY: St Vladimir's Seminary Press, 2002), 28/11,17,31.

43. Gill, *The Doctrine of the Trinity*, 4. Regarding the Trinity as mystery, Poythress notes, "The Father is God, not a part of God. The Father manifests in himself the whole of what God is. He has all of God's attributes, including simplicity. And so it is with the Son. The Son is God, fully God. The Holy Spirit is God. This is a mystery. We cannot comprehend it because God alone is God and we are not. Nothing in the created world offers a full model for the Trinity." Vern S. Poythress, *The Mystery of the Trinity: A Trinitarian Approach to the Attributes of God* (Phillipsburg, NJ: P&R, 2020), 81; also, see John Thompson, *Modern Trinitarian Perspectives* (New York: Oxford University Press, 1994), 22-23.

44. Augustine, *The Trinity*, 15.2.

45. Regarding the subtle relationship between the Trinity and the Bible (the Old and New Testaments), Scott Swain asserts, "we cannot fully appreciate how 'the Trinity is in the Bible' without observing how 'the Bible is in the Trinity.' While the Bible is the cognitive principle of the Trinity, the supreme source from which our knowledge of the Trinity is drawn, the Trinity is the ontological principle of the Bible. The Trinity is not simply one of the things about which the Bible speaks. The Trinity is the speaker from whom the Bible and all things proceed: 'For us there is one God, the Father, from whom are all things . . . and one Lord, Jesus Christ, through whom are all things' (1 Cor 8:6). All things in heaven and on earth, including holy Scripture, are 'produced by the creative breath of the Almighty' (See Ps 33:6; 2 Tim 3:16)." Scott R. Swain, *The Trinity and the Bible: On Theological Interpretation* (Bellingham, WA: Lexham, 2021), 9-10.

that there is but one God; (2) a plurality in the Godhead, which is delimited by three; (3) personal relations of the three divine persons in the Godhead.[46]

The Unity of God

For Gill, the unity of God or the one and only God is inextricably and essentially linked to all the "glorious perfections" that God embraces as his attributes.[47] Thus, Gill, taking quite a big portion of his first book of the *Divinity*, deals with each divine attribute of God, which reflects the perfection of God in the finest way before he jumps into the theological formulation of God himself as the Trinity.

Listing several scriptural passages to buttress the unity of God, Gill continues to elaborate on the perfections of God.[48] Gill begins with the origin or existence of God in discussing the concept of perfection, which will later lead to an idea that God is the "first Cause" from which every other being is possible to be.[49] While asserting that "the necessary existence of God is a proof of his unity," Gill continues,

46. Affirming the Bible as the primary discourse of trinitarian theology, Swain, as Gill's threefold framework of the Trinity, provides three patterns of the Trinity; that is, "The Bible's Trinitarian discourse consistently," (1) "affirms the existence of the one God," (2) "identifies the Father, the Son, and the Holy Spirit with the one God," (3) "distinguishes the Father, the Son, and the Holy Spirit by their mutual relations, which are 'relations of origin.'" Scott R. Swain, *The Trinity: An Introduction*, Short Studies in Systematic Theology (Wheaton: Crossway, 2020), 28-32.

47. Gill, *Divinity: Book I*, 133. Gill's term "glorious perfections" in plural denotes that each attribute of God, e.g., infinity, omnipotence, wisdom, love, righteousness, etc., cannot be divided into or be shared with others in its pure sense. It is because each attribute is perfect. In other words, each attribute carries the perfect notion by itself, and nothing can add to or subtract from the attribute of God. Thus, the God who possesses such attributes must be one. In a slightly different nuance, Frame also indicates, "God's oneness is related to all his lordship attributes. Only one being can be fully in control of all other beings, so that no one can deliver out of his hand. He is the God of all things in heaven, earth, and sea (Deut. 4:39; 2 Kings 19:15) because he created them all (Neh. 9:6; Mal. 2:10)." Frame, *Systematic Theology*, 424.

48. Deut 6:4; Ps 86:10; Isa 43:10, 44:6, 8, 45:5, 6, 14, 18, 21, 22, 46:9; Mark 12:29; John 17:3; Rom 3:30; 1 Cor 8:4-6; Eph 4:6; 1 Tim 2:5. Gill focuses on two aspects to explain the unity of God: (1) *ad intra*: the perfections of God; (2) *ad extra*: God's relation to his creatures. Regarding the latter, Gill states, "He is their creator, their king, their judge, and lawgiver . . . As God is one in his nature or essence, and cannot be multiplied or divided, so he is one in his relation to his creatures." Gill, *The Doctrine of the Trinity*, 8.

49. Gill, *Divinity: Book I*, 133. Craig Carter agrees with what Gill tried to convey, saying, "God cannot be self-caused or have a cause external to himself; otherwise, it would be impossible for him to have been the First Cause of all things. Any actualizer that is itself actualized by another is by definition not the *first* actualizer. For God to be

The existence of God must be either or necessity, or of will and choice; if of will and choice, then it must be either of the will and choice of another, or of his own; not of another, for then that other would be prior and superior to him, and so be God, and not he: not of his own will and choice, for then he must be before himself, and be and not be at the same instant; which is such an absurdity and contradiction as is not to be endured. It remains, therefore, that he necessarily exists; and if so, there can be but one God; for no reason can be given why there should be, or can be, more than one necessarily existent Being.[50]

This ontological perfection of God in the necessary existence is manifested by his unique attributes. First, eternity that "is peculiar to him; so as not to be ascribed to any other being" is a strong proof of his unity.[51] Gill affirms, "God is infinite and incomprehensible; as he is not bounded by time, so not by space; he is not contained or included anywhere, nor

---

the First Cause, he must be the unactualized actualizer. Few would deny that the Bible clearly teaches that God is the creator of all things; can the 'Creator' be anything other than the First Cause? It would seem not." Craig A. Carter, *Contemplating God with the Great Tradition: Recovering Trinitarian Classical Theism* (Grand Rapids: Baker, 2021), 58. This 'first Cause' might remind one of Aristotle's term unmoved mover. Definitely, when Aristotle's works were translated in Latin, he made a huge impact on the thought of the West Christians. However, Poythress notes "classical Christian theologians have uniformly rejected some aspects of Aristotle's conception." Regarding the differences between Aristotle's conception and the Christian God, Poythress makes some points: (1) "Aristotle has no mention of anything resembling the Trinity;" (2) "Aristotle appeals to *other* eternal things in order to infer the existence of the unmoved mover;" (3) "Aristotle fatally compromises the uniqueness of God," (4) "the unmoved mover is not an efficient cause that actually pushes other movers around;" finally, (5) "Aristotle describes the unmoved mover as 'Mind,' but it is a 'Mind' that thinks only of itself." For more explanations concerning the unmoved mover, see Poythress, *The Mystery of the Trinity*, 283-90. Italics original.

50. Gill, *Divinity: Book I*, 133. From God's being first Cause concomitant with the necessary existence of God, Gill brings the thoughts of Pythagoras and Plato into the relation of the independent and the dependent, stating, "unity is the principle of all things. God, the first Cause, who is without a cause, and is the Cause of all, is independent; all owe their existence to him, and so depend upon him for the preservation, continuance, and comfort of their being; all live, and move, and have their being in him; but he, receiving his being from none, is independent of any; which can only be said of one; there is but one independent Being, and therefore but one God." Gill, *Divinity: Book I*, 133-34. As the apostle Paul asserts, "For in him we live and move and have our being," in Acts 17:28, "the natural life which men live is from God; and they are supported in it by him; and from him they have all the comforts and blessings of life; and all motions, whether external or internal, of body or of mind, are of God . . . ; and their being, and the maintenance of it, and continuance in it, are all owing to the power and providence of God." Gill, *An Exposition of the New Testament*, 2:311.

51. Gill, *The Doctrine of the Trinity*, 6.

comprehended by any."[52] Secondly, God's omnipotence demonstrates the unity of God as well. Power is in control of everything; therefore, "the word, almighty, admits of no degrees; it cannot be said that there is one that is almighty, and another that is more almighty and another that is most almighty; no, there is but one almighty, and therefore but one God."[53] Finally, the perfection of God in his attributes converges into "El-Shaddai, God all-sufficient" whose perfection is revealed not only in his nature but also in works.[54] The one and only God in unity "stands in need of nothing, for of him, and by him, and for him, are all things," says Gill, "All-sufficiency can only be said of One, of Him who is the first Cause and last End of all things; and which, as he is but one, so but one God."[55]

---

52. Gill, *Divinity: Book I*, 134. Instancing Isaiah 43:10, "... No god was formed before me, and there will be none after me," Gill exposes fabrication of idols which "were formed by the hands of men, and yet none of these were formed before him, and therefore could make no pretensions to deity, or to an equality with him; nor should any be formed afterwards, that could be put in competition with him." Gill, *An Exposition of the Old Testament*, 5:248.

53. Gill, *The Doctrine of the Trinity*, 7.

54. Gill, *Divinity: Book I*, 134; Gill, *The Doctrine of the Trinity*, 7. Recognizing the relation of the unity of God to the work of the Trinity, Garrett observes, "The work of the Father, of the Son, and of the Spirit can be identified and even differentiated, but the work of each is not exclusive. The work of each is in a sense the work of the Godhead. God the Father may be called Creator, but the Son and the Spirit are not excluded from the work of creation. God the Son may be called Redeemer, but the Father and the Spirit are not excluded from the work of redemption. The Holy Spirit may be called Sanctifier, but the Father and the Son are not excluded from the work of sanctification." Garrett, *Systematic Theology*, 1:328.

55. Gill, *Divinity: Book I*, 134. Poythress approaches God's all-sufficiency from the aspect of God's glory which cannot be shared with another except for the eternal co-relationship between the Father, Son, and Holy Spirit (Isa 42:8; Heb 1:3): "God is sufficient in himself. He is absolute, not dependent on the world. He does not have an inner 'need' to create the world in order to enhance or develop himself. He has all glory in himself.... This all-sufficient glory is the archetype. Precisely *because* of its complete sufficiency, it is the archetype, and can be reflected in creation as an ectype. The glory of God in the created world reflects the original glory of God in the Son and in the Spirit." Vern S. Poythress, *Knowing and the Trinity: How Perspectives in Human Knowledge Imitate the Trinity* (Phillipsburg, NJ: P&R, 2018), 205-6. Italics original. God's glory does not rely on his creation because God is one and only God the creator who is all-sufficient in himself. God says, "I will not give my glory to another or my praise to idols." However, the prayer of the Son to the Father in John 17:4-5 shows that this unique concept of glory, never allowed to be shared with any other, proves the unity of God, "I have glorified you on the earth by completing the work you gave me to do. Now Father, glorify me in your presence with that glory I had with you before the world existed." For more theological meaning of the glory of God in general, see Christopher W. Morgan and Robert A. Peterson, eds., *The Glory of God*, Theology in Community (Wheaton: Crossway, 2010), 153-87.

With regard to the understanding of the unity of God, Gill avoids three heretical conceptions in Christian history: Arianism, Sabellianism, and Tritheism. Being aware of the theological setting of his contemporary flowed from and challenged by the previous unitarian thoughts, Gill first rejects Arianism, the root of Unitarianism, that senses "there is one supreme God and two subordinate or inferior ones."[56] Gill criticizes the Arian's implied denigration of the Son and the Spirit, which is clearly confronted by the Scripture, Jeremiah 10:11. Gill writes,

> if two subordinate and inferior deities may be admitted, consistent with one God, why not two hundred, or two thousand? no reason can be given why the one should not stand as much excluded as the other: and again, those deities are either creators or creatures; if creators, then they are the one supreme God; for to create is peculiar to him; but if creatures, for there is no medium between the Creator and the creature, then they are not gods that made the heavens and the earth; and so come under the imprecation of the prophet, "The gods that have not made the heavens and the earth, even they shall perish, or may they perish from the earth, and from under these heavens."[57]

Secondly, Gill rejects Sabellianism, which claims "God is but one person," not three persons in one Godhead.[58] Gill traces the roots of

---

56. Gill, *Divinity: Book I*, 134. What caused Arius a heretic though he emphasized one supreme God? "His [Arius] dominant idea was the monotheistic principle of the Monarchians, that there is only one unbegotten God, one unoriginated Being, without any beginning of existence. He distinguished between the Logos that is immanent in God, which is simply a divine energy, and the Son or Logos that finally became incarnate. The latter had a beginning: He was generated by the Father, which in the parlance of Arius was simply equivalent to saying that He was created." Louis Berkhof, *The History of Christian Doctrines* (1937; Edinburgh, UK: The Banner of Truth Trust, 1969), 84. In other words, according to Thiselton, "He [Arius] perhaps aimed at showing the uniqueness and transcendence of God as an 'Origin and Source.' Hence he made the genuine mistake of bracketing Christ *with creation* as 'having a beginning,' rather than *with God*." Thiselton, *Systematic Theology*, 38. Italics original. Also, see Garrett, *Systematic Theology*, 1:319; Harwood, *Christian Theology*, 410-12; Carter, *Contemplating God with the Great Tradition*, 210-18. Sanders's words on the Arian controversy hints to the way of the EFS, "It was clear to every interpreter that numerous passages of Scripture ranked the Son as subordinate to the Father; *the Arian argument maintained that the reason Scripture spoke this way reflected actual ontological subordination. The Son, on the Arian reading, was in his essence less than the Father, even if certain other passages identified him so closely with God that he had to be recognized as highly exalted above mere humanity.*" Sanders, *The Triune God*, 114. Italics added. The dispute on the EFS issue will be more deeply considered later in this chapter.

57. Gill, *Divinity: Book I*, 135.

58. Gill, *Divinity: Book I*, 135.

Sabellianism from Noetians and Patripassians through Victorinus, Praxeas, and Cataphrygians, and finally to the oldest version of Sabellianism, that is, Simon Magus who argued, "Father, Son, and Holy Ghost, were only different names of one and the same person, according to his different way of operation."[59]

Watching out for such Monarchianism not to be disseminated as in the previous generations, Gill gives a word of warning to the contemporary evangelicals in a rebuking sense,

> Our Socinians and modern Unitarians are much of the same sentiment with the Sabellians in this respect; and some who profess evangelical doctrines have embraced it, or are nibbling at it; fancying they have got new light, when they have only imbibed an old stale-error, an ancient work of darkness, which has been confuted over and over.[60]

Then, he cites John 10:30, "I and the Father are one," to which both Unitarians and Trinitarians appeal for their own arguments. Denouncing the Unitarian's reason that the Son and the Father are one person, Gill asserts, "His meaning is, that they were one in nature, essence, power, and glory."[61]

---

59. Gill, *Divinity: Book I*, 135. Noetus, Victorinus, Praxeas, and Cataphrygians (so called, Montanism known as advocating the New Prophecy), were the debate objects by Tertullian with special regard to the doctrine of the Trinity. Against Tertullian's trinitarian concept of God, these asserted, "Jesus Christ was both Son and Father." Gill, *Divinity: Book I*, 135. Willem Oliver writes in his article directly on the thoughts of Praxeas that Hippolytus "pointed to the doctrine of Praxeas (which the latter has adopted from the Christian philosopher, Noetus of Smyrna, . . .), in the words of Noetus: [W]hen indeed, then, the Father had not been born, He [yet] was justly styled Father; and when it pleased Him to undergo generation, having been forgotten, He Himself became His own Son, not another's." The Monarchians believed the Son and the Father as "not two beings, but only one,"; "it was therefore God who was born from a virgin and who confessed himself to humankind as the Son of God." Willem H. Oliver, "The Praxis of Adversus Praxeam: Tertullian's Views on the Trinity," *Verbum et Ecclesia* 42, no. 1 (2021): 2-3. For more about the relation of Montanism to Tertullian and its evaluation, see Jaroslav Pelikan, "Montanism and its Trinitarian Significance," *Church History* 25, no. 2 (1956): 99-109; Douglas L. Powell, "Tertullianists and Cataphrygians," *Vigiliae christianae* 29, no. 1 (1975): 33-54. For the study of the Tertullian's trinitarian theology itself, see Bryan M. Litfin, "Tertullian on the Trinity," *Perichoresis: The Theological Journal of Emanuel University* 17, no. 1 (2019): 81-98. Regarding the story of Simon Magus, read Acts 8:9-24.

60. Gill, *Divinity: Book I*, 135.

61. Gill, *The Doctrine of the Trinity*, 11. Interesting to see a slightly different nuance in interpreting this verse between a functional unity and the unity of nature or an ontological unity though both reject Unitarianism. G. R. Beasley-Murray points out, "The setting of v 30 in relation to vv 28-29 shows that a functional unity of the Son and the

Thirdly, Gill rejects tritheism, which claims of God that "there are three essences, or beings numerically distinct, which may be said to be one essence or being, because they are all three of one and the same nature."[62]

Father in their case for the sheep is in mind. From earliest times it has been observed that Jesus says, 'I and the Father are ἕν,' not 'εἷς,' i.e., one in action, not in person." Beasley-Murray, *John*, 174. D. A. Carson also states, "In short, although the words *I and the Father are* one do not affirm complete identity, in the context of this book they certainly suggest more than that Jesus' will was one with the will of his Father, at least in the weak sense that a human being may at times regulate his own will and deed by the will of God. If instead Jesus' will is exhaustively one with his Father's will, some kind of metaphysical unity is presupposed, even if not articulated." Carson, *The Gospel According to John*, 395. Italics original. Capturing both the movement of the Jewish leaders to take up stones to kill Jesus right after 10:30 and Jesus' perichorestic words, "the Father is in me, and I in the Father," in 10:38, Richard Bauckham stresses on "the uniquely intimate communion" between the Father and the Son, saying, "This strongly supports the view that the unity between the Father and the Son is not just their unity of will in Jesus's mission from the Father, the unity of words and works by which Jesus conveys what he has heard from the Father and does the works of the Father. . . . (the view) points to a relational intimacy of Jesus and the Father within the identity of the one God." Richard Bauckham, *Gospel of Glory: Major Themes in Johannine Theology* (Grand Rapids: Baker, 2015), 33-34. Gill clearly writes from the trinitarian perspective, "Not in person, for the father must be a distinct person from the son, and the son a distinct person from the father; and which is further manifest, from the use of the verb plural, *I and my father*, εσμεν, *we are one*; that is, in nature and essence, and perfections, particularly in power; since Christ is speaking of the impossibility of plucking any of the sheep, out of his own and his father's hands; giving this as a reason for it, their unity of nature, and equality of power; so that it must be as impracticable to pluck them out of his hands, as out of his father's, because he is equal with God the father, and the one God with him." Gill, *An Exposition of the New Testament*, 2:19. Italics original. Also, see Adonis Vidu, *The Same God who Works All Things: Inseparable Operations in Trinitarian Theology* (Grand Rapids: Eerdmans, 2021), 42-43; Mark DelCogliano, "The Interpretation of John 10:30 in the Third Century: Antimonarchian Polemics and the Rise of Grammatical Reading Techniques," *Journal of Theological Interpretation* 6, no. 1 (2012): 117-38.

62. Gill, *The Doctrine of the Trinity*, 11. Regarding historical developments of the tritheistic thought, D. Glenn Butner Jr. provides two key figures: one is John Philoponus in the sixth century in the East; the other is Roscelin of Compiegne in the tenth century in the West. Butner notes, "Both of these examples reveal the serious risk that the distinctions between the persons may become so pronounced that they overcome the unity of the divine being. Both East and West, however, have striven to avoid this risk by insisting on the simplicity of God." D. Glenn Butner Jr., *Trinitarian Dogmatics: Exploring the Grammar of the Christian Doctrine of God* (Grand Rapids: Baker, 2022), 123. Butner explains more on the unity and simplicity in the same section. Gavin Ortlund also agrees with the unity of God through the divine simplicity, criticizing the common contemporary notion of *perichoresis* to establish the monotheistic Trinity. Especially, mentioning Moltmann's advocating *perichoresis* for the unity and triunity of God; who says, "The unity of the triunity lies in the eternal perichoresis of the Trinitarian persons. Interpreted perichoretically, the Trinitarian persons form their own unity by themselves in the circulation of the divine life," Ortlund claims, "(But) perichoresis

was always used in conjunction with divine simplicity, which was the more recurrent and consistent basis for divine unity throughout church history. Today, by contrast, it has become common to seek to establish the Trinity as one through perichoresis *instead of* divine simplicity.... I want to suggest that divine simplicity ... may provide a more solid grounding for a monotheistic Trinity than perichoresis alone. The reason is that divine simplicity is able to bind the three persons not merely into *each other* but into the one divine essence." See respectively, Jürgen Moltmann, *The Trinity and the Kingdom: The Doctrine of God* (Minneapolis: Fortress Press, 1993), 175; Gavin Ortlund, *Theological Retrieval for Evangelicals: Why we Need our Past to have a Future* (Wheaton: Crossway, 2019), 137-38. For the detailed explication of Moltmann's trinitarian theology, see Veli-Matti Kärkkäinen, *The Trinity: Global Perspectives* (Louisville, KY: Westminster John Knox Press, 2007), 100-122. For the early usage of the *perichoresis* in Christology and the Trinity, see Verna Harrison, "Perichoresis in the Greek Fathers," *St Vladimir's Theological Quarterly* 35, no. 1 (1991): 53-65. Back to the risk of the tritheistic thought, Garrett, indicating potential risks to fall into the tritheism, writes, "Present-day usage of language such as 'cooperating within the Godhead,' 'conferring among persons of the Trinity,' and 'the councils of eternity' can easily lead to a tritheistic interpretation. Furthermore, some present-day usage of the historic term 'person' in reference to Father, Son, and Holy Spirit, when devoid of understanding about its patristic origin, tends to fall into the trap of tritheism." Garrett, *Systematic Theology*, 1:324. Among Garrett's risky terms, 'the councils of eternity' might be related to the basic concept of the *pactum* in the wrong understanding. Garett is correct to take precaution of the tritheism with regard to the *pactum*, i.e., three covenantal acts of the eternal council by three different wills, which assumes three independent beings with three essences. Regarding this issue, see note 64 in the chapter three. Does the *pactum* in eternity make a covenant within three wills of the independent three beings because the *pactum* is actually made by three different acts of the three persons, the Father, Son, and Holy Spirit? Gill rejects such an idea of the three wills that join the covenant because Gill fully recognizes that the one will of God comes with a pure act and also definitely with the divine simplicity. The three distinct acts of the three persons should not be presumed as 'three separated acts' by three different wills. God is a pure act. This act/will conception is closely connected to the doctrine of the Trinity itself: i.e., God is one nature and three persons, which is ultimately the very mystery to creation. If this writer attempts to explain that the *pactum* cannot fall into the tritheism, based on Gill's 'distinct acts of will,' the beginning point will be the relations of both *nature-will* and *person-act*. Acknowledging one will of God, Gill explains distinct acts of the one will in three persons. Does it make sense for the three divine persons to make a covenant in eternity? In terms of making a normal covenant, it does not make sense because a covenant is made in agreement between a will and another will. This way or understanding of making a covenant, however, stems from the men's practice in the ancient Near East including the people in the Old Testament. The point is that the Father is person, the Son is person, and the Holy Spirit is person according to the classical and traditional orthodox teaching of the Trinity. Moreover, each divine person possesses the full deity, that is, the perfect essence of God. Thus, one might come to a logical conclusion that the Father in the first person of the Godhead must have the will of God because the Father possesses the full essence or nature in the Godhead. And so does the Son and the Spirit. In that sense, one might say that the Father has his own will, the Son has his own will, and the Holy Spirit has his own will. However, these three 'wills' does not make 'three wills' in God and the three divine persons as if a human person and another human person have their own will respectively. God's nature-will and person-act structure or mechanism

The Doctrine of the Trinity According to John Gill 143

Thus, tritheism practically asserts that there are three Gods because the Father is God, the Son is God, and the Holy Spirit is God.

Explaining the three 'rejections' in Church history, Gill affirms the unity of God: "There is but one divine essence, undivided, and common to Father, Son, and Spirit, and in this sense but one God; since there is but one essence, though there are different modes of subsisting in it which are called persons; and these possess the whole essence undivided."[63] Due to the simplicity and incompositeness of God in three persons, no concept is allowed that the Father has a part, the Son another, and the Spirit has the third. A beautiful description regarding God's being against the partitive ontology, Gill writes:

> the whole divine nature or essence is in the Father; and that
> the whole divine nature or essence is in the Son; and that
> the whole divine nature or essence is in the Holy Ghost;
> and that it is simple and undivided, and common to all three.[64]

---

should not and cannot be appreciated in a human level because God's being and action are archetype, not ectype. God's covenant in eternity, i.e., the eternal covenant, the archetype of human covenants, is not an actual time-consuming covenant like human's one. It just happens in the three divine eternal persons' mind, in his one will; Gill says, "consultations on an affair have been sometimes held many days successively; but so it is not with God, counsel with him is as quick as thought, yea, it is no other than his thought, and therefore they go together." Gill, *Divinity: Book II*, 45.

63. Gill, *Divinity: Book I*, 135.

64. Gill, *The Doctrine of the Trinity*, 11. As biblical evidence of the unity of God in the Father, Son, Holy Spirit, Gill offers three examples in demonstrating the God of the Old Testament is the same God in the New Testament in relation to God's names and expressions which indicate the one God, e.g., Jehovah, Lord, the first and the last: (1) Deuteronomy 6:4 and Mark 12:28-29; (2) Isaiah 44:6 and Revelation 1:8; (3) Isaiah 45:23 and Romans 14:10-11. See Gill, *Divinity: Book I*, 136. For instance, it is interesting to observe the biblical image in Mark 12. Namely, Jesus' two citations from the Old Testament (Deut 6:4 and Ps 110:1) in the narrative of Mark 12:28-37 have subtly connected each other and depict that Jesus is Lord and God. "The Lord our God is one Lord," explains Gill of Deuteronomy 6:4, "the doctrine of which is, that the Lord, who was the covenant God and Father of his people Israel, is but one Jehovah; he is Jehovah, the Being of beings, a self-existent Being, eternal and immutable; and he is but one in nature and essence; this appears from the perfection of his nature, his eternity, omnipotence, omnipresence, infinity, goodness, self-sufficiency, and perfection. . . . And for this purpose these words are cited in Mark 12:29, 30. but then they no ways contradict the doctrine of a trinity of persons in the unity of the divine essence, the Father, Word, and Holy Spirit, which three are one." Gill, *An Exposition of the Old Testament*, 2:27-28. For the basic understanding of Shema, see Bill T. Arnold, *The Book of Deuteronomy: Chapters 1-11*, NICOT (Grand Rapids: Eerdmans, 2022), 380-89. Gill's description of divine attributes of God as Lord which were applied to God the Father is also applied to God the Son and the Spirit as Jesus cited Psalm 110:1, "This is the declaration of the Lord to my Lord." Gill explains the meaning of the phrase, "The Targum is, 'the Lord said in his Word.' Galatinus says the true Targum of Jonathan has it, 'the Lord said to his

Summary

To Gill, the ontological perfection must be one who is infinite, incomprehensible, and omnipotent. The unity of God proves itself by being necessary. The one God whose being is of necessity does not share his glory and unique attributes. This is the one and only God in unity. Thus, the traditional trinitarian heresies, namely Arianism, Sabellianism, and Tritheism, cannot fully emulate or fully embrace the biblical truth of one God in unity. Each person of the one Godhead is the whole divine essence, which mysteriously means that God is one.

Plurality in the Unity of the Godhead

Knowing that it is not enough only to deal with the unity of God, i.e., there is but one God, in order to fully draw the doctrine of God the Trinity, Gill enters squarely into the plurality in the Godhead that will ultimately reach the three persons.[65] This section of the plurality of persons in the one God consists of two proof points. First, Gill notes that God's names signify there is more than one person in the Godhead. Secondly, Gill offers his unique method to prove both God's plurality of persons and the fact that the plurality is "neither more nor fewer than three."[66] In other words, Gill, thoroughly based on the Scripture, investigates that God's plurality of persons and the three persons in the one God are revealed in the special economy, especially in creation, providence, and grace. Gill finds the plurality of God not only in God's works of creation and "spiritual communion with God" in grace

---

Word;' and produces an authority for it. These are the words of Jehovah the Father to his Son the Messiah. . . . The words said to him by Jehovah, as follow, were said in his mind, in his eternal purpose and decree; to which he, lying in his bosom, was privy, when he fore-ordained him to be the Redeemer; and in the council and covenant of grace, when he promised him this glory as the reward of his sufferings." Gill, *An Exposition to the Old Testament*, 4:181. In sum, the names and expressions in Scripture applied to the Father are to be in the same meaning applied to the Son and the Spirit; in other words, in Gill's word, "there is but one Jehovah; but not that this is peculiar to the Father, and as exclusive of the Son and Spirit." Gill, *Divinity: Book I*, 136.

65. Regarding the theological meaning of the trinitarian term 'person' and 'personhood,' see Rudi A. Te Velde, "The Divine Person(s): Trinity, Person, and Analogous Naming," in *The Oxford Handbook of the Trinity*, ed. Gilles Emery, O.P. and Matthew Levering (Oxford: Oxford University Press, 2011), 359-68; Butner, *Trinitarian Dogmatics*, 101-31; John D. Zizioulas, *Being as Communion: Studies in Personhood and the Church* (Crestwood, NY: St. Vladimir's Seminary Press, 1985), 27-66.

66. Gill, *Divinity: Book I*, 141.

but also in "some particular affairs of providence."⁶⁷ It is the very exclusive way of proving the plurality and three persons in the one God that the sovereign and transcendent Lord and covenant God manifests himself through the economic relations with men throughout the whole Scripture. By taking and unfolding this method, Gill not only has a way of vindicating the plurality of the one God but also attains the doctrine of the Trinity that is Scripture-based and not made by the early church fathers in metaphysical speculation.

Plurality in the Godhead

First, Gill's concern to prove the plurality in the one God goes with the comparison of God's names between Jehovah and Elohim. Jehovah, according to Gill, is the "great and incommunicable name" and "always in the singular number, and is never used plurally; the reason of which is because it is expressive of his essence, which is but one; it is the same with 'I AM that I AM.'"⁶⁸ Though the name Jehovah in Scripture fundamentally and essentially delineates who God is, including the noted articulation of God himself in Exodus 3:14, Gill instead focuses on the plural expression of God, Elohim, as Moses recorded in the very first verse of the whole Scripture, which "may seem strange."⁶⁹ It is because "one end of the writing of Moses is to extirpate the polytheism of the heathens, and to prevent the people of Israel from going into it."⁷⁰ From this 'strange' expression in Genesis 1:1,

---

67. Gill, *Divinity: Book I*, 140.

68. Gill, *Divinity, Book I*, 138. For the basic background and information of Jehovah, see Elmer A. Martens, "God, Names of," in *Evangelical Dictionary of Biblical Theology*, 297-300; Walter A. Elwell, ed., "Jehovah," in *Baker Encyclopedia of the Bible*, 2 vols. (Grand Rapids: Baker Book House, 1988), 2:1106. Also, regarding the general background of the divine name in Exodus 3:14, see R. W. L. Moberly, *The God of the Old Testament: Encountering the Divine in Christian Scripture* (Grand Rapids: Baker, 2020), 51-91. With respect to Gill's understanding of the expression of Jehovah as 'his essence,' Eichrodt in the same context writes, "In Deutero-Isaiah, . . . the name Yahweh is associated with *the concept of eternity* and is emphatically designated as the name of the God who is the First and the Last, before whom no being was formed and after whom nothing will exist." Eichrodt stressing also the "constant immutability of his nature" in the name of Jehovah discloses God's one and unique nature that indicates the only God. See Eichrodt, *Theology of the Old Testament*, 1:191-92.

69. Gill, *Divinity: Book I*, 138.

70. Gill, *Divinity: Book I*, 138. Practically, polytheism in the ancient Near East was prevalent and "awash with gods – it was polytheistic through and through – and inhabitants of the ANE would have been surprised to hear that the gods might not exist." Craig Bartholomew, as an example, continues to write how such gods were shown even in a humanlike image, saying, "The gods were finite; only a few had power outside a

however, Gill finds what Moses intends to convey concerning the mystery of the being of God: "this plural word Elohim, is, in this passage, in construction with a verb singular, 'bara,' rendered 'created'; which some have thought is designed to point out a plurality of persons, in the unity of the divine essence."[71]

Secondly, Gill pays attention to God's plural expressions, particularly in relation to men, regarding redemptive history, specifically, creation, providence, and grace. With regard to creation, Genesis 1:26 reads, "Then God said, 'Let us make man in our image, according to our likeness. . . .'" In the act of God as the creator of man, Gill fixes his eyes on the four meaningful terms: "us," "our," "image," and "likeness."[72] Seeing each two terms making a pair, Gill writes, "the pronouns 'us' and 'our,' manifestly express

---

town, a nome, a region. Generally, the gods' efficacy decreased as distance increased, so that travellers prayed to local gods. The gods could be male or female and in some cases androgynous." Craig G. Bartholomew, *The Old Testament and God: Old Testament Origins and the Question of God* (Grand Rapids: Baker, 2022), 204, 226. Regarding the Egyptian religion, Safwat Marzouk indirectly implies the polytheism in ancient Egypt, saying, "Ancient Egyptians had an unshaken belief in the presence of the divine in all aspects of the cycle of life, which led them to consider all of life's activities to be numinous. Thus ancient Egyptian religion created multiple layers for human-divine interaction. . . . In addition, ancient Egyptians used 'local chapels' in order to offer their prayers to the gods." Safwat Marzouk, "The Egyptians," in *The Baker Illustrated Bible Background Commentary*, ed. J. Scott Duvall and J. Daniel Hays (Grand Rapids: Baker, 2020), 44.

71. Gill, *Divinity: Book I*, 138. Also, see Gill, *An Exposition of the Old Testament*, 1:3. Robert Jamieson adds a similar point to Gill, "The choice of Elohim, therefore, in preference to all other names for the Divine Being, must have been dictated by some special reason of great utility and importance. . . . therefore we are led to conclude that by its use here in the plural form is obscurely taught, at the opening of the Bible, a doctrine clearly revealed in the later portions of it–viz., that though God is one, there is a plurality of persons in the Godhead, who were engaged in the creative work." Robert Jamieson, A. R. Fausset, and David Brown, *A Commentary, Critical, Experimental, and Practical on the Old and New Testaments: Genesis-Deuteronomy*, 3 vols. (London; Glasgow: William Collins, Sons, & Company, 1874), 1:1. Yarnell also writes, "perhaps, the plurality of אלהים; who nevertheless acts in a singular way in the biblical context, provides a linguistic hint toward a vital multiplicity within the unity of God." Yarnell, *God the Trinity*, 67. Another reason why this plural-singular (Elohim-bara) combination is peculiar for a special purpose, comes with other passages, which "the word Elohim is sometimes in construction with a verb plural"; e.g., Gen 20:13; Gen 35:7; 2 Sam 7:23.

72. Gill, *Divinity: Book I*, 139. Goldingay notes, "Strikingly, the act is not initially described as 'creation' but simply as 'making.' But the novelty of this act of making is further underlined by God's saying not 'I am going to make' but 'We are going to make.'" Goldingay, *Genesis*, 35.

a plurality of persons; these being personal plural characters; as image and likeness being the singular number, secure the unity of the divine essence."[73]

73. Gill, *Divinity: Book I*, 139. Gill provides other scriptural passages that use the plural words of God as creator: Job 35:10; Ps 149:2; Eccl 12:1; and Isa 54:5, which includes in the original text, "Where is God, my Makers," "Let Israel rejoice בְּיֹ in his Makers," "Remember בֹּרְאֶיךָ thy Creators in the days of thy youth," and "For בְּעָלַיִךְ thy husbands are thy Makers; the Lord of Hosts is his name." Gill, *The Doctrine of the Trinity*, 20. Pointing to the same theological meaning but accessing from a different focus in looking at Genesis 1:26, Anthony Hoekema notes that "the main *verb* is in the plural." While rejecting the plural expression applied to angels, Hoekema asserts, "Rather, we should interpret the plural as indicating that God does not exist as a solitary being, but as a being in fellowship with 'others.' Though we cannot say that we have here clear teaching about the Trinity, we do learn that God exists as a 'plurality.' What is here merely hinted at is further developed in the New Testament into the doctrine of the Trinity." Anthony A. Hoekema, *Created in God's Image* (Grand Rapids: Eerdmans, 1994), 12. Also, see Derek Kidner, *Genesis: An Introduction and Commentary*, Tyndale Old Testament Commentaries (Downers Grove: IVP, 1967), 56. Other OT scholars approach this plural usage in various meanings. Gordon Wenham provides several options regarding this plural: (1) heavenly court, the angles; (2) a reference to Christ; (3) reflecting the polytheistic account; (4) a plural of majesty; (5) a plural of self-deliberation, self-encouragement; (6) the plurality in the Godhead. See Gordon J. Wenham, *Genesis 1-15*, WBC, vol. 1 (Waco, TX: Word Books, 1987), 27-28; Also, see Claus Westermann, *Genesis 1-11: A Commentary*, trans. John J. Scullion S.J. (Minneapolis: Augsburg Publishing House, 1984), 144-45. U. Cassuto argues for the "plural of exhortation" or encouragement in Genesis 1:26, rejecting the idea that "God took the counsel with the ministering angels." The reasons are logical: (1) "God *alone* created the entire world;" (2) "the expression *Let us make* is not one of consultation." Umberto Cassuto, *A Commentary on the Book of Genesis*, trans. Israel Abrahams (Jerusalem: Magnes Press; Hebrew University, 1961), 55. Victor Hamilton, seeing the Trinity in this plural is "going too far to call Israel's here a trinitarian monotheist," explains, "The question remains whether that was the author's intention and understanding. The theological battle of Moses' day was not trinitarianism versus unitarianism. The battle centered around the belief in one God who is himself uncreated, merciful, and sovereign versus the belief in multiple gods and demons who are capricious, unpredictable, and often immoral." Victor P. Hamilton, *The Book of Genesis: Chapters 1-17*, NICOT (Grand Rapids: Eerdmans, 1990), 132-33. Acknowledging the intra-trinitarian dialogue of the plural expression, Kenneth Mathews states, "However, this position can only be entertained as a possible 'canonical' reading of the text since the first audience could not have understood it in the sense of the trinitarian reference." Finally, by appealing the New Testament Mathews writes, "Our passage describes the result of God's creative act by both plural and singular pronouns: the plural possessive 'our image' in v. 26 and the singular pronoun 'his image' in v. 27. Here the unity and plurality of God are in view." Kenneth A. Mathews, *Genesis 1-11:26*, NAC, vol. 1A (Nashville: B&H, 1996), 162-63. Gill also refutes the interpretation of angels in the plurality, "as for the angels, they are creatures themselves, and not possessed of creative powers; nor were they concerned in the creation of man, nor was he made after their image and likeness; nor can it be reasonably thought, that God spoke to them, and held a consultation with them about it; for 'with whom took he counsel?' (Isa. 40:14). Not with any of his creatures; no, not with the highest angel in heaven; they are not of his privy council." Gill, *Divinity: Book I*, 139. Gill's final comment regarding the creator is worth of citing in full length: "That the

After dealing with God's self-involvement with creation as a plurality of divine persons, Gill demonstrates another biblical usage of the plural persons in God's "speaking of himself, with respect to some particular affairs of providence."[74] In other words, with regard to God's providence of a sort of reproof, Isaiah 6:8 reads, "Then I heard the voice of the Lord asking: Who should I send? Who will go for us?..."[75] The mystery of one Jehovah in more persons than one suggested by the plural pronoun 'us' is revealed, according to Gill, by John 12:40-41 and Acts 28:25-26, which describes the situation of the prophet Isaiah in Isaiah 6:[76]

Word and Spirit were concerned with God in the creation of man, is a truth, and is the true reason of this plural expression; but then, there are not to be considered as mere characters, under which God acted; for mere names and characters cannot be consulted with; nor can creative powers be ascribed to them; nor have they any image and likeness after which man could be made. The words are a manifest proof of a plurality of divine persons, who were equal to one another, and to the work of man's creation, in which they were jointly concerned." Gill, *The doctrine of the Trinity*, 22.

74. Gill, *Divinity: Book I*, 140.

75. Gill's first *particular affair of providence* showing the plural number of God happens in Genesis 11:7, "Come, let's go down there and confuse their language so that they will not understand one another's speech." The situation of this verse depicts a kind of judgment of God in plural expression from the perspective of the grand providence of God. Later, confounding the language of men in the New Testament is used as a great blessing and opportunity for the whole world to listen to the gospel of Christ, which belongs to the particular affair of God's providence (Acts 2:8-11). In addition, most of scholars agree that the plural sense in Genesis 11:7 is in the same context with Genesis 1:26. Thus, for the meaning of the plurality in Genesis 11:7, see note 73 above. Isaiah 6:8 presents the negative word that when God is to send someone, it is "to the people of Israel, to reprove them for their blindness and stupidity, and to threaten them, and foretell unto them their ruin and destruction." At the same time, it also conveys a positive and hopeful sense when God is "not directing his discourse to the seraphim . . . ; as if he consulted with them: for who of all the creatures is the Lord's counsellor? but to the Son and Spirit, who 'tis certain were concerned in this mission." Gill, *An Exposition of the Old Testament*, 5:37. In the end, God's self-plural expressions imply the reproof, judgment, and hope to salvation in his special relation with men through the redemptive history.

76. What is the identity of 'us'? "The plural is no doubt used here with reference to the seraphim," says Delitzsch, "who formed, together with the Lord, one deliberative council." Franz Delitzsch, *Biblical Commentary on the Prophesies of Isaiah*, trans. James Martin (Grand Rapids: Eerdmans, 1967), 198. Different from Delitzsch, however, Edward Young asserts, "In carrying out his sovereign purposes God consults only with himself. He has no need of counseling with His creatures, even with angelic creatures. . . . Let us not fear to acknowledge that here is an adumbration of the doctrine of the Trinity which in the New Testament receives its fuller revelation." Edward J. Young, *The Book of Isaiah: The English Text, with Introduction, Exposition, and Notes*, 3 vols. (Grand Rapids: Eerdmans, 1965), 254; also, see Larry L. Walker, "Isaiah," in *Cornerstone Biblical Commentary*, vol. 8 (Wheaton: Tyndale House Publishers, 2005), 36. J. Alec Motyer is exactly in the same line with Gill's approach with the interpretation of the plural, saying,

He has blinded their eyes and hardened their hearts, so that they would not see with their eyes or understand with their hearts, and turn, and I would heal them. Isaiah said these things because *he saw his glory* and spoke about him (John 12:40-41). Disagreeing among themselves, they began to leave after Paul made one statement: "*The Holy Spirit was right in saying to your ancestors through the prophet Isaiah when he said*, Go to these people and say: You will always be listening, but never understanding; and you will always be looking, but never perceiving (Acts 28:25-26).[77]

Through the interconnected setting of Isaiah 6:8-10, John 12:40-41, and Acts 28:25-26, Gill corroborates the fact that the divine plural persons are revealed in the particular affair of providence in God's speaking of himself. Moreover, it is not just a plural pronoun; it indicates three divine persons. The Father speaks in asking; the Son is with the Father in his glory, and the Holy Spirit is saying to the ancestors of the Israelites.[78]

With regard to grace, especially to "spiritual communion with God," Gill cites John 14:23, "Jesus answered, 'If anyone loves me, he will keep my word. My Father will love him, and we will come to him and make our home with him.'" The threefold economy revealed in the plurality of God's self-expression, i.e., creation, providence, and grace, demonstrates God's care and concern for his people. As this plurality is getting more specified by the Father, Son, and Holy Spirit in the NT than in the OT, Gill attempts to prove that God the Trinity is associated with his people's birth, life, and

---

"a plural of consultation (1 Kgs 22:19-23), but the New Testament relates these verses to both the Lord Jesus (John 12:41) and the Holy Spirit (Acts 28:25), thus finding here what will yet accommodation the full revelation of the Holy Trinity." Motyer, *Isaiah*, 83.

77. In both citations of John and Acts, the italics are added for emphases.

78. Regarding the meaning of 'he saw his glory,' Gill affirms that Isaiah saw Jesus' glory: "Agreeably to which our Lord says here, that he saw his glory, the glory of his majesty, the glory of his divine nature, the train of his divine perfections, filling the temple of the human nature; and he spoke of him as the true Jehovah, the Lord of hosts; and which therefore is a very clear and strong proof of the proper divinity of Christ." Gill, *An Exposition of the New Testament*, 2:43. While mentioning, "It means that in his vision Isaiah saw (the pre-incarnate) Jesus," Carson agrees, "What is remarkable, on this rendering of the passage, is the statement that *Isaiah* saw Jesus' glory. This may be no more than the conclusion of a chain of Christian reasoning: if the Son, the Word, was with God in the beginning, and was God, and if he was God's agent of creation, and the perfect revelation of God to humankind, then it stands to reason that in those Old Testament passages where God is said to reveal himself rather spectacularly to someone, it must have been through the agency of his Son, his Word, however imperfectly the point was spelled out at the time. Therefore Isaiah said these words *because* (a stronger reading than 'when', AV) he saw Jesus' glory." Carson, *The Gospel according to John*, 449-50. Italics original.

final destiny. Jesus clearly avers, "We [Jesus and the Father] will come to him and make our home with him." Gill explains that these personal actions of "coming and making abode," are "expressive of communion and fellowship, are said of more than one; and we cannot be at a loss about two of them, Christ and his Father, who are expressly mentioned; and hence we read of fellowship with the Father, and his Son Jesus Christ; and also of the communion of the Holy Ghost"[79] The contour of the plurality in the Godhead is manifested by three as Gill has "before taken for granted." In the next section, Gill lastly proves that this plurality of God is exactly three, i.e., God is the unity in the three divine persons.

Three Persons in the Godhead

The truth that God is one essence and three persons comes into view, according to Gill, throughout the whole Scripture.[80] Not only through a

79. Gill, *Divinity: Book I*, 140. Where and what is the point of grace as God's particular relation to men in this verse? What about the Holy Spirit? Is the Spirit related to the spiritual communion as indicated here by the relation of the Father and the Son? Then how? Making two points of John 14:23, Gill elucidates: first, the Father's love should "be understood not of the love of the father, as in his own heart, which is not taken up in time, but was in him from all eternity; nor of the first discovery of it to his people, but great manifestations of it to them . . . ; such as larger measures of grace, more communion with him here, and eternal honour and glory hereafter"; secondly, the Father and the Son will come spiritually and will make habitation; "for the saints are the dwelling-places or temples of the living God, Father, Son, and Spirit; and the constancy and perpetuity of their residence in them . . . ; and is a wonderful instance of the grace and condescension of God to dwell on earth with sinful men." Gill, *An Exposition of the New Testament*, 2:61. It is genuine grace of God to see the three divine persons in the heart of a believer. John 14:20 reads, "On that day you will know that I am in my Father, you are in me, and I am in you." The mutual indwelling of the Father and the Son lies in the heart of a believer; also, the Spirit of God lives in the believer, the temple of God (1 Cor 3:16). Therefore, the Father, the Son, and the Holy Spirit all three divine persons are in the heart of the believer. This is the point of grace poured upon a believer with all three persons. Gerald Borchert writes, "the idea of the 'indwelling' of the Godhead in the postresurrection period naturally raises again the question of the relationship of this idea to the Paraclete theme in the whole section. Indeed, Augustine much earlier argued that 'the God of the Trinity' was here in the mind of John so that the Father, Son, and Holy Spirit 'come to us as we come to them.'" Gerald L. Borchert, *John 12-21*, NAC, vol. 25B (Nashville: B&H, 2002), 131.

80. Gill in his early work on the Trinity defines both essence and person in his words: "An essence is, that by which a person or thing is what it is," and "A person is an individual, that subsists, lives, understands, etc. but such is the Father, therefore a person; such is the Son, therefore a person; such is the Holy Ghost, and therefore a person." Then, Gill opens his method to prove the Trinity by the testimonies of Scripture because "being a doctrine of pure revelation, it cannot be expected that it should be demonstrated by arguments taken from the reason of things" or "by natural similes."

simple and plain scriptural passage but also through the essential Christian doctrines revealed by the redemptive history, e.g., creation, providence, grace, and God's acts of grace through the office and work of Christ.[81]

As the most obvious and simple evidence of the three divine persons in the Godhead, Gill chooses 1 John 5:7, "For there are three that bear record in heaven, the Father, the Word, and the Holy Ghost; and these three are one."[82] Already knowing the criticism of the text's authenticity by "the enemies" who "have pushed hard to extirpate it from a place in the sacred writings," Gill replies in defending the authority of the text regarding the points of the criticism, e.g., wanting in the Syriac version, not being found in Greek manuscripts, no citations by the ancient fathers.[83] Gill asserts

---

Interestingly, Gill neither brings nor mentions 1 John 5:7, which later in *Divinity* he takes as the direct evidence of the Trinity, to prove the Trinity as the scriptural evidence in his early writing. See Gill, *The Doctrine of the Trinity*, 32-34.

81. Gill, *Divinity: Book I*, 142-43.

82. Gill, *Divinity: Book I*, 142. Contemporarily, this textual translation is only found in KJV and NKJV among major and popular Bible versions.

83. Gill, *Divinity: Book I*, 142. Arguing that this text is an interpolated gloss, so-called the Johannine Comma, Westcott briefly summarizes the external evidence of the words as being not found "(1) In any independent Greek MS (more than 180 MSS and 50 lectionaries are quoted). Both the late MSS which contain it have unquestionably been modified by the Latin Vulgate. (2) In any independent Greek writer. The very few Greek writers who make use of the words derived their knowledge of them from the Latin. (3) In any Latin Father earlier than Victor Vitensis or Vigilius Tapsensis. (4) In any ancient version except the Latin; and it was not found (a) in the old Latin in its early form, or (b) in the Vulgate as issued by Jerome or (c) as revised by Alcuin." Brooke Foss Westcott, *The Epistles of St John: The Greek Text with Notes and Essays* (Grand Rapids: Eerdmans, 1957), 202. As internal probabilities, Bruce Metzger makes two points: (1) "As regards transcriptional probability, if the passage were original, no good reason can be found to account for its omission, either accidently or intentionally, by copyists of hundreds of Greek manuscripts, and by translators of ancient versions. (2) As regards intrinsic probability, the passage makes an awkward break in the sense." Bruce M. Metzger, *A Textual Commentary on the Greek New Testament*, Second Edition (Stuttgart: Deutsche Bibelgesellschaft, 2000), 648-49. Scholars agree that the words are spurious: see Robert W. Yarbrough, *1-3 John*, BECNT (Grand Rapids: Baker, 2008), 293; Stephen S. Smalley, *1, 2, 3 John*, WBC, vol. 51 (Waco, TX: Word Books, 1984), 273; Karen H. Jobes, *1, 2, and 3 John*, Exegetical Commentary on the New Testament (Grand Rapids: Zondervan, 2014), 222-23; Constantine R. Campbell, *1, 2 and 3 John*, The Story of God Bible Commentary (Grand Rapids: Zondervan, 2017), 156n10; Arthur W. Wainwright, *The Trinity in the New Testament* (1962; Eugene, OR: Wipf and Stock, 2001), 245. Akin writes a concluding remark, "Is the Johannine Comma Scripture? The evidence seems to say no. Is the Johannine Comma truthful? Is it sound theology? Yes. It is not necessary, however, to place the Johannine Comma in the text of Scripture. The Trinity can be adduced from many other texts of Scripture.... We are warned in the Bible neither to take away nor add to its words. On this basis it is best to leave out the disputed words." Daniel L. Akin, *1, 2, 3 John*, NAC, vol. 38 (Nashville: B&H, 2001), 199-200.

that this text was quoted by many ancient fathers, e.g., Jerome, Athanasius, Cyprian, Tertullian, and Clements of Alexandria; moreover, even "the Socinians themselves have not dared to leave it out in their German Racovian version, A. C. 1630."[84]

Gill goes further and takes evidence from the essential Christian doctrines through the redemptive history to prove the divine three persons. As in the previous section, Gill sees the Trinity in the works of creation, providence, and grace. First, the Father, Son, and Holy Spirit participate in the critical incidents of economy in Scripture from the creation of the entire universe through men's birth, nurture, punishment, and to the end in the providence of the one Godhead.[85] In other words, in Gill's expression, "the three divine persons appear in that remarkable affair of providence, the deliverance of Israel out of Egypt, and the protection and guidance of them through the wilderness to the land of Canaan."[86]

---

84. Gill, *Divinity: Book I*, 143. Regarding the church fathers who quoted 1 John 5:7 by the trinitarian translation, Gill does not provide any proof-resources except for naming them. Based on Deuteronomy 4:2 and following Akin's comment on the dispute of Johannine Comma mentioned in the note 83 above, this section is not going to deal with 1 John 5:7 any longer to prove the divine three persons.

85. For instance, Psalm 33:6 is the abstract verse to show the three persons' work together in creation, which reads, "The heavens were made by the word of the Lord, and all the stars, by the breath of his mouth." Gill notes, "Where by the Lord, is meant God the Father; and by his word, the Logos, or Word that was with him from everlasting; and by the breath or spirit of his mouth, the Holy Ghost. Now here are three who were manifestly concerned in the production of all creatures, into being; nor can any one of them be dropped, nor can a fourth be added to them. It remains then, that there is a Trinity in the Godhead." Gill, *The Doctrine of the Trinity*, 35. Samuel Pierce adds, "Here we have the whole creation ascribed to Jehovah, Father, Word, and Spirit. These words are a comment on the three first verses of the first chapter in Genesis. There we read, ... Here is *God*, the *Spirit of God*, and *God said*, the Three in the one Incomprehensible Essence, declared by Moses to be the creators of the heavens and the earth." Samuel Eyles Pierce, *An Exposition of the Book of Psalms: Set Forth as Prophetic of Christ & His Church*, Newport Commentary Series, vol. 1 (Springfield, MO: Particular Baptist Press, 2009), 305. Susan Gillingham points out that the church fathers acknowledged Ps 33:6 as indicating the Trinity. Origen as one of the first person who remarks Ps 33:6 as a trinitarian work comments, "And David also points us to the mystery of the Trinity when he says, 'By the word of the Lord all the heavens were made strong; and all their power by the Spirit of his mouth.' So by reading the Hebrew word for 'breath' as 'spirit,' Origen sees the twin agencies in creation as the Word/Logos and the Spirit." Gillingham continues to name Theodoret, Hilary of Poitiers, Jerome, and Gregory of Nyssa. See Susan Gillingham, *Psalms through the Centuries: A Reception History Commentary on Psalms 1-72*, vol. 2 (Chichester: Wiley Blackwell, 2018), 202; also, see Craig A. Blaising and Carmen S. Hardin, eds., *Psalm 1-50*, Ancient Christian Commentary on Scripture, vol. 7 (Downers Grove: IVP, 2008), 249-51.

86. Gill, *Divinity: Book I*, 144.

Secondly, God's redemptive works appearing by means of his grace attest to the three divine persons. The grace of God initiating from eternity in three persons of the one Godhead guarantees the whole process of economic salvation of men as already sealed in eternity by the covenant of grace among the Father, Son, and Holy Spirit. Gill affirms,

> This covenant was made by Jehovah the Father, and was made with his Son, who condescended and agreed to be the surety, mediator, and messenger of it; yea he is said to be the covenant itself; and in which the Holy Spirit is promised, and whose part in it is, and to which he agreed, to be the applier of the blessings and promises of it to those interested therein; ... and they are all three mentioned together as concerned in this covenant.[87]

This covenantal agreement for men's salvation among the three persons in eternity moves toward its realization and application in time. Gill observes that the economic shape of the eternal covenant among the three persons for men's salvation is actualized by threefold action: namely, "the election of men to salvation is usually ascribed to the Father; redemption, or the impetration of salvation, to the Son; and sanctification, or the application of salvation, to the Spirit."[88] Then, Gill finds one scriptural passage to which the *pactum* and economic redemption perfectly fit in the works of the three divine persons: 1 Peter 1:2, which reads, "(chosen) according to the foreknowledge of God the Father, through the sanctifying work of the Spirit, to be obedient and to be sprinkled with the blood of Jesus Christ ... "[89] Finally, Gill, conveying that the special relation of the three divine persons

---

87. Gill, *Divinity: Book I*, 144.

88. Gill, *Divinity: Book I*, 144.

89. Gill, *Divinity: Book I*, 144. Also, see Gill, *An Exposition of the New Testament*, 3:529-530. Scholars acknowledge the divine three persons in one Godhead. "In this verse we have God the Father, the Spirit and Jesus Christ mentioned alongside one another; we have here the beginning of Trinitarian doctrine." Earnest Best, *1 Peter: Based on the Revised Standard Version*, New Century Bible Commentary (1971; Grand Rapids: Eerdmans, 1982), 72; Jobes writes, "This triadic structure describes the relationship of the Christians to whom Peter writes to each member of the Godhead, particularly in reference to their conversion. ... Although it would be anachronistic to call this a reference to the Trinity, surely such verses as this one later issued in the orthodox doctrine of the Trinity at the First Council of Nicaea (AD 325), which was located in Bithynia, one of the regions to which Peter writes." Karen H. Jobes, *1 Peter*, BECNT (Grand Rapids: Baker, 2005), 68; also, Thomas Schreiner notes, "The Father foreknows, the Spirit sanctifies, and the Son cleanses. The idea is close to the traditional theological formulation of the Father as Creator, the Son as Redeemer, and the Spirit as Sanctifier. ... Peter, of course, did not articulate in a full-fledged way the doctrine of the Trinity, but from verses such as this the doctrine was hammered out." Thomas R. Schreiner, *1, 2 Peter, Jude*, NAC, vol. 37 (Nashville: B&H, 2003), 57.

to men in salvific economy confirms God's perfection in and for himself, avouches for the plurality in the one Godhead, which should only be three,

> That a plurality of Persons in the Godhead, seems necessary from the nature of God himself, and his most complete happiness; for as he is the best, the greatest and most perfect of Beings, his happiness in himself must be the most perfect and complete; now happiness lies not in solitude, but in society; hence the three personal distinctions in Deity, seem necessary to perfect happiness, which lies in that most glorious, inconceivable, and inexpressible communion the three Persons have with one another; and which arises from the, incomprehensible in being and unspeakable nearness they have to each other.[90]

Summary

Recognizing that it is not enough to argue for the doctrine of the Trinity with the one God concept only, Gill explicates the plurality and three persons of the one God to reveal the biblical completion of the doctrine of God. God is one and three. The plurality of God is manifested not only by God's names internally but also by God's special economic relation with his people externally, i.e., creation, providence, and grace. The eternal covenant of grace for men's salvation in God's economy demonstrates who is engaged in redemptive work. The Father, Son, and Holy Spirit getting involved with his creation by his providential grace are always in perfection in terms of lovely fellowship, happiness, and satisfaction. It is because the three divine persons making the perfect and harmonious eternal society coexist within themselves.

Personal Relations of the Three Divine Persons in the Godhead

This section, following Gill's doctrine of the Trinity, has so far demonstrated the unity and plurality of the one Godhead. In addition, it has also proved that the plurality is none other than three. Thus, God is one and three. In other words, God is three distinct persons in the one Godhead. At this point, while repulsing Sabellianism's one person in three names by Father, Son, and Spirit like one man who has three names, Gill asks a final question regarding the doctrine of the Trinity: "So that the Father is not the Son,

---

90. Gill, *Divinity: Book I*, 147. Regarding the office and work of Christ in relation to the three divine persons, see the section of *Incarnation* in the chapter three above.

nor the Son the Father, nor the Holy Spirit either the Father or the Son; but the difficulty is, what that is which gives or makes the distinction between them?"[91]

By two points, does Gill's approach answer the question: (1) the distinction of the three divine persons "must be as early as the existence of God itself" and (2) the distinction of the three divine persons comes from "the personal relations, or distinctive relative properties, which belong to each Person."[92]

First, according to Gill, the origin of the three divine persons, if it is possible to describe the existence or origin of God in human words, is "from everlasting to everlasting."[93] In other words, God is eternal, which entails immutability, one of the most crucial attributes of God. Thus, God is "the Lord who changes not, who is subject to no variation whatever."[94] To put it concretely, if God is eternal and immutable, so are the three divine persons, which affirms the mode of existence of God in eternity as the three divine persons in the one Godhead demonstrates that God is always one God in three persons; then, no human terms like origin or development leave room to be applied. Gill explains, "If the one God existed from eternity; and if the three Persons are the one God, they must exist from eternity, and exist as distinct Persons; and consequently, what gives them their distinction must exist as early."[95] Therefore, the distinction of the three divine persons has

---

91. Gill, *Divinity: Book I*, 147. As the argument proceeds, Gill's antagonist proves to be the Socinians. This will be the point of discussion later with regard to the Son's eternal generation and further to the EFS. Matthew Emerson describes the question as "how to differentiate these three hypostases without falling into subordinationism on the one hand or modalism on the other." Matthew Y. Emerson, "The Role of Proverbs 8: Eternal Generation and Hermeneutics Ancient and Modern," in *Retrieving Eternal Generation*, ed. Fred Sanders and Scott R. Swain (Grand Rapids: Zondervan, 2017), 46.

92. Gill, *Divinity: Book I*, 147-48.

93. Gill, *Divinity: Book I*, 147.

94. Gill, *The Doctrine of the Trinity*, 51.

95. Gill, *Divinity: Book I*, 147. Zizioulas in the same vein presents his famous thesis, "The being of God could be known only through personal relationships and personal love. Being means life, and life means *communion*." Zizioulas, *Being as Communion*, 16. Italics original. In other words, "there is no true being without communion; nothing exists as an 'individual' in itself. Therefore, to be a 'person' in contrast to an 'individual,' there needs to be communion, relation, and opening to the Other ... " Kärkkäinen, *The Trinity*, 90. Zizioulas means that the being of God in eternity necessarily exists in communion. Ontologically, therefore, one God in three persons perfects as what it is supposed to be called God. Millard Erickson depicts the necessity of the distinct three persons in the one Godhead in love, one of God's another perfect attributes. Looking at the ontological statement "God is love" in 1 John, Erickson notes, "God being love virtually requires that he be more than one person. Love, to be love, must have both a subject and an object. Thus, if there were not multiplicity in the person of the

nothing to do with the works done by the Father, Son, and Holy Spirit in relation to creation. God's economy in creation, redemption, and consummation makes no effect on distinguishing the three divine persons in the one Godhead: "These do not make God to be, but to appear to be what he is."[96]

Secondly, the first point above regarding the distinction of the three divine persons leads under no coercion to the eternal act of God among the three persons. Again, "it is the personal relations, or distinctive relative properties, which belong to each Person, which distinguish them one from another; as paternity in the first Person, filiation in the second, and spiration in the third."[97] Gill draws a biblical and eidetic image of begetting (Ps 2:7), begotten (John 1:14), and breathed (Job 33:4; Ps 33:6) to the personal

---

Godhead, God could not really be love prior to this creation of other subjects." Regarding the three persons, he says, "With three persons, there must be a greater quality of selflessness, of genuine *agape*. Thus the Trinity founded upon love is a demonstration of the full nature of *agape*." Millard J. Erickson, *God in Three Persons: A Contemporary Interpretation of the Trinity* (Grand Rapids: Baker, 1995), 221-22.

96. Gill, *Divinity: Book I*, 148. While considering "the missions as the foundation of our knowledge of the distinction of the persons," Sanders approaches it slightly different from Gill in terms of economic works of God, "What preserves our distinguishing of the persons by reflection on the missions from being merely economic is the confession that missions reveal processions. Economic sendings . . . make known eternal processions. And immanent processions . . . are extended or elongated into economic missions." Sanders argues it based on that "the origin point of a divine mission is not different from the origin point . . . of an eternal divine procession. That is, the eternal Son is eternally from the Father as his origin point, and the incarnate Son is identically from that paternal origin point–unless he is two different Sons. But the Son does have two distinct termination points, one in the divine nature and one in the human nature." Sanders, *The Triune God*, 124-25. Sanders's mission-based distinction of the divine persons appears that it does not fully reflect the demarcation between eternity and time. As Sanders mentioned, the Son assumes the humanity in being sent to the world, which is the works of the Son and the Father. This act of sending and being sent belong to the function or role of the divine persons for human redemption in economy, not demonstrating the personal distinction in eternity. Gill asserts, "it must be something in the divine nature, and not anything out of it, that distinguishes them; not any works 'ad extra', done by them; nor their concern in the economy of man's salvation . . . " Gill, *Divinity: Book I*, 148.

97. Gill, *Divinity: Book I*, 148. Swain, stressing God's single divine name among the three persons, points out that "the distinction between the persons is indicated by their '*personal names*': 'Father,' 'Son,' and 'Holy Spirit.'" And these names signify *relations*. The Father is Father to the Son ('paternity' is thus his unique personal property); the Son is Son to the Father ('filiation is thus his unique personal property); the Spirit is the Spirit of the Father and the Son ('spiration' is thus his unique personal property). These personal properties are not interchangeable." Scott R. Swain, "The Radiance of the Father's Glory: Eternal Generation, the Divine Names, and Biblical Interpretation," in *Retrieving Eternal Generation*, 36. Italics original.

relations.[98] Gill puts his emphasis on the connecting link of the three concepts: generation–relation–distinct personality:

> If one of these distinct Persons is a Father, in the divine nature, and another a Son in the divine nature, there must be something in the divine nature which is the ground of the relation, and distinguishes the one from the other; and can be nothing else than generation, and which distinguishes the third Persons from them both, as neither begetting nor begotten. *From generation arises the relation, and from relation distinct personality.* And as an ancient writer says, "unbegotten, begotten, and proceeding" are not names of essence, . . . but are modes of subsistence; and so distinguish persons.[99]

In the end, the internal and eternal act of generation exists with the concept of relation, which also comes with the distinct personality. This notion is closely related to the biblical understanding of eternity as a grand presupposition in Gill's covenantal theological system, explained in chapter two above. God's being in the three distinct persons pertains to God's own unique and mysterious realm; thus, no creation is allowed to define the existence of God.[100]

---

98. For Gill's explanation of the begetting in Ps 2:7 and begotten in John 1:14, see Gill, *An Exposition of the Old Testament*, 3:531; Gill, *An Exposition of the New Testament*, 1:745. Also, see Jonathan E. Swan, "John Gill (1697-1771) and the Eternally Begotten Word of God," *Perichoresis* 20, no. 1 (2022): 53-69; Swan, "The Divine Word in the Theology of John Gill (1697-1771)," *SBJT* 25, no. 1 (2021): 131-53. Regarding the proceeding of the Spirit, Gill, giving John 15:26 as biblical evidence, interestingly writes, "I take no notice of the procession of the Spirit from Father and Son, . . . , yet rather seems to be understood of his coming forth from them, not with respect to his Person, but his office, in a way of mission by them, to be the Convincer and Comforter of men . . . " Gill, *Divinity: Book I*, 165. In this regard, Yarnell notes, "Proceeding from the Father eternally, the Holy Spirit is also sent into the world to lead the disciple into the truth. This is only one biblical text, but it is nevertheless a strong one. The Cappadocian fathers helped make it widely accepted, and the language of procession with regard to the eternal relation of the Father and the Holy Spirit has entered into the theological vocabulary of Christianity through the Niceno-Constantinopolitan Creed they influenced." Yarnell, *God the Trinity*, 153. Also, see R. Lucas Stamps, "The Trinity," in *Historical Theology for the Church*, ed. Jason G. Duesing and Nathan A. Finn (Nashville: B&H, 2021), 47-58.

99. Gill, *Divinity: Book I*, 149. Italics added. In addition to the connecting link Gill makes, see Duby, *Jesus and the God of Classical Theism*, 76-87, esp. 80-81.

100. "Time being nothing else but the measure of a creature's duration; as soon as a creature was, time was; time begins with that, let it be when it will . . . time must be reckoned from the existence of that creature; . . . for if there was anything created before time, or before the world was, whether an angel or a man, or a part of man, the human soul, or the whole human nature of Christ, our Bible must begin with a falsehood." Gill,

Gill's main point with respect to the 'begetting,' the Father's relative property, characterizes the fact that the economic works in creation "does not give him the name of Father in the Trinity."[101] The Father is the Father, specifically not because he is the Father of all creatures, though it is true, but because he is the Father begetting the Son and proceeding the Spirit in the one Godhead.[102] This is the unique distinction of the Father to be the Father among the divine persons, according to Gill, and "it being never attributed to any other."[103] Another point that Gill makes regarding the second person of the Trinity, who is the 'begotten' in eternity and the Son of God, is deeply linked to a critical dispute that is so called the eternal functional subordination of the Son (and the Spirit) to the Father (EFS) or eternal relational authority-submission (ERAS). Due to the importance of the issue and the length of time it takes to deal with the arguments, the eternal generation with regard to EFS will take a separate section.

Eternal Generation and Eternal Relational Authority

The Niceno-Constantinopolitan and the Athanasian Creeds state,

> And in one Lord Jesus Christ, the only Son of God; who was begotten from the Father before all the ages, light from light, true God from true God, begotten not made, one essence with the Father; through whom all things came into existence.
> ... thus also not three uncreated nor three infinites, but one uncreated and one infinite. Likewise, omnipotent Father, omnipotent Son, omnipotent Holy Spirit–and nevertheless not three omnipotents, but one omnipotent.[104]

Divinity: Book I, 161-62.

101. Gill, *Divinity: Book I*, 149.

102. Gill clearly states that the three persons "are the one Father of us, even the second and third Persons, as well as the first." Gill, *Divinity: Book I*, 149. See Isaiah 9:6, "For a child will be born for us, a son will be given to us, and the government will be on his shoulders. He will be named Wonderful Counselor, Might God, Eternal Father, Prince of Peace." Gill asserts, "Christ is a Father with respect to chosen men, who were given him as his children and offspring in covenant; who are adopted into that family that is named of him, and who are regenerated by his spirit and grace: and to these he is an *everlasting Father*." Gill, *An Exposition of the Old Testament*, 5:56.

103. Gill, *Divinity: Book I*, 150.

104. The translation for both Niceno-Constantinopolitan and Athanasian Creeds comes from Yarnell, *God the Trinity*, 241-42. For the relation of the Nicene Creed and EFS, see Thomas Brand, "Nature, Person and will: An Argument from the Church Fathers and the Ecumenical Councils against the Eternal Subordination of the Son," *Foundations* 73 (Fall 2017): 51-54.

The Doctrine of the Trinity According to John Gill

Since the early church, the ceaseless attempt to denigrate the deity of Christ (and the Holy Spirit), as the major Creeds demonstrate against the challenge, has been pertaining to the issue of subordinationism. From Ante-Nicene fathers like Irenaeus, Arius, and Origen through Arminians, George Bull, and Samuel Clarke in the seventeenth century to contemporary theologians like John V. Dahms, Stephen Kovach, and Peter Schemm, subordinationism has emphasized "the absolute uniqueness and transcendence of God the Creator, who was identified with God the Father."[105]

Bruce Ware, one of the most recent and critical contemporary proponents of ERAS, answers Gill's question of what makes the distinction between the Father, Son, and Holy Spirit:

> What distinguishes the Father from Son and Spirit is not the divine nature of the Father. This–the one and undivided divine nature–is also possessed equally and fully by the Son and Spirit. Therefore, what distinguishes the Father is his particular *role* as Father in relation to the Son and Spirit and the *relationships* that he has with each of them.[106]

---

105. Kevin Giles, *The Trinity and Subordinationism: The Doctrine of God and the Contemporary Gender Debate* (Downers Grove: IVP, 2002), 64. For the historical details of subordinationism, see Giles, *The Trinity and Subordinationism*, 60-85. Giles in contrast points out that, according to subordinationism, because the Son and the Spirit is begotten by and proceeding from the Father, they are created in time, which implies, "creation or begetting presupposes subordination in being and function." Giles, *The Trinity and Subordinationism*, 65. For the ERAS, see John V. Dahms, "The Subordination of the Son," *JETS* 37, no. 3 (September 1994): 351-64; Stephen D. Kovach and Peter R. Schemm Jr., "A Defense of the Doctrine of the Eternal Subordination of the Son," *JETS* 42, no. 3 (September 1999): 461-76.

106. Bruce A. Ware, *Father, Son, and Holy Spirit: Relationships, Roles, and Relevance* (Wheaton: Crossway, 2005), 43. Italics original. Regarding the two words, relationships and role, Ware names them as ontological relation and functional relation respectively. First, "each is distinct most fundamentally in *ontological relation* due to the eternal relations of origin or modes of subsistence that identify each of the trinitarian persons uniquely"; in other words, unbegotten, begotten, and proceeding. Secondly, "the trinitarian persons are also distinct in functional relation within the Godhead such that each expresses outwardly, as it were, who he is ontologically and hypostatically as defined by and flowing from their respect eternal relations of origin." This means the Father is the eternal Father, the Son is the eternal Son, and the Spirit is the eternal Spirit. See Bruce A. Ware, "Unity and Distinction of the Trinitarian Persons," in *Trinitarian Theology: Theological Models and Doctrinal Application*, ed. Keith S. Whitfield (Nashville: B&H, 2019), 20-21. Interestingly, Ware thinks that the term and concept of the eternal generation for both the Son and the Spirit, i.e., begotten and procession, appear speculative: "The conceptions of both the 'eternal begetting of the Son' and 'eternal procession of the Spirit' seem to me highly speculative and not grounded in biblical teaching. Both the Son as only-begotten and the Spirit as proceeding from the Father (and the Son) refer, in my judgment, to the historical realities of the incarnation and

Because the particular role of each person in the Godhead, according to Ware, makes the distinctions between the three divine persons even in eternity, the Father, who functions as the planner, schemer, sender, and the head of the Son, should be eternally "supreme over all, and in particular, he is supreme within the Godhead as the highest in authority and the one deserving of ultimate praise."[107] According to the same manner, therefore, the Son who functions as being sent and the executor in relation to the Father should always be given the status of submitting himself to the Father's authority.[108] In addition, since the distinction by role and function is eternal, i.e., the Father is the eternal Father, so do the Son and the Holy Spirit, the relation of the authority-submission given by names should be the same in time as well as in eternity, says Ware,

> Eternal paternal authority and eternal filial submission give expression, therefore, to a portion of the meaning contained within the divine personal names of Father and Son, which in turn flow from their eternal hypostatic identities as eternal Father and eternal Son, which in turn flow from their respective eternal relations of origin.[109]

Pentecost, respectively." Ware, *Father, Son, and Holy Spirit*, 162n3. Wayne Grudem gives a similar answer to the same question of Gill on what makes the distinction between the divine persons. Taking the functions of the three persons in relating to the world as the first cause of the distinction, in other words, focusing on the economic Trinity, Grudem asserts, "while the persons of the Trinity are equal in all their attributes, they nonetheless differ in their relationships to the creation. The Son and Holy Spirit are completely equal in deity to God the Father, but they are subordinate in their roles. Moreover, these differences in role are not temporary but will last forever." Then, Grudem brings as a biblical evidence 1 Corinthian 15:28. Grudem, *Systematic Theology*, 293.

107. Ware, *Father, Son, and Holy Spirit*, 51.

108. Regarding the functional subordination between the three divine persons in eternity, Thomas McCall raises a question, "What *is* this functional subordination in all these possible worlds? What *are* these functions? What *could* they be? A possible world containing no sin needs neither Judge nor Savior. A possible world with no creation needs no Governor. In fact, it is hard to even conceive of 'functional subordination' in a possible world in which only God exists – in which there is only the triune communion of holy love. It is also hard to imagine what the motivation might be for holding to such a view." Thomas H. McCall, *Which Trinity? Whose Monotheism?: Philosophical and Systematic Theologians on the Metaphysics of Trinitarian Theology* (Grand Rapids: Eerdmans, 2010), 178. Italics original. Regarding the distinction of persons, Matthew Barrett pinpoints, "EFSers were adamant that these indications of supremacy and subordination tell us who the persons are apart from creation and salvation. They are even person-defining. Just as subordination distinguishes the Son *as Son*, so too does supremacy distinguish the Father *as Father* within the Trinity. Apart from these roles there is no Trinity." Matthew Barrett, *Simply Trinity: The Unmanipulated Father, Son, and Spirit* (Grand Rapids: Baker, 2021), 217.

109. Ware, "Unity and Distinction of the Trinitarian Persons," in *Trinitarian*

This point is emphasized by Ware's threefold submission of the Son to the Father in the most appropriate way: (1) "The Son's submission to the Father during his incarnation and earthly mission;" (2) "The Son's submission to the Father in eternity past;" (3) "The Son's submission to the Father in eternity future."[110]

No theologian sets forth a counterargument on the first point. The issue comes from the second and third points. Regarding the Son's submission to the Father in eternity past, Ware appeals to 1 Corinthians 11:3,

> That God is the head of Christ is not presented here as an ad hoc relationship for Christ's mission during the incarnation. It is rather stated as an absolute fact regarding this relationship. God is the head of Christ. The Father has authority over the Son. There is a relationship of authority and submission in the very Godhead on which the other authority-submission relationships of Christ and man, and man and woman, depend. The *taxis* of God's headship over his Son accounts for the presence of *taxis* in man's relationship with Christ and the woman's relationship with man.[111]

Theology, 23.

110. Ware, *Father, Son, and Holy Spirit*, 73, 76, 83.

111. Ware, *Father, Son, and Holy Spirit*, 77. Italics original. Concerning the interpretation of κεφαλὴ in 1 Corinthians 11:3, Mark Taylor provides a helpful summary of three views: (1) the traditional view indicating "a hierarchy that entails authoritative leadership, that is, the man (husband) as the head of the woman (wife) occupies a position of superior relational authority that corresponds to the principle of subordination within the Godhead"; (2) the meaning of the head as "source" or "origin" in which "the 'head' is the one through whom others exist"; (3) "the terms means something along the lines of 'that which is most prominent, foremost, uppermost, preeminent.'" Mark Taylor, *1 Corinthians*, NAC, vol. 28 (Nashville: B&H, 2014), 258-59; also, see Paul Gardner, *1 Corinthians*, ECNT, vol. 7 (Grand Rapids: Zondervan, 2018), 480-85. For the meaning of *source* in κεφαλὴ, see Stephen Bedale, "The Meaning of κεφαλὴ in the Pauline Epistles," *JTS* 5, no. 2 (1954): 211-215. Millard Erickson properly indicates that Ware puts the core of his trinitarian theology in authority-submission and *taxis*, that is, ordering within the Trinity. See Millard J. Erickson, *Who's Tampering with the Trinity?: An Assessment of the Subordination Debate* (Grand Rapids: Kregel, 2009), 36-42. Yarnell writes, "there is 'a proper ordering within the eternal Trinity.' The Cappadocian fathers detected a τάξις (*taxis*) between the Father, the Son, and the Holy Spirit, and I concur with their exegetical conclusion. However, like the same Nicene fathers, I also indicated that this ordering 'does not entail any loss of equality.'" Yarnell, "From God to Humanity," in *Trinitarian Theology*, 82; also, see Yarnell, *God the Trinity*, 229-30. Emerson and Stamps add, "To be clear, there is an order (Greek, *taxis*) to trinitarian action, which is reflective of the order of the eternal relations of origin. The works of God are carried out from the Father through the Son by the Spirit . . . But order here does not imply *sub*-order, so to speak. Nor does it imply merely harmonious but ultimately independent action. The ordered work of the Triune remains undivided. As God is one,

Also, by drawing 1 Corinthians 15:24-28, Ware attempts to justify the third point, the Son's submission to the Father in eternity future,

> In full acknowledgment of the Father's supremacy, the Son displays his submission to the Father by delivering up the kingdom that he gains to the Father, and then, remarkably, by subjecting himself also to his Father. Though all of creation is subject to him, he himself is subject to his Father. There is no question that this passage indicates the eternal future submission of the Son to the Father, in keeping with his submission to the Father both in the incarnation and in eternity past.[112]

When inferring from the above discussion regarding the EFS or ERAS, it appears excessive to put the eternal subordination of the Son to the Father into the category in line with Arius, who advocated subordinationism in the fourth century. Ware explains what the ERAS holds by its essential

---

so are his works." Matthew Y. Emerson and Luke Stamps, "On Trinitarian Theological Method," in *Trinitarian Theology*, 126; also, see Madison N. Pierce, "Trinity without Taxis?: A Reconsideration of 1 Corinthians 11," in *Trinity without Hierarchy: Reclaiming Nicene Orthodoxy in Evangelical Theology*, ed. Michael F. Bird and Scott Harrower (Grand Rapids: Kregel, 2019), 39-55.

112. Ware, *Father, Son, and Holy Spirit*, 83-84. Especially, because 1 Corinthians 15:24-28 is one of the core biblical passages on which the EFS proponents heavily rely, Glenn Butner, who has argued against the eternal submission of the Son throughout his book, spends an entire chapter of his book refuting the interpretation of 1 Corinthians 15:24-28 for EFS argument. In contrast with James Hamilton's essay on 1 Corinthians 15 which "lines up with the chronology of Revelation 19-20" without looking carefully at the intention of Paul and the context of 1 Corinthians 15, Butner, emphasizing on the Adam/Christ typology in 1 Corinthians 15 with Paul's citations of Psalm 110:1 and 8:6, notes that "Paul's purpose here is to connect the significance of Jesus's bodily resurrection to the expected viceregency of the second Adam." Then, he asserts, "What Paul has in mind in verse 28 has nothing to do with the eternal relation between Father and Son, and everything to do with Christ's human status as second Adam, a status that Paul reveals will one day be supplanted by the even greater grace of God's direct rule." D. Glenn Butner Jr., *The Son Who Learned Obedience: A Theological Case Against the Eternal Submission of the Son* (Eugene, OR: Pickwick, 2018), 168-71; James M. Hamilton Jr., "'That God May Be All in All': The Trinity in 1 Corinthians 15," in *One God in Three Persons: Unity of Essence, Distinction of Persons, Implications for Life*, ed. Bruce A. Ware and John Starke (Wheaton: Crossway, 2015), 95-108; also, see Barrett, *Simply Trinity*, 242-46; Taylor writes, "The relational language of Father (15:24) and Son (15:28) underscores Christ the Son's redemptive work in accomplishing the will of God the Father (cf. John 5:19-30). The submission language is functional and does not imply that the Son is inferior to the Father in essence of being." Taylor, *1 Corinthians*, 389-90. For the *homoousios* argument regarding the authority-submission, see Erickson, *Who's Tampering with the Trinity?*, 172; McCall, *Which Trinity?*, 179-82; Bruce A. Ware, "Does Affirming an Eternal Authority-Submission Relationship in the Trinity Entail a Denial of Homoousios?: A Response to Millard Erickson and Tom McCall," in *One God in Three Persons*, 237-48.

conception, which indicates and has no problem with the classical trinitarian theology, "God reveals himself in Scripture as one God in three persons, such that the Father, Son and Holy Spirit are fully equal in their deity as each possesses fully and eternally the one and undivided divine nature." A couple of issues, however, occur when Ware goes further with defining ERAS,

> yet the Father is revealed as having the highest authority among the Trinitarian persons, such that the Son, as agent of the Father, eternally implements the will of the Father and is under the Father's authority, and the Holy Spirit likewise serves to advance the Father's purposes fulfilled through the Son, under the authority of the Father and also of the Son.[113]

With regard to the issues that can occur, the rest of this section is going to address and attempt to refute Ware's ERAS argument using Gill's theological perspectives on the second person of the Trinity in special terms of eternal generation.

First, the Son's eternal generation, i.e., begotten, that makes the distinction between the Father and the Son, is established by and presupposes "the Son of God as equal to his Father, as one who thought it not robbery to be equal with God; being of the same nature, and having the same *perfections* with him." Moreover, the most crucial point, according to Gill, is that "he [the Son] is equal to him with respect to *power* and *authority*."[114] In 1 Corinthians 12:3, Paul says, "No one can say, 'Jesus is Lord,' except by the Holy Spirit." If confessed with the help of the Spirit, Jesus is Lord; it must be a true statement. In addition, if Jesus is Lord, then his lordship in perfection is revealed by his power and authority, to which no being can compare. The concept of submission of Christ as Lord and God to a certain being in eternity is unthinkable. Gill also mentions 1 Corinthians 15:24, 28, which "is perverted by some to the sense of subordination and subjection of the Son of God to the Father."[115] Christ's Sonship by generation may imply that he is subordinate to the Father; however, not as the Son of God: "Whatever inequality sonship may imply among men, it implies no such thing in the

---

113. Ware, "Does Affirming an Eternal Authority-Submission Relationship in the Trinity Entail a Denial of Homoousios?," in *One God in Three Persons*, 237-38.

114. Gill, *Divinity: Book I*, 154. Italics added.

115. Gill, *Divinity: Book I*, 154. As aforementioned, Gill also focuses on the context of the passage and remarks, "This is to be learnt from the context, where he is spoken of throughout as man, as man who died, and rose again from the dead; from whence, by various arguments, is proved the general resurrection. . . . and then God, Father, Son, and Spirit will be all in all; and there will be no more distinction of offices among them; only the natural and essential distinctions of the divine Persons will always continue." Gill, *Divinity: Book I*, 155.

divine nature, among the divine natures; who in it subsist in perfect equality with one another."[116] Even though one argues that the three divine persons are equal and share the one essence and nature in the one Godhead, his or her sincerity and legitimacy concerning the doctrine of the Trinity cannot avoid being doubted or suspicious if there is no proper explanation given regarding the Son's perfection and having the same power and authority with the other two divine persons. It is because God is a pure act in his divine simplicity.

Secondly, does the eternal begotten Son by generation take place later than the Father who begets the Son? Is the begotten Son dependent on or subordinate to the Father because he is begotten later? Ware's usage of eternity as eternity past and eternity future appears to give a twofold dimension of eternity by infusing a temporal concept into the second level of eternity so that the begotten Son who comes later is supposed to be included by the second level, and then subject or subordinate to the Father who is in the primary level. These seemingly artificial terms are not allowed by Gill, who cannot imagine the temporal order in eternity, i.e., before and after: "It seems to be contrary to his eternity, independence, and equality."[117] If so, there might come with a potential risk of Arian sense regarding the concept of the begotten, says Gill, "If the Father begat the Son, he that is begotten must have a beginning of his existence; and from hence it must be evident that there was a time when he was not a Son; and therefore it must necessarily follow, that he has his subsistence out of nothing."[118] Instead, Gill asserts that there is no temporal concept of before and after: "Now father and son are correlates, they suppose each other; a father supposes a son and a son supposes a father; they commence and exist together, they co-exist, they are not one before nor after another."[119]

Thirdly, the distinction between Creator and creation, as well as between the immanent Trinity and the economic Trinity, must be maintained in relation to the divine names and the personal relations of the Father, Son, and Holy Spirit. Wayne Grudem states,

---

116. Gill, *Divinity: Book I*, 154.

117. Gill, *Divinity: Book I*, 153. In relation to Ware's concept of eternity, Yarnell states, "he presents God in such a way that God has both a past and a future within or alongside his eternity. God is said to experience 'eternity past' and 'eternity future,' which are then related to another level of eternity, that which is 'absolute eternal.'" Yarnell, "Response to Bruce A. Ware, Matthew Y. Emerson, and Luke Stamps," in *Trinitarian Theology*, 146. For Gill's understanding of eternity, see the chapter one of this volume above.

118. Gill, *Divinity: Book I*, 153.

119. Gill, *Divinity: Book I*, 153.

> The eternal names Father and Son indicate differences in the relationship. In the biblical world, the father in a family had a leadership role, an authority, that a son did not have even as an adult, and the authors and original readers of Scripture would have naturally associated such a relationship with the names Father and Son.... The doctrine of the eternal generation of the Son indicates that the Son is eternally "from" the Father, which indicates that the Father has always had some kind of priority in the relationship. More specifically, the Son's submission to the Father's authority is appropriate to and flows from the eternal generation of the Son by the Father.[120]

It is not a sound theological method to attempt to explain the ontological relation of the Trinity by bringing creation's wrongly formulated concept of the names Father and Son. The human notion of authority-submission and generation cannot and should not be applied to a totally different realm. Yarnell notes, "We must proceed from theology toward anthropology, and we must move with great caution in the reverse direction."[121] Gill notes the possibility that those terms of generation, like begetting and begotten, could be used to refer to human generation. Gill also, however, recognizes and gives a caveat when one seeks to apply those theological terms to human usage:

> Care must be taken to remove from our minds everything carnal and impure; and what implies an imperfection; as division of nature, multiplication of essence, priority and posteriority, motion, mutation, alteration, corruption, diminution, cessation from operation, to reason from the one to the other, as running parallel to each other, is unreasonable; to argue from human to divine generation; from that which is physical or natural, to what which is hyperphysical or supernatural; from what is in finite nature, to that which is in a nature infinite, ... , is very irrational ... is very unsafe and dangerous.[122]

Ultimately, "because the Ontological Trinity exists in eternity, and the Economic Trinity describes activities in time," says McGregor Wright, "it will be obvious that to impose temporal relations on the eternal being of God will violate the Creator-creature distinction.... The economy manifests the

---

120. Grudem, *Systematic Theology*, 302.
121. Yarnell, "From God to Humanity: A Trinitarian Method for Theological Anthropology," in *Trinitarian Theology*, 91.
122. Gill, *Divinity: Book I*, 152-53.

plan in eternity, but its subordination cannot be imposed on the Persons in the eternal ontology."[123]

The divine three persons, Father, Son, and Holy Spirit, make distinctions through the eternal processions. The Father is unbegotten, the Son is begotten, and the Holy Spirit proceeds. The ontological distinction of God only happens in himself, i.e., the eternal realm. No creature or artificially created concept or formulation of humans is allowed to intervene in the pure personal relations of the essential Triune God. Thus, the EFS or ERAS is a theological error. Finally, after devoting his whole book to opposing the idea of the eternal submission of the Son, Glenn Butner gives his appraisal with which this writer agrees:

> Lacking explicit endorsement in the Bible, EFS becomes a second-order inference from Scripture, but I have demonstrated in previous chapters that EFS fails to be an adequate second-order account of Scripture, for it neither provides conceptual clarity, fits scriptural patterns well, nor offers precision of theological language.[124]

Summary

God is one and three persons. Then, what makes the distinction between the Father, Son, and Holy Spirit? With this deep connection with the origin of the three divine persons, Gill matches the distinction between the divine persons and God's existence itself. The divine persons are distinguished not by their association with creatures in economic works but by the inner relations of begetting, begotten, and proceeding whose shape and mechanism can never be comprehensible by human minds. Thus, the way of approaching the origin of personal relations by role or function cannot help but fall into the error of ignoring the difference between eternity and time, as well as the difference between the ontological Trinity and the economic Trinity. Since each person of the one Godhead is perfect and equal in power and authority, the concept of authority submission between the Father and the Son in eternity is unimaginable. God is one and three persons in the Godhead, and all concerning God's ontology takes place in eternity. Therefore, no human notion is allowed to be mixed with God's eternal being and act.

---

123. R. K. McGregor Wright, *The Two Trinities: A Study in Apologetic Strategy* (Johnson City, TN: Worldview Heritage Press, 2011), 7-8, cited by Francis Geis, "The Trinity and the Eternal Subordination of the Son," *Priscilla Papers* 27, no. 4 (2013): 24.

124. Butner, *The Son Who Learned Obedience*, 162.

CONCLUSION

At the beginning of this chapter, one significant question was raised, "Does the Trinity pertain to the *pactum* and to the central locus of the *pactum* directly in Gill's systematic theology?" Throughout the sections, the doctrine of the Trinity, i.e., God is one and three persons, has been confirmed as the very presupposition for the *pactum* to be an eternal act. One might say that the eternal subordination of the Son to the Father appropriately works with the *pactum* when he looks at the covenant concept between God and man, or man and man in the Scripture. Then, one must ask if the authority-submission formula works for the *pactum*? Not at all. As Gill clearly asserted in the previous chapter, the *pactum* can only happen among the three divine persons, which indicates Gill firmly presupposes that each person of the Godhead is perfect and equal in power and authority. Therefore, to maintain the classical orthodox trinitarian theology, it was important for Gill to set up the covenantal theological system.

This chapter investigates the historical background of the trinitarian controversy in the sixteenth and seventeenth centuries and constructs a scaffold for Gill's doctrine of the Trinity to unfold in opposition to unitarian thoughts, especially those of the Socinians. The existence of the *pactum* goes together with the one God in three persons. The eternal act of God belongs only to God himself; therefore, in that sense, the *pactum* is a mystery as God himself exists as a mystery. However, God has revealed himself in accommodation and condescension. As far as the doctrine of the Trinity is manifested, therefore, the *pactum* should be affirmed.

Now, the long story of Gill's eternal covenant of redemption reaches the final destination of the doctrine of Jesus Christ, without whose person and work no one can access the mystery of the *pactum*.

CHAPTER 5

The Doctrine of Jesus Christ According to John Gill

THE PREVIOUS CHAPTER HAS dealt with the ontological necessity of the doctrine of God the Trinity, i.e., one nature in three persons, from the perspective of the classical orthodox trinitarian tradition to legitimize both the conceptual substance and the function of the *pactum* in Gill's systematic theology. The notion and reality of the *pactum* are inextricably linked to the existence of one God in three persons. Thus, the concept of the *pactum* is deeply associated with the works and acts of God the Trinity, which, according to Gill, "may be distinguished into internal and external."[1]

Such distinctions of the works and acts of God match the conceptual definitions of Gill's twofold *pactum*: the eternal council of God and the eternal covenant of grace; namely, the former is "held between the three divine persons, Father, Son, and Spirit, concerning the affair of man's salvation before the world was" while the latter is "a compact or agreement made from all eternity among the divine Persons, more especially between the Father and the son concerning the salvation of the elect" respectively.[2] As aforementioned in chapter three on Gill's *pactum*, the council of God is "considered as leading on, and as preparatory and introductory to" the covenant of grace, which indicates the council is more concerned with the

---

1. Gill, *Divinity: Book II*, 8. Gill continues in the same page, "The 'external' acts and works of God, are such as done in time, visible to us, or known by us; as creation, providence, redemption, etc. His 'internal' acts and works, which will be first considered, and are what were done in eternity, are commonly distinguished into personal and essential. Personal acts are such as are peculiar to each person, . . . , in treating of the doctrine of the Trinity. 'Essential' acts are such as are common to them all."

2. Gill, *Divinity: Book II*, 45, 49.

The Doctrine of Jesus Christ According to John Gill 169

immanent and internal acts of God than the covenant of grace.[3] Though the covenant of grace also happens from all eternity and is related to the internal works of God, it is associated with the economic and external acts of God effectively.

The introductory connection between the internal and external acts of God in relation to the conceptual definitions of Gill's twofold *pactum* is good enough to highlight and properly help give prominence to the doctrine of Jesus Christ with special regard to the role of Christ in the *pactum*. As far as the whole decree of God regarding the redemption of man is concerned, Gill explains that internally, Christ occupies the central stage in terms of election and justification; externally, Christ becomes the covenantal or federal head of the elect and the mediator of the covenant of grace.[4] Christ's role in the works of election, justification, and of becoming the covenant head and mediator in his two natures presupposes or is based on God's immutability and the close connection between eternity and time within God's sovereign will and decrees, which makes two radical notions possible: election of the particular persons in eternity and eternal justification.[5] In the beginning of the internal works of God, Gill affirms that God as a pure act,

> never was without the thoughts of his heart, the acts of his understanding, and the volitions of his will. The 'Sovereignty' of God over all, and his 'independency', clearly show, that whatever is done in time, is according to his decrees in eternity; for if anything comes to pass without the will of God, or contrary to it, or what he has not commanded, that is decreed, (Lam. 3:37) how is he a sovereign Being, that does according to his will in heaven and in earth, and works all things after the counsel of his will?[6]

---

3. Gill, *Divinity: Book II*, 45.

4. As the role of Christ in the *pactum*, Gill mentions four functions: the covenant head of the elect, the mediator of the covenant, the surety of the covenant, and the testator of the covenant. This chapter only delves into the first two roles that carry more related concerns to the theological flow of the chapter than the other two. Gill even says, "the suretyship of Christ is a branch of his mediatorial office." Gill, *Divinity: Book II*, 72. For the functions of Christ as the surety and testator in the *pactum*, see Gill, *Divinity: Book II*, 72-78.

5. These two radical and provocative issues among theologians will be examined in detail below.

6. Gill, *Divinity: Book II*, 9. In the beginning of the external works of God, Gill confirms the same concept, "I proceed to consider the external acts and works of God, or his goings forth out of himself, in the exercise of his power and goodness in the works of creation, providence, redemption, and grace; which works of God, without himself, in time, are agreeable to the acts of his mind within himself, in eternity. These are no other than his eternal purposes and decrees carried into execution; for 'he worketh all things after the counsel of his own will' (Eph. 1:11)." Gill, *Divinity: Book III*, 90.

On the basis of such unique and absolute attributes of God, the rest of this chapter unfolds how the *pactum* controls all the works and acts of God regarding man's salvation from all eternity and time in virtue of Christ's two natures: namely, in Christ. Gill's twofold definitions of the *pactum* in God's eternal decrees and sovereign will lucidly describe that the covenant among the three divine persons pertains to "the affair of man's salvation," that is, "the salvation of the elect." Three questions are raised in terms of these two expressions in the *pactum*: the affair of the salvation and the elect. First, who is the elect? Secondly, related to the first question, if the election of the particular persons, according to Gill, happens in eternity, why do the particular persons, i.e., the elect, need the affair of salvation?[7] Thirdly, how do Christ's two natures in one person work and affect the salvation of the elect in and according to the noble and divine scheme of the *pactum*?

Following the questions above, this chapter first examines Gill's understanding of the election. Secondly, with regard to the meaning of the salvation of the elect, it attempts to elucidate that Gill's doctrine of the eternal justification opens and accounts for the reality of salvation in eternity and time. Then, lastly, it unfolds the redemptive history shaped and affected by the trinitarian economic works centered on Christ's two roles as the covenant head and the mediator in virtue of his two natures, all of which are willed and planned by the eternal decrees of the Trinity, specifically the Father, in the *pactum*. In this regard, the apostle Paul sums up and articulates the whole work of the triune God in Christ as the locus, on whom both eternity and time converge:

> He made known to us the mystery of his will, according to his good pleasure that he purposed in Christ as a plan for the right time–to bring everything together in Christ, both things in heaven and things on earth in him (Eph 1:9-10).

ELECTION[8]

Acknowledging God's incomprehensibility in his eternal decrees regarding the doctrine of election, Jonathan Dickinson (1688-1747), a Presbyterian

---

7. This second question includes an assumption that the elect is the saved. As will be seen in Gill's argument regarding God's election, Gill believes the goal of God's election of his chosen people is to lead them to salvation. Also, in the fact that election happens in eternity, Gill affirms that salvation of the elect is fixed and confirmed as an eternal act of God, which makes no change with the elect's status before God.

8. The scope and depth of the doctrine of election are wide, deep, and profound in relation to other doctrinal areas. Thus, this section only attempts to understand what

pastor and theologian who served a local church in New Jersey for almost forty years, articulates,

> I shall accordingly endeavour to treat upon the arduous Theme, which my Text leads me to contemplate, with a humble sense, that *God is in Heaven, and I upon Earth*; and to avoid plunging into this Ocean beyond my Depth. I shall purposely overlook all the curious Questions and scholastic Distinctions, so commonly found in Authors upon this Subject, as *Things too wonderful for me, which I know not*; and with all the Plainness and Perspicuity

---

Gill means when he concerns with the doctrine of election below. This note deals briefly with the introduction of the doctrine of election. As James Leo Garrett states, this doctrine of election by some theologians is placed in the doctrine of God in connection to the decrees of God whereas others put the election under the doctrine of salvation. Garrett, *Systematic Theology*, 2:432. Gill handles the election in the doctrine of God due to the close connection with God's decrees and the *pactum*. Kenneth Keathley defines election as "the gracious decision of God by which he chooses certain ones to be the recipients of salvation," and continues to classify the points of argument, "whether God chooses the elect individually or as a group and whether he bases his choice on the foreseen faith of the elect are issues of intense debate. Also, some contend that election in the Bible refers only to service and not to salvation." Kenneth Keathley, "The Work of God: Salvation," in *A Theology for the Church*, 558. From the biblical usage, Klooster unfolds five aspects of God's sovereign election: (1) "the elect angels"; (2) "election to service or office"; (3) "the election of Abraham's descendants to form the theocratic nation of Israel; (4) "the election of the Messiah"; and (5) "election to salvation." Then, he lists six features of the principles of election: (1) "election is a sovereign, eternal decree of God"; (2) "the presupposition of God's eternal decree of election is that the human race is fallen"; (3) "election is 'election in Christ'"; (4) "election involves both the elect's salvation and the means to that end"; (5) "election (as well as reprobation) is individual, personal, specific, particular"; (6) "finally, the ultimate goal of election is the glory and praise of God." F. H. Klooster, "Elect, Election," in *Evangelical Dictionary of Theology*, ed. Walter A. Elwell, Second Edition (Grand Rapids: Baker, 2001), 370-71. More specifically, Daniel Treier explains four views of the doctrine of election: the Calvinist, the classical Arminian, some contemporary Arminians in corporate terms, and finally, Barthian christological focus position. See Treier, *Introducing Evangelical Theology*, 233-35. The essential point of the doctrine of election is the difference between the Calvinist unconditional election and the classical Arminian election whose distinction is whether there is a "consideration of any foreseen merit or faith on the part of the elect." Keathley, "The Work of God: Salvation," 559. For more explanation of each view of election in detail, see Chad Owen Brand, ed., *Perspectives on Election: Five Views* (Nashville: B&H, 2006); Harwood, *Christian Theology*, 579-606; especially, for the view of corporate election and solidarity, see William W. Klein, *The New Chosen People: A Corporate View of Election* (Grand Rapids: Zondervan, 1990). Also, regarding the purpose of election as a service, see H. H. Rowley, *The Biblical Doctrine of Election* (London: Lutterworth, 1950), who notes, "Election is for service. This is not to ignore the fact that it carries with it privilege. For in the service of God is man's supreme privilege and honour" (45).

I am capable of, consider the Doctrine as it is set before us in the Words of the Text.⁹

Though standing on the quite opposite side against Dickinson in terms of infant baptism and church government, Gill agrees, at least in approaching the concept of election in God's eternal decrees, with Dickinson's self-recognition that man must bring to a screeching halt where God ceases revealing himself in Scripture as well as that God is in heaven and man upon earth.¹⁰

Accordingly, Gill begins the doctrine of election with God himself in the person and work of Jesus Christ, i.e., "the election of Christ," who is "God's first and chief elect."¹¹ "You prepared a body for me," does Gill

---

9. Jonathan Dickinson, *The True Scripture-Doctrine concerning Some Important Points of Christian Faith, particularly Eternal Election, Original Sin, Grace in Conversion, Justification by Faith, and the Saints Perseverance. Represented and Apply'd in Five Discourses* (Boston: G. Rogers, for S. Eliot in Cornhill, 1741), 3. For more about Jonathan Dickinson, especially his life, writings, and theological context, see Gary L. Steward, "The Calvinistic Soteriology of Jonathan Dickinson," *The Confessional Presbyterian* 7 (2011): 78-81.

10. See Jonathan Dickinson, *Remarks upon Mr. Gale's Reflections on Mr. Wall's History of Infant Baptism* (New York: William Bradford for and sold by T. Wood, 1721); Jonathan Dickinson, *A Defence of Presbyterian Ordination: In Answer to a Pamphlet, Entituled, A Modest Proof, of the Order and Government Settled by Christ, in the Church* (Boston: Printed for Daniel Henchman, and sold at his shop, over-against the Brick Meeting-House in Cornhill, 1724); also, see John Gill, *The Argument from Apostolic Tradition, in Favour of Infant-Baptism, with Others, Advanced in a Late Pamphlet, Called the Baptism of Infants a Reasonable Service, &c. Consider'd* (London printed. Boston, New-England: re-printed by Z. Fowle, in Back-Street, near the Mill-Bridge, 1765).

11. Gill, *Divinity: Book II*, 12. As biblical evidence for the election of Christ, Gill presents Isa 42:1; Ps 89:3; Luke 23:25; and 1 Pet 2:4. Regarding the expression "this is my chosen one" in Isa 42:1, Gill explains, "this character of *elect* may respect the choice of the human nature to the grace of union with the son of God; ... and was pre-ordained to be the Lamb slain for the redemption of man, and appointed to glory." Gill, *An Exposition of the Old Testament*, 5:238. In Ps 89:3, God's chosen pertains to the eternal covenant. Gill asserts that this chosen is neither Abraham nor David "but mystical David, the Messiah, David's son and antitype; after, on this account, called David in Scripture," and "with him the covenant of grace was made from all eternity, and all the blessings and promises of it were put it into his hands. ... the Septuagint render it, in the plural number, *with mine elect ones*; and it is a truth, that the covenant of grace is made with all the elect, considered in Christ, and is made with them as such, and not as believers, converted persons," "election is the foundation of the covenant, and the source of all covenant-blessings." Gill, *An Exposition of the Old Testament*, 4:75. Emphasis original. Barth, arguing Jesus Christ as the electing and the elected, stresses Christ as the basis and foundation of God's election, "He [Christ] is the election of God before which and without which and beside which God cannot make any other choices. Before Him and without Him and beside Him God does not, then, elect or will anything." Barth, *CD*, II/2: 94. For the evaluation of Barth's doctrine of election, see

The Doctrine of Jesus Christ According to John Gill

appeal to Hebrews 10:5 and emphasizes the human nature of Christ for election in God's eternal purposes and decrees. Therefore, persons who have been given to the Son by the Father "were fashioned, when as yet, before there were none of them;" in other words, "among all the individuals of human nature, which rose up in the divine mind, to be brought into being by him, this was singled out from among them, and appointed to union with the second Person in the Godhead."[12]

As a pastoral theologian who experienced and served a local church for over fifty years, Gill attempts to explain God's election in Christ from two viewpoints: one is from eternity, and the other is from time. First, instancing two biblical passages, i.e., Acts 13:48 and Revelation 13:8, Gill draws two related concepts in terms of election and elect from eternity: eternal life and names written in heaven.[13] Gill sees that God's perfection of the eternal decrees in the *pactum* knows the chief elect, Christ, and the particular persons in Christ. From the eternal perspective, it is a certain and perfect number of the elect in God's eternal divine mind, that is, *before the foundation of the world*, even "before men were born," regarding which no one is privy to the perfect knowledge of election except the Father, Son, and Holy Spirit.[14] Gill asserts,

---

Bird, *Evangelical Theology*, 574-76.

12. Gill, *Divinity: Book II*, 13. For the passages of those who are given to the Son by the Father, see John 6:37, 39, 64-65; 17:6, 12; 18:9.

13. Gill, *Divinity: Book II*, 14-15.

14. Emphasis added. Based on Romans 9:11; Jeremiah 1:5; 2 Thessalonians 2:13, Gill firmly avers that "this act of election is an eternal act, or from eternity," which may be concluded, Gill argues, from two ideas: (1) God's immutability, "which could not be established if any new thoughts and resolutions arose in time, or new decrees in time were made by him; and therefore it may be reckoned a sure point, that such a special decree as this, respecting so important an affair as the salvation of all his people, as well as his own glory, must be eternal"; (2) The covenant of grace is an eternal covenant, "from everlasting to everlasting; in which the goings of Christ as Mediator were of old; and promises were made before the world began; and grants of grace were made, and blessings of grace provided as early; and which covenant was made with the 'chosen' of God; with Christ, the chosen Head, and with his people, as chosen in him; so that if this covenant was from everlasting, and made with chosen ones in Christ, their representative, then the choice of them in him must be as early." Gill, *Divinity: Book II*, 22. Regarding God's immutability in election, Barth also notes on God's works in eternity and time, "It is as God's election that we must understand the Word and decree and beginning of God over against the reality which is distinct from Himself. When we say this, we say that in His decision all God's works, both 'inward,' and 'outward,' rest upon His freedom. We say, too, that in so far as these works are done in time, they rest upon the eternal decision of God by which time is founded and governed. God elects. It is this that precedes absolutely all other being and happening." Barth, *CD*, II/2: 99. After affirming that nothing, e.g., good works of men, holiness of men, faith, perseverance, can be the cause of God's election and "Christ, as God, is the efficient cause of election,"

> As many as were ordained to eternal life, believed; by which ordination is meant to no other than the predestination, choice, and appointment of men to everlasting life and salvation by Jesus Christ; and from whence it appears that this of particular persons, of some and not all, though many; that it is not to temporary privileges and enjoyments, but to grace and glory; and that faith is not the cause, but the sure and certain fruit and effect of it.
>
> All [Luke 10:20; Heb 12:22; Phil 4:3; Rev 13:8] which shows that it is an act of God in heaven, and respects the happiness of men there; is of particular persons, whose names are in a special manner known of God, and as distinct from others; and is sure and certain, and will abide.[15]

Presenting more passages, e.g., Ephesians 1:4; 2 Thessalonians 2:13; and Romans 8:33, Gill leads his arguments of "chosen" and "elected" to the concept of "a remnant according to the election of grace," whose meaning is to entail "only some, and not all men," that is, particular persons.[16]

Secondly, though conceding God's election of particular persons from eternity as clearly revealed in the Scripture, Gill's intention is far from opening "a door to all licentiousness" of the elect.[17] He says, "It is true. Indeed,

---

Gill continues and makes concluding words, "In short, these maxims are certainly true, and indisputable, that nothing in time can be the cause of what was done in eternity; to believe, to be holy, to do good works, and persevere in them, are acts in time, and so cannot be causes of election, which was done in eternity." Gill, *Divinity: Book II*, 24. The issue of locus and function of 'faith' will be handled later in the section of Gill's eternal justification.

15. Gill, *Divinity: Book II*, 14, 15. With regard to "the authority of the predestinating action of God" in Acts 13:48, see Jaroslav Pelikan, *Acts*, Brazos Theological Commentary on the Bible (Grand Rapids: Brazos, 2005), 159-61; David E. Garland, *Acts*, Teach the Text Commentary (Grand Rapids: Baker, 2017), 142. "Not everyone is affected in the same way by the preaching of the gospel. God must open hearts, to enable people to listen and respond with faith." Peterson, *The Acts of the Apostles*, 399. Regarding those whose names were written in the book of life in Revelation 13:8, Thomas Schreiner notes, "John probably speaks of those who were inscribed in the book of life before history began. After all, the death of Christ was *predetermined* before history began, but it is quite another thing to say he was actually *slain* before the world began, for the Lamb was slain in history, but before the world began. On the other hand, God decided before history began who would be inscribed in the book of life." Thomas Schreiner, "Revelation," in *Expository Commentary, vol. XII, Hebrews–Revelation* (Wheaton: Crossway, 2018), 670; also, see Hoskins, *The Book of Revelation*, 243, saying, "While God and the Lamb have known the names of their own, since 'the foundation of the world' (13:8), the people of God become evident in history due to their perseverance and faith. They do not worship the Beast, as the rest of the world does."

16. Gill, *Divinity: Book II*, 15.

17. In Gill's other writing, the concept of 'particular persons' in election is in stark

it cannot be said of particular persons that such a man is elected, and such a man is reprobated, especially when both appear to be in a state of unregeneracy; yet when men, in a judgment of charity, may be hoped to be called by grace, they may be concluded to be the elect of God, though it cannot be said with precision."[18] Thus, what is important to ask for Gill "is not, am I elected; but, am I born again? Am I a new creature? Am I called by the grace of God and truly converted? If a man can arrive to satisfaction in this matter, he can have no doubt about his election."[19]

---

contrast to Daniel Whitby's concept of election which indicates nations, or churches, or communities. For example, Whitby comments on Romans 9, "that suitable to this notion of the word election, where it respects the Jewish nation, or the Jewish converts, is the import of it in these epistles, where whole nations, communities, or churches, are styled the elect." Whitby also explains on 2 Tim 2:10, "if we compare this with a parallel place in Col. 1:24, 25, we shall find the elect to be no other than the whole church of Christ, of which he was a minister." Daniel Whitby, "Discourse I: Concerning Election and Reprobation," in *Discourse on the Five Points*, Third Edition, corrected (1710; London: F. C. and J. Rivington, 1816), 61, 62. In response, Gill, while asserting the "whole nations are never styled the elect," states, "it appears that the church of which the apostle was a minister, is no other than the body of Christ; and intends *the general assembly and church of the first-born which are written in heaven*, and not any particular society, or community of men, under a profession of Christianity." John Gill, *The Cause of God and Truth*, 155-56.

18. Gill, *Divinity: Book II*, 13.

19. Gill, *Divinity: Book II*, 13. From this twofold concept of election, Gill satisfies both God's sovereign, gracious, and merciful work of election from eternity and man's recognition of and responsibility for confirmation of one's status by the grace of God in time. Election of particular persons, a remnant according to Gill, therefore, does not violate the teaching of Scripture. Man's comprehension of salvation in Scripture can be represented by twofold examples: first, "everyone who calls on the name of the Lord will be saved"; secondly, "all who had been appointed to eternal life believed." Both God's sovereignty and man's volition are in the Scripture with regard to the salvation. Both the universal redemption and the election of particular persons have a potential problem, however, in light of that the understanding of God the Trinity and his attributes, the only subject or main agent of man's salvation, might be distorted and broken by the already-framed perspective of man who is to be called righteous in order to live before God the righteous judge. In this regard, Elwell, examining Pauline concept of election, asserts, "In order to understand Paul's doctrine of election and predestination one must begin with the doctrine of God, because it is God who elects, who calls, who purposes and who predestinates." W. A. Elwell, "Election and Predestination," in *Dictionary of Paul and His Letters*, ed. Gerald F. Hawthorne, Ralph P. Martin, Daniel G. Reid (Downers Grove: IVP, 1993), 225. Man's logic based on the reasonable thought-process does not allow a 'both-and' frame but pursue a sharp and clear answer due to his limit of only having temporal perspective. The mystery of God's eternal being in one essence and three persons is never located solitarily without regard to God's economic acts in man's salvation, which is also mystery. The mystery of particular persons in salvation is hidden to man. As God's love and wrath work perfectly together in harmony in the divine simplicity, Gill presents twofold of God's election, which is the unique joy and hidden delight given, revealed, and allowed only to the elect. Gill mentions, "though

The last point Gill makes regarding the doctrine of election pertains to the agent and instrument of the decree, that is, "by whom election is made, and in whom it is made."[20] First, election is made by God. When Gill terms God, it indicates not just God the Father; it includes Christ and the Spirit as well.[21] Based on Ephesians 1:4 and 1 Peter 1:2, Gill notes that "the God and Father of our Lord Jesus Christ" chose the elect "according to the foreknowledge of God the Father."[22] In addition, Gill cites Jesus' words in John 13:18 to prove that "sometimes it [election] is ascribed to Christ": "I speak not of you all; I know whom I have chosen."[23] The Spirit, as involved

indeed no man, be he ever so vile, is out of the reach of powerful and efficacious grace; and therefore it cannot be absolutely said that he is rejected of God: and whereas there may be only the appearance of grace, and not the truth of it, in such that profess to have it; it cannot be said with certainty that such an one is an elect persons, yet in charity it may be so concluded: however, *a truly gracious man may know for himself his 'election of God.'*" Gill, *Divinity: Book II*, 13. Emphasis added.

20. Gill, *Divinity: Book II*, 16.

21. "Election is a Trinitarian event. . . . Election follows from creation and salvation being works of God." Letham, *Systematic Theology*, 406.

22. "The author of this choice is God, God the father, who is distinguished from Christ, in whom this act is made; and it is according to his fore-knowledge, and is an act of his grace, and is entirely sovereign." Gill, *An Exposition of the New Testament*, 3:61. What the Father "as the ultimate source of all blessing" dispenses is election, the first spiritual blessing. Constantine Campbell analyses Ephesians 1:4, "The election of God [the Father] is modified by three phrases: first, God chose us 'in him,' . . . God is the subject of 'he chose' and Christ is the one through him this election took place. . . . The second phrase, 'before the foundation of the world,' underscores God's *electing* in the election of God. That is, God's choosing of his people could not have been influenced by human decision, human action, or human responsibility since it occurred before God laid the foundation of the world–before any human had being. . . . The third phrase indicates the purpose of God's election; namely, that he chosen people would 'be holy and blameless before him in love.'" Constantine R. Campbell, *The Letter to the Ephesians*, PNTC (Grand Rapids: Eerdmans, 2023), 42, 44, 46. Emphasis original. Grudem suggests and considers the meaning of "according to the foreknowledge" as "according to God's fatherly care for you before the world was made." For details, see Wayne Grudem, *1 Peter: An Introduction and Commentary*, TNTC (Downers Grove: IVP, 1988), 54.

23. Gill, *Divinity: Book II*, 17. Gill adds, "this cannot be understood of Christ's choosing his disciples to the office or apostleship, for all the twelve were chosen to that; but of his choosing them to eternal life; and this is what he could not say of them all, for one of them was the son of perdition; and hence the elect are called Christ's elect; not only because chosen in him, and given to him, but because chosen by him." In this regard, Carson notes, "The reason why he now takes the pains to show that inclusion of Judas was not an oversight or a sign of weakness on his part is so that their faith might be strengthened for the critical hour. As in 6:70, the argument assumes that not all election is to salvation." Carson, *The Gospel According to John*, 470. Namely, the election may function as a certain service for the purpose of God as Rowley mentioned above. Jobes also denotes, "Although election is often individualized as a matter of personal salvation, in the Old Testament it is set in the context of God's universal authority and

with all the internal decrees and external acts and works of God, including the *pactum*, is also engaged in and not "to be excluded" from the decree of election.[24] The Spirit's actions in making all the "blessings, gifts, and operations of grace" of the election effective becomes the "efficient cause of it."[25]

Secondly, election is made in Christ. Gill's idea of election in Christ is closely related to the concept of corporate solidarity revealed in Christ's being the covenantal head of the elect in eternity and time.[26] Gill makes a helpful comment,

> Election does not find men in Christ, but puts them there; it gives them a being in him, and union to him; which is the foundation of their open being in Christ at conversion, which is the manifestation and evidence of this; "If any man be in Christ", even in the secret way, by electing grace, "he is a new creature", sooner or later; which is an evidence of it.[27]

From the reference above, Gill provides two kinds of elected beings in Christ: open being and secret being; in other words, Gill means "these two, an open and secret being in Christ, differ in this, that the one is in time, . . . , the other from eternity; the one is the evidence of the other."[28] Therefore, there is a temporal order in becoming a Christian within the concept of the open being in Christ, whereas no order makes an effect in the secret being in Christ because of the "electing grace" that completes "the whole body of the elect being chosen together in Christ" in eternity.[29] This notion of twofold being in Christ makes a distinction between election and salvation in terms of the cause. Gill asserts that the temporal works of Christ, e.g., his blood, sacrifice, obedience, sufferings, and death, are not the cause of election but "the meritorious cause" of redemption. The efficient cause of election is only the electing grace and Christ himself as God. Consequently, not only men's good works, holiness, and perseverance but even faith itself cannot be "the moving cause of election" because "the one is in time, the other in eternity."[30]

---

his desire to bless all nations (Ge 12:1-3). The election of Israel was the means by which salvation would come to the human race and is part of God's commitment to work within human history." Jobes, *John*, 216.

24. Gill, *Divinity: Book II*, 17.

25. Gill, *Divinity: Book II*, 17.

26. Thus, Christ's being the head and mediator of the elect in the *pactum* necessarily follows by the 'in Christ' formula, which will be dealt with more deeply below.

27. Gill, *Divinity: Book II*, 17.

28. Gill, *Divinity: Book II*, 17.

29. Gill, *Divinity: Book II*, 17.

30. Gill, *Divinity: Book II*, 23. The issue of faith in Gill's soteriology relates more

Summary

Though Gill's doctrine of election pertains primarily to God's free and sovereign and absolute and unconditional selection of particular persons from eternity, it does not lead the elect to a licentiousness in time. Based on the election in Christ by God and through the Spirit, Gill distinguishes two concepts of being in Christ: open being in time and secret being in eternity. The elect of the open being in Christ is a new creature, being called and converted, which happens as evidence or manifestation of the electing grace that makes the whole body of the elect of the secret being in Christ. However, neither does this mean God's election is "begun in eternity and completed in time, nor takes its rise from the will of God, and is finished by the will of man; nor is made perfect by faith, holiness, obedience, and persevering in well doing, but has its complete being in the will of God at once."[31] Rather, God's perfection and completion of the election in Christ are manifested as evidence by faith, holiness, and obedience. Also, because "no man can know his election of God until he is called," no one is allowed to conclude oneself as God's elect or a reprobate.[32] After all, Gill offers two viewpoints regarding the doctrine of election: the unlimited and eternal perspective of God and the limited and temporal perspective of man. What man sees and experiences in time with regard to the election is the very evidence and manifestation of the perfect plan and decree of God's eternal election in Christ.

JUSTIFICATION FROM ETERNITY

In the big picture of Gill's *pactum* that controls both realms of eternity and time, the doctrines of election and justification are closely related, as the internal and immanent acts of God constitute the foundation and substance of the *pactum* in Gill's soteriological system. Based on God's unique, sovereign, and eternal election, Gill sets up the doctrine of justification from eternity as a necessary corollary. Examining Karl Barth's doctrine, especially of justification, Hans Küng also notes, "the justification of sinners is grounded in the unique eternal election of the individual as a member of the people

---

to justification, a secret branch of election, rather than election. Gill categorizes faith as one of the spiritual blessings flowing from election, which also includes effectual calling, holiness, communion with God, justification, adoption, and glorification. See Gill, *Divinity: Book II*, 26.

31. Gill, *Divinity: Book II*, 26.
32. Gill, *Divinity: Book II*, 27.

of God in Jesus Christ."³³ However, Küng, in thoughts of Barth does not embrace the notion of justification from eternity,

> Justification as a temporal event must not be dissociated from eternity. Does this mean that the divine election—and with it justification—was "fixed" in advance, the consequence of an inflexible eternal decree? In no sense. While the gracious election is the work of the unchangeable God, nonetheless this God is also very much alive. Justification is eternal, yet it is a living and present event."³⁴

Is justification eternal? In other words, when is the date of the justification? If the election of God is eternal and the ultimate goal of the elect is salvation and eternal life, what is the meaning of the Protestant soteriological principle, i.e., justification by faith alone, which appears to happen in time by one's faith? Finally, what does Gill mean by his justification? Why does Gill's concept of justification raise an issue or even provoke such severe criticism?

Below, we will examine Gill's doctrine of justification from eternity and how it relates to the reality of salvation in eternity and time. Prior to exploring Gill's justification, this section will briefly look into the core concept of classical Protestant Reformed justification.

Justification

The doctrine of justification has always been one of the provocative issues in Christian history. J. V. Fesko delivers what it means,

> Whether in the Augustine-Pelagius debates in the patristic era, the disputes that sparked and fueled the Reformation with Martin Luther's ninety-five theses, the contentions over the center of Paul's theology in the nineteenth century, or the current debates

---

33. Hans Küng, *Justification: The Doctrine of Karl Barth and a Catholic Reflection*, trans. Thomas Collins, Edmund E. Tolk, and David Granskou (Philadelphia: Westminster, 1981), 14.

34. Küng, *Justification*, 16. For Barth's understanding of justification, see Barth, *CD*, IV/1; also, see Paul T. Nimmo, "Reforming *simul iustus et peccator*: Karl Barth and the 'Actualisation' of the Doctrine of Justification," *Zeitschrift für Dialektische Theologie*, Supplement Series 6 (2014): 91-104; Paul D. Molnar, "The Importance of the Doctrine of Justification in the Theology of Thomas F. Torrance and of Karl Barth," *Scottish Journal of Theology* 70, no. 2 (2017): 199-209.

surrounding justification and the New Perspective on Paul, the doctrine of justification has always been a subject of contention.[35]

Among various issues concerning justification, the debate between the Roman Catholic and the Protestant theologies regarding its definition has helped to disclose what the biblical and theological meaning of justification indicates. Based on the ideas of Chrysostom, Augustine, and Roman Catholic theologians throughout the medieval era, and prompted by and responding to the Protestant Reformation, the Council of Trent (1545-1563) affirmed justification embraces a transformational process; moreover, "justification requires man's co-operation with God."[36] However, the "classical

---

35. J. V. Fesko, *Justification: Understanding the Classic Reformed Doctrine* (Phillipsburg, NJ: P&R, 2008), 1. Fesko, making this statement, suggests some related resources of the issues of justification in the note 1. Most of all, the New Perspective on Paul (NPP) has made a huge impact on the current conversations of justification. Regarding more resources for the NPP in particular, see Krister Standahl, "The Apostle Paul and the Introspective Conscience of the West," *Harvard Theological Review* 56, no. 3 (1963): 199-215; E. P. Sanders, *Paul and Palestinian Judaism: A Comparison of Patterns of Religion* (Philadelphia: Fortress, 1977); N. T. Wright, *The Climax of the Covenant: Christ and the Law in the Pauline Theology* (London: T&T Clark, 1991); Peter Stuhlmacher, *Revisiting Paul's Doctrine of Justification: A Challenge to the New Perspective* (Downers Grove: IVP, 2001); Stephen Westerholm, *Perspectives Old and New on Paul: The "Lutheran" Paul and His Critics* (Grand Rapids: Eerdmans, 2004); D. A. Carson, Peter T. O'Brien, and Mark A. Seifrid, eds., *Justification and Variegated Nomism: Volume 2-The Paradoxes of Paul* (Tübingen: Mohr Siebeck, 2004); James D. G. Dunn, *The New Perspective on Paul: Collected Essays*, Wissenschaftliche Untersuchungen zum Neuen Testament 185 (Tübingen: Mohr Siebeck, 2005); Michael F. Bird, *The Saving Righteousness of God: Studies on Paul, Justification, and the New Perspective*, Paternoster Biblical Monographs (Eugene, OR: Wipf and Stock, 2007); N. T. Wright, *Paul: In Fresh Perspective*, paperback edition (Minneapolis: Fortress, 2009); John M. G. Barclay, *Paul and the Gift* (Grand Rapids: Eerdmans, 2015); Scot McKnight and B. J. Oropeza, eds., *Perspectives on Paul: Five Views* (Grand Rapids: Baker, 2020).

36. Cross, ed., "justification," in *The Oxford Dictionary of the Christian Church*, 914. For more about Augustine's justification in general and especially as being *made righteous*, see Jack D. Kilcrease, *Justification by the Word: Restoring Sola Fide* (Bellingham, WA: Lexham, 2022), 118-27; also, see Saint Augustine, *On Grace and Free Will*, ed. Philip Schaff (Louisville, KY: GLH Publishing, 2017). Piggin further explains, "The Tridentine doctrine on justification was expressed in sixteen chapters. Chapters 1-9 stress man's incapacity to save himself but confirm the necessity for the cooperation of his free will, including his resolve to receive baptism and begin a new life. Justification results not only in the remission of sin but also in 'sanctification and renewal of the whole man.'" F. S. Piggin, "Trent, Council of," in *Evangelical Dictionary of Theology*, 1216. Regarding personal righteousness and merit of Romish practice, Buchanan describes, "By the infusion of a principle of grace into his heart at baptism, the sinner was supposed to be made inherently righteous, so as to be entitled to claim eternal life on that ground, and enabled also to do good works which were properly meritorious." James Buchanan, *The Doctrine of Justification: An Outline of its History in the Church and of its Exposition from Scripture* (Grand Rapids: Baker, 1955), 106. Relying on the

Protestant theology" has recognized that "'justification' was interpreted as God 'declaring man to be righteous' . . . , to be distinguished from sanctification, in which man is 'made righteous.'"[37] In other words, the Reformed theologians, including Calvin, clarify that justification is by grace alone and through faith alone. Justification is God's act; thus, it comes with God's grace. Then, what does it mean by that justification is through faith alone?

Nathan Busenitz provides three "core components" of the Reformers' teaching on the justification by faith alone: "(1) the forensic nature of justification, (2) a distinction between justification and sanctification (or regeneration), and (3) the imputed righteousness of Christ."[38] Thomas Sch-

---

Council of Trent, Ott a Catholic theologian also confirms, "Besides faith, further acts of disposition must be present" as the preparation for justification; in other words, "In addition to faith, Holy Writ demands other acts of preparation, for example: the fear of God . . . , hope . . . , love of God . . . , sorrow and penance . . . ." " . . . faith alone does not suffice for justification." Ludwig Ott, *Fundamentals of Catholic Dogma*, trans. Patrick Lynch (Rockford, IL: Tan Books, 1974), 253-54.

37. Cross, ed., "justification," in *The Oxford Dictionary of the Christian Church*, 914. Buchanan stresses, "The doctrine of Justification, by grace, through faith in Christ, . . . resting solely on the redemption and righteousness of the Lord Jesus Christ" stands "as the actual and immediate privilege of every sinner, on the instant when he begins to rely on Christ alone for salvation, as He is offered to *him* individually in the Gospel." Buchanan, *The Doctrine of Justification*, 3. Emphasis original. Michael Horton explains, "the Reformers taught and evangelicals teach that justification is distinct from sanctification. Although both are inseparable gifts of union with Christ through faith, justification is a verdict that declares sinners to be righteous even while they are inherently unrighteous, simply on the basis of Christ's righteousness imputed to them. Where Rome teaches that one is finally justified by being sanctified, the Reformed conviction is that one is being sanctified because one has already been justified. Rather than working toward the verdict of divine vindication, the believer leaves the court justified in the joy that bears the fruit of faith: namely, good works." Michael S. Horton, "Traditional Reformed View," in *Justification: Five Views*, ed. James K. Beilby and Paul Rhodes Eddy (Downers Grove: IVP, 2011), 85-86; also, for the relation of justification and sanctification, see R. Michael Allen, *Justification and the Gospel: Understanding the Contexts and Controversies* (Grand Rapids: Baker, 2013), 127-51.

38. Nathan Busenitz, "The Substance of *Sola Fide*: Justification Defended from Scripture in the Writings of the Reformers," *TMSJ* 32, no. 1 (Spring 2021): 80. Fesko, similar but slightly different elements of justification by faith alone, writes: "(1) it is by faith alone; (2) it is the remission of sins; and (3) it is the imputation of righteousness." Fesko, *Justification*, 189. Also, see John P. Burgess, "Justification and Sanctification: Implications for Church Life Today," in *What Is Justification About?: Reformed Contributions to an Ecumenical Theme*, ed. Michael Weinrich and John P. Burgess (Grand Rapids: Eerdmans, 2009), 63-64. Thomas Oden also notes on justification of Reformers, "Its Source: God. Its Nature: a gracious act. Its Elements: pardon and acceptance. Its Scope: all believers. Its Ground: the imputed righteousness of Christ. Its Condition: faith alone." Then, Oden lists the confessions and positions of each denomination on justification in consensus, e.g., Reformed Confessions (Belgic, Westminster), Lutheran Formula of Concord, New Hampshire Baptist Confession, and Anglican, Wesleyan,

reiner, bringing McGrath's arguments regarding the main characteristics of Lutheran and Protestant doctrine of justification, supports Busenitz's three elements of justification by faith alone. Schreiner denotes that (1) the term forensic indicates "a change in status rather than a change in nature"; (2) "justification refers to the declaration that one stands in the right before God, while sanctification denotes the ongoing renewal and transformation in one's life"; and lastly (3) "justification denotes alien righteousness, which means that Christ's righteousness is imputed to the believer."[39]

Then, on what basis have the Reformers come to such a notion of justification and attained the three core components? Busenitz appeals to the works and thoughts of the key Reformers, viz. Luther, Melanchthon, Calvin, and Chemnitz prove the justification by faith alone by presenting defending

---

Pentecostal traditions. See Thomas C. Oden, *The Justification Reader*, Classic Christian Readers (Grand Rapids: Eerdmans, 2002), 37, 38-43. James Renihan compares the Second London Confession, Savoy Declaration, and Westminster Confession concerning *Of Justification*, and notes, "The three Confessions agree that justification is not the result of infused righteousness, nor 'for anything wrought in them' or their own efforts, nor on the basis of the act of faith or believing or any other gospel-oriented righteousness. *Westminster* then states truly but simply that justification flows from the imputation of Christ's obedience and satisfaction, while *Savoy*, followed by *Second London*, adds that justification is based solely upon the imputation of the work of Christ considered from two perspectives–His life of holy and perfect obedience to the law of God and His sacrificial death." James M. Renihan, "God Freely Justifieth . . . by Imputing Christ's Active . . . and Passive Obedience," *TMSJ* 32, no. 1 (Spring 2021): 65-66. For more detailed explication for the imputation, see J. V. Fesko, *Death in Adam, Life in Christ: The Doctrine of Imputation*, Reformed, Exegetical and Doctrinal Studies (Fearn, Ross-shire: Mentor, 2016).

39. Thomas Schreiner, *Faith Alone: The Doctrine of Justification: What the Reformers Taught . . . and Why It Still Matters*, The Five Solas Series (Grand Rapids: Zondervan, 2015), 39. Alister McGrath delves deeply and massively into the history of justification from pre-Augustine and Augustine through the Middle Ages and the Reformation to the modern thoughts of justification. Regarding the medieval notion of justification, McGrath points out, "Justification refers not merely to the beginning of the Christian life, but also to its continuation and ultimate perfection, in which Christians are made righteous in the sight of God and of humanity through a fundamental change in their nature, and not merely in their status." Also, mentioning justifying righteousness with the relation of justification to sanctification, he states, "The notional distinction, necessitated by a forensic understanding of justification, between the external act of God in pronouncing sentence, and the internal process of regeneration, along with the associated insistence upon the alien and external nature of justifying righteousness, must be considered to be the most reliable *historical* characterization of Protestant doctrines of justification." Alister E. McGrath, *Iustitia Dei: A History of the Christian Doctrine of Justification*, Third Edition (Cambridge: Cambridge University Press, 2005), 59, 209-10. For the short and rough history and theology of justification, see Robert Letham, *The Work of Christ*, Contours of Christian Theology (Downers Grove: IVP, 1993), 186-94.

biblical references for each component of justification.⁴⁰ Above all things, the understanding of the concept of faith and the related biblical verses have led the Reformers to focus on the genuine and essential meaning of biblical justification and to distinguish themselves from the Roman Catholics and other theological notions, e.g., a new perspective on Paul.

The concept of faith in Scripture is crucial to understanding what justification is. For example, Sam Waldron deals with the relation between Genesis 15:6 and Romans 4:3 regarding Abraham's faith. In this study, Waldron argues for justification by faith against the NPP's claim as "contemporary Judaic tendencies to read the OT as supporting a soteriology of human achievement or 'the works of the law.'"⁴¹ After looking into the righteousness of God and Abraham's faith, Waldron notes on faith, "We must, rather, remember that faith is oriented toward and, we may even say, shaped by the promise of God. Faith is what it is because of the promise of God. Its content is the content of the promise of God."⁴² Malcolm Yarnell, as a part of defining justification, gives an insightful definition of faith as instrumentality. It deserves to load the full definition of faith,

> From the numerous Scriptures mentioned, it should be evident that our participation in Christ is activated instrumentally by the gift of faith (cf. Phil 3:8-9). This faith does not have any value in itself. Faith is merely the free reception of the divine power of the gospel. The General Baptist *Orthodox Creed* of 1679 said there are six necessary causes of justification, all of which have God as the primary actor. The fifth cause is faith, which is the instrumental cause. Faith is a divine gift, and man is a secondary actor. As noted above, faith is a mere reception dependent upon its object for its effective power. Dagg would agree: "Nothing can be accounted the meritorious cause of justification, but the obedience and sufferings of Christ: yet faith is indispensable."⁴³

---

40. For the forensic feature, Busenitz lists Acts 13:38-39, 15:11; Rom 3:24, 4, 5:10-11, 19, 8:33-34; 1 Cor 4:3-4; Gal 2:16; Eph 2:5; and 1 Tim 3:16. For the distinction between justification and sanctification, 1 Cor 1:30, 6:11; Rev 22:11; Rom 6:15-23. Lastly, for the imputed righteousness of Christ, Acts 13:38-39; Rom 3:21-4:25; 5:18-19, 10:4; 1 Cor 1:30; 2 Cor 5:21; and Phil 3:7-9. See Busenitz, "The Substance of Sola Fide," 81-92.

41. Sam Waldron, "Paul's Use of Genesis 15:6 in Romans 4:3," *TMSJ* 32, no. 1 (Spring 2021): 115.

42. Waldron, "Paul's Use of Genesis 15:6 in Romans 4:3," 129. For more relation of Romans 4 to the NPP, see Michael Horton, *Justification*, New Studies in Dogmatics, 2 vols. (Grand Rapids: Zondervan, 2018), 2:309-17.

43. Malcolm B. Yarnell III, "Christian Justification: A Reformation and Baptist View," *CTR* 2, no. 2 (Spring 2005): 82-83. Yarnell's two proof texts (Rom 1:15-18 and Luke 18:9-14) for justification, through which many other biblical references follow, help understand why justification comes from "the faithfulness of God and being

In sum, the classical Protestant Reformers have maintained the doctrine of justification by grace through faith (Rom 3:24; Eph 2:8). In other words, the forensic distinction between justification and sanctification, and the imputed righteousness of God, these three core components of justification by faith alone, *sola fide*, have strenuously opposed the synergistic concept of justification of Roman Catholic and the NPP. The righteousness of God in Christ's suffering, death, and resurrection is only received by faith, not by works of the law. As Roger Duke delivers, "Faith is but the instrument and not the basis of justification. 'We are not justified because we believe, but we are justified through faith, faith being the "appropriating organ" by which justification comes.'"[44]

The following, based on the Reformers' doctrine of justification, deals with Gill's justification from eternity within Gill's grand presupposition of eternity and time frame.

Justification from Eternity

Theological issues pertaining to eternity have been damaged or at least disparaged by the human notion of time frame. With notions of pushing God's

---

transmitted to the faith of man" and why the synergistic feature of "a self-righteous Pharisee," which is "advocated in Tridentine Catholic expositions and in the 'covenantal nomism' of the NP on Paul," must be rejected. From the biblical passages to support justification, as the title of the article implies, Yarnell makes a significant point that justification should find its right place beyond the theological conversations in Pauline cartel because "Jesus Christ also taught the doctrine of justification by grace alone." He notes, "Justification is not just a Pauline doctrine; it is a Christian doctrine." See Yarnell, "Christian Justification," 76-77, 78, 79. For more explanation of justifying faith in *An Orthodox Creed*, see Article XXIII on *Of Justifying, or Saving Faith* in Thomas Monck et al., "An Orthodox Creed," 158. Also, see the Heidelberg Catechism question 61, "Why sayest thou that thou art righteous by faith only?" It answers, "Not that I am acceptable to God on account of the worthiness of my faith, but because only the satisfaction, righteousness, and holiness of Christ is my righteousness before God, and that I cannot receive and apply the same to myself any other way than by faith only." Regarding this issue, Zacharias Ursinus comments, "Because we are justified by the object of faith alone, that is by the merits of Christ only, without which we can have no righteousness whatever: for we are justified for Christ's sake. Nothing but the merit of Christ can be our righteousness in the sight of God, either as a whole, or a part only. We are justified only by believing, and receiving the righteousness of another, and not by our own works, or merit. All works are excluded from our justification, yea even faith itself in as far as it is a virtue, or work." Zacharias Ursinus, *The Commentary of Zacharias Ursinus on the Heidelberg Catechism*, trans. G. W. Williard (Cincinnati: Elm Street Printing Company, 1888; reprint, Miami, FL: HardPress, 2012), 331.

44. Roger Duke, "The Most Important Question One Can Ask!" *Founders Journal* 110 (Fall 2017): 26.

sovereign, free, and immanent acts into the box of the limited human mind and, at the same time, putting the already fixed frame of man on the mysterious but truthful words and works of the triune God revealed in Scripture, the concept of eternity has been treated as a mere theological idea or object to be analyzed so as to support man's reasonable logic in doing theology and to help understand Scripture in man's easiness. As mentioned in chapter two, Gill's concept of eternity and time, as a grand presupposition of the entire volume, God is eternal, and the concept of eternity should be found and established in and by the three divine *persons* in the Godhead.[45] A good example of distortion in the usage of eternity is the terms like "eternity past" and "eternity future." These expressions within themselves show an inconsistency or contradiction in the respect that such language makes eternity dance to creation's tune.

The reason why the beginning of this section goes back to the discussion of eternity and reminds us of its meaning in connection with God's attribute is that to Gill, justification is an act of the eternal God in grace as God does in election, neither just happening by *ordo salutis* appeared in the timeline of man's reason nor depending on man's meritorious decision, but solely complete and perfect in the eternal divine mind.[46] Every process seen in the timeline for justification through Christ's righteousness, i.e., Christ's suffering, death, and resurrection, is in the eternal divine mind of God. Thus, according to Gill, justification that man sees in the temporal realm is not the reality of the concept, but the substance rather lies in the

---

45. Italics added for emphasis. Eternity is not just an object of man's analysis that belongs to timeframe which is a product of God's creation. Eternity is one of God's essential attributes. For more concept of personal characteristic of eternity in Gill's theology, refer to chapter two of this volume.

46. Regarding the reason of focusing on God himself and his sovereign divine grace in terms of justification, David Rathel notes on the historical circumstances of Gill's contemporary as aforementioned, "The time in which Gill ministered, often labeled the 'Age of Reason,' witnessed considerable theological upheavals, and Gill was, overall, troubled by these changes. He believed that the era's strong commitment to rationalism created theologies that deemphasized the necessity of divine grace. The popularity of such theologies–most notably various forms of deism and the theology of Daniel Whitby–pushed him into a defensive position." David Mark Rathel, "John Gill and the Charge of Hyper-Calvinism: Assessing Contemporary Arguments in Defense of Gill in Light of Gill's Doctrine of Eternal Justification," *SBJT* 25, no. 1 (2021): 44. Pertaining to the historical conditions, for more about the relation between eternal justification and the antinomianism, and Arminianism in the context of seventeenth-century English Reformed theology, see Robert J. McKelvey, "'That Error and Pillar of Antinomianism': Eternal Justification," in *Drawn into Controversie: Reformed Theological Diversity and Debates within Seventeenth-Century British Puritanism*, ed. Michael A. G. Haykin and Mark Jones, Reformed Historical Theology 17 (Göttingen: Vandenhoeck & Ruprecht, 2011), 223-62.

will of God. While observing a concept of will, "as God's will to elect, is the election of his people, so his will to justify them, is the justification of them," Gill presents his conceptual definition of justification,

> as it is an immanent act in God, it is an act of his grace towards them, is wholly without them, entirely resides in the divine mind, and lies in his estimating, accounting, and constituting them righteous, through the righteousness of his Son; and, as such, did not first commence in time, but from eternity.[47]

Based on the definition of justification above, the rest of this section will examine Gill's understanding of the date of justification, which entails the notion and function of faith, and then Gill's answers to the expected objections to justification from eternity.[48] This also is the most clearly different point from the classical Reformed understanding of justification above.[49]

First, justification "does not begin to take place in time, or at believing, but is antecedent to any act of faith."[50] Gill's first and foremost biblical basis for this argument is Romans 3:24, in which Paul strongly affirms God's grace and redemption in Christ as the source of justification, "They are justified freely by his grace through the redemption that is in Christ Jesus."[51] Thus, there is no place for faith to become the cause of justification.[52] Gill explains,

---

47. Gill, *Divinity: Book II*, 39.

48. Such two choices of 'the date of justification' and 'answers to objection' as contents for this section follow Gill's order of contents dealing with justification in *Divinity* that is the essence of Gill's theology and written in 1767. In fact, Gill wrote and published a small book regarding this topic titled, *The Doctrine of Justification* (1756), in which Gill makes several points of justification, including act, author, matter, form, objects, effects, and properties of justification. See John Gill, *The Doctrine of Justification, by the Righteousness of Christ, Stated and Maintained, Being the Substance of Several Sermons*, Fourth Edition (London: Printed, and sold by G. Keith, at the Bible and Crown in Gracechurch-Street, and J. Robinson, at Dockhead, Southwark, 1756), 6.

49. Gill does not deny the classical Reformed three core components of justification, which includes forensic, distinction between justification and sanctification, and the imputed righteousness of God. See Gill, *The Doctrine of Justification*, 11, 18, 37-38.

50. Gill, *Divinity: Book II*, 39.

51. God's grace is the moving cause of justification, says Gill, "for by *the grace of God* here, is not meant the Gospel, or what some men call the terms of Gospel, and the constitution of it; nor the grace of God infused into the heart; but the free love and favour of God, as it is in his heart; which is wonderfully displayed in the business of a sinner's justification before him." Then, he continues, "The meritorious cause of justification is, *the redemption that is in Jesus Christ*, which signifies, "as all the blessings of grace come through redemption by Christ, so does this of justification, and after this manner." Gill, *An Exposition of the New Testament*, 2:438. Emphasis original.

52. While agreeing with Gill's concept of faith, saying, "Faith is not the impulsive

It [faith] is the effect of justification: all men have not faith, and the reason why some do not believe is, because they are none of Christ's sheep; they were not chosen in him, nor justified through him; but justly left in their sins, and so to condemnation; the reason why others believe is, because they are ordained to eternal life, have a justifying righteousness provided for them, and are justified by it, and shall never enter into condemnation: the reason why any are justified, is not because they have faith; but the reason why they have faith, is because they are justified.[53]

In other words, Gill's concept of faith in relation to justification is abridged by four propositions: (1) "Faith is the evidence and manifestation of justification"; (2) "Faith adds nothing to the 'esse' only to the 'bene esse' of justification . . . it is a complete act in the eternal mind of God"; (3) "Justification is the object, and faith the act that is conversant with it. Now every object is prior to the act that is concerned with it"; and (4) "All the elect of God were justified in Christ, their Head, and Representative when he rose from the dead, and therefore they believe."[54]

---

or moving cause of justification. It is an act of pure and free grace, without any motive in the creature," John Brine even before Gill asserts, "faith is a work or act of ours." John Brine, *A Defence of the Doctrine of Eternal Justification, from some Exceptions made to it by Mr. Bragge, and others* (London: Printed and sold by A. Ward, at the *King's-Arms* in *Little Britain*; and H. Whitridge, at the Corner of Castle-Alley, near the Royal-Exchange, 1732), 4.

53. Gill, *Divinity: Book II*, 39.

54. Gill, *Divinity: Book II*, 40. "Faith is the hand which receives the blessing of justification from the Lord, and righteousness, by which the soul is justified from the God of its salvation, but then this blessing must exist before faith can receive it." Gill, *The Doctrine of Justification*, 43. One might have a question about the date of justification in Gill's propositions. How does it make sense between justification from eternity and being justified in Christ when they believe? Johannes Steenbuch delivers Gill's design and explains, "Justification happens from eternity, as God's decision to justify the elect is in itself a justification of the elect, says Gill. But it also happens in time. Christ had the sins of the elect imputed to him when he died on the cross, and they were justified again, when Christ in his resurrection was justified 'as a public person.' Justification in time, understood as the public declaration of an already existing righteousness, further happens by faith in the consciousness of the justified, on the one hand, and by works in the eyes of others, on the other hand. By this distinction Gill manages to harmonise the idea of justification from eternity with Paul's remarks on justification by faith in the Epistle to the Romans, as well as notion of justification by works in the Epistle of James. Again there seem to have been pastoral concerns, as this distinction makes it clear that our eternal righteousness depends neither on our degree of faith nor on good works in time." Johannes A. Steenbuch, "Always Already Loved: Recovering the Doctrine of Justification from Eternity," *Journal of European Baptist Studies* 18, no. 2 (Fall 2018): 38. Gill also borrows Ames' words using two terms, 'conceived' and 'pronounced': "The sentence of justification was, 1. As it were conceived in the mind of God, by the decree

Moreover, Gill's justification is not just before faith but from eternity, "being an immanent act in the divine mind."[55] The concept of eternal election in Gill's system is deeply related to and logically brings about eternal adoption and eternal justification.[56] If the elect persons are in Christ, chosen from eternity, i.e., before the foundation of the world, then they "must be acquitted, discharged, and justified so early" as the election.[57] It is because "as a branch of election," justification is "as of the same date with it [election]."[58] In addition, as a proof text for justification from eternity, Gill appeals to Ephesians 1:3-4. If the electing grace is given to the chosen in Christ from eternity, every spiritual blessing from the grace must be granted to the elect, one of which is justification. Thus, justification is from eternity. Lastly, it is the eternal will of God "not to punish sin in the persons of his elect, but to punish it in the person of Christ."[59] Below is Gill's thought regarding God's will in punishing sin,

> This will was notified to man, quickly after the fall, though it did not then begin, for no new will can arise in God; he wills

---

of justifying. 2. Pronounced in Christ our Head, when he rose from the dead." Gill, *The Doctrine of Justification*, 46.

55. Gill, *Divinity: Book II*, 40. Gill does not believe that the elect, though justified from eternity, "had an actual personal existence from eternity"; rather Gill says, "they had a representative one in Christ." Gill, *The Doctrine of Justification*, 49.

56. These two spiritual blessings are, strictly speaking, linked to the eternal union with Christ, which is described and performed by the *pactum* in Gill's system. David Rathel explains, "In Gill's system, election creates an eternal union between the elect and God.... The *pactum salutis* explains how the elect are able to receive these spiritual blessings in this eternal union." Rathel, "John Gill and the Charge of Hyper-Calvinism," 45. Ultimately, the *pactum* that embraces all God's immanent and economic works in both eternity and time in and through Jesus Christ, is also closely connected to the doctrine of justification. Then, it is interesting or even not understandable to see that Benjamin Keach who affirmed the *pactum* could not consider the concept of justification from eternity in light of Hicks' explanation that Keach's theological doctrines were all "interconnected" and he "never isolated the doctrine of justification from other doctrines of Scripture, but always discussed it within the broader framework of soteriology, ecclesiology, covenant theology, anthropology, Christology, eschatology, and theology proper." Tom Hicks, "Benjamin Keach's Doctrine of Justification," *TMSJ* 32, no. 1 (Spring 2021): 93. According to Hicks, Keach made his effort to defend the Reformed position of the doctrine of justification against Richard Baxter's Neonomian doctrine of justification. So Keach used the *pactum* to advocate the covenantalism is not man-merit based theology but Christ-centered (103-4).

57. Gill, *Divinity: Book II*, 41. Gill brings Romans 8:1, "there is now no condemnation for those in Christ Jesus." Thus, if one is in Christ, he or she must be in a state of righteousness, which denotes justification.

58. Gill, *Divinity: Book II*, 41.

59. Gill, *Divinity: Book II*, 41-42.

nothing in time, but what he willed from eternity. If it was God's eternal will not to punish sin in his people, but in his Son, then they were eternally discharged, acquitted from sin, and secured from everlasting wrath and destruction; and, if they were eternally discharged from sin, and freed from punishment, they were eternally justified.[60]

Secondly, Gill, answering some objections to justification from eternity, solidifies what he means by the doctrine. The first and primary objection is that "men cannot be justified before they exist."[61] Gill penetrates the opponent's mind and sees through what the objection attempts to shake and attack, i.e., eternal election.[62] As a branch of and reckoned as the same date with election, justification may lose its foundation as election loses its biblical and theological ground. However, as aforementioned, Gill argues, based on Ephesians 1:3-4 and 2 Timothy 1:9, that the meaning of 'chosen in Christ' has "an 'esse representativum,' a representative being in Christ; which is more than other creatures have, whose future existences are certain."[63] Also, Gill directly asserts, "though God's elect have not an actual

60. Gill, *The Doctrine of Justification*, 60. When Gill says, "he wills nothing in time," it means God's will never changes. Eternity with immutability makes such a firm sovereignty in God. The affirmed will of God confirms what is determined in God himself. Thus, as in the case of election, God's will to punish sin in his Son is the fundamental and eternal concept of punishment. Such a firmly established will of God in eternity is revealed and manifested by the person and work of Jesus Christ, and Christian's faith is the evidence of God's will that is manifested in the temporal realm. Gill leaves no room for faith to function as an intellectual work of man, which makes a subtle difference in function of faith from the classical Reformed understanding as an instrument. To Gill, faith is "the sense, perception, and evidence of our justification." Gill, *The Doctrine of Justification*, 65. In this regard, George Ella states, "One of the reasons for the modern unwillingness to examine Gill's doctrine of justification in the light of Scripture is that it has become 'sound' amongst evangelicals to view justification as occurring through believing, making personal belief the cause of justification." However, Gill thought "justification as being determined by the mind and will of God in providing a Bride for His Son and thus justification, along with the whole of redemption both accomplished and applied, was a gift of God." George M. Ella, *John Gill and Justification from Eternity: A Tercentenary Appreciation 1697-1997* (Durham, England: Go Publications, 1998), 49.

61. Gill, *Divinity: Book II*, 42.

62. This question may become the objection to the *pactum* as well. By definition, one might think that it is absurd or invalid to consider man's redemption in eternity even before they have an actual existence or form in person.

63. Gill, *Divinity: Book II*, 42. With regard to this 'non-existence in substance,' the author of Hebrews writes in 7:9-10, "And in a sense Levi himself, who receives a tenth, has paid a tenth through Abraham, for he was still within his ancestor when Melchizedek met him." Levi did not even exist when Abraham met and paid a tenth to Melchizedek. But the author says Levi was there. This gives a hint of the relationship between being and act in the big frame of the concept of representative, which is

being from eternity, yet it is certain, by the prescience and predetermination of God, that they shall have one."[64]

The second objection is extended by the first question concerning a substance of the justified in eternity, which claims justification from eternity is not only ridiculous in terms of men who do not exist to be justified, but it also "seems absurd to say, that they are justified from sins, before they were committed, or any charge was brought against them for sin."[65] Gill approaches this objection and attempts to answer with a more absurd doctrine, "which is most certainly true of all those that live, since the coming and death of Christ," i.e., the doctrine of the imputation of sin to Christ.[66] In other words, if men's sins "were imputed to Christ, and laid upon him, and he was delivered up to justice, and died for them before they were committed," and this doctrine of the imputation of sin to Christ is accepted by every Christian, says Gill, one cannot deny that being justified from their sins before they were committed in eternity.

Lastly, one might have an objection to reading Scripture, "Then, what about those many passages of Scripture that include the expression, 'justified through and by faith'? Is it not that one is justified when they believe?" In response, Gill acknowledges two sorts of justification: i.e., justification by faith in time and justification before faith in eternity,

> the one being an immanent act in God, all which sort of acts are eternal, and so before faith; the other being a transient declarative act, terminating on the conscience of the believer; and so is by and through faith, and follows it. But then these do not contradict each other, the one being a declaration and manifestation of the other.[67]

---

connected to Adam-Christ headship matter. Gill also senses the similar concept with respect to justification issue from these verses, "Abraham; namely, Levi and his whole posterity; which is to be understood seminally, just as all mankind were in the loins of Adam, when he sinned and fell, and so they sinned and fell in him; and so Levi was in Abraham's loins, when Melchisedec met him: which, as it proves Melchisedec to be greater than Levi, and much more Jesus Christ, who is a priest of his order, which is the grand thing the apostle has in view; so it serves to illustrates several points of doctrine, in which either of the public heads, Adam and Christ, are concerned, with respect to their seed and offspring; such as personal election in Christ, an eternal donation of all blessings of grace to the elect in him, eternal justification in him, the doctrine of original sin, and the saints' crucifixion, burial, resurrection, and session in Christ, and together with him." Gill, *An Exposition of the New Testament*, 3:415-16.

64. Gill, *Divinity: Book II*, 42.
65. Gill, *The Doctrine of Justification*, 71.
66. Gill, *Divinity: Book II*, 42.
67. Gill, *Divinity: Book II*, 43.

To prove his point, Gill takes an example in Galatians 2:16, " ... even we ourselves have believed in Christ Jesus. This was so that we might be justified by faith in Christ." In this passage, Gill tries to highlight the object of belief by which men might be justified, namely, Jesus Christ. The expression 'by faith' itself is not given such an emphasis in this passage.[68] "The apostle's meaning then is that we have believed in Christ, or have looked to him for justification, that we might have the comfortable sense and apprehension of it, through faith in him; or that we may appear to be justified, or to expect justification alone by his righteousness, received by faith, and not by the works of the law," says Gill.[69]

Summary and Evaluation

Gill's justification is a spiritual blessing with adoption derived from the eternal election and union with Christ, explained by the *pactum*. The elect in Christ is also justified in Christ. Because the will of God in his divine mind from eternity is in control, all phenomena seen in the temporal realm are the manifestation of the will determined in eternity. God's immanent acts in the eternal decrees, including election and justification, possess twofold characteristics: eternal substance and temporal reflection or manifestation. Thus, based on this principle of Gill's doctrine of God, justification by grace through Christ's righteousness conceptually precedes justification through and by faith. Consequently, faith is the evidence and manifestation of justification. This unique feature of justification from eternity and the difference from the classical Reformed concept of faith as an instrument emphasizes the triune God's sovereign grace more than any other Protestant denomination.

However, accepting faith's instrumentality in the temporal realm never damages God's sole and sovereign grace in both immanent and economic

---

68. However, F. F. Bruce, citing Bornkamm's words, denotes, "'Paul never defines faith. The nature of faith is given in the object to which that faith is directed . . . . Faith always means faith in . . . or faith that . . . ' . . . it is the personal faith that unites one to Christ along with all fellow-members of the new covenant community–all those who, in Paul's idiom, are 'in Christ.'" F. F. Bruce, *The Epistle to the Galatians: A Commentary on the Greek Text*, NIGTC (Grand Rapids: Eerdmans, 1982), 139.

69. Gill, *The Doctrine of Justification*, 78. In the expression, "received by faith," one might guess Gill also accepts the usage of faith as an instrument. Due to so much emphasis on God's sole work of justification in his sovereignty, Gill sees the function of faith as a mere sense, perception, and evidence of justification. However, if that is the case, it might be difficult how to explain or be ambiguous to figure out the interrelation between eternal justification and the moment of man's temporal recognition of himself in Christ's righteousness.

acts. As Yarnell mentioned above, faith is a divine gift, and man is a secondary actor. The redemptive work of God can only be performed by the Father, Son, and Spirit. Man recognizes God's eternal and marvelous work of election and justification through a gift of faith. By faith, in other words, regardless of the debate, so-called subjective or objective genitive with regard to πίστις Χριστοῦ, by exercising one's intellectual agreement, as recorded in Scripture, which is a gift from above, that Jesus is Lord, man confesses what has come to his heart and mind, expresses his salvation through the mouth by faith only.[70] Paul and Silas, when asked, "What must I do to be saved?" answered, "Believe in the Lord Jesus, and you will be saved." Exercising one's heart for God, that is, expressing one's belief, comes out of a person and is manifested by faith, an instrument revealing and connecting the eternal reality of justification with man's temporal self-recognition that he can confess Jesus is Lord.

JESUS CHRIST

The covenantal scheme of the triune God in the *pactum*, through which the glory of God is pursued as the primary and ultimate goal, demands two concepts in order to unfold what God has in his eternal divine mind: spiritual perfection and historical evidence.[71] As the plan of God to save his people begins from eternity and at the same time, the perfection of God's saving plan in eternity must be revealed and accomplished in the perfect way in time, for Gill, Jesus Christ is the best method to satisfy the two demands of the *pactum* in perfection. The already-existing God's eternal covenantal scheme in the *pactum* is clearly manifested in time through the temporal course of creation, redemption, and consummation. In other words, "as God's eternal plan is enacted on the stage of human history, it moves from creation in Adam to consummation in Christ."[72]

---

70. For further and detailed explication regarding πίστις Χριστοῦ and the concept of faith in Paul's writings, see Kevin W. McFadden, *Faith in the Son of God: The Place of Christ-Oriented Faith within Pauline Theology* (Wheaton: Crossway, 2021). McFadden explores the πίστις Χριστοῦ debate in Introduction, the concept of faith and subject and object issue in chapter one.

71. These two demands are directly related to Christ's two natures: divinity and humanity, which also will be helpful and working for the next section of Christ the Mediator of the covenant.

72. Gentry and Wellum, *Kingdom through Covenant*, 36. They, introducing the *pactum* as "the foundation to the outworking of God's plan," and serves also as "an 'archetype for the historical covenants,'" mention Christ's two functions regarding which Gill is to explain, "It also provides the grounding for our covenantal union with Christ as our mediator and representative substitute in the covenant of grace" (78-79).

The Doctrine of Jesus Christ According to John Gill   193

Two previous sections of this chapter, i.e., eternal election and justification, confirmed that these immanent acts of God happen in Christ. Namely, the union with Christ depicts the complete scheme of the *pactum* from God's election through adoption to justification in Christ. These eternal acts of God, in particular the union with Christ, are revealed in the temporal realm by Christ's two specific and crucial roles: the covenantal Head and the Mediator of the covenant.[73] The rest of this chapter will examine Christ's two roles in manifesting the triune God's eternal and perfect redemption for man, which is derived from the *pactum*.

Christ as the Covenantal Head

Gill first indicates the different biblical usages of the head concept applied to Christ, i.e., natural, political, and economical senses.[74] Christ, as the "head of the church" (Eph 5:23), becomes the origin, source of life, and the unique figure under and through whom all beings belong to or participate in the figure's fate or destiny.[75] This headship is, therefore, according to Gill, inextricably linked to Christ as the representative of human society in the covenant of grace and the spiritual life through corporate solidarity, contrasting with Adam, who is the negative representative in the natural world.

Emphasis added.

73. Almost every chapter of the rest in Gill's *Divinity* converge toward these two significant works of Christ. See Book V and VI of the *Divinity*. Gill deals with the most temporal works of God in the concept of both 'of Christ and by Christ.'

74. The natural sense is the relation between the natural head and the natural body (Eph 4:15-16); the political means Christ is the political head as "a captain general is head of his army, and a king is head of his subjects" (Judg 10:18; Hos 1:11). Lastly, the economical sense concerns as "the husband is the head of the wife, and a father the head of his children, and a master the head of his servants and of his whole family" (Num 1:4; Eph 5:23-24). Gill, *Divinity: Book II*, 63. For more about the correlation among God, Christ, church, husband, and wife, see E. Earle Ellis, *Pauline Theology: Ministry and Society* (Eugene, OR: Wipf and Stock, 1997), 57-62; also, see Taylor, *1 Corinthians*, 257-59.

75. In this regard, Christ does not exist as a private person only. In the big umbrella of the 'in Christ formula,' "It is not only an individual believer who exists and does certain things in Christ, but believers as a whole also exist and do certain things in Christ." Sang-Won (Aaron) Son, *Corporate Elements in Pauline Anthropology: A Study of Selected Terms, Idioms, and Concepts in the Light of Paul's usage and background* (Roma, Italia: Editrice Pontificio Istituto Biblico, 2001), 16.

Representative

From eternal election and union, Christ is the head and representative of the chosen people. Those who are in Christ as his members from eternity "did not personally exist, but Christ did, who represented them, and therefore were capable of being chosen in him, as they were (Eph. 1:4)."[76] Galatians 3:16-17, Gill's primary passage in the context for Jesus Christ to be the head and representative of the elect, reads,

> Now the promises were spoken to Abraham and to his seed. He does not say, "And to seeds," as referring to many, but rather to one, "And to your seed," that is, Christ. What I am saying is this: the Law, which came four hundred and thirty years later, does not invalidate a covenant previously ratified by God, so as to nullify the promise.[77]

Gill makes two significant points from these two verses in connection with Christ's being the head and representative according to the *pactum*: one is from 3:17 concerning the date of covenant promises, the other from 3:16 presenting Christ as the seed of Abraham embracing all the spiritual descendants through the redemptive history of the Israelites.

First, Gill argues that the covenant *promises* the Lord gave to Abraham and to his seed in Genesis are before the foundation of the world; namely, they are from the eternal covenant.[78] That is, all the blessings promised to God's elect in eternity are confirmed in Christ their head though "as yet they had not an actual being, only a representative one in Christ," before those covenant blessings were manifested to Abraham and to his spiritual seed as a revelation.[79] Thus, Gill interprets Galatians 3:17, "'The law, which was four hundred and thirty years after' revelation and manifestation of the

---

76. Gill, *Divinity: Book II*, 63.

77. The passage is from NASB.

78. Emphasis added.

79. Gill, *Divinity: Book II*, 63. Gill means by the covenant as "*confirmed of God in Christ*: a covenant in which Christ is concerned; a covenant made with him, of which he is the sum and substance, the Mediator, surety, and messenger; and such is what the Scriptures call the covenant of life and peace, and what we commonly style the covenant of grace and redemption; because the articles of redemption and reconciliation, of eternal life and salvation, by the free grace of God, are the principal things in it. This is said to be *in Christ*, ας Χριςον, with respect to Christ: . . . meaning either that this covenant has respect to Christ personal, he having that concern in it, as just now mentioned, and as it was made manifest and confirmed to Abraham, was promised in it to spring from him; or rather that it has respect to Christ mystical, as before, to all Abraham's spiritual seed, both Jews and Gentiles: and this is said to be *confirmed of God*, with respect thereunto." Gill, *An Exposition of the New Testament*, 3:19.

covenant to Abraham, 'cannot disannul, that it should make the promise of none effect'; for what commences in time, can never make void what was confirmed in eternity."[80]

Is Gill's interpretation correct to see the promises 'to Abraham and to his seed' in Galatians 3:17 stemming from the eternal covenant? The next question is helpful to approach the issue: what accurate verse of Scripture did Paul have in mind when he quotes the narrative of the Abrahamic covenant? There are three candidates to precisely satisfy the key citation of Paul in Galatians 3:16 pertaining to the Abrahamic covenant, "καὶ τῷ σπερματί σου ('and to your seed')": Genesis 13:15; 17:8; and 24:7, all of which include "וּלְזַרְעֲךָ ('and to your seed')."[81] Scholars consider Genesis 17:8 as the basis for Paul's citation.[82] If that is so, Gill's understanding concerning the promises from the eternal covenant is advocated by the verse, which reads,

> I will establish My covenant between Me and you and your descendants after you throughout their generations for an *everlasting covenant*, to be God to you and to your descendants after you. I will give *to you and to your descendants* after you, the land of your sojournings, all the land of Canaan, for an everlasting possession; and I will be their God (Genesis 17:7-8).[83]

---

80. Gill, *Divinity: Book II*, 63.

81. The LXX of those three Genesis passages also match the Greek New Testament. Some scholars claim that Genesis 22:17-18 is the most appropriate verse for Paul's allusion in citation. See T. Desmond Alexander, "Further Observations on the Term 'Seed' in Genesis," *Tyndale Bulletin* 48, no. 2 (1997): 363-67; C. John Collins, "Galatians 3:16: What Kind of Exegete was Paul?," *Tyndale Bulletin* 54, no. 1 (2003): 75-86. However, Thomas Schreiner, opposing Collins's argument for Genesis 22, states, "The use of the word 'and' (καί) as part of the OT citation 'and to your offspring' (καὶ τῷ σπερματί σου) is lacking in Gen 22:18. If Paul were merely alluding to a text, it is unlikely that he would use the word 'and' (καί). The presence of 'and' (καί) is a stubborn piece of evidence that calls into question Collins's interpretation, indicating that Paul is actually quoting the OT here. And if he is quoting the OT, he is not referring to Gen 22:17-18, since 'and' (καί) is omitted there." Thomas R. Schreiner, *Galatians*, Zondervan Exegetical Commentary on the New Testament (Grand Rapids: Zondervan, 2010), 230.

82. See J. Louis Martyn, *Galatians: A New Translation with Introduction and Commentary*, The Anchor Bible 33A (New York: Doubleday, 1997), 339; Ben Witherington III, *Grace in Galatia: A Commentary on St Paul's Letter to the Galatians* (Grand Rapids: Eerdmans, 1998), 244; Schreiner, *Galatians*, 230. On the other hand, Robby Kagarise says Paul's point is to concern with the particular passage but to "call attention to the fact that all the promises made to Abraham were made not only to the patriarch but to his seed as well." Robby J. Kagarise, "The 'Seed' in Galatians 3:16–A Window to Paul's Thinking," *Evangelical Journal* 18, no. 2 (Fall 2000): 69.

83. NABS. Emphasis added.

As it happens, Abraham records that God will establish his covenant not only between him [God] and Abraham but also between him [God] and Abraham's seed, who is ultimately revealed, according to Paul in Galatians 3:16, as Christ.

This Christ as the seed of Abraham in Galatians 3:16 is Gill's second point to manifest Christ's role as the head and representative of the elect who are revealed in and by faith according to the grand scheme of the *pactum*. The eternal blessings and inheritance derived from the promises of the *pactum* "were made to them [the elect], as considered in Christ, their head and representative."[84] Thus, the promises of God, which were made to Abraham and to his seed, are essentially meant to be made to Christ. Is it legitimate to consider Paul's interpretation of the 'seed' indicating Christ as singular, not as the plural or collective noun normally understood by the usage of Jews? Then, who is the 'seed' of Abraham?

Max Wilcox notes that the seed can be used in both collective and individual sense, "The term 'seed' usually interpreted in the Targumim and Rabbinic sources generally as a collective, meaning 'sons' (and hence, 'sons of Israel'), can also have an 'individual' meaning, e.g., Isaac, Solomon, Seth."[85] Specifically, Trent Hunter and Stephen Wellum present four categories of who the seed of Abraham is: (1) Abraham's children by natural birth; (2) the promised seed, e.g., God's choice of Jacob over Esau though both are Abraham's natural children; (3) those who are circumcised of the heart even among the chosen covenant people; and finally (4) the true and singular seed who is Jesus Christ, the fulfillment of the protevangelium in Genesis 3:15.[86] In connection with the fourth category above, scholars agree with Richard Longenecker's suggestion of the corporate solidarity comprehension, which implies and embraces the idea of representative:

> Paul understood 'seed' here as a specific singular rather than a generic singular. Later in v 29 Paul treats 'seed' as a collective, as he does also in Rom 4:13-18. So, it seems that Paul is here invoking a *corporate solidarity understanding of the promise of Abraham* wherein the Messiah, as the true descendant of Abraham and the true representative of the nation, is seen as the true

---

84. Gill, *Divinity: Book II*, 63.

85. Max Wilcox, "The Promise of the 'Seed' in the New Testament and the Targumim," *Journal for the Study of the New Testament* 2, no. 5 (September 1979): 2.

86. Trent Hunter and Stephen Wellum, *Christ from Beginning to End: How the Full Story of Scripture Reveals the Full Glory of Christ* (Grand Rapids: Zondervan, 2018), 125.

'seed' of Abraham–as are, of course, also the Messiah's own, as v 29 insists.⁸⁷

87. Richard N. Longenecker, *Galatians*, Word Biblical Commentary (Dallas, TX: Word Books, 1990), 132. Emphasis added. Kagarise, considering Paul's "Jewish background and his Christian experience" in mind, explains, "In spite of the fact that 'seed' is used in the context of the Abrahamic covenant as a collective singular, because it is grammatically singular it would also be justifiable to interpret it as referring to an individual. Although Paul's familiarity with this method may have provided him an exegetical device in his approach in Galatians 3:16, another aspect of his Jewish mind set may be of far more significance. His Semitic background allowed him to comprehend 'a corporate solidarity understanding of the promise of Abraham wherein the Messiah, as the true descendant of Abraham and the true representative of his people . . . [would have been] seen as the legitimate [inheritor] of God's promises.' 'Corporate solidarity' refers here to the ancient Semitic ability to comprehend a whole host of individuals as summed up in a single representative. *The Apostle has the ability to see an individual as representative of a group and a group as embodied in an individual.*" Kagarise, "The 'Seed' in Galatians 3:16," 71. Also, see Schreiner, *Galatians*, 229; G. Walter Hansen, *Galatians*, IVP New Testament Commentary Series (Downers Grove: IVP, 1994), 98; Leonhard Goppelt, *Typos: The Typological Interpretation of the Old Testament in the New*, trans. Donald H. Madvig (Grand Rapids: Eerdmans, 1982), 138; Letham, *The Work of Christ*, 43; Paul R. Williamson, *Sealed with an Oath: Covenant in God's Unfolding Purpose*, New Studies in Biblical Theology 23 (Downers Grove: IVP, 2007), 198; Timothy George, *Galatians*, NAC, vol. 30 (Nashville: B&H, 1994), 247; Andrew T. Abernethy and Gregory Goswell, *God's Messiah in the Old Testament: Expectations of a Coming King* (Grand Rapids: Baker, 2020), 26-27. Abernethy and Goswell say, "the corporate is not entirely discarded if Christ is the corporate representative" (27). While agreeing with the solidarity concept like others, Earle Ellis states a helpful remark regarding the grammar and interpretation, "Paul was not unaware of the grammar; his point was that the grammar was aptly suited to contain his exegesis. The grammar alone could never do more than circumscribe the meaning; while most often it was a collective denoting one's posterity in general, זֶרַע also represented a restricted class of posterity and sometimes even an individual. Paul found the true meaning of the promise by interpreting it of Christ. In the end, then, the passage does not involve a question of grammatical accuracy but of theological interpretation, and Paul's interpretation involves no rabbinical sophistry. He notes that it is a collective and not a simple plural, and within the limits of the grammar interprets it of Christ, or better, of that particular type of seed which is identified with and headed up in Christ." E. Earle Ellis, *Paul's Use of the Old Testament* (Edinburgh: Oliver and Boyd, 1957), 72-73. G. K. Beale and D. A. Carson also say, "It would be ludicrous to suggest that Paul was unaware of the collective sense of *sperma* or that he was hoping that his readers would not detect this 'logical flaw.' In this very passage–indeed, at its climax–he affirms, 'if you are of Christ, then you [plural!] are Abraham's seed, heirs according to the promise' (3:29). The collective meaning of the term is fundamental for Paul's argument, and thus we can hardly read 3:16 as though he were wishing to exclude such a meaning." G. K. Beale and D. A. Carson, eds., *Commentary on the New Testament Use of the Old Testament* (Grand Rapids: Baker, 2007), 807. N. T. Wright, however, noting that "Paul exploits the collective sense of *sperma*, very similar to our 'family,' explains, "Paul's point is not, as has usually been assumed, that the promise of the singular 'seed' necessarily points to the 'singular' person Jesus of Nazareth, here denoted as *Christos*. Paul knows perfectly well that *sperma* is collective. Rather, his point is that *God promised Abraham a single family*, one 'seed,' not more,

The corporate solidarity in understanding the seed of Abraham in Galatians 3:16 is fully agreed by Gill as well because the concept reflects Christ's role as the head and representative of all his spiritual offspring in and from the covenant of grace. Thus, Gill affirms, "all the promises made, manifested, and applied to Abraham, and his spiritual seed was originally made to Christ, the everlasting Father of his spiritual offspring, the common Head and Parent of them."[88]

Adam and Christ

According to Gill, the role of Jesus Christ as the head and representative according to the *pactum* is not confined by the corporate solidarity notion in the seed of Abraham; it is also depicted in the parallel between Adam and Christ as the federal headship in a more detailed picture of the two contrasting figures.[89] The headship is closely linked to the concept of representative: in other words, Adam is the representative of all his natural offspring, and Christ is the representative of all the spiritual offspring. The apostle Paul manifestly articulates the typological relationship between Adam and Christ in Romans 5:12-21 and 1 Corinthians 15:45, 47.

The apostle Paul avers, "He [Adam] is the type of the Coming one" in Romans 5:14. In what sense is Adam the type of the coming Christ? Karl Barth sees the Adam and Christ typology from the perspective of "the fundamental truth of anthropology"; in other words, "the relationship between

---

and that that family consists of the Messiah and his people." N. T. Wright, *Galatians*, Commentaries for Christian Formation (Grand Rapids: Eerdmans, 2021), 223-24. He did already mention the concept of 'a single family' in Galatians 3:16. See Wright, *The Climax of the Covenant*, 163. While Wright's notion of 'corporate' and 'representative' in the seed concept is accepted in connection with 3:29, Paul clearly says that the promises were made to Abraham and to his seed, i.e., "and to your seed," who is Christ. Thus, primarily the seed is Christ, not a single family. Thus, to acknowledge both collective and individual idea of the seed considered not just by grammatical matter but also through the theological interpretation, makes the concept of corporate solidarity.

88. Gill, *Divinity: Book II*, 63.

89. Gill, *Divinity: Book II*, 64. In his other writing, Gill mentions Adam and Christ as the federal heads, "as such it [a covenant of works] was made with *Adam*, the federal head of all his posterity, in which he was a figure and type of the Messiah that was to come, the covenant-head of his spiritual offspring. This covenant *Adam* broke, and all his posterity in him; and so he conveyed sin and death to them, from which there is no deliverance but by Christ the second *Adam*." Gill, "Sermon XVII: The Law in the Hand of Christ," in *A Collection of Sermons and Tracts*, 1:279. Emphasis original; also, see Gill, "Sermon XIII: The Law Established by the Gospel," in *A Collection of Sermons and Tracts*, 1:211-12.

Adam and us reveals not the primary but only the secondary anthropological truth and ordering principle." Rather, Barth continues,

> The primary anthropological truth and ordering principle, which only mirrors itself in that relationship, is made clear only through the relationship between Christ and us.... Man's essential and original nature is to be found, therefore, not in Adam but in Christ. In Adam we can only find it prefigured. Adam can therefore be interpreted only in the light of Christ and not the other way round.[90]

Barth, implying that the structural frame of the two worlds of Adam and Christ is similar though the internal character of each world is utterly different, denotes, "The relationship that existed between Adam and us is, according to v. 12, the relationship that exists originally and essentially between Christ and us."[91] Robert Peterson, in the same line with Barth, uses a slightly different term to describe the meaning of "the type of the Coming one," that is, "a covenant head."[92] Aaron Son also describes Adam and Christ as corporate persons, "Paul understands Adam and Christ not only

---

90. Karl Barth, *Christ and Adam: Man and Humanity in Romans 5*, trans. T. A. Smail (New York: Harper and Brothers, 1956), 29.

91. Barth, *Christ and Adam*, 30. Herman Ridderbos adds, "Adam and Christ here stand over against each other as the two great figures at the entrance of two worlds, two aeons, two 'creations,' the old and the new; and in their actions and fate lies the decision for all who belong to them, because these are comprehended in them and thus are reckoned either to death or to life. This is now expressed by 'in Adam' and 'in Christ.' And it is therefore in this sense that Adam can be called the type of him who was to come." Herman Ridderbos, *Paul: An Outline of His Theology*, trans. John Richard De Witt, Paperback edition (1975; Grand Rapids: Eerdmans, 1997), 60-61.

92. Robert A. Peterson, *Salvation Accomplished by the Son: The Work of Christ* (Wheaton: Crossway, 2012), 472. Peterson writes, "Adam and Christ are the two covenant heads of their respective races. Adam is the covenant head of all humankind; Christ the covenant head of the race of the redeemed. Though Eve sinned first, she is not mentioned in Romans 5 or 1 Corinthians 15. Instead, Adam is. He stands for humankind, and his fall is the fall of the race" (472-73). Gentry and Wellum, emphasizing that the "typological patterns of Scripture are developed through the progression of the covenants," indicates, "Adam, as the covenant head of the old creation, anticipates and looks forward to the coming of the 'last Adam,' our Lord Jesus, who is the head of the new covenant." Then, they mention "other Adams," e.g., Noah, Abraham, Israel, and David, who come on the historical stage of the progressive and developed covenants until the last Adam who can accomplish the first Adam's role comes out. Gentry and Wellum, *Kingdom through Covenant*, 657, 658. Gordon Fee considers Adam and Christ as the forerunners of each respective initiation, "there is considerable emphasis on Adam and Christ as standing at the *beginning of something*. For Paul they are the progenitors of the two creations, a fallen one that has issued in sin and death and a new one that has been issued in by crucifixion and resurrection." Gordon D. Fee, *Jesus the Lord according to Paul the Apostle: A Concise Introduction* (Grand Rapids: Baker, 2018), 55.

as two great individuals but also as corporate beings in whom the whole humanity is included, the old humanity in Adam and the new humanity in Christ."[93] Interpreting 1 Corinthians 15:22, Earle Ellis, stressing "all in Adam die" and "all in Christ shall be made alive," shows how the parallel between Adam and Christ works, "the Apostle expresses the most comprehensive human solidarity as one that embraces in two groups the whole of humanity, man-in-Adam and man-in-Christ. In designating two 'Adams,' he identifies two worlds or societies made up of those who belong to the one or to the other . . . "[94]

Each explanation above manifests through the redemptive history of the whole Scripture that Adam is the head and representative of the natural seed of the world; Christ is the head and representative of all the spiritual seed in the grand scheme of the *pactum*. Gill finally confirms Adam and Christ as,

> heads and representatives of their respective offspring: Adam, through his fall, conveying sin and death to all his natural descendants; and Christ, through the free gift of himself, communicating grace, righteousness, and life to all his spiritual seed, the elect, the children his Father gave him: and hence these two are spoken of as the first and last Adam, and the first and second man; as if they were the only two men in the world, being the representatives of each of their seeds, which are included in them.[95]

Christ as the Mediator of the Covenant[96]

The idea of the mediator presupposes that there is a disharmony between two parties: God and man, i.e., God and the elect. Thus, the matter of the mediator introduces the whole discussion into the concept of reconciliation between God and the elect.[97] The Scripture manifestly demonstrates that

---

93. Son, *Corporate Elements in Pauline Anthropology*, 61.
94. Ellis, *Pauline Theology*, 10.
95. Gill, *Divinity: Book II*, 64.
96. See chapter VIII, Of Christ the Mediator in Westminster Assembly, *The Westminster Confession of Faith: Edinburgh Edition*, 51-52; also, see article XVII in Thomas Monck et al., "An Orthodox Creed," 153. The Baptist London Confession of Faith in 1689 follows the Westminster Confession in terms of the 'Of Christ the Mediator' in chapter VIII.
97. Gill sees "the elect of God are considered in the covenant of grace as fallen creatures"; thus, they need Christ as "being a mediator of reconciliation and satisfaction for

"Christ is the mediator" between "the offended party" and "the offending party," as the apostle Paul writes in 1 Timothy 2:5, "For there is one God and one mediator between God and mankind, the man Christ Jesus."[98] Gill figures out the truth of the mediatorship of Christ in Hebrews 8:6 and gives an essential abstract of the whole biblical and theological discourse on the mediatorship:

> Christ is the Mediator between God and man, a middle person between both, being both God and man, the days-man, who lays his hands on both; who brings men to God that were afar off, and makes peace for them by the blood of his cross, and satisfies the justice of God, which he has done by the sacrifice of himself; and now appears in the presence of God for them, and intercedes for them, and applies the blessings of the covenant to them by his spirit, and keeps and preserves them safe to his everlasting kingdom.[99]

Thus, based on Gill's basic and foundational concept of Christ's mediatorship, as explained above, the last section of this chapter will delve into the two significant points regarding Christ as the mediator of the covenant of grace: Christ's mediation and the fitness of Christ as the mediator of the covenant of grace.

Christ's Mediation

Gill's first question is, "in what sense Christ is the mediator of the covenant."[100] Gill answers, "Christ is a mediator of reconciliation," whose implication includes the flow of the biblical redemptive history, i.e., innocence, fall, and restoration. Reconciliation, in Gill's expression, "supposes a former state of friendship, a breach of that friendship, and a renewal of it; or a bringing into open friendship again."[101] In other words, due to the entrance of sin into the

---

them." Gill, *Divinity: Book II*, 65.

98. Gill, *Divinity: Book II*, 65.

99. Gill, *An Exposition of the New Testament*, 3:424.

100. Gill, *Divinity: Book II*, 65.

101. Gill, Divinity: Book II, 65. An English independent minister, William Bridge (1600-1670) before Gill used the similar terms and made the same points concerning the proper work of a mediator, "It is to make peace and reconciliation between God and us. At the first, in the state of innocency, there was peace and friendship between God and Man, . . . but upon the Fall, a breach and separation was made between God and us, insomuch as we are all by Nature the children of wrath, God is angry . . . Now therefore, the work of a Mediator is to reconcile God to us, and to reconcile us unto God." William Bridge, *Christ and the Covenant the Work and Way of Meditation: Gods Return to the*

world by the first man, Adam's rebellion, offense comes into existence in the holistic person of man, which inevitably creates a rupture between the holy God and sinful man. Thus, reconciliation in the critical separation demands a mediator; so, "Christ acts as the mediator by proposing to his Father to satisfy the offense committed and appease injured justice. . . . this is what was proposed in covenant, and what he therein agreed to do, and therefore is called the mediator of the covenant."[102]

The second crucial thought concerning the reconciliation through Christ's mediation comes with the love of God. Namely, Christ's being the mediator to satisfy the justice of God is "the fruit and effect" of God's love.[103] The love of God in the eternal and sovereign will of God is "from everlasting to everlasting, invariably the same: with him, there is no shadow of turning; there is no change in God, as not from love to hatred, so not from hatred to love; he is in one mind, and none can turn him, no, not Christ himself."[104]

Soul, or Nation; Together with his Preventing Mercy (London: Printed for N. Ranew, and J. Robinson at the Angel in Jewen-Street, 1667), 83.

102. Gill, *Divinity: Book II*, 65. The relation of Christ's being the mediator to the everlasting covenant is also found in Gill's other writings: "Christ was set up from everlasting, as the Mediator of this covenant: his goings forth, and acting therein, on the behalf of his people, were of old, from everlasting." Gill, "The Doctrine of Justification by the Righteousness of Christ: Stated and Maintained," in *A Collection of Sermons and Tracks*, 3:169; also, see "he loved his people from eternity, is manifest from his engaging as a Surety for them; his becoming the Mediator of an everlasting covenant; in which he agreed to take care of their persons, and by dying to redeem their lives from destruction, and to bring them to eternal glory." John Gill, *An Exposition of the Book of Solomon's Song; Commonly Called Canticles* (London: William Hill Collingridge, 1854), 14. More clear remark of Gill on the *pactum* and Christ's being mediator is shown in a sermon delivered at the ordination of John Reynolds. Long, it is worth citing the whole words, "The doctrine of the covenant of grace is to be held fast, made between the eternal three, when there were none in being but themselves; no creature, neither an angel, nor a man, nor the soul of a man; none but God, Father, Son and Spirit, between whom and them alone the covenant-transactions were; even before the world was, or any creature whatever in being, hence it is called an *everlasting covenant*, being from everlasting; as well as it will continue to everlasting; which appears from Christ's being set up so early as the mediator of it, from the provision of blessings of grace in it so early, which were given to the elect in Christ, and they were blessed with them in him before the world was; and from promises made in it so early, particularly the promise of *eternal life, which God, that cannot lie, promised before the world began*." Gill, "Sermon XL: The Form of sound Words to be held fast," in *A Collection of Sermons and Tracks*, 2:58-59. Emphasis original.

103. Gill, *Divinity: Book II*, 66.

104. Gill, *Divinity: Book II*, 66. Gill gets this idea from 1 John 4:10, "Love consists in this: not that we loved God, but that he loved us and sent his Son to be the atoning sacrifice for our sins." See Gill's explanation in Gill, *An Exposition of the New Testament*, 3:647. That the mediation of Christ is the fruit and effect is also proved by other biblical passages, e.g., John 3:16; Rom 5:8, which reads respectively, "For God loved the world

Therefore, Gill asserts that the mediating work of Christ does not change the will of God to love his people because God loves the elect from everlasting to everlasting. The reconciliation through the work of Christ's mediation is not to gain the love of God but to satisfy the justice of God because the love and affection of God are never separated from his people.[105] The immutable love of God wills the restoration of his elect people, which results,

> Christ interposed, and offered himself in the covenant, to be a Mediator of reconciliation, or to make satisfaction for sin; and so mercy and truth have met together, and righteousness and peace have kissed each other. Reconciliation then is the principal branch of Christ's office in the covenant as Mediator.[106]

The Fitness of Christ as the Mediator

The second point Gill makes for Christ's being the mediator of the covenant of grace pertains to the essential requirement that the mediator between God and man must be a God-man; in other words, the mediator must be fully God and fully man. Moreover, Gill notes that Jesus Christ, not just having both natures in his person, should have a necessary but mysterious relationship between the two natures in himself: "the principal fitness of Christ for his office, as Mediator, at least for the execution of it, lies in the union of the two natures, human and divine, in his one Person."[107]

The matter of Christ's two natures in one person has always provoked or stirred up Christianity as one of the most important issues in Christian history. A key reason for that, except for the trinitarian controversies, is the person of Jesus Christ, with special regard to the notions of the hypostatic union and *communicatio idiomatum*, becomes the fundamental ground in building up the utmost principles with regard to man's salvation.[108] The

---

in this way: He gave his one and only Son . . ." "God proves his own love for us in that while we were still sinners, Christ died for us."

105. Gill, *Divinity: Book II*, 66.

106. Gill, *Divinity: Book II*, 66.

107. Gill, *Divinity: Book II*, 67. For a theological concept of the two terms, nature and person, with respect to the person of Christ, see Stephen Wellum, *The Person of Christ: An Introduction*, Short Studies in Systematic Theology (Wheaton: Crossway, 2021), 186-87; also, see Garrett J. DeWeese, "One Person, Two Natures: Two Metaphysical Models of the Incarnation," in *Jesus in Trinitarian Perspective: An Intermediate Christology* by Fred Sanders and Klaus Issler (Nashville: B&H, 2007), 114-53.

108. Craig Blaising explains the hypostatic union, "In the incarnation of the Son of God, a human nature was inseparably united forever with the divine nature in the one person of Jesus Christ, yet with the two natures remaining distinct, whole, and

work of Christ as the mediator of the covenant, therefore, puts its basis on the unique feature of the person of Christ. Before a further examination of Christ's two natures in one person, it deserves a mention of the creed of Chalcedon (AD 451) in its entirety, which is inextricably linked to both Christological concepts, i.e., the hypostatic union and *communicatio idiomatum*:

> Following, then, the holy fathers, we unite in teaching all men to confess the one and only Son, our Lord Jesus Christ. This selfsame one is perfect both in deity and also in human-ness; this selfsame one is also actually God and actually man, with a rational soul and a body. He is of the same reality [*homoousion*] as we are ourselves as far as his human-ness is concerned; thus like us in all respects, sin only excepted. Before time began he was begotten of the Father, in respect of his deity, and now in these "last days," for us and on behalf of our salvation, this selfsame one was born of Mary the virgin, who is God-bearer [*theotokos*] in respect of his human-ness.
>
> [We also teach] that we apprehend this one and only Christ-Son, Lord, only-begotten–in two natures; without confusing the two natures, without transmuting one nature into the other, without dividing them into two separate categories, without contrasting them according to area or function. The distinctiveness of each nature is not nullified by the union. Instead, the "properties" of each nature are conserved and both natures concur in one "person" [*prosōpon*] and in one hypostatsis. They are not divided or cut into two "persons" [*prosōpa*], but are together the one and only and only-begotten *Logos* of God, the Lord Jesus Christ. Thus have the prophets of old testified; thus the Lord Jesus Christ himself taught us; thus the Symbol of the Fathers has handed down to us.[109]

---

unchanged, without mixture or confusion, so that the one person, Jesus Christ, is truly God and truly man." Craig A. Blaising, "Hypostatic Union," in *Evangelical Dictionary of Theology*, 583. The *communicatio idiomatum* means that "whatever can be attributed to (said about) either the divine or the human nature in Christ is to be attributed to the entire person. Whatever is true of either nature is true of the person. This is only a detailed discussion of the fact that Jesus Christ is one person, not two. It does not add to the statement that the God-man is one person." John M. Drickamer, "Communication of Attributes, Communicatio Idiomatum," in *Evangelical Dictionary of Theology*, 277.

109. The whole statement is cited from Daniel L. Akin, "The Person of Christ," in *A Theology for the Church*, 426. Emphasis original. Akin continues to mention that "the creed of Chalcedon sought to summarize and address every problem that had plagued the church with regard to the person of Christ"; e.g., Docetism, Adoptionism, Modalism, Arianism, Apollinarianism, Nestorianism, and Eutychianism. See Akin, "The Person of Christ," 426-27. Akin proves the importance of the creed of Chalcedon

1. *Christ as Man.* Deep concern for the phrase "You prepared a body for me" in Hebrews 10:5, indicating Christ's incarnation, drives Gill to affirm that "the Father prepared a body, an human nature in his purpose, council, and covenant, for another, and not for himself, even for his Son, as he acknowledges"[110] When the time comes to completion, the Holy Spirit makes the virgin birth of the second person of the Trinity feasible by assuming "human nature into union with his divine Person, even a true body, and a reasonable soul."[111] In other words, a body has a significant meaning to all three divine persons in both realms from eternity to time. Why are the Father, Son, and Holy Spirit so firmly concerned with a human body with regard to man's salvation, in particular, Christ's being a body?[112] Gill provides three reasons.

First, the right to be a redeemer, mediator, and Savior of people, says Gill, might be "their brother, their near kinsman" according to the law.[113] Gill brings Leviticus 25:48-49 as a proof text regarding who has the right to be a redeemer of one's kinsman, relative, and the same people. Leviticus 25:47 introduces an incident in which one of the Israelites is in debt to a foreigner and is unable to pay for it, so he must sell himself and even his

---

in terms of the hypostatic union of two natures in one person by listing and showing various related heresies that attack either deity or humanity of Jesus Christ. Lucas Stamps also, after enumerating the same christological heresies' concepts, sums up, "Chalcedon laid down the coordinates for the orthodox doctrine of the incarnation: true God (against the created Son of the Arians), true man (against the partial incarnation of the Apollinarians), two distinct natures (against the merged nature of the Eutychians), and one united person (against the divided persons of the Nestorians)." R. Lucas Stamps, "Baptists, Classic Christology, and the Christian Tradition," in *Baptist and the Christian Tradition: Towards an Evangelical Baptist Catholicity*, ed. Matthew Y. Emerson, Christopher W. Morgan, and R. Lucas Stamps (Nashville: B&H, 2020), 89; also, see Gill, *Divinity: Book V*, 8-19; Harwood, *Christian Theology*, 410-15. Though this creed of Chalcedon was formulated to advocate the biblical truth that Jesus Christ is fully God and fully man in one person, it does not explain us how the mystery of the hypostatic union of the two natures in the second person of the Trinity identify itself in description. Craig Carter clarifies, "Does Chalcedon explain how this [Christ's being fully God and fully man] can be so? No, it has a different purpose. The purpose of the Chalcedonian Definition is to define our confession, not to define the God-Man. What does Holy Scripture require us to say about Jesus Christ? . . . It ensures that we confess the totality of biblical revelation about Jesus Christ, but it never presumes to explain the 'how' of the hypostatic union." Carter, *Contemplating God with the Great Tradition*, 82.

110. Gill, *Divinity: Book V*, 8.

111. Gill, *Divinity: Book II*, 67.

112. For the details and proofs concerning Christ's genuine human nature and the theological significance of incarnation, see Garrett, *Systematic Theology*, 1:621-24; Thomas F. Torrance, *Incarnation: The Person and Life of Christ*, ed. Robert T. Walker (Downers Grove: IVP, 2008), 37-104.

113. Gill, *Divinity: Book II*, 67.

family to the foreigner. In that situation, verses 48-49 read, "he has the right of redemption after he has been sold. One of his brothers may redeem him. His uncle or cousin may redeem him, or any of his close relatives from his clan may redeem him. If he prospers, he may redeem himself."[114] God's becoming a man in the second person of the Trinity, assuming human nature as the same property of his creation, is demanded to fulfill the justice of the law of God. In order to make a close relation with man even further, to be one of them, God became a kinsman, relative, and the same blood of a human being.[115] In the exposition of Leviticus 25:49, Gill interprets the verse in relation to Christ's assuming human nature for man's salvation,

> Indeed the whole of this case is applicable to the spiritual and eternal redemption of the people of God by Christ: they through the fall, and in a state of nature, are become poor and helpless, and in a spiritual sense have neither bread to eat, nor clothes to wear, nor money to buy either; and are in debt, owe ten thousand talents, and have nothing to pay, and so are brought into bondage to sin, Satan, and the law; nor can they redeem themselves from these by power or price; nor can a brother, or the nearest relation redeem them, or give to God a ransom for them; none but Christ could do this for them, who through his incarnation, whereby he became of the same nature, of the same flesh and blood with them, and in all things like unto them, is their *goel*, and so their Redeemer, and has obtained eternal redemption for them, not with silver and gold, but by his own precious blood.[116]

Secondly, Christ assumes that human nature, being fully man, is a prerequisite to being capable of obeying the law and suffering death. Christ

---

114. "From whence it appears, that it must be a near kinsman that has to be the redeemer, as in another case, the redemption of inheritances; hence the same word *goel* signifies both a redeemer and a near kinsman." Gill, *An Exposition of the Old Testament*, 1:690. Regarding the scope of the redeemer, Christopher Wright notes, "The whole clan had the duty of preserving its constituent families and their inherited land." Christopher J. H. Wright, *Walking in the Ways of the Lord: The Ethical Authority of the Old Testament* (Downers Grove: IVP, 1995), 205; also, see Jacob Milgrom, *Leviticus 23-27: A New Translation with Introduction and Commentary*, The Anchor Bible, vol. 3B (New York: Doubleday, 2001), 2237-38.

115. To be the same nature with man is to follow the God's arranged principle for man to be redeemed according to the Scripture. Christ had to be a human being who is with blood to make atonement for the sin of his people. It is because the Scripture says, "For the life of a creature is in the blood, and I have appointed it to you to make atonement on the altar for your lives, since it is the lifeblood that makes atonement" (Lev 17:11), and "According to the law almost everything is purified with blood, and without the shedding of blood there is no forgiveness" (Heb 9:22).

116. Gill, *An Exposition of the Old Testament*, 1:690.

The Doctrine of Jesus Christ According to John Gill

"as a divine Person could not be subject to the law, and yield obedience to it; and had he assumed the angelic nature, that would not have been capable of obeying all the precepts of the law, which are required of men."[117] Thus, Christ was "born of a woman, born under the law, to redeem those under the law," which means that Christ came in the flesh under the law not as a teacher or encourager to urge his people to keep the law but as the one who fulfills the whole law by putting himself on the cross for the sake of his people.[118] Gill denotes the meaning of "born under the law,"

> since he [Christ] was the principal end of it [the law], in whom it centres, and for whose sake it was made; and that he might completely fulfill it, and by so doing put a period to it: and he was made under the moral law, both as a man and the surety of his people, and *was subject to all the precepts of it, and bore the penalty of it, death, in their room and stead, and thereby fulfilled it*, and delivered them from its curse and condemnation.[119]

---

117. Gill, *Divinity: Book II*, 68.

118. The quotation is from Galatians 4:4-5. Regarding the sense of obedience to the law, Thomas Blanton argues from the interpretation of Matthew 1:21, "(Jesus) will save his people from their sin," that because sin can be defined as not observing the Torah, Jesus came to teach his people the Torah and encourage them to observe it to be saved. Blanton, asserting Jesus's advocacy of Torah observance in the Gospel of Matthew, sums up, "Jesus 'saves his people from their sins' not primarily by forgiving sin or by his death on the cross but by exhorting his audience to follow the Torah with perfect obedience." Thomas R. Blanton IV, "Saved by Obedience: Matthew 1:21 in Light of Jesus' Teaching on the Torah," *Journal of Biblical Literature* 132, no. 2 (2013): 393. However, Paul clearly articulates in his writing to the churches to the Galatia, "For all who rely on the works of the law are under a curse, because it is written, 'Everyone who does not do everything written in the book of the law is cursed.' Now it is clear that no one is justified before God by the law, because 'The righteous will live by faith'" (Gal 3:10-11). Daniel Kirk is also on the same page with Paul on this issue, "Humanity cannot be justified by the law, not simply because we as fallen people cannot fulfill its precepts, but also, and even more importantly, because we see that even the One who lived perfectly (a) saved us through his death rather than through the law, and (b) was himself cursed rather than blessed by the law." J. R. Daniel Kirk, "The Sufficiency of the Cross (I): The Crucifixion as Jesus' Act of Obedience," *Scottish Bulletin of Evangelical Theology* 24, no. 1 (Spring 2006): 40. For more relation between law and gospel, see Greg L. Bahnsen et al., *Five Views on Law and Gospel* (Grand Rapids: Zonderan, 1999).

119. Gill, *An Exposition of the New Testament*, 3:28. Emphasis added. Brian Rosner investigates the sense of 'under the law' as "can be equivalent to being 'under the penalty and power of sin', and is thus something from which Jews need to be released (and something to which being under grace can be favourably contrasted)." Rosner continues, while delving into Leviticus 18:5, to say that "For Paul, the essence of the law as law-covenant or legal code is its call for something to be done in order to find life, and this path has failed, due to the universal sinfulness of humanity." As a conclusion and summary of the section, Rosner writes, "Even though the law promises life to those who keep it, it is evident that no one keeps the law. Consequently, no one

As seen above, Christ's ultimate accomplishment as a mediator in obedience to the law is fulfilled by the suffering death. The subsequent outcome of Christ's suffering death on the cross proves that the second divine person of the Trinity assumed human nature and became a real man. It is because "as God he could not die, and had he assumed the nature of an angel, that is uncapable of dying," he could not die the suffering death with "shedding blood ... without which he could not be made sin, and a curse for men, as the law required he should."[120] Gill, reasoning that "God should make the pioneer of their salvation perfect through suffering" in Hebrews 2:10, appeals to 2:14 for the legitimacy of Christ's being a man: "Now since the children have flesh and blood in common, Jesus also shared in these, so that through his death he might destroy the one holding the power of death–that is, the devil."[121]

---

receives life through the law. The law used as law is for the lawless. Christ has abolished the law with its commandments and ordinances." Brian S. Rosner, *Paul and the Law: Keeping the Commandments of God*, NSBT (Downers Grove: IVP, 2013), 48, 72, 81. Gill also compares Adam to Christ in terms of obedience. Romans 5:19 reads, "For just as through one man's disobedience the many were made sinners, so also through the one man's obedience the many will be made righteous." Gill clarifies that this obedience to be made righteous is "not by their own obedience, nor by their own obedience and Christ's together; but by his [Christ's] sole and single obedience to the law of God." Gill, *An Exposition of the New Testament*, 2:456. This simple but profound comparison denotes that the first actual man Adam is compared to the second or last actual man Jesus Christ in functioning as the representatives of the people group respectively. Jesus was an actual man who was able to obey the law as an actual man Adam disobeyed and was against the will of God. Frame says, "Jesus came in the flesh, to be a true man, as Adam was a true man. Like Adam and Adam's descendants, Jesus lived in a body that was made of dust, part of the creation." Frame, *Systematic Theology*, 883.

120. Gill, *Divinity: Book II*, 68.

121. From the interpretation of Hebrews 2, Wellum denotes, "Unless the Son took upon himself our humanity and suffered for us, there would be no suffering to help humanity, no fulfillment of God's promises for humanity, and no return to the planned glory of humanity. Jesus's suffering and death, then, was not a failed end to the incarnation but the precise purpose of the incarnation, all of which fulfills the Creator-Covenant Lord's plan to perfect a new humanity to rule over his good creation." Stephen J. Wellum, *God the Son Incarnate: The Doctrine of Christ*, Foundations of Evangelical Theology Series (Wheaton: Crossway, 2016), 221. Frame also answers the question why it was necessary for Christ to become flesh, "His work is to bring sacrifice to God on behalf of men. As we will see, Jesus' sacrifice, fulfilling all sacrifices, was the sacrifice of his own perfect flesh, bearing the death that we all deserved. For that work, it was necessary, except for sin." Frame, *Systematic Theology*, 884. Gill asserts regarding Christ's assuming a human nature, "Christ's participation of human nature, and the children's, in some things agree, in others they differ, they agree in this, that it is real flesh and blood they both partake of; that Christ's body is not spiritual and heavenly, but natural as theirs is; and that it is a complete, perfect, human nature, and subject to mortality and infirmity like theirs: but then Christ took his nature of a virgin, and is without

Third and lastly, a holy and righteous body is required to satisfy the justice of God and offer oneself to God without spot, which is one of the reasons why Christ, the divine person, must assume human nature.[122] The author of Hebrews, recognizing Christ being able to be the guarantee of a better covenant because of his permanent and eternal holding of the priesthood, asserts that "it was indeed fitting that we should have such a high priest, holy, innocent, unstained, separated from sinners, and exalted above the heavens" (7:26, ESV). The apostle John stresses that "Jesus Christ the righteous one," being the propitiation for the sins of his people, "was revealed so that he might take away sins," and emphasizes, "there is no sin in him" (1 John 2:1, 3:5). Gill mentions, "such an one [holy by nature; being typified by the high priest] becomes us, for had he not been holy he could not have entered into the holy place for us, or have appeared there on our account."[123] Gill continues to say, however, "It was not enough to be truly man, and an innocent person; he must be more than a man, to be a mediator between God and man."[124] Jesus Christ, the second person of the Trinity, is Lord and God.

---

sin; nor has it any distinct personality, but from the moment of its being subsisted in his divine person: and now the true reason of Christ's assuming such a nature was on account of the children, which discovers great love to them, and shews that it was with a peculiar view to them that he became man; hence they only share the special advantages of his incarnation, sufferings, and death: and his end in doing this was, *that through death he might destroy him that had the power of death, that is, the devil.*" Gill, *An Exposition of the New Testament*, 3:385. Whitney Gamble in understanding of the Westminster Confession of faith gives a summing-up word on Christ's obedience in his work of redemption, "Christ as mediator came under the law and perfectly fulfilled it. Christ's active obedience to the law during His life and His passive obedience of enduring the cross fully discharged the debt of 'all those that are thus justified, and did make a proper, real and full satisfaction to His Father's justice in their behalf.'" Whitney G. Gamble, *Christ and the Law: Antinomianism at the Westminster Assembly*, Studies on the Westminster Assembly (Grand Rapids: Reformation Heritage Books, 2018), 141.

122. Gill, *Divinity: Book II*, 68.

123. Gill, *An Exposition of the New Testament*, 3:420. Athanasius in his writing, one of the most important apologetic writings on the incarnation, describes, "He did not will simply to become embodies, or merely to appear; for He might, if He willed simply to appear, as well have made His Divine Manifestation through some other and more excellent method: but He took our body, and not simply so, but from a spotless and stainless virgin, knowing not a man–a body pure and truly untarnished by intercourse with men." Athanasius of Alexandria, *On the Incarnation of the Word of God*, trans. T. Herbert Bindley, Second Edition Revised (London: The Religious Track Society, 1903), 56. The incarnation, therefore, with the doctrine of the Trinity, is the very mystery among God's marvelous works. The holiness and righteousness of Christ free from all sin could be kept, even in assuming a human nature, through the virgin conception by the work of the Holy Spirit.

124. Gill, *Divinity: Book II*, 68.

2. *Christ as God.* Gill perceives Christ's works as a mediator of the covenant of grace by two senses in accordance with his two natures. One pertains to Christ's actual existence of human nature, which is required, as aforementioned, in order to accomplish some works as a mediator, i.e., being a kinsman, obeying the law, and suffering death. The other is related to Christ's divinity through which some specific works can be performed without the actual human existence.[125] Below, we will focus on Christ's mediating works as God.

First, Christ as God can "draw nigh to God, and treat with him about terms of peace, and covenant with him; all which a mere man could not do."[126] This idea of an internal and intimate relationship between the Father and the Son only happens in eternity, which is closely connected with the *pactum* itself, i.e., the covenant of redemption for his people. The council is only allowed between the divine persons as Gill quotes the word of the Lord through the prophet Jeremiah while promising the restoration for Israel and Judah, saying, "Jacob's leader will be one of them; his ruler will issue from him. I will invite him to me, and he will approach me. *Who would otherwise risk his life by approaching me?* This is the Lord's declaration" (30:21).[127] There is no one who can access the divine and holy God so as to make a covenant and to bring reconciliation to man except for Jesus Christ, the second divine person of the Trinity, only "Jehovah's fellow could or dared to do this."[128]

Secondly, Christ's existence and status as God grants a theological meaning to the mediating works of Christ as a man; namely, Christ's

---

125. Gill, *Divinity: Book II*, 71.

126. Gill, *Divinity: Book II*, 68. In this regard, it is correct to say that with Christ as man, "Christ *represents God* to humanity, and *represents humanity* to God." Thiselton, *Systematic Theology*, 252.

127. Emphasis added. Gill supports that Christ's divinity only works as mediation for the redemption of his people in relation to the Father, "his [Christ's] drawing to God *in the council and covenant of grace*, to be surety of his people, and his undertaking for them, were quite free and voluntary; he came of himself, and surrendered himself into the hands of justice at the time of his sufferings and death; and *his intercession in heaven flows from his hearty love to his people; his heart has been, and is, engaged in every branch of his mediatorial work*, which is a very singular and wonderful thing. No mere man could have engaged his heart to draw nigh to God, who is a consuming fire; no angel in heaven could have presumed to have done it on the behalf of sinful men; none but Christ himself could, and which is owing to the dignity of his person, and to his wondrous love." Gill, *An Exposition of the Old Testament*, 5:567. Emphasis added. Gill through this expression in Jeremiah 30:21 makes sure that the mediating work between God and man can only be done by Christ who is fully man and fully God, neither mere man, nor an angel.

128. Gill, *Divinity: Book II*, 68.

divinity invests his works of obedience and sufferings as man with "virtue and value."[129] Below is Gill's further explanation:

> For if he had been a mere man, his obedience and righteousness would not have been sufficient to justify men, nor his sufferings and death a proper sacrifice and atonement for sin. But being God as well as man, his righteousness is the righteousness of God; and so sufficient to justify all that believe in him, and them from all their sins; and *his blood is the blood of the Son of God*, and so cleanses from all sin, and is a proper atonement for it.[130]

Citing Hebrews 5:8, which reads, "Although he was the Son, he learned obedience from what he suffered," Gill recognizes that one can perceive Christ's both natures in his obedience by sufferings and death on the cross. Christ himself, the Son of God, learned obedience through suffering, which implies that the suffering does not just remain as the judgment without hope to be saved. Because the one who suffered and died on the cross is the Son of God, the divine person, the sufferings are not mere sufferings any longer but *virtued and valued* sufferings and death, which can be offered up to the Father by his eternal Spirit to satisfy his justice of God.[131] Knowing the truth of the mystery of the two natures in the person of Jesus Christ, therefore, Paul could vouch and affirm " . . . the church of God, which he purchased with his own blood" (Acts 20:28). God purchased his church with his own blood. Does God as a spirit have blood?[132] Gill explains, "The

---

129. Gill, *Divinity: Book II*, 68.

130. Gill, *Divinity: Book II*, 68. Emphasis added.

131. "Through sufferings he became obedient to death, even the death of the cross: and this he learnt; not that he was ignorant of the nature of it; nor was he destitute of an obedient disposition to it; but the meaning is, he had an experience of it, and effected it; and which was voluntary, and done in our room and stead." Gill, *An Exposition of the New Testament*, 3:400.

132. Regarding the issue, see Charles F. Devine who investigates the blood of God indicating the divinity of Christ in "The 'blood of God' in Acts 20:28," *The Catholic Biblical Quarterly* 9, no. 4 (October 1947): 381-408; William J. Larkin, *Acts*, IVP New Testament Commentary Series 5 (Downers Grove: IVP, 1995), 296; John D. Harvey and David Gentino, *Acts: A Commentary for Biblical Preaching and Teaching*, Kerux Commentaries (Grand Rapids: Kregel, 2023), 452; also, Wellum denotes, "God does not have blood to shed. But what is true of his human nature is also true of God the Son incarnate. Thus, we must confess that God the Son died." Wellum, *God the Son Incarnate*, 438. Brian Vickers gives a warning that this expression may lead some to the interpretation of patripassianism: "Paul is not making a Trinitarian assertion about the blood of the Father, much less offering a foundation for the suffering of the Father-what later theologians referred to as patripassianism, an error made by Praxeas in the third century, as well as many others. That error is linked to ancient and related heresies known as modalism, Sabellianism, and Monarchianism. Modern versions of

purchase price, or the price of redemption, is his precious blood, his blood as man; but what gave virtue to that blood, and made it a sufficient ransom price, is, that it was the blood of him that is God as well as man."[133] Such an interpretation of the blood of God and Gill's concept of virtue and value affecting the works of Christ as man presuppose the unique mechanism of *communicatio idiomatum* in the hypostatic union of Christ's two natures. Treier, linking the last section of Acts 20:28 to the notion of *communicatio idiomatum*, indicates, "redemption is attributed to God, in the person of the Son, while, properly speaking, the blood is attributed to him by virtue of his human nature."[134]

It is the reason why Gill deals with the christological principle as the next topic in the discourse of Christ, the mediator of the covenant of grace. Later, Gill puts this concept in the incarnation of Christ in Book V of *Divinity* concretely, saying,

> A communication of idioms, or properties, as the ancients express it; that is, of the properties of each nature; which are, in common, predicated of the Person of Christ, by virtue of the union of natures in it; for though each nature retains its peculiar properties, and does not communicate them to each other; yet they may be predicated of the Person of Christ.[135]

Richard Muller also gives a typical understanding of the Reformed Christology of *communicatio idiomatum*: "The two natures are here considered as joined in the person, and the interchange of attributes is understood

---

this ancient heresy are found in various 'oneness' theologies.... Such a view does not stand up under the scrutiny of the rest of the NT, even if Acts 20:28 is offered in support of it. The rest of Paul's teaching makes clear that the 'blood' through which the church was obtained was the blood of Jesus." Brian J. Vickers, "The Acts of the Apostles," in *Expository Commentary, Vol. IX: John–Acts* (Wheaton: Crossway, 2019), 526-27.

133. Patrick Schreiner based on 1 Peter 1:19 says, "The blood indicates an infinite and precious cost." Schreiner, *Acts*, 554. Gill adds why it deserves 'an infinite and precious cost': "which being the blood not only of a pure and innocent man, but of one that is truly and properly God as well as man, was a sufficient ransom-price to redeem the church and people of God from sin, the law, its curse and condemnation: so that this is no inconsiderable proof of the true and proper deity of Christ." Gill, *An Exposition of the New Testament*, 2:341.

134. Treier, *Evangelical Theology*, 185. Concerning the *communicatio idiomatum* in Acts 20:28, Schreiner also notes, "it is better simply to acknowledge the doctrine of inseparable operations What Jesus does, so does the Father and Spirit. The church is birthed by blood, the blood of God. The verse is an application of the *communicatio idiomatum*. God can truly be said to have suffered and have shed his blood in virtue of the hypostatic union." Schreiner, *Acts*, 554.

135. Gill, *Divinity: Book V*, 16.

as taking place at the level of the person and not between the natures."[136] In other words, each nature is directly related to the person of Christ, not between the two natures.[137] Therefore, such an ostensibly contradictory work of Christ in Scripture is acknowledged as a legitimate mediating work of Christ for the sake of his people.[138] Gill lists those mysterious works of Christ by virtue of *communicatio idiomatum*: "Thus the Lord of glory is said

136. Muller, "communicatio idiomatum / communicatio proprietatum," in *Dictionary of Latin and Greek Theological Terms*, 69. Different from the Reformed, Steven Duby explains the Lutheran orthodox's three kinds of christological communication: "First, there is a *genus idiomaticum*, wherein the essential properties of each nature are really communicated to or belong to the one person of Christ, the divine properties being communicated to Christ on account of his deity and the human properties being communicated to Christ on account of his humanity. Second, there is a *genus majestaticum*, wherein the majesty or glory and excellence of the divine nature is communicated to the human nature on account of the hypostatic union, so that Christ's humanity has an excellence and power that surpasses that of ordinary humanity.... Third, there is a *genus apotelesmaticum*, wherein the economic offices and works (*apotelesmata*) of Christ belong to the person of Christ on account of both his deity and his humanity because Christ always acts by both natures together to accomplish his works." Duby, *Jesus and the God of Classical Theism*, 167. Muller while introducing Lutheranism's three *genera of communicatio*, points out, "The greatest difference between the Lutherans and the Reformed appears in the *genus maiestaticum*, which the Reformed utterly reject. The Reformed view of the *communicatio*, which tends to be restricted to the *genus idiomaticum*, approaches the communication more as a *praedicatio verbalis*, or verbal predication, of *idiomata* from both natures of the person; but the Lutheran view insists that the person actually bears the *idiomata* of both natures." Muller, "communicatio idiomatum / communicatio proprietatum," in *Dictionary of Latin and Greek Theological Terms*, 71. Wellum, indicating the Creator-creature distinction even in Christ's hypostatic union, states, "Although theologians have different conceptions of the *communicatio*, they typically agree on two points: (1) each nature retained its own attributes, and (2) the attributes of each nature may be predicated of the Son since he is the person of both natures." Wellum, *The Person of Christ*, 167.

137. This person is the second person of the Trinity, who is eternal and divine. Regarding Herman Hoeksema's criticism that the covenant party in the biblical covenants is related to the Christ who is the Servant of Jehovah or the Head of the elect, not the divine Son who is equal to the Father and the Spirit, Gill answers the covenant Head of the elect is from eternity. In addition, as aforementioned, the concept of 'in Christ' is a formula in Gill's system, which embraces both eternity and time. Before assuming the human nature, Christ as the divine person is already the covenant Head according to the *pactum*. Also, as the christological principle, i.e., *communicatio idiomatum*, indicates, every act or work of Christ regardless of the nature is the act of the second person of the Trinity because act is a persons' job. Christ assumed the human nature, which means it is the fulfillment of the *pactum*. In eternity, the Father prepared a body for the Son. Through the eternal plan and scheme of the incarnation, the second person of the Trinity is a party of the *pactum* with the Holy Spirit as well.

138. "The *communicatio* is vital for making sense of seemingly contradictory biblical data, and it helps in thinking through Christ's dual agency." Wellum, *The Person of Christ*, 167.

to be crucified; God is said to purchase the church with his blood; and the Son of man is said to be in heaven, while he was here on earth."[139] Then, he finally confirms the relevance between the christological principle and the mediating works of Christ in the covenant of grace, "the divine nature has an influence upon and gives virtue and dignity to whatsoever is done or suffered in the human nature; which is of the utmost concern in the mediation of Christ."[140]

Summary

The second half of this chapter deals with Gill's Christology, which makes two components of Christ's work in large: (1) Christ as the covenantal head and (2) Christ as the mediator of the covenant. Christ is the head of the elect, which signifies that from the Abrahamic covenant through David to Jesus Christ, the seed of Abraham, Christ is the representative and person in whom God's elect people find and confirm their identity in Christ. The concept of representative is connected to the Adam and Christ typology through which these two emblematic figures become the head of their respective offspring.

Christ is also the mediator of the covenant of grace. In such a terrible reality of sin's entrance into the world, Christ is the only way and the unique person who can approach the Father and supplicate for reconciliation. Based on the eternal love of God, Christ becomes the mediator to satisfy the justice of God, which is nothing but the fruit and effect of God's love. Christ is the perfect person to be a mediator between God and man. From eternity, precisely, in the *pactum*, the three divine persons plan, agree and apply that the second person of the Trinity becomes a man by assuming human nature. It is necessary for Christ to be a man so as to fulfill what is required by the law. Also, Christ must be a divine person, without which the works of Christ as man, i.e., obedience to the law and the suffering of death, are mere works of man. Christ, as God, gives virtue and value to the obedience and suffering of death. Finally, the relation of two natures in the hypostatic union to complete the redemption requires one of the greatest mysteries, that is, the christological principle, *communicatio idiomatum*.

---

139. Gill, *Divinity: Book II*, 70.

140. Gill, *Divinity: Book II*, 70. Aaron Riches, considering *communicatio idiomatum* in relating to "the reality of cross as the place where the exchange of divine and human properties in Jesus," mentions, "*Communicatio idiomatum* is nothing other than the traditional safeguard and expression of the apostolic declaration that the Crucified truly is the one Lord." Aaron Riches, *Ecce Homo: On the Divine Unity of Christ* (Grand Rapids: Eerdmans, 2016), 6.

Therefore, every work of Jesus Christ in both eternity and time schemed in the *pactum* is by and through the second person of the Trinity only, who is eternal and divine.

CONCLUSION

Jesus Christ is the central locus in whom both realms of eternity and time coexist and meet. Through Jesus Christ, therefore, the realm of eternity is revealed to the other realm. One cannot deny that God is creator and man is creation; thus, the work of God must be beyond man's calculation. The doctrine of the covenant of redemption is solely the work of the triune God. God is there to act as he will be, and man is there to see what he can do to live. The *pactum*, therefore, is God's pure grace. The notion of salvation, as none of the creation has perceived yet any concept of it, is planned, executed, and applied by God the Trinity, who is spirit. Ultimately, Gill implies that all redemptive ideas, e.g., election, justification, hypostatic union, and *communicatio idiomatum*, handled in this chapter, belong to Jesus Christ. Man attempts to find what he can see and do; however, even those perceptions and actions of man happen in Christ. Jesus Christ is the window through which the reality of eternity is manifested and seen.

Gill's *pactum*, the central locus of his systematic theology, begins with the triune God and ends with the triune God. Gill's *pactum* functions as a bridge to connect the creator and creation, which only occurs in Jesus Christ, who is the creator and who became creation.

CHAPTER 6

Conclusion

THE WHOLE STUDY OF this volume begins with two research questions. The first is related to the methodology of picturing the whole biblical narrative colored by various covenantal images. Unfortunately, however, Baptists historically have not fully and properly benefited from the rich biblical theology based on a covenant concept. The second pertains to the theological status of the doctrine of the covenant of redemption. The typical Reformed covenant theology has, since the sixteenth century, developed the threefold form of covenant theology: the covenant of redemption, works, and grace. This framework has considered the covenant of redemption as a mere foundation or supplement for a better explanation of the covenant of grace.

Such recognitions bring about paying attention to the theological system of John Gill, an eighteenth-century Particular Baptist theologian and pastor. Gill, though deeply saturating himself in a strict Calvinism, was a Baptist. His "Calvinism stood in broad continuity with the Baptist revision of the WCF [Westminster Confession of Faith], the Second London Baptist Confession of Faith (SLBCF)."[1] As a Baptist, Gill embraced the covenant

---

1. R. Lucas Stamps, "John Gill's Reformed Dyothelitism," *The Reformed Theological Review* 74, no. 2 (August 2015): 82. Garrett explains five differences between those two confessions (1644 and 1677). Among the differences, two deserve a mention: (1) "the 1677 confession greatly expanded the Westminster's chapters on the church from six to fifteen sections, thus incorporating Baptist teachings on membership, polity, elders and deacons, and discipline, and made significant additions relative to perseverance of saints; (2) "some articles, notably those on repentance and on baptism and the Lord's Supper–devoid of sacramental language, were completely rewritten for the 1677 confession." James Leo Garrett Jr., *Baptist Theology: A Four-Century Study* (Macon, GA: Mercer University Press, 2009), 73. In addition, one of the features of the Second London Confession with regard to the threefold covenantal form, according to Garrett, is that "The Westminster's teaching about a covenant of works was omitted, but the covenant of grace was still founded on the eternal covenant between the Father and the

of redemption as the primary and comprehensive concept of his systematic theology, *A Body of Doctrinal Divinity* (1767). Thus, this volume has attempted to demonstrate Gill's *pactum* plays a critical role, occupying a central locus in his systematic theology with various major theological doctrines.

Summary of the Study

Chapter two serves as a grand presupposition of the whole volume. The *pactum*, by definition, is inextricably linked to the distinctive notion between the two realms, eternity and time. Throughout the entire Book I of *Divinity*, which deals with God's ontological attributes, Gill maintains his demonstration of God the Trinity on the basis of his being creator whose corollary includes immutability, simplicity, and eternity. For Gill, therefore, eternity is not just a philosophical or scientific idea that is an object of critical study but the very mystery attribute of God, even tantamount to dealing with God himself.

Chapter three deals with that; based on the key groundwork of the two realms, Gill sets out the internal and external works of God. Because there is only one genuine covenant in Gill's mind, i.e., the covenant of grace, the *pactum* in Gill's system takes control of both realms from the perspective of God's own being.[2] Gill's unique twofold *pactum*, the everlasting council and the everlasting covenant of grace, encompasses all realms with regard to both the eternal plan and scheme of man's salvation and the temporal, historical, redemptive narrative. For Gill, therefore, the *pactum* is the most foundational and fundamental framework and structure to understand the whole picture of the full narrative of the biblical redemption of man.

Chapter four attempts to explicate that the doctrine of the Trinity, i.e., one essence in three divine persons, is ontologically essential to establish the existence of the *pactum* and to support the *pactum*'s occupation of the core locus in Gill's systematic theology as its corollary. In Gill's system, the *pactum* is allowed only to be made among equal authorities or at the same level as covenantal parties. Thus, the so-called eternal functional subordination of the Son to the Father or eternal relational authority-submission cannot be accepted. In this regard, this chapter investigates the historical

---

Son and still traced to the promise of salvation to Adam through the seed of Eve. None has ever been saved apart from this covenant." Garrett, *Baptist Theology*, 75.

2. Gill takes and understands the *pactum* in the same notion of other descriptions in Scripture: that is, the covenant of life; covenant of peace; covenant of grace; and the covenant of redemption. For details, see Gill, *Divinity: Book II*, 51-52.

movement of Unitarianism, which Gill's contemporary and his preceding generation had to face. In the end, classical orthodox trinitarian theology supports the *pactum* in Gill's systematic theology.

Chapter five attempts to confirm that Gill's *pactum* is not only theoretical but also practical in both realms. The *pactum*'s twofold definition or concept in terms of the internal and external decrees is unfolded by Jesus Christ, who exists as both God and man in the hypostatic union. Internally, Christ is the center of election and justification. Due to the eternal relation, will, and plan of the three divine persons, all theological events, whether eternal or temporal, are centered *in Christ*. Externally, the notion of *Christ* becomes a formula in the temporal realm. In other words, Jesus Christ as God and man becomes the covenantal or federal head of the elect and the mediator of the covenant of grace. That Gill's *pactum* occupies the central locus in his systematic theology with special respect to man's salvation is finally proved by the person and work of Jesus Christ, who is the unique window through which the redemptive reality in eternity is seen, manifested, and applied to the elect in time.

Further Research and Concluding Thought

Gill devoted almost his entire life to serving a local Baptist church for over fifty years. Though he fully studied and mastered the biblical languages and understood various kinds of theologies, especially Calvinism in the Reformed tradition, he remained a Baptist theologian and pastor throughout his whole life. Gill prioritized the *pactum* over any other theological notion or doctrine in unfolding the whole systematic theology. In other words, covenant theology, though it is considered fundamental to the Reformed theological tradition, was Gill's center of gravity in doing and setting up his theological system as a Baptist pastor. At present, though some good works on covenant theology are attempting to retrieve the Baptist covenantal tradition and practice, more research is needed to elaborate, especially the connection or relation of Gill's *pactum* to his other theological details of the Baptist distinctive.[3]

Establishing one's own theological system might fall into personal speculation and rely heavily on a philosophical route or critical

---

3. For those that tried to get involved with the covenant notion regarding the Baptist theology, see Gentry and Wellum, *Kingdom through Covenant*; Pascal Denault, *The Distinctiveness of Baptist Covenant Theology: A Comparison between Seventeenth-Century Particular Baptist and Paedobaptist Federalism* (Birmingham, AL: Solid Ground Christian Books, 2013); Richard C. Barcellos, ed., *Recovering the Covenantal Heritage: Essays in Baptist Covenant Theology* (Palmdale, CA: RBAP, 2014).

methodology, which, for some, might be thought of as more reasonable, logical, persuasive, and fitting the contemporary context without noticing what basis Christianity is established. However, any person who is engaged in such a way of approaching a biblical and theological system ought seriously to consider what he or she is trying to accomplish in writing. It is simply because the work of systematicians dealing with Scripture affects not just a way of a person's lifestyle or how to pursue a better life in convenience; in stark contrast, setting up the biblical and theological frame to see the whole Scripture might affect and change one's own life entirely. In this respect, Gill's conviction with the *pactum* and his method based on Scripture teach contemporary Christians how to receive the word of God, how to understand the heart of God in his Word, and how to work with theology as a systematician.

Bibliography

PRIMARY SOURCES

Gill, John. *A Body of Doctrinal Divinity.* Books I-VII. Fareham, U.K.:Bierton Particular Baptists, 2020-2021.

———.*A Collection of Sermons and Tracts.* 3 vols. London: George Keith, 1773.

———.*An Exposition of the Book of Solomon's Song; Commonly Called Canticles.* London: William Hill Collingridge, 1854.

———.*An Exposition of the New Testament.* Vol. I-III. London: Mathews and Leigh, 1809. Reprinted by Paris, AR: The Baptist Standard Bearer, Inc., 2006.

———.*An Exposition of the Old Testament.* Vol. I-VI. London: Mathews and Leigh, 1810. Reprinted by Paris, AR: The Baptist Standard Bearer, Inc., 2006.

———.*The Argument from Apostolic Tradition, in Favour of Infant-Baptism, with Others, Advanced in a Late Pamphlet, Called the Baptism of Infants a Reasonable Service, &c. Consider'd.* London printed. Boston, New-England: re-printed by Z. Fowle, in Back-Street, near the Mill-Bridge, 1765.

———.*The Cause of God and Truth: In Four Parts: with a Vindication of Part IV from the Cavils, Calumnies, and Defamations, of Mr. Henry Heywood.* A New Edition. London: W. H. Collingridge, 1855. Reprinted by Atlanta, GA: Turner Lassetter, 1962.

———.*The Doctrines of God's Everlasting Love to His Elect, and their Eternal Union with Christ: Together with Some Other Truths, Stated and Defended, in a Letter to Dr. Abraham Taylor.* London: G. Keith, 1732. Reprinted by Paris, AR: The Baptist Standard Bearer, Inc., 1987.

———.*The Doctrine of Justification, by the Righteousness of Christ, Stated and Maintained, Being the Substance of Several Sermons.* Fourth Edition. London: G. Keith, 1756. Reprinted by Gale ECCO, 2010.

———.*The Doctrine of the Trinity Stated and Vindicated Being the Substance of Several Discourses on that Important Subject.* Paris, AR: The Baptist Standard Bearer, Inc., 1999.

Bibliography

SECONDARY SOURCES

BOOKS

Abernethy, Andrew T. and Gregory Goswell. *God's Messiah in the Old Testament: Expectations of a Coming King*. Grand Rapids: Baker, 2020.

Akin, Daniel L. *A Theology for the Church*. Revised Edition. Nashville: B&H, 2014.

———. *1, 2, 3 John*. NAC vol. 38. Nashville: B&H, 2001.

Allen, Michael. *Ephesians*. Grand Rapids: Brazos, 2020.

———. *Justification and the Gospel: Understanding the Contexts and Controversies*. Grand Rapids: Baker, 2013.

Allison, Gregg R. *Historical Theology: An Introduction to Christian Doctrine*. Grand Rapids: Zondervan, 2011.

Anonymous. *The Unreasonableness of the Doctrine of the Trinity Briefly Demonstrated, In a Letter to a Friend*. London: s.n., 1692.

Anselm, Saint. *Complete Philosophical and Theological Treatises of Anselm of Canterbury*. trans. Jasper Hopkins and Herbert Richardson. Minneapolis, MN: Arthur J. Banning Press, 2000.

———. *St. Anselm's Proslogion with A Reply on Behalf of the Fool by Gaunilo and The Author's Reply to Gaunilo*. Translated by M. J. Charlesworth. Notre Dame: University of Notre Dame, 1979.

Arnold, Bill T. *The Book of Deuteronomy: Chapters 1-11*. NICOT. Grand Rapids: Eerdmans, 2022.

Athanasius of Alexandria. *On the Incarnation of the Word of God*. Translated by T. Herbert Bindley. 2nd ed. Revised. London: The Religious Track Society, 1903.

Aquinas, Saint Thomas. *Summa Contra Gentiles*. Book One: God. Translated by Anton C. Pegis, F.R.S.C. Nortre Dame: University of Notre Dame Press, 1975.

———. *Summa Theologiae: Latin Text and English Translation, Introductions, Notes, Appendices and Glossaries*. Blackfriars: Eyre and Spottiswoode, 1964.

Augustine, Saint. *Confessions*. Translated by Henry Chadwick. Oxford University Press, 2009.

———. *On Grace and Free Will*. ed. Philip Schaff. Louisville, KY: GLH Publishing, 2017.

———. "The City of God." In *A Select Library of the Nicene and Post-Nicene Fathers of the Christian Church*. ed. Philip Schaff. Vol. II: St. Augustin's City of God and Christian Doctrine. 14 vols. Edinburgh: T&T Clark, 1988.

———. *The Trinity*. Translated by Edmund Hill, O.P. Edited by John E. Rotelle, O.S.A. The Works of Saint Augustine: A Translation for the 21st Century. Hyde Park, NY: New City Press, 1991.

Bahnsen, Greg L. et al. *Five Views on Law and Gospel*. Grand Rapids: Zondervan, 1999.

Barcellos, Richard C, ed. *Recovering the Covenantal Heritage: Essays in Baptist Covenant Theology*. Palmdale, CA: RBAP, 2014.

Barclay, John M. G. *Paul and the Gift*. Grand Rapids: Eerdmans, 2015.

Barnes, Albert. *Notes on the New Testament: Acts*. Edited by Robert Frew. London: Blackie & Son, 1884-85.

Barr, James. *Biblical Words for Time*. Revised Edition. Naperville, Ill: Alec R. Allenson, 1969.

Barrett, Helen M. *Boethius: Some Aspects of his Times and Work*. New York: Russell & Russell, 1965.

Barrett, Jordan P. *Divine Simplicity: A Biblical and Trinitarian Account*. Minneapolis, MN: Fortress Press, 2017.
Barrett, Matthew. *Simply Trinity: The Unmanipulated Father, Son, and Spirit*. Grand Rapids: Baker, 2021.
Barth, Karl. *Christ and Adam: Man and Humanity in Romans 5*. Translated by T. A. Smail. New York: Harper and Brothers, 1956.
———.*Church Dogmatics*. Edited by G. W. Bromiley and T. F. Torrance. Translated by G. W. Bromiley. Edinburgh: T&T Clark, 1956.
———.*The Epistle to the Romans*. Translated by Edwyn C. Hoskyns. 6th ed. Oxford: Oxford University Press, 1968.
Bartholomew, Craig G. *The Old Testament and God: Old Testament Origins and the Question of God*. Grand Rapids: Baker, 2022.
Bavinck, Herman. *Reformed Dogmatics*. vol. 2: God and Creation. Edited by John Bolt. Translated by John Vriend. Grand Rapids: Baker, 2004.
_____, *Reformed Dogmatics*. vol. 3: Sin and Salvation in Christ. Edited by John Bolt. Translated by John Vriend. Grand Rapids: Baker, 2006.
Bauckham, Richard. *Gospel of Glory: Major Themes in Johannine Theology*. Grand Rapids: Baker, 2015.
Beale, G. K. and D. A. Carson, ed. *Commentary on the New Testament Use of the Old Testament*. Grand Rapids: Baker, 2007.
Beasley-Murray, G. R. *John*. Word Biblical Commentary. vol. 36. Dallas: Word, 1999.
Beeke, Joel R. and Paul M. Smalley. *Reformed Systematic Theology*. vol. 2: Man and Christ. Wheaton: Crossway, 2020.
———.*Reformed Systematic Theology*. vol. 3: Spirit and Salvation. Wheaton: Crossway, 2021.
Beilby, James K. and Paul Rhodes Eddy, eds. *Justification: Five Views*. Downers Grove: IVP, 2011.
Berkhof, Louis. *Systematic Theology*. New Combined Edition. Grand Rapids: Eerdmans, 1996.
———.*The History of Christian Doctrines*. 1937; Edinburgh, UK: The Banner of Truth Trust, 1969.
Best, Earnest. *1 Peter: Based on the Revised Standard Version*. New Century Bible Commentary. 1971; Grand Rapids: Eerdmans, 1982.
Bidle, John. "A Letter written to Sir H. V. a Member of the Honourable House of Commons." In *The Apostolical and True Opinion concerning the Holy Trinity, Revived and Asserted*. 1653; repr., London: s.n., 1691.
———."A Short Account of the Life of John Bidle." In *The Apostolical and True Opinion concerning the Holy Trinity, Revived and Asserted: Partly by Twelve Arguments levied against the Traditional and False Opinion about the Godhead of the Holy Spirit. Partly by a Confession of Faith touching the Three Persons*, by John Bidle. 1653; repr., London: s.n., 1691.
Bird, Michael F. *Evangelical Theology: A Biblical and Systematic Introduction*. 2nd ed. Grand Rapids: Zondervan, 2020.
———.*The Saving Righteousness of God: Studies on Paul, Justification, and the New Perspective*. Paternoster Biblical Monographs. Eugene, OR: Wipf and Stock, 2007.
Bird, Michael F. and Scott Harrower, eds. *Trinity without Hierarchy: Reclaiming Nicene Orthodoxy in Evangelical Theology*. Grand Rapids: Kregel, 2019.

Blaising, Craig A. and Carmen S. Hardin, eds. *Psalm 1-50*. Ancient Christian Commentary on Scripture. vol. 7. Downers Grove: IVP, 2008.
Block, Daniel I. *Covenant: The Framework of God's Grand Plan of Redemption*. Grand Rapids: Baker, 2021.
Bloesch, Donald G. *Essentials of Evangelical Theology: Volume One: God, Authority, and Salvation*. 2 vols. Peabody, MA: Prince Press, 2001.
———. *God the Almighty: Power, Wisdom, Holiness, Love*. Downers Grove: IVP, 2006.
Boethius, Anicius Manlius Severinus. *The Consolation of Philosophy*. Translated by Victor Watts. Revised Edition. London: Penguin Books, 1999.
Boice, James Montgomery. *The Gospel of John: An Expositional Commentary: John 18:1-21:25*. vol. 5. Grand Rapids: Zondervan, 1979.
Borchert, Gerald L. *John 12-21*. NAC. vol. 25B. Nashville: B&H, 2002.
Bower, John R. *The Confession of Faith: A Critical Text and Introduction*. Grand Rapids: Reformation Heritage Books, 2020.
Brabant, Frank Herbert. *Time and Eternity in Christian Thought: Being Eight Lectures Delivered before the University of Oxford, in the Year 1936, on the Foundation of the Rev. John Bampton, Canon of Salisbury*. London: Longmans, Green, 1937.
Brand, Chad Owen, ed. *Perspectives on Election: Five Views*. Nashville: B&H, 2006.
Bridge, William. *Christ and the Covenant the Work and Way of Meditation: Gods Return to the Soul, or Nation; Together with his Preventing Mercy*. London: Printed for N. Ranew, and J. Robinson at the Angel in Jewen-Street, 1667.
Brine, John. *A Defence of the Doctrine of Eternal Justification, from some Exceptions made to it by Mr. Bragge, and others*. London: Printed and sold by A. Ward, at the King's-Arms in Little Britain; and H. Whitridge, at the Corner of Castle-Alley, near the Royal-Exchange, 1732.
Brown, Francis, S. R. Driver, and Charles Briggs. *The Abridged Brown-Driver-Briggs Hebrew-English Lexicon of the Old Testament: From A Hebrew and English Lexicon of the Old Testament*. Edited by Richard Whitaker. Boston, MA: Houghton, Mifflin and Company, 1906.
Bruce, F. F. *The Epistle to the Galatians: A Commentary on the Greek Text*. NIGTC. Grand Rapids: Eerdmans, 1982.
Buchanan, James. *The Doctrine of Justification: An Outline of its History in the Church and of its Exposition from Scripture*. Grand Rapids: Baker, 1955.
Büchsel, Rostock Friedrich. "ἀλλάσσω, ἀντάλλαγμα, ἀπ-, δι-, καταλλάσσω, καταλλαγή, ἀποκατ-, μεταλλάσσω." In *Theological Dictionary of the New Testament*. Edited by Gerhard Kittel. Translated by Geoffrey W. Bromiley, 10 vols. 1964; repr. Grand Rapids: Eerdmans, 2006.
Burrell, David B. C.S.C. "Aquinas and Islamic and Jewish thinkers" In *The Cambridge Companion to Aquinas*. Edited by Norman Kretzmann and Eleonore Stump. Cambridge: Cambridge University Press, 1993.
Butner Jr., D. Glenn. *The Son Who Learned Obedience: A Theological Case Against the Eternal Submission of the Son*. Eugene, OR: Pickwick, 2018.
———. *Trinitarian Dogmatics: Exploring the Grammar of the Christian Doctrine of God*. Grand Rapids: Baker, 2022.
Calvin, John. *Institute of the Christian Religion*. Edited by John T. McNeill. Translated by Ford Lewis Battles. Louisville, KY: Westminster John Knox, 2011.
Campbell, Constantine R. *1, 2 and 3 John*. The Story of God Bible Commentary. Grand Rapids: Zondervan, 2017.

———. *The Letter to the Ephesians*. PNTC. Grand Rapids: Eerdmans, 2023.
Carson, D. A. *The Gospel According to John*. The Pillar New Testament Commentary. Grand Rapids: Eerdmans, 1991.
Carson, D. A., Peter T. O'Brien, and Mark A. Seifrid, eds. *Justification and Variegated Nomism: Volume 2-The Paradoxes of Paul*. Tübingen: Mohr Siebeck, 2004.
Carter, Craig A. *Contemplating God with the Great Tradition: Recovering Trinitarian Classical Theism*. Grand Rapids: Baker, 2021.
Cassuto, Umberto. *A Commentary on the Book of Genesis*. Translated by Israel Abrahams. Jerusalem: Magnes Press; Hebrew University, 1961.
Childs, Brevard S. *The Book of Exodus: A Critical, Theological Commentary*. The Old Testament Library. paperback edition. Louisville: Westminster John Knox, 2004.
Collier, Thomas. *The Exaltation of Christ In the dayes of the Gospel: as the alone High-Priest, Prophet, and King of Saints*. London, 1641.
Coxe, Nehemiah and John Owen, *Covenant Theology: From Adam to Christ*. Edited by Ronald D. Miller, James M. Renihan, and Francisco Orozco. Palmdale, CA: Reformed Baptist Academic Press, 2005.
Craig, William Lane. *Time and Eternity: Exploring God's Relationship to Time*. Wheaton: Crossway, 2001.
Crisp, Oliver D. "Incarnation." In *The Oxford Handbook of Systematic Theology*. Edited by John Webster, Kathryn Tanner, and Iain Torrance. Oxford: Oxford University Press, 2007.
Crisp, Tobias and John Gill. *Christ Alone Exalted: The Complete Works of Tobias Crisp*. 2 vols. London: John Bennett, 1832.
Cross, F. L. "Socinus." In *The Oxford Dictionary of the Christian Church*. Oxford: Oxford University Press, 1997.
Cullmann, Oscar. *Christ and Time: The Primitive Christian Conception of Time and History*. Translated by Floyd V. Filson. Revised Edition. Philadelphia: The Westminster Press, 1964.
———. *Salvation in History*. Translated by Sidney G. Sowers. New York: Harper & Row, 1967.
Dalferth, Ingolf U. "Gott und Zeit." In *Religion und Gestaltung der Zeit*. Edited by D. Georgi, H-G. Heimbrock, and M. Moxter. Kampen: Kok Pharos, 1994.
Dam, Cornelis Van. *In the Beginning: Listening to Genesis 1 and 2*. Grand Rapids: Reformation Heritage Books, 2021.
Daniel, Curt. *The History and Theology of Calvinism*. Darlington, U.K.: Evangelical Press, 2019.
Davidson, Robert. "Covenant." In *The Oxford Companion to Christian Thought*. Edited by Adrian Hastings, Alistair Mason, and Hugh Pyper. Oxford University Press, 2000.
Davies, Brian. *The Thought of Thomas Aquinas*. Oxford: Clarendon, 1992.
Davies, Brian and G. R. Evans, ed. *Anselm of Canterbury: The Major Works*. Oxford: Oxford University Press, 2008.
Delitzsch, Franz. *Biblical Commentary on the Prophesies of Isaiah*. Translated by James Martin. Grand Rapids: Eerdmans, 1967.
Demarest, Bruce. *The Cross and Salvation*. Foundations of Evangelical Theology. Wheaton: Crossway, 2006.

Denault, Pascal. *The Distinctiveness of Baptist Covenant Theology: A Comparison between Seventeenth-Century Particular Baptist and Paedobaptist Federalism.* Birmingham, AL: Solid Ground Christian Books, 2013.

DeWeese, Garrett J. *God and the Nature of Time.* Burlington, VT: Ashgate, 2004.

Dickinson, Jonathan. *A Defence of Presbyterian Ordination: In Answer to a Pamphlet, Entituled, A Modest Proof, of the Order and Government Settled by Christ, in the Church.* Boston: Printed for Daniel Henchman, and sold at his shop, over-against the Brick Meeting-House in Cornhill, 1724.

———.*Remarks upon Mr. Gale's Reflections on Mr. Wall's History of Infant Baptism.* New York: William Bradford for and sold by T. Wood, 1721.

———.*The True Scripture-Doctrine concerning Some Important Points of Christian Faith, particularly Eternal Election, Original Sin, Grace in Conversion, Justification by Faith, and the Saints Perseverance. Represented and Apply'd in Five Discourses.* Boston: G. Rogers, for S. Eliot in Cornhill, 1741.

Dockery, David S. *The Doctrine of the Bible.* Fort Worth, TX: Seminary Hill Press, 2020.

Duby, Steven J. *Divine Simplicity: A Dogmatic Account.* T&T Clark Studies in Systematic Theology. London: Bloomsbury T&T Clark, 2018.

———.*Jesus and the God of Classical Theism: Biblical Christology in Light of the Doctrine of God.* Grand Rapids: Baker, 2022.

Dumbrell, William J. *Covenant and Creation: An Old Testament Covenant Theology.* Revised and Enlarged Edition. Nashville: Thomas Nelson, 1984; reprint, Milton Keynes, England: Paternoster, 2013.

Dunn, James D. G. *The New Perspective on Paul: Collected Essays.* Wissenschaftliche Untersuchungen zum Neuen Testament 185. Tübingen: Mohr Siebeck, 2005.

Dyken, Seymour Van. *Samuel Willard, 1640-1707: Preacher of Orthodoxy in an Era of Change.* Grand Rapids: Eerdmans, 1972.

Eichrodt, Walther. *Theology of the Old Testament.* Translated by J. A. Baker. The Old Testament Library. 2 vols. Philadelphia: The Westminster Press, 1961.

Ella, George M. *John Gill and Justification from Eternity: A Tercentenary Appreciation 1697-1997.* Durham, England: Go Publications, 1998.

Elliott, Mark W, ed. *Isaiah 40-66.* Ancient Christian Commentary on Scripture. Old Testament XI. Downers Grove: IVP, 2007.

Ellis, E. Earle. *Pauline Theology: Ministry and Society.* Eugene, OR: Wipf and Stock, 1997.

———.*Paul's Use of the Old Testament.* Edinburgh: Oliver and Boyd, 1957.

Elwell, Walter A, ed. *Baker Encyclopedia of the Bible.* 2 vols. Grand Rapids: Baker Book House, 1988.

———.*Evangelical Dictionary of Biblical Theology.* Grand Rapids: Baker, 1996.

———.*Evangelical Dictionary of Theology.* 2nd ed. Grand Rapids: Baker, 2001.

Emerson, Matthew Y. "The Role of Proverbs 8: Eternal Generation and Hermeneutics Ancient and Modern." In *Retrieving Eternal Generation.* Edited by Fred Sanders and Scott R. Swain. Grand Rapids: Zondervan, 2017.

Emerson, Matthew Y., Christopher W. Morgan, and R. Lucas Stamps, eds. *Baptist and the Christian Tradition: Towards an Evangelical Baptist Catholicity.* Nashville: B&H, 2020.

Enns, Peter. *Exodus.* The NIV Application Commentary. Grand Rapids: Zondervan, 2000.

Erickson, Millard J. *Christian Theology.* 3rd ed. Grand Rapids: Baker, 2103.

———.*God in Three Persons: A Contemporary Interpretation of the Trinity*. Grand Rapids: Baker, 1995.

———.*Who's Tampering with the Trinity?: An Assessment of the Subordination Debate*. Grand Rapids: Kregel, 2009.

Estep, W. R. *The Reformation: Luther, the Anabaptists*. Christian Classics. Nashville: Broadman Press, 1979.

Estes, Douglas. "Eternity." In *The Encyclopedia of Christian Civilization*. Vol. II. Edited by George Thomas Kurian. Chichester, West Sussex: Wiley-Blackwell, 2009.

Fee, Gordon D. *Jesus the Lord according to Paul the Apostle: A Concise Introduction*. Grand Rapids: Baker, 2018.

Feinberg, John S. *No One Like Him: The Doctrine of God*. Foundations of Evangelical Theology. Wheaton: Crossway, 2001.

Fesko, J. V. *Death in Adam, Life in Christ: The Doctrine of Imputation*. Reformed, Exegetical and Doctrinal Studies. Fearn, Ross-shire: Mentor, 2016.

———.*Justification: Understanding the Classic Reformed Doctrine*. Phillipsburg, NJ: P&R, 2008.

———.*The Covenant of Redemption: Origins, Development, and Reception*. Göttingen: Vandenhoeck & Ruprecht, 2015.

———.*The Trinity and the Covenant of Redemption*. Fearn, Ross-shire, U.K.: Mentor, 2016.

Fowler, Edward. *A Second Defence of the Propositions, by which the Doctrine of the Holy Trinity is so Explained, according to the Ancient Fathers, as to speak it not contradictory to Natural Reason: in Answer to a Socinian Manuscript*. London: B. Aylmer, 1695.

Frame, John M. *Systematic Theology: An Introduction to Christian Belief*. Phillipsburg, NJ: P&R, 2013.

———.*The Doctrine of God*. Phillipsburg, NJ: P&R, 2002.

Fretheim, Terence E. *Exodus*. Interpretation: A Bible Commentary for Teaching and Preaching. Louisville: Westminster John Knox, 1991.

Gamble, Whitney G. *Christ and the Law: Antinomianism at the Westminster Assembly*, Studies on the Westminster Assembly. Grand Rapids: Reformation Heritage Books, 2018.

Gardner, Paul. *1 Corinthians*. ECNT. vol. 7. Grand Rapids: Zondervan, 2018.

Garland, David E. *Acts*. Teach the Text Commentary. Grand Rapids: Baker, 2017.

———.*2 Corinthians*. Christian Standard Commentary. Nashville: Holman, 2021.

Garrett, Jr., James Leo. *Baptist Theology: A Four-Century Study*. Macon, GA: Mercer University Press, 2009.

———.*Systematic Theology: Biblical, Historical, and Evangelical*, 4th ed. 2 vols. North Richland Hills, TX: Bibal, 2011.

Geisler, Norman. *Systematic Theology: God and Creation*. 4 vols. Minneapolis, MN: Bethany House, 2003.

Gentry, Peter J. and Stephen J. Wellum, *Kingdom through Covenant: A Biblical-Theological Understanding of the Covenants*, 2nd ed. Wheaton: Crossway, 2018.

George, Timothy. "St. Augustine and the Mystery of Time." In *What God Knows: Time, Eternity, and Divine Knowledge*. Edited by Harry Lee Poe and J. Stanley Mattson. Waco, TX: Baylor University Press, 2005.

———.*Galatians*. NAC. vol. 30. Nashville: B&H, 1994.

Giles, Kevin. *The Trinity and Subordinationism: The Doctrine of God and the Contemporary Gender Debate*. Downers Grove: IVP, 2002.

Gillespie, Patrick. *The Ark of the Covenant Opened: Or, A Treatise of the Covenant of Redemption between God and Christ, as the Foundation of the Covenant of Grace*. London: Tho. Parkhurst, 1677.

Gillingham, Susan. *Psalms through the Centuries: A Reception History Commentary on Psalms 1-72*. vol. 2. Chichester: Wiley Blackwell, 2018.

Goldingay, John. *Genesis*. Baker Commentary on the Old Testament: Pentateuch. Grand Rapids: Baker, 2020.

Goppelt, Leonhard. *Typos: The Typological Interpretation of the Old Testament in the New*. Translated by Donald H. Madvig. Grand Rapids: Eerdmans, 1982.

Gregory, Francis. *The Doctrine of the Glorious Trinity, not Explained, but Asserted by Several Texts, as they are expounded by the ancient Fathers and later Divines*. London: Walter Kettilby, 1695.

Gregory of Nazianzus. *On God and Christ: The Five Theological Orations and Two Letters to Cledonius*. Translated by Frederick Williams and Lionel Wickham. St Vladimir's Seminary Press Popular Patristics Series 23. Crestwood, NY: St Vladimir's Seminary Press, 2002.

Grudem, Wayne. *Systematic Theology: An Introduction to Biblical Doctrine*. 2nd ed. Grand Rapids: Zondervan, 2020.

———. *1 Peter: An Introduction and Commentary*. TNTC. Downers Grove: IVP, 1988.

Hagner, Donald A. *Hebrews*. NIBC. Peabody, MA: Hendrickson, 1990.

Hamilton, Victor P. *The Book of Genesis: Chapters 1-17*. NICOT. Grand Rapids: Eerdmans, 1990.

Hansen, G. Walter. *Galatians*. IVP New Testament Commentary Series. Downers Grove: IVP, 1994.

———. *The Letter to the Philippians*. The Pillar New Testament Commentary. Grand Rapids: Eerdmans, 2009.

Hanson, R. C. P. "Biblical Exegesis in the Early Church." In *The Cambridge History of the Bible: From the Beginnings to Jerome*. Edited by P. R. Ackroyd and C. F. Evans. 3 vols. London: Cambridge University Press, 1970.

Harris, Murray J. *The Second Epistle to the Corinthians: A Commentary on the Greek Text*. NIGTC. Grand Rapids: Eerdmans, 2005.

Harvey John D. and David Gentino. *Acts: A Commentary for Biblical Preaching and Teaching*. Kerux Commentaries. Grand Rapids: Kregel, 2023.

Harwood, Adam. *Christian Theology: Biblical, Historical, and Systematic*. Bellingham, WA: Lexham, 2022.

Hawkins, Ralph K. *Discovering Exodus: Context, Interpretation, Reception*. Grand Rapids: Eerdmans, 2021.

Hawthorne, Gerald F., Ralph P. Martin, and Daniel G. Reid, ed. *Dictionary of Paul and His Letters*. Downers Grove: IVP, 1993.

Haykin Michael A. G. and Mark Jones, eds. *Drawn into Controversie: Reformed Theological Diversity and Debates within Seventeenth-Century British Puritanism*. Reformed Historical Theology 17. Göttingen: Vandenhoeck & Ruprecht, 2011.

Helm, Paul. *Eternal God: A Study of God without Time*. Oxford: Clarendon Press, 1988.

Hillers, Delbert R. *Covenant: The History of a Biblical Idea*. Baltimore: The Johns Hopkins University Press, 1969.

Hinlicky, Paul R. *Divine Simplicity: Christ the Crisis of Metaphysics.* Grand Rapids: Baker, 2016.
Hodge, Charles. *Systematic Theology.* 3 vols. Peabody, MA: Hendrickson Publishers, Inc., 2008.
Hoehner, Harold W. *Ephesians: An Exegetical Commentary.* Grand Rapids: Baker, 2002.
Hoekema, Anthony A. *Created in God's Image.* Grand Rapids: Eerdmans, 1994.
Hoeksema, Herman. *Reformed Dogmatics.* Grand Rapids: Reformed Free Publishing Association, 1966.
Horton, Michael. *Introducing Covenant Theology.* Grand Rapids: BakerBooks, 2006.
———.*Justification.* New Studies in Dogmatics. 2 vols. Grand Rapids: Zondervan, 2018.
———.*The Christian Faith: A Systematic Theology for Pilgrims on the Way.* Grand Rapids: Zondervan, 2011.
Hoskins, Paul M. *The Book of Revelation: A Theological and Exegetical Commentary.* North Charleston, SC: ChristoDoulos, 2017.
Howell, Robert Boyte C. *The Cross.* Charleston, SC: Southern Baptist Publication Society, 1854.
Hunter, Trent and Stephen Wellum, *Christ from Beginning to End: How the Full Story of Scripture Reveals the Full Glory of Christ.* Grand Rapids: Zondervan, 2018.
Jackelen, Antjie. *Time and Eternity: The Question of Time in Church, Science, and Theology.* Philadelphia: Templeton Faoundation Press, 2005.
Jamieson, Robert, A. R. Fausset, and David Brown. *A Commentary, Critical, Experimental, and Practical on the Old and New Testaments: Genesis-Deuteronomy.* 3 vols. London; Glasgow: William Collins, Sons, & Company, 1874.
Jobes, Karen H. *John: Through Old Testament Eyes.* Grand Rapids: Kregel, 2021.
———.*1, 2, and 3 John.* Exegetical Commentary on the New Testament. Grand Rapids: Zondervan, 2014.
———.*1 Peter.* BECNT. Grand Rapids: Baker, 2005.
Kärkkäinen, Veli-Matti. *The Trinity: Global Perspectives.* Louisville, KY: Westminster John Knox Press, 2007.
Katz, Sheri. "Person." In *Augustine through the Ages: An Encyclopedia.* Edited by Allan D. Fitzgerald, O.S.A. Grand Rapids: Eerdmans, 1999.
Keach, Benjamin. *The Everlasting Covenant: A Sweet Cordial for a Drooping Soul.* Edited by Quinn R. Mosier. Kansas City, MO: Baptist Heritage Press, 2022.
Kidner, Derek. *Genesis: An Introduction and Commentary.* Tyndale Old Testament Commentaries. Downers Grove: IVP, 1967.
Kilcrease, Jack D. *Justification by the Word: Restoring Sola Fide.* Bellingham, WA: Lexham, 2022.
Kline, Meredith G. *Treaty of the Great King: The Covenant Structure of Deuteronomy.* Eugene: Wipe&Stock, 1963.
Klein, George L. *Zechariah.* The New American Commentary. vol. 21B. Nashville: B&H, 2008.
Klein, William W. *The New Chosen People: A Corporate View of Election.* Grand Rapids: Zondervan, 1990.
Kot, Stanislas. *Socinianism in Poland: The Social and Political Ideas of the Polish Antitrinitarians in the Sixteenth and Seventeenth Centuries.* Translated from the Polish by Earl Morse Wilbur. Boston: Starr King Press, 1957.

Küng, Hans. *Justification: The Doctrine of Karl Barth and a Catholic Reflection.* Translated by Thomas Collins, Edmund E. Tolk, and David Granskou. Philadelphia: Westminster, 1981.

Larkin, William J. *Acts.* IVP New Testament Commentary Series 5. Downers Grove: IVP, 1995.

Leftow, Brian. "Anselm's perfect-being theology." In *The Cambridge Companion to Anselm.* Edited by Brian Davies and Brian Leftow. Cambridge: Cambridge University Press, 2004.

———. *Time and Eternity.* Ithaca, NY: Cornell University Press, 1991.

Letham, Robert. "John Owen's Doctrine of the Trinity in its Catholic Context." In *The Ashgate Research Companion to John Owen's Theology.* Edited by Kelly M. Kapic and Mark Jones. London: Routledge, 2012.

———. *Systematic Theology.* Wheaton: Crossway, 2019.

———. *The Holy Trinity: In Scripture, History, Theology, and Worship.* Phillipsburg, NJ: P&R, 2004.

———. *The Work of Christ: Contours of Christian Theology.* Downers Grove: IVP, 1993.

———. *Union with Christ: In Scripture, History, and Theology.* Phillipsburg, NJ: P&R, 2011.

Lewis, Gordon R. and Bruce A. Demarest. *Integrative Theology, Volume 1: Knowing Ultimate Reality: The Living God.* 3 vols. Grand Rapids: Zondervan, 1987.

Liddel, Henry George and Robert Scott. comp. *A Greek-English Lexicon.* Oxford: Clarendon Press, 1996.

Lillback, Peter A. *The Binding of God: Calvin's Role in the Development of Covenant Theology.* Grand Rapids: Baker, 2001.

Longenecker, Richard N. *Galatians.* Word Biblical Commentary. Dallas, TX: Word Books, 1990.

Loonstra, Bertus. *Verkiezing – Verzoening – Verbond: Beschrijving en beoordeling van de leer van het pactum salutis in de gereformeerde theologie.* Gravenhage: Uitgeverij Boekencentrum, 1990.

Lumpkin, William L. *Baptist Confessions of Faith.* Second Revised Edition. rev. Bill J. Leonard. Valley Forge, PA: Judson Press, 2011.

Magee, Gregory S. and Jeffrey D. Arthurs, *Ephesians: A Commentary for Biblical Preaching and Teaching.* Kerux Commentaries. Grand Rapids: Kregel, 2021.

Mann, William E. "Simplicity and Immutability in God." In *The Concept of God.* Edited by Thomas V. Morris. Oxford: Oxford University Press, 1987.

Marshall, I. Howard. *The Gospel of Luke: A Commentary on the Greek Text.* NIGTC. Exeter, England: Paternoster Press, 1978.

Martyn, J. Louis. *Galatians: A New Translation with Introduction and Commentary.* The Anchor Bible 33A. New York: Doubleday, 1997.

Marzouk, Safwat. "The Egyptians." In *The Baker Illustrated Bible Background Commentary.* Edited by J. Scott Duvall and J. Daniel Hays. Grand Rapids: Baker, 2020.

Mathews, Kenneth A. *Genesis 1-11:26.* NAC. vol. 1A. Nashville: B&H, 1996.

McCall, Thomas H. *Which Trinity? Whose Monotheism?: Philosophical and Systematic Theologians on the Metaphysics of Trinitarian Theology.* Grand Rapids: Eerdmans, 2010.

McFadden, Kevin W. *Faith in the Son of God: The Place of Christ-Oriented Faith within Pauline Theology.* Wheaton: Crossway, 2021.

McGrath, Alister E. *Iustitia Dei: A History of the Christian Doctrine of Justification*. 3rd ed. Cambridge: Cambridge University Press, 2005.

McGuire-Moushon J. A. and Rachel Klippenstein. "Eternity." In *The Lexham Theological Wordbook*. Edited by Douglas Mangum, Derek R. Brown, Rachel Klippenstein, and Rebekah Hurst. Bellingham, WA: Lexham, 2014.

McKnight, Scot and B. J. Oropeza, eds. *Perspectives on Paul: Five Views*. Grand Rapids: Baker, 2020.

McLachlan, H. John. *Socinianism in Seventeenth-Century England*. London: Oxford University Press, 1951.

Mendenhall, George E. *Law and Covenant in Israel and the Ancient Near East*. Pittsburgh: The Biblical Colloquium, 1955.

Merkle, Benjamin L. *United to Christ, Walking in the Spirit: A Theology of Ephesians*. New Testament Theology. Wheaton: Crossway, 2022.

Metzger, Bruce M. *A Textual Commentary on the Greek New Testament*. 2nd ed. Stuttgart: Deutsche Bibelgesellschaft, 2000.

Milgrom, Jacob. *Leviticus 23-27: A New Translation with Introduction and Commentary*. The Anchor Bible, vol. 3B. New York: Doubleday, 2001.

Moberly, R. W. L. *The God of the Old Testament: Encountering the Divine in Christian Scripture*. Grand Rapids: Baker, 2020.

Moltmann, Jürgen. *The Trinity and the Kingdom: The Doctrine of God*. Minneapolis: Fortress Press, 1993.

Morgan, Christopher W. and Robert A. Peterson, eds. *The Glory of God*. Theology in Community. Wheaton: Crossway, 2010.

Morris, Leon. *Luke: An Introduction and Commentary*. TNTC. vol. 3. Downers Grove: IVP, 1988.

———.*The Gospel according to John*. NICNT. Revised Edition. Grand Rapids: Eerdmans, 1995.

Mortimer, Sarah. *Reason and Religion in the English Revolution: The Challenge of Socinianism*. Cambridge Studies in Early Modern British History. Cambridge: Cambridge University Press, 2010.

Motyer, J. Alec. *Isaiah: An Introduction and Commentery*. Tyndale Old Testament Commentaries, vol. 20. Downers Grove: IVP, 1999.

Muller, Richard A. "pactum salutis." In *Dictionary of Latin and Greek Theological Terms: Drawn Principally from Protestant Scholastic Theology*. 2nd ed. Grand Rapids: Baker, 2017.

Nicholls, William. *An Answer to an Heretical Book Called the Naked Gospel, which was condemned and ordered to be publicly burnt by the Convocation of the University of Oxford, Aug. 19, 1690*. London: Bishop's Head in St. Paul's Church-Yard, 1691.

Nimmo, Paul T. and Keith L. Johnson, eds. *Kenosis: The Self-Emptying of Christ in Scripture & Theology*. Grand Rapids: Eerdmans, 2022.

Ney, Stephen. *A Letter of Resolution concerning the Doctrines of the Trinity and the Incarnation*. London: s.n., 1691.

———.*Doctor Wallis's Letter Touching the Doctrine of the Blessed Trinity Answer'd by his Friend*. London: s.n., 1691.

Oden, Thomas C. *The Justification Reader*. Classic Christian Readers. Grand Rapids: Eerdmans, 2002.

Oliver, Robert W. "John Gill (1697-1771): His Life and Ministry." In *The Life and Thought of John Gill (1697-1771): A Tercentennial Appreciation*. Edited by Michael A. G. Haykin. Studies in the History of Christian Thought. Leiden: Brill, 1997.

Origen. *Contra Celsum*. Translated by Henry Chadwick. Cambridge: University Press, 1953.

Ortlund, Gavin. *Theological Retrieval for Evangelicals: Why we Need our Past to have a Future*. Wheaton: Crossway, 2019.

Osborne, Grant R. and George H. Guthrie, *Hebrews: Verse by Verse*. Osborne New Testament Commentaries. Bellingham, WA: Lexham, 2021.

Ott, Ludwig. *Fundamentals of Catholic Dogma*. Translated by Patrick Lynch. Rockford, IL: Tan Books, 1974.

Paul, Shalom M. *Isaiah 40-66: Translation and Commentary*. Grand Rapids: Eerdmans, 2012.

Peckham, John C. *Divine Attributes: Knowing the Covenantal God of Scripture*. Grand Rapids: Baker, 2021.

Pedersen, Johannes. *Israel: Its Life and Culture*. Vols. I-II. Oxford University Press, 1926.

Pelikan, Jaroslav. *Acts*. Brazos Theological Commentary on the Bible. Grand Rapids: Brazos, 2005.

———. *The Emergence of the Catholic Tradition (100-600)*. The Christian Tradition: A History of the Development of Doctrine. 5 vols. Chicago: The University of Chicago Press, 1971; Paperback edition, 1975.

Peterson, David G. *The Acts of the Apostles*. The Pillar New Testament Commentary. Grand Rapids: Eerdmans, 2009.

Peterson, Robert A. *Salvation Accomplished by the Son: The Work of Christ*. Wheaton: Crossway, 2012.

———. *Salvation Applied by the Spirit: Union with Christ*. Wheaton: Crossway, 2015.

Petterson, Anthony R. *Behold Your King: The Hope for the House of David in the Book of Zechariah*. Library of Hebrew Bible/Old Testament Studies 513. New York: T&T Clark, 2009.

Petto, Samuel. *The Difference between the Old and New Covenant Stated and Explained*. London, 1674.

Pfizenmaier, Thomas C. *The Trinitarian Theology of Dr. Samuel Clarke (1675-1729): Context, Sources, and Controversy*. Studies in the History of Christian Thought. Leiden: Brill, 1997.

Picirilli, Robert E. *God in Eternity and Time: A New Case for Human Freedom*. Nashville: B&H, 2022.

Pierce, Madison N. *Divine Discourse in the Epistle to the Hebrews: The Recontextualization of Spoken Quotations of Scripture*. SNTSMS 178. Cambridge: Cambridge University Press, 2020.

Pierce, Samuel Eyles. *An Exposition of the Book of Psalms: Set Forth as Prophetic of Christ & His Church*, Newport Commentary Series. vol. 1. Springfield, MO: Particular Baptist Press, 2009.

Plantinga, Alvin. *Does God have a Nature?*. The Aquinas Lecture 1980. Milwaukee, WI: Marquette University Press, 2007.

Platter, Jonathan M. *Divine Simplicity and the Triune Identity: A Critical Dialogue with the Theological Metaphysics of Robert W. Jenson*. Theologische Bibliothek Töpelmann. Berlin: De Gruyter, 2021.

Pollock, Algernon J. *Unitarianism: The Negation of the Christian Faith*. London: Central Bible Truth Depot, 1951.
Poythress, Vern S. *Knowing and the Trinity: How Perspectives in Human Knowledge Imitate the Trinity*. Phillipsburg, NJ: P&R, 2018.
———. *The Mystery of the Trinity: A Trinitarian Approach to the Attributes of God*. Phillipsburg, NJ: P&R, 2020.
———. *Truth, Theology, and Perspective: An Approach to Understanding Biblical Doctrine*. Wheaton: Crossway, 2022.
Preuss, Neuendettelsau H. D. "סָלוּעַ." In *Theological Dictionary of the Old Testament*. Edited by G. Johannes Botterweck, Helmer Ringgren, and Heinz-Josef Fabry. Translated by Douglas W. Stott. 15 vols. Grand Rapids: Eerdmans, 1999.
Pusey, E. B. *Notes on the Old Testament: The Minor Prophtes: Micah to Malachi*. vol. 2. New York: Funk and Wagnalls, 1885; reprint, Grand Rapids: Baker Book House, 1983.
Rees, Thomas. *The Racovian Catechism: with Notes and Illustrations, translated from the Latin; to which is prefixed a sketch of the history of Unitarianism in Poland and the adjacent countries*. London: Longman, Hurst, Rees, Orme and Brown, 1818; repr., Lexington, KY: American Theological Library Association, 1962.
Rendtorff, Rolf. *Die „Bundesformel": eine exegetisch-theologische Untersuchung*. Stuttgarter Bibelstudien 160. Stuttgart: Verlag Katholisches Bibelwerk, 1995.
Renihan, Samuel D. *From Shadow to Substance: The Federal Theology of the English Particular Baptists (1642-1704)*. Centre for Baptist History and Heritage Studies. Oxford: Regent's Park College, 2018.
Richard, Guy M. "The Covenant of Redemption." In *Covenant Theology: Biblical, Theological, and Historical Perspectives*. Edited by Guy Prentiss Waters, J. Nicholas Reid, and John R. Muether. Wheaton: Crossway, 2020.
Richard of Saint Victor. *On the Trinity*. Translated by Ruben Angelici. Eugene, OR: Cascade Books, 2011.
Ridderbos, Herman. *Paul: An Outline of His Theology*. Translated by John Richard De Witt. Paperback edition. 1975; Grand Rapids: Eerdmans, 1997.
Rine, C. Rebecca. "Interpretations of Genesis 1-2 among the Nicene and Post-Nicene Fathers." In *Since the Beginning: Interpreting Genesis 1 and 2 through the Ages*. Edited by Kyle R. Greenwood. Grand Rapids: Baker, 2018.
Rippon, John. *A Brief Memoir of the Life and Writings of the late Rev. John Gill*. London: John Bennett, 1838.
Robertson, O. Palmer. *The Christ of the Covenants*. Phillipsburg, NJ: P&R, 1980.
Robinson, Michael D. *Eternity and Freedom: A Critical Analysis of Divine Timelessness as a Solution to the Foreknowledge/Free Will Debate*. Lanham, MD: University Press of America, 1995.
Rose, Wolter H. *Zemah and Zerubbabel: Messianic Expectations in the Early Postexilic Period*. Journal for the Study of the Old Testament Supplement Series 304. England: Sheffield Academic Press, 2000.
Rosner, Brian S. *Paul and the Law: Keeping the Commandments of God*. NSBT. Downers Grove: IVP, 2013.
Rowley, H. H. *The Biblical Doctrine of Election*. London: Lutterworth, 1950.
Rusch, William G, ed. and trans. *The Trinitarian Controversy*. Sources of Early Christian Thought. Philadelphia: Fortress, 1980.

Ryken, Philip Graham. *Luke*. Reformed Expository Commentary. vol. 2. Phillipsburg, NJ: P&R, 2009.
Sanders, E. P. *Paul and Palestinian Judaism: A Comparison of Patterns of Religion*. Philadelphia: Fortress, 1977.
Sanders, Fred. *The Triune God*. NSD. Grand Rapids: Zondervan, 2016.
Sanders, Fred and Klaus Issler. *Jesus in Trinitarian Perspective: An Intermediate Christology*. Nashville: B&H, 2007.
Sasse, Hermann. "αἰών, αἰώνιος." In *Theological Dictionary of the New Testament*, Edited by Gerhard Kittel. Translated by Geoffrey W. Bromiley. 10 vols. 1964; repr. Grand Rapids: Eerdmans, 2006.
Schreiner, Patrick. *Acts*. Christian Standard Commentary. Nashville: Holman, 2021.
Schreiner, Thomas R. *Faith Alone: The Doctrine of Justification: What the Reformers Taught ... and Why It Still Matters*. The Five Solas Series. Grand Rapids: Zondervan, 2015.
———.*Galatians*. Zondervan Exegetical Commentary on the New Testament. Grand Rapids: Zondervan, 2010.
———."Revelation." In *Expository Commentary, vol. XII, Hebrews–Revelation*. Wheaton: Crossway, 2018.
———.*1, 2 Peter, Jude*. NAC. vol. 37. Nashville: B&H, 2003.
Servetus, Michael. "On the Errors of the Trinity." In *The Two Treatises of Servetus on the Trinity*. Translated by Earl Morse Wilbur. Harvard Theological Studies 16. Cambridge: Harvard University Press, 1932.
Smalley, Stephen S. *1, 2, 3 John*. WBC. vol. 51. Waco, TX: Word Books, 1984.
Smith, Gary V. *Isaiah 40-66*. The New American Commentary. vol. 15B. Nashville: B&H, 2009.
Son, Sang-Won (Aaron). *Corporate Elements in Pauline Anthropology: A Study of Selected Terms, Idioms, and Concepts in the Light of Paul's usage and background*. Roma, Italia: Editrice Pontificio Istituto Biblico, 2001.
Sproul, R. C. *The Promises of God: Discovering the One who keeps his Word*. Colorado Springs, CO: David C Cook, 2013.
Stillingfleet, Edward. *A Discourse in Vindication of the Doctrine of the Trinity: with An Answer to the Late Socinian Objections Against it from Scripture, Antiquity and Reason and a Preface concerning the different Explications of the Trinity, and the Tendency of the present Socinian Controversie*. London: Henry Mortlock, 1697.
Stott, John. *The Cross of Christ*. Stott Centennial Edition. Downers Grove: IVP, 2021.
Stuhlmacher, Peter. *Revisiting Paul's Doctrine of Justification: A Challenge to the New Perspective*. Downers Grove: IVP, 2001.
Stamps, R. Lucas. "The Trinity." In *Historical Theology for the Church*. Edited by Jason G. Duesing and Nathan A. Finn. Nashville: B&H, 2021.
Stump, Eleonore. *Aquinas*. London: Routledge, 2003.
Swain, Scott R. "Covenant of Redemption." In *Christian Dogmatics: Reformed Theology for the Church Catholic*. Edited by Michael Allen and Scott R. Swain. Grand Rapids: Baker, 2016.
———."The Radiance of the Father's Glory: Eternal Generation, the Divine Names, and Biblical Interpretation." In *Retrieving Eternal Generation*. Edited by Fred Sanders and Scott R. Swain. Grand Rapids: Zondervan, 2017.
———.*The Trinity: An Introduction*. Short Studies in Systematic Theology. Wheaton: Crossway, 2020.

———. *The Trinity and the Bible: On Theological Interpretation*. Bellingham, WA: Lexham, 2021.

Swanson, James. "רָמָא." In *A Dictionary of Biblical Languages: Hebrew (Old Testament)*. Electronic ed. Oak Harbor: Logos Research Systems, 1997.

Taylor, Mark. *1 Corinthians*. NAC. vol. 28. Nashville: B&H, 2014.

Tan, Randall, David A. DeSilva, and Isaiah Hoogendyk, eds. *The Lexham Greek-English Interlinear Septuagint: H. B. Swete Edition*. vol. 2. Bellingham, WA: Lexham, 2012.

Thiselton, Anthony C. *Systematic Theology*. Grand Rapids: Eerdmans, 2015.

Thompson, John. *Modern Trinitarian Perspectives*. New York: Oxford University Press, 1994.

Tillotson, John. *A Seasonable Vindication of the B. Trinity Being an Answer to this Question, Why do you believe the Doctrine of the Trinity?* London: B. Aylmer, 1697.

Torrance, Thomas F. *Incarnation: The Person and Life of Christ*. Edited by Robert T. Walker. Downers Grove: IVP, 2008.

Towne, Robert. *A Re-Assertion of Grace, Or, Vindiciae Evangelii: A Vindication of the Gospel-truths, from the unjust censure and undue aspersions of Antinomians*. London, 1654.

Treier, Daniel J. *Introducing Evangelical Theology*. Grand Rapids: Baker, 2019.

Ursinus, Zacharias. *The Commentary of Zacharias Ursinus on the Heidelberg Catechism*. Translated by G. W. Williard. Cincinnati: Elm Street Printing Company, 1888; reprint, Miami, FL: HardPress, 2012.

Vanhoozer, Kevin J. *Dictionary for Theological Interpretation of the Bible*. Grand Rapids: Baker, 2005.

Velde, Rudi A. Te. "The Divine Person(s): Trinity, Person, and Analogous Naming." In *The Oxford Handbook of the Trinity*. Edited by Gilles Emery, O.P. and Matthew Levering. Oxford: Oxford University Press, 2011.

Vickers, Brian J. "The Acts of the Apostles." In *Expository Commentary, Vol. IX: John–Acts*. Wheaton: Crossway, 2019.

Vidu, Adonis. *The Same God who Works All Things: Inseparable Opertations in Trinitarian Theology*. Grand Rapids: Eerdmans, 2021.

Wainwright, Arthur W. *The Trinity in the New Testament*. 1962; Eugene, OR: Wipf and Stock, 2001.

Walker, Larry L. "Isaiah." In *Cornerstone Biblical Commentary*. vol. 8. Wheaton: Tyndale House Publishers, 2005.

Wallis, John. *The Doctrine of the Blessed Trinity Briefly Explained, In a Letter to a Friend*. London: Tho. Parkhurst, 1690.

Waltke, Bruce K. *An Old Testament Theology: An Exegetical, Canonical, and Thematic Approach*. Grand Rapids: Zondervan, 2007.

Ware, Bruce A. *Father, Son, and Holy Spirit: Relationships, Roles, and Relevance*. Wheaton: Crossway, 2005.

Ware, Bruce A. and John Starke, eds. *One God in Three Persons: Unity of Essence, Distinction of Persons, Implications for Life*. Wheaton: Crossway, 2015.

Waters, Guy Prentiss, J. Nicholas Reid, and John R. Muether, eds. *Covenant Theology: Biblical, Theological, and Historical Perspectives*. Wheaton: Crossway, 2020.

Webster, John. "Gospel." In *Dictionary for Theological Interpretation of the Bible*. Edited by Kevin J. Vanhoozer. Grand Rapids: Baker, 2005.

Weinrich, Michael and John P. Burgess, ed. *What Is Justification About?: Reformed Contributions to an Ecumenical Theme*. Grand Rapids: Eerdmans, 2009.

Wellum, Stephen J. *God the Son Incarnate: The Doctrine of Christ*. Foundations of Evangelical Theology Series. Wheaton: Crossway, 2016.

———.*The Person of Christ: An Introduction*. Short Studies in Systematic Theology. Wheaton: Crossway, 2021.

Wenham, Gordon J. *Genesis 1-15*. WBC. vol. 1. Waco, TX: Word Books, 1987.

Wesley, John. *Predestination Calmly Considered*. London: Printed by Henry Cock, 1755.

Westcott, Brooke Foss. *The Epistles of St John: The Greek Text with Notes and Essays*. Grand Rapids: Eerdmans, 1957.

Westerholm, Stephen. *Perspectives Old and New on Paul: The "Lutheran" Paul and His Critics*. Grand Rapids: Eerdmans, 2004.

Westermann, Claus. *Genesis 1-11: A Commentary*. Translated by John J. Scullion S.J. Minneapolis: Augsburg Publishing House, 1984.

Westminster Assembly. *The Westminster Confession of Faith: Edinburgh Edition*. Philadelphia: William S. Young, 1851.

Westminster Confession of Faith. Glasgow: Free Presbyterian Publications, 1994.

Whitby, Daniel. "Discourse I: Concerning Election and Reprobation." In *Discourse on the Five Points*. 3rd ed. corrected. 1710; London: F. C. and J. Rivington, 1816.

Whitfield, Keith S, ed. *Trinitarian Theology: Theological Models and Doctrinal Application*. Nashville: B&H, 2019.

Wiles, Maurice. *Archetypal Heresy: Arianism through the Centuries*. Oxford: Clarendon, 1996.

Willard, Samuel. *The Doctrine of the Covenant of Redemption: Wherein is laid the Foundation of all our Hopes and Happiness: Briefly Opened and Improved*. Boston: Benj. Harris, 1693.

Williamson, Paul R. *Sealed with an Oath: Covenant in God's Unfolding Purpose*. New Studies in Biblical Theology 23. Downers Grove: IVP, 2007.

Witherington III, Ben. *Grace in Galatia: A Commentary on St Paul's Letter to the Galatians*. Grand Rapids: Eerdmans, 1998.

Witsius, Herman. *The Economy of the Covenants Between God and Man: Comprehending A Complete Body of Divinity*. vol. 1. Translated by William Crookshank. London: Baynes, 1882.

Woo, B. Hoon. *The Promise of the Trinity: The Covenant of Redemption in the Theologies of Witsius, Owen, Dickson, Goodwin, and Cocceius*. Göttingen: Vandenhoeck & Ruprecht, 2018.

Wright, G. Ernest. *The Old Testament against its Environment*. Studies in Biblical Theology. London: SCM, 1950.

Wright, Christopher J. H. *Walking in the Ways of the Lord: The Ethical Authority of the Old Testament*. Downers Grove: IVP, 1995.

Wright, N. T. *Galatians*. Commentaries for Christian Formation. Grand Rapids: Eerdmans, 2021.

———.*Paul: In Fresh Perspective*. paperback edition. Minneapolis: Fortress, 2009.

———.*The Climax of the Covenant: Christ and the Law in the Pauline Theology*. London: T&T Clark, 1991.

Wright, R. K. McGregor. *The Two Trinities: A Study in Apologetic Strategy*. Johnson City, TN: Worldview Heritage Press, 2011.

Yarbrough, Robert W. "Eternal Life, Eternality, Everlasting Life." In *Evangelical Dictionary of Biblical Theology*. Edited by Walter A. Elwell. Grand Rapids: Baker Books, 1996.

———. *1-3 John*. BECNT. Grand Rapids: Baker, 2008.
Yarnell III, Malcolm B. *God the Trinity: Biblical Portraits*. Nashville: B&H, 2016.
———. *Who Is the Holy Spirit: Biblical Insights into His Divine Person*. Hobbs College Library. Nashville: B&H, 2019.
Yates, John C. *The Timelessness of God*. Lanham, MD: University Press of America, 1990.
Young, Edward J. *The Book of Isaiah: The English Text, with Introduction, Exposition, and Notes*. 3 vols. Grand Rapids: Eerdmans, 1965.
Zizioulas, John D. *Being as Communion: Studies in Personhood and the Church*. Crestwood, NY: St. Vladimir's Seminary Press, 1985.

ARTICLES

Agus, Jacob B. "The Covenant Concept – Particularistic, Pluralistic, or Futuristic?" *JES* 18, no. 2 (Spring 1981): 217-230.
Alexander, T. Desmond. "Further Observations on the Term 'Seed' in Genesis." *Tyndale Bulletin* 48, no. 2 (1997): 363-367.
Azkoul, Michael. "On Time and Eternity: The Nature of History According to the Greek Fathers." *St Vladimir's Seminary Quarterly* 12, no. 2 (1968): 56-77.
Babcock, William S. "A Changing of the Christian God: The Doctrine of the Trinity in the Seventeenth Century." *Interpretations* 45, no. 2 (April 1991): 133-146.
Baddorf, Matthew. "Divine Simplicity, Aseity, and Sovereignty." *Sophia* 56, no. 3 (September 2017): 403-418.
Bainton, Roland H. "Burned Heretic: Michael Servetus." *The Christian Century* 70, no. 43 (October 1953): 1230-1231.
Baker, Bruce A. "A Biblical and Theological Examination of the Glory of God." *JMAT* 22, no. 1 (Spring 2018): 5-25.
Baugh, S. M. "Galatians 3:20 and the Covenant of Redemption." *WTJ* 66, no. 1 (2004): 49-70.
Beach, J. Mark. "The Doctrine of the *Pactum Salutis* in the Covenant Theology of Herman Witsius." *MJT* 13 (2002): 101-142.
Beacham, Roy. "Ancient Near Eastern Covenants." *JMAT* 15, no. 1 (Spring 2011): 110-128.
Bedale, Stephen. "The Meaning of κεφαλή in the Pauline Epistles." *JTS* 5, no. 2 (1954): 211-215.
Blanton IV, Thomas R. "Saved by Obedience: Matthew 1:21 in Light of Jesus' Teaching on the Torah." *Journal of Biblical Literature* 132, no. 2 (2013): 393-413.
Blocher, Henri. "Yesterday, Today, Forever: Time, Times, Eternity in Biblical Perspective." *Tyndale Bulletin* 52, no. 2 (2001): 183-202.
Brand, Thomas. "Nature, Person and Will: An Argument from the Church Fathers and the Ecumenical Councils against the Eternal Subordination of the Son." *Foundations* 73 (Fall 2017): 51-64.
Brown, Michael G. "Samuel Petto (c. 1624-1711): A Portrait a Puritan Pastor Theologian." *PRJ* 2, no. 1 (2010): 75-91.
Busenitz, Irvin A. "Introduction to the Biblical Covenants; The Noahic Covenant and the Priestly Covenant." *TMSJ* 10, no. 2 (Fall 1999): 173-189.

Busenitz, Nathan. "The Substance of *Sola Fide*: Justification Defended from Scripture in the Writings of the Reformers." *TMSJ* 32, no. 1 (Spring 2021): 77-92.

Cary, Phillip. "The Incomprehensibility of God and the Origin of the Thomistic Concept of the Supernatural." *Pro Ecclesia* 11, no. 3 (2002): 340-355.

Chase, Michael. "Time and Eternity From Plotinus and Boethius to Einstein." *Schole Ancient Philosophy and the Classical Tradition* 8, no. 1 (2014): 67-110.

Chaves, Joao. "The Servetus Challenge: Eisegesis and the Problematic of Differing Chronologies of Ecclesiastical Corruption." *Journal of Reformed Theology* 10, no. 3 (2016): 195-214.

Collins, C. John. "Galatians 3:16: What Kind of Exegete was Paul?" *Tyndale Bulletin* 54, no. 1 (2003): 75-86.

Dahms, John V. "The Subordination of the Son." *JETS* 37, no. 3 (September 1994): 351-364.

DelCogliano, Mark. "The Interpretation of John 10:30 in the Third Century: Antimonarchian Polemics and the Rise of Grammatical Reading Techniques." *Journal of Theological Interpretation* 6, no. 1 (2012): 117-138.

Devine, Charles F. "The 'blood of God' in Acts 20:28." *The Catholic Biblical Quarterly* 9, no. 4 (October 1947): 381-408.

Duke, Roger. "The Most Important Question One Can Ask!" *Founders Journal* 110 (Fall 2017): 22-31.

Everts, W. W. "The Rise and Spread of Socinianism." *Review and Expositor* 11, no. 4 (October 1914): 518-535.

Fesko, J. V. "The Covenant of Redemption and the Ordo Salutis." *TMSJ* 33, no. 1 (Spring 2022): 5-19.

Fortaci, Talha. "The Trinity in the Theology of Michael Servetus." *Oksident* 4, no. 2 (2022): 173-206.

Geis, Francis. "The Trinity and the Eternal Subordination of the Son." *Priscilla Papers* 27, no. 4 (2013): 23-28.

Gentry, Peter J. "'The Glory of God'--The Character of God's Being and Way in the Word: Some Reflections on a Key Biblical Theology Theme." *SBJT* 20, no. 1 (2016): 149-161.

Gomes, Alan W. "Some Observations on the Theological Method of Faustus Socinus (1539-1604)." *WTJ* 70 (2008): 49-71.

Harrison, Verna. "Perichoresis in the Greek Fathers." *St Vladimir's Theological Quarterly* 35, no. 1 (1991): 53-65.

Haykin, Michael A. G. "A Socinian and Calvinist Compared: Joseph Priestley and Andrew Fuller on the Propriety of Prayer to Christ." *Nederlands archief voor kerkgeschiedenis* 73, no. 2 (1993): 178-82.

Hicks, Tom. "Benjamin Keach's Doctrine of Justification." *TMSJ* 32, no. 1 (Spring 2021): 93-113.

Hilgert, Earle. "Some Reflections on Cullmann's New Edition of *Christ and Time*." *Andrew University Seminary Studies* 2 (1964): 27-39.

Hillar, Marian. "Laelius and Faustus Socinus, Founders of Socinianism: Their Lives and Theology." Part One and Two, *A Journal from the Radical Reformation: A Testimony to Biblical Unitarianism* 10, no. 2-3 (2001-2): 19-38.

———. "The Polish Socinians: Contribution to Freedom of Conscience and the American Constitution." *Dialogue and Universalism* 19, no. 3-5 (2009): 45-75.

Jackelen, Antjie. "A Relativistic Eschatology: Time, Eternity, and Eschatology in Light of the Physics of Relativity." *Zygon* 41, no. 4 (2006): 955-973.

———."Where Time and Eternity Meet." *Dialog* 39, no. 1 (2000): 15-20.

Jauhiainen, Marko. "Turban and Crown Lost and Regained: Ezekiel 21:29-32 and Zechariah's Zemah." *Journal of Biblical Literature* 127, no. 3 (2008): 501-511.

Jones, David W. and John K. Tarwater. "Are Biblical Covenants Dissoluble?" *SWJT* 47, no. 1 (Fall 2004): 1-11

Jordan, W. K. "Sectarian Thought and Its Relation to the Development of Religious Toleration, 1640-1660; Part III: 'The Socinians.'" *Huntington Library Quarterly* 3, no. 4 (1940): 403-418.

Kagarise, Robby J. "The 'Seed' in Galatians 3:16–A Window to Paul's Thinking." *Evangelical Journal* 18, no. 2 (Fall 2000): 67-73.

Kim, Hyo-Nam. "Eternal God and Temporal World: The Reformed Understanding of Divine Affections as an Evidence of Eternal God Walking in the Temporal World." *Korea Reformed Theology* 59 (2018): 175-217.

Kirk, J. R. Daniel. "The Sufficiency of the Cross (I): The Crucifixion as Jesus' Act of Obedience." *Scottish Bulletin of Evangelical Theology* 24, no. 1 (Spring 2006): 36-64.

Kovach, Stephen D. and Peter R. Schemm Jr. "A Defense of the Doctrine of the Eternal Subordination of the Son." *JETS* 42, no. 3 (September 1999): 461-476.

Levering, Matthew and George Kalantzis. "Introduction: Why Think About Divine Simplicity?" *Modern Theology* 35, no. 3 (July 2019): 411-417.

Litfin, Bryan M. "Tertullian on the Trinity." *Perichoresis: The Theological Journal of Emanuel University* 17, no. 1 (2019): 81-98.

Loftin, R. Keith. "A Barthian Critique of the Covenant of Redemption." *TRINJ* 38, no. 2 (2017): 203-222.

Lombardo, Nicholas E. OP. "Divine Persons and Notional Acts in the Trinitarian Theology of Thomas Aquinas." *Theological Studies* 82, no. 4 (December 2021): 603-625.

Michelson, Jared. "Contemplating the One Who Remains the Same: Augustine, Swinburne, and Psalm 102 on the Relation between Divine Immutability and Theological Reason." *Modern Theology* 36:4 (October 2020): 803-825.

Molnar, Paul D. "The Importance of the Doctrine of Justification in the Theology of Thomas F. Torrance and of Karl Barth." *Scottish Journal of Theology* 70, no. 2 (2017): 199-209.

Monck, Thomas. "An Orthodox Creed." *SWJT* 48, no. 2 (Spring 2006): 133-182.

Muller, Richard A. "Toward the Pactum Salutis: Locating the Origins of a Concept." *MJT* 18 (2007): 11-65.

Nimmo, Paul T. "Reforming *simul iustus et peccator*: Karl Barth and the 'Actualisation' of the Doctrine of Justification." *Zeitschrift für Dialektische Theologie, Supplement Series* 6 (2014): 91-104.

Ogonowski, Zbigniew. "Antitrinitarianism in Poland before Socinus: A Historical Outline." *Roczniki Filozoficzne* 70, no. 4 (2022): 87-142.

Oliver, Willem H. "The Praxis of Adversus Praxeam: Tertullian's Views on the Trinity." *Verbum et Ecclesia* 42, no. 1 (2021): 1-9.

Parr, Thomas. "English Puritans and the Covenant of Redemption: The Exegetical Arguments of John Flavel and William Strong." *PRJ* 12, no. 1 (2020): 55-74.

———. "Patrick Gillespie on the Covenant of Redemption: Exegetical Arguments." *PRJ* 13, no. 1 (2021): 48-77.

Pelikan, Jaroslav. "Montanism and its Trinitarian Significance." *Church History* 25, no. 2 (1956): 99-109.

Pester, John. "'And God Said, Let Us Make...And Let Them'–The Body of Christ as the Corporate Manifestation of the Triune God in the Flesh." *Affirmation & Critique* 18, no. 2 (Fall 2013): 15-32.

Playoust, Marc R. "Oscar Cullmann and Salvation History." *Heythrop Journal* 12, no. 1 (1971): 29-43.

Powell, Douglas L. "Tertullianists and Cataphrygians." *Vigiliae christianae* 29, no. 1 (1975): 33-54.

Rathel, David Mark. "John Gill and the Charge of Hyper-Calvinism: Assessing Contemporary Arguments in Defense of Gill in Light of Gill's Doctrine of Eternal Justification." *SBJT* 25, no. 1 (2021): 43-62.

———. "John Gill and the History of Redemption as Mere Shadow: Exploring Gill's Doctrine of the Covenant of Redemption." *JRT* 11, no. 4 (2017): 377-400.

Reedy, S.J., Gerard. "Socinians, John Toland, and the Anglican Rationalists." *Harvard Theological Review* 70, no. 3-4 (July-October 1977): 285-304.

Renihan, James M. "God Freely Justifieth...by Imputing Christ's Active...and Passive Obedience." *TMSJ* 32, no. 1 (Spring 2021): 61-75.

Rogers, Katherin A. "Anselmian Eternalism: The Presence of a Timeless God." *Faith and Philosophy* 24, no. 1 (2007): 3-27.

Rust, Eric C. "Time and Eternity in Biblical Thought." *Theology Today* 10, no. 3 (1953): 327-356.

Sammons, Peter. "The Eternal God of a Vanishing Creation: Recovering the Doctrine of Divine Timelessness." *TMSJ* 31, no. 2 (2020): 189-211.

Scheiderer, Daniel D. "John Gill and the Continuing Baptist Affirmation of the Eternal Covenant." *SBJT* 25, no. 1 (2021): 65-90.

Schwöbel, Christoph. "The Eternity of the Triune God: Preliminary Considerations on the Relationship between the Trinity and the Time of Creation." *Modern Theology* 34, no. 3 (2018): 345-355.

Shimko, Tim. "Divine Incomprehensibility in Eastern Orthodoxy and Reformed Theology." *Theological Reflections* 19, no. 1 (2021): 15-26.

Stamps, R. Lucas. "John Gill's Reformed Dyothelitism." *The Reformed Theological Review* 74, no. 2 (August 2015): 77-93.

Standahl, Krister. "The Apostle Paul and the Introspective Conscience of the West." *Harvard Theological Review* 56, no. 3 (1963): 199-215.

Steenbuch, Johannes A. "Always Already Loved: Recovering the Doctrine of Justification from Eternity." *Journal of European Baptist Studies* 18, no. 2 (Fall 2018): 31-44.

Steward, Gary L. "The Calvinistic Soteriology of Jonathan Dickinson." *The Confessional Presbyterian* 7 (2011):

Streett, Andrew D. "New Approaches to the Use of the Old Testament in the New Testament," *SWJT* 64, no. 1 (2021): 77-86.

Swan, Jonathan E. "John Gill (1697-1771) and the Eternally Begotten Word of God." *Perichoresis* 20, no. 1 (2022): 53-69.

———. "The Divine Word in the Theology of John Gill (1697-1771)." *SBJT* 25, no. 1 (2021): 131-53.

Taggar-Cohen, Ada. "Biblical Covenant and Hittite išḫiul reexamined." *Vetus Testamentum* 61, no. 3 (2011): 461-488.
Thompson, J. A. "Non-Biblical Covenants in the Ancient Near East." *ABR* 8, no. 1 (1960): 38-45.
Waldron, Sam. "Paul's Use of Genesis 15:6 in Romans 4:3." *TMSJ* 32, no. 1 (Spring 2021): 115-130.
Webster, John. "Trinity and Creation." *International Journal of Systematic Theology* 12, no. 1 (January 2010): 4-19.
Weinfeld, M. "The Covenant of Grant in the Old Testament and in the Ancient Near East." *JAOS* 90, no. 2 (1970): 184-203.
Welker, Michael. "God's Eternity, God's Temporality, and Trinitarian Theology." *Theology Today* 55, no. 3 (1998): 317-328.
Wilcox, Max. "The Promise of the 'Seed' in the New Testament and the Targumim." *Journal for the Study of the New Testament* 2, no. 5 (September 1979): 2-20.
Williamson, Paul R. "The *Pactum Salutis*: A Scriptural Concept or Scholastic Mythology?" *TB* 69, no. 2 (2018): 259-281.
Yarnell III, Malcolm B. "Christian Justification: A Reformation and Baptist View." *CTR* 2, no. 2 (Spring 2005): 71-89.
Young III, William W. "Toward an inclusive conception of eternity." *International Journal for Philosophy of Religion* 89, no. 2 (2021): 171-187.

DISSERTATIONS

Daniel, Curt D. "Hyper-Calvinism and John Gill." Ph.D. diss., University of Edinburgh, 1983.
Godet, Steven Tshombe. "The Trinitarian Theology of John Gill (1697-1771): Context, Sources, and Controversy." Ph.D. diss., The Southern Baptist Theological Seminary, 2015.
Hicks, Thomas Eugene, Jr. "An Analysis of the Doctrine of Justification in the Theologies of Richard Baxter and Benjamin Keach." Ph.D. diss., The Southern Baptist Theological Seminary, 2009.
Ladd, Steven W. "Theological Indicators Supporting an Evangelical Conception of Eternity: A Study of God's Relation to Time in Light of the Doctrine of Creation *ex nihilo*." Ph.D. diss., Southeastern Baptist Theological Seminary, 2002.
Park, Hong-Gyu. "Grace and Nature in the Theology of John Gill." Ph.D. diss., University of Aberdeen, 2001.
Seymour, Robert Edward. "John Gill, Baptist Theologian (1697-1771)." Ph.D. diss., University of Edinburgh, 1954.
White, Jonathan Anthony. "A Theological and Historical Examination of John Gill's Soteriology in Relation to Eighteenth-Century Hyper-Calvinism." Ph.D. diss., The Southern Baptist Theological Seminary, 2010.
Williams, Carol. "The Decree of Redemption is in Effect a Covenant: David Dickson and the Covenant of Redemption." Ph.D. diss., Calvin Theological Seminary, 2005.
Yazawa, Reita. "Covenant of Redemption in the Theology of Jonathan Edwards: the Nexus between the Immanent and Economic Trinity" Ph.D. diss., Calvin Theological Seminary, 2013.

Names Index

A
Abernethy, Andrew T., 197
Agus, Jacob B., 3
Akin, Daniel L., 151, 204
Alexander, T. Desmond, 195
Allen, R. Michael, 111, 181
Allison, Gregg R., 128
Anselm of Canterbury, 24, 28–30, 36, 112
Aquinas, Thomas, 24, 30–31, 36, 41, 59
Aristotle, 137
Arius, 39, 159
Arnold, Bill T., 143
Arthurs, Jeffrey D., 111
Ashford, Bruce Riley, 45
Athanasius of Alexandria, 152, 209
Augustine of Hippo, 24–26, 28, 30, 36, 57, 58, 134, 135, 180, 182
Azkoul, Michael, 24

B
Babcock, William S., 126
Baddorf, Matthew, 50
Bahnsen, Greg L., 207
Bainton, Roland H., 127
Baker, Bruce A., 69
Barrett, Matthew, 160, 162
Bauckham, Richard, 141
Barcellos, Richard C., 218
Barclay, John M. G., 180
Barns, Albert, 76
Barr, James, 21
Barrett, Helen M., 28
Barrett, Jordan P., 48

Barth, Karl, 5, 10, 14, 41–43, 90, 92, 94, 100, 121, 172–173, 178–179, 199
Bartholomew, Craig G., 145
Basil the Great, 24
Baugh, Steven M., 15, 16
Bavinck, Herman, 3–4, 16, 50, 53, 55, 57, 65, 99–100
Beach, J. Mark, 12
Beacham, Roy, 3
Beale, G. K., 197
Beasley-Murray, G. R., 39, 140–141
Bedale, Stephen, 161
Beeke, Joel R., 7, 108
Berkhof, Louis, 3–4, 65, 139
Best, Earnest, 153
Biddle, John, 130–132, 134
Bird, Michael F., 100, 173, 180
Blaising, Craig A., 152, 203–204
Blanton IV, Thomas R., 207
Blocher, Henri, 22
Block, Daniel I, 2–5, 14
Bloesch, Donald G., 53, 121
Boethius, Anicius Manlius T. S., 24, 26–28, 30, 36, 58
Boice, James Montgomery, 105
Borchert, Gerald L., 150
Brabant, Frank Herbert, 27, 31
Brand, Chad Owen, 171
Brand, Thomas, 158
Bridge, William, 201
Briggs, Charles, 56
Brine, John, 187
Brown, David, 146
Brown, Francis, 56

Brown, Michael G., 81
Bruce, F. F., 191
Brunner, Emil, 59
Buchanan, James, 180–181
Büchsel, Rostock Friedrich, 96
Bulkeley, Peter, 5
Bull, George, 159
Bullinger, Heinrich, 128
Bultmann, Rudolf, 32
Burgess, John P., 181
Burrell, David B., 31
Bury, Arthur, 123
Busenitz, Irvin A., 3
Busenitz, Nathan, 181–182
Butner Jr., D. Glenn, 141, 144, 162, 166

C

Calvin, John, 57, 128, 181–182
Campbell, Constantine R., 151, 176
Carson, D. A., 39, 141, 149, 176, 180, 197
Carter, Craig A., 136, 139
Cassuto, Umberto, 147
Cary, Phillip, 41
Chase, Michael, 24
Chaves, Joao, 127
Childs, Brevard S., 120
Chrysostom, 180
Clarke, Samuel, 159
Clement of Alexandria, 24, 152
Cloppenburg, Johannes, 5
Cocceius, Johannes, 5
Collier, Thomas, 88
Collins, C. John, 195
Coxe, Nehemiah, 66
Craig, William Lane, 23
Crisp, Oliver D., 54
Crisp, Tobias, 85
Cross, F. L., 128, 180–181
Cullmann, Oscar, 32–33, 36
Cyprian, 152
Cyril of Jerusalem, 24

D

Dahms, John V., 159
Dalferth, Ingolf, 35
Dam, Cornelis Van, 74

Daniel, Curt, 7
Davidson, Robert, 3
Davies, Brian, 31
DelCogliano, Mark, 141
Delitzsch, Franz, 148
Demarest, Bruce A., 44, 112
Denault, Pascal, 218
DeSilva, David A., 101
Devine, Charles F., 211
DeWeese, Garrett J., 22, 29, 203
Dickinson, Jonathan, 170, 172
Dickson, David, 5, 13
Dockery, David S., 56
Drickamer, John M., 204
Driver, S. R., 56
Duby, Steven J., 48, 104, 213
Duke, Roger, 184
Dumbrell, William J., 82
Dunn, James D. G., 180
Dyken, Seymour Van, 9

E

Eichrodt, Walther, 81, 145
Ella, George M., 189
Elliot, Mark W., 72
Ellis, E. Earle, 193, 197, 200
Elwell, Walter A., 3, 145, 175
Emerson, Matthew Y., 155, 161, 162
Enns, Peter, 120
Erickson, Millard J., 12, 42–43, 51, 155–156, 161–162
Estep, W. R., 126
Estes, Douglas, 21
Everts, W. W., 126, 128

F

Fausset, A. R., 146
Fee, Gordon D., 199
Feinberg, John S., 25, 27–28, 45
Fesko, John V., 4–5, 7, 13, 63, 78–79, 121, 179, 180–182
Fisher, Edward, 5
Flavel, John, 4
Fortaci, Talha, 127, 128
Fowler, Edward, 133
Frame, John M., 45, 53, 57–58, 69, 77, 91, 136, 208
Fretheim, Terence E., 120

Names Index

G
Gamble, Whitney G., 209
Gardner, Paul, 161
Garland, David E., 96, 174
Garrett Jr., James Leo, 41–42, 45, 53, 59, 108, 138, 139, 142, 171, 205, 216–217
Geis, Francis, 166
Geisler, Norman, 59
Gentino, David, 211
Gentry, Peter J., 10, 69, 192, 199, 218
George, Timothy, 25, 56, 197
Giezek, Peter, 130
Giles, Kevin N., 12, 159
Gillespie, Patrick, 1, 4, 8–9, 12, 78
Gillingham, Susan, 152
Godet, Steven Tshombe, 124
Goldingay, John, 75, 146
Gomes, Alan W., 128
Goppelt, Leonhard, 197
Goswell, Gregory, 197
Gregory, Francis, 133
Gregory of Nazianzus, 135
Gregory of Nyssa, 24
Groningen, Gerard Van, 3
Grudem, Wayne, 12, 42, 160, 164, 176
Guthrie, George H., 101

H
Hagner, Donald A., 101
Hamilton Jr., James M., 162
Hamilton, Victor P., 147
Hansen, G. Walter, 104, 197
Hanson, R. C. P., 57
Hardin, Carmen S., 152
Harris, Murray J., 96
Harrison, Verna, 142
Harvey, John D., 211
Harwood, Adam, 108, 139, 171, 205
Hawkins, Ralph K., 120
Haykin, Michael A. G., 125
Helm, Paul, 23, 26
Heokema, Anthony A., 147
Heoksema, Herman, 15–17, 86–87, 213
Hicks, Tom, 188
Hilary of Poitiers, 24
Hilgert, Earle, 32
Hillar, Marian, 128, 130
Hillers, Delbert R., 3, 82
Hinlicky, Paul R., 48
Hodge, Charles, 65
Hoehner, Harold W., 111–112
Hoogendyk, Isaiah, 101
Horton, Michael, 2, 50, 60, 181, 183
Hoskins, Paul M., 37, 174
Howell, Robert Boyte C., 106
Hunter, Trent, 196

I
Ignatius of Antioch, 24
Irenaeus of Lyons, 24, 159

J
Jackelen, Antjie, 23–24, 32–35
Jamieson, Robert, 146
Jauhiainen, Marko, 78
Jerome, 152
Jobes, Karen H., 105, 151, 153, 176, 177
John of Damascus, 24
Johnson, Keith L., 54
Jones, David W., 3
Jordan, W. K., 130
Justin Martyr, 24

K
Kagarise, Robby J., 195, 197
Kalantzis, George, 49
Kärkkäinen, Veli-Matti, 142, 155
Kats, Sheri, 91
Keach, Benjamin, 66, 87, 89, 118, 188
Keathley, Kenneth, 171
Kidner, Derek, 147
Kilcrease, Jack D., 180
Kim, Hyo-Nam, 26
Kirk, J. R. Daniel, 207
Klein, George L., 78
Klein, William W., 171
Kline, Meredith G., 3
Klippenstein, Rachel, 22
Klooster, F. H., 171
Kot, Stanislas, 125–126, 128, 130
Kovach, Stephen D., 159
Küng, Hans, 178, 179

L

Larkin, William J., 211
Leftow, Brian, 23, 30
Letham, Robert, 5, 11, 12, 14–15, 176, 182, 197
Levering, Matthew, 49
Lewis, Gordon R., 44
Liddel, Henry George, 83
Lillback, Peter A., 3
Lindsey, Theophilus, 133
Litfin, Bryan M., 140
Loftin, Keith, 14
Lombardo, Nicholas E., 92–93
Longenecker, Richard N., 196, 197
Loonstra, Bertus, 7, 13
Lumpkin, William L., 66
Luther, Martin, 182

M

Magee, Gregory S., 111
Mann, William E., 51
Marshall, I. Howard, 83
Martens, Elmer A., 145
Martyn, J. Louis, 195
Marzouk, Safwat, 146
Mathews, Kenneth A., 147
Maximus the Confessor, 24
McCall, Thomas H., 160, 162
McDowell, Mark I., 92
McFadden, Kevin W., 192
McGrath, Alister E., 182
McGuire-Moushon, J. A., 22
McKelvey, Robert J., 185
McKnight, Scot, 180
McLachlan, H. John, 125–126, 128–129
Melanchthon, Philip, 182
Mendenhall, George E., 3
Merkle, Benjamin L., 112
Metzger, Bruce M., 151
Michelson, Jared, 52
Milgrom, Jacob, 206
Moberly, R. W. L., 145
Molnar, Paul D., 179
Moltmann, Jürgen, 141, 142
Monck, Thomas, 66
Morgan, Christopher W., 138
Morris, Leon, 83, 105

Mortimer, Sarah, 126, 129–132
Motyer, J. Alec, 72, 148–149
Muller, Richard A., 5–6, 212–213

N

Nimmo, Paul T., 54, 179
Nicholls, William, 123, 133
Nye, Stephen, 132–133

O

O'Brien, Peter T., 180
Oden, Thomas C., 181–182
Oecolampadius, Johannes, 128
Ogonowski, Zbigniew, 130
Oliver, Robert W., 123
Oliver, Willem H., 140
Origen, 57, 72, 159
Oropeza, B. J., 180
Ortlund, Gavin, 141
Osborne, Grant R., 101
Ott, Ludwig, 181
Owen, John, 5, 8, 66

P

Parr, Thomas, 4
Paul, Shalom M., 72
Peckham, John C., 60
Pedersen, Johannes, 22
Pelikan, Jaroslav, 53, 140, 174
Pester, John, 74, 75
Peterson, David G., 76
Peterson, Robert A., 74, 138, 199
Petterson, Anthony R., 78
Petto, Samuel, 81, 89–90
Pfizenmaier, Thomas C., 123–124
Philoponus, John, 141
Picirilli, Robert E., 48, 59
Pierce, Madison N., 7, 162
Pierce, Samuel Eyles, 152
Piggin, F. S., 180
Plantinga, Alvin, 49
Plato, 24, 137
Platter, Jonathan M., 48
Playoust, Marc R., 33
Plotinus, 24
Pollock, Algernon. J., 125, 133
Powell, Douglas L., 140
Poythress, Vern S., 76, 135, 137–138

Names Index

Preuss, Neuendettelsau H. D., 22
Priestley, Joseph, 125, 133
Pusey, E. B., 79
Pythagoras, 137

R
Rae, Murray A., 44–45
Rainwater, Jacob, 12
Rathel, David Mark, 63, 185, 188
Reedy, Gerard, S.J., 123, 129, 132
Rees, Thomas, 130
Rendtorff, Rolf, 81–82
Renihan, James M., 182
Renihan, Samuel D., 66
Richard, Guy M., 5
Richard of Saint Victor, 61
Ridderbos, Herman, 199
Rine, C. Rebecca, 75
Rippon, John, 18, 63, 122–124
Robertson, O. Palmer, 2, 14, 86–87
Robinson, Michael D., 27
Rogers, Katherin A., 28–29
Roscelin of Compiegne, 141
Rose, Wolter H., 78
Rosner, Brian S., 207–208
Rowley, H. H., 171, 176
Rusch, William G., 124
Rust, Eric C., 23
Ryken, Philip Graham, 83

S
Sabellius, 125
Sammons, Peter, 24
Sanders, E. P., 180
Sanders, Fred, 11, 139, 156
Sasse, Hermann, 22
Scheiderer, Daniel D., 63
Schemm Jr., Peter R., 159
Schreiner, Patrick, 76, 212
Schreiner, Thomas R., 153, 174, 181–182, 195, 197
Schweitzer, Albert, 32
Schville, Keith N., 60
Schwöbel, Christoph, 34, 35
Scott, Robert, 83
Seifrid, Mark A., 180
Servetus, Michael, 125–128, 130, 134
Shimko, Tim, 41

Smalley, Paul M., 7, 108
Smalley, Stephen S., 151
Smith, Gary V., 72
Socinus, Faustus, 125, 128–130, 134
Socinus, Laelius, 129, 130
Son, Sang-Won (Aaron), 194, 200
Sproul, R. C., 114
Stamps, R. Lucas, 157, 161–162, 205, 216
Standahl, Krister, 180
Steenbuch, Johannes A., 187
Steward, Gary L., 172
Stillingfleet, Edward, 133
Stott, John, 106
Streett, Andrew D., 7
Stuhlmacher, Peter, 180
Stump, Eleonore, 30
Swain, Scott R., 6, 7, 135–136, 156
Swan, Jonathan E., 157
Swanson, James, 76

T
Taggar-Cohen, Ada, 3
Tan, Randall, 101
Tarwater, John K., 3
Taylor, Mark, 161–162, 193
Tertullian, 24, 152
Thiselton, Anthony C., 59, 70, 108, 139, 210
Tillotson, John, 133
Thompson, J. A., 3
Torrance, Thomas F., 205
Towne, Robert, 88
Treier, Daniel J., 56, 58, 71, 171, 212
Twisse, William, 1

U
Ursinus, Zacharias, 184

V
Velde, Rudi A. Te, 144
Vickers, Brian J., 212
Vidu, Adonis, 141

W
Wainwright, Arthur W., 151
Waldron, Sam, 183
Walker, Larry L., 148

Wallis, John, 132
Waltke, Bruce K., 82
Ware, Bruce A., 12, 159, 160–163
Webster, John, 77, 92–93
Weinfeld, M., 3
Welker, Michael, 34
Wellum, Stephen J., 10, 192, 196, 199, 203, 208, 211, 213, 218
Wenham, Gordon J., 147
Wesley, John, 86
Westcott, Brooke Foss, 151
Westerholm, Stephen, 180
Westermann, Claus, 147
Whitby, Daniel, 175
Whitfield, Keith, 45
Wilcox, Max, 196
Wiles, Maurice, 123
Willard, Samuel, 9–11, 78
Williams, Carol, 13
Williamson, Paul R., 16, 197
Witherington III, Ben, 195
Witsius, Herman, 4, 6, 12, 65
Woo, B. Hoon, 7, 13
Wright, Christopher J. H., 206
Wright, G. Ernest, 81
Wright, N. T., 180, 197, 198
Wright, R. K. McGregor, 165–166

Y

Yarnell III, Malcolm B., 11, 39, 50, 53, 74, 103, 108, 122–123, 146, 157, 158, 161, 164, 165, 183, 184, 192
Yarbrough, Robert W., 22, 151
Yates, John C., 31
Yazawa, Reita, 13
Young, Edward J., 148
Young III, William W., 26

Z

Zizioulas, John D., 144, 155
Zwingli, Huldrych, 128

Scripture Index

OLD TESTAMENT

Genesis

1:1-2	40
1:1	145
1:2	74n25
1:26-27	75n27
1:26	74n27, 75, 92n64, 146, 147n73, 148n75
3:15	70n15, 196
11:7	148n75
12:1-3	177n23
13:15	195
15:6	183
15:12	82n39
15:17	82n39
17	37n55
17:7-8	37, 37n55, 82n39, 195
17:7	81n39
17:8	195
20:13	146n71
22:17-18	195n81
22:18	83n43, 195n81
24:7	195
35:7	146n71

Exodus

3	60n116
3:7-8	104n88
3:12	121n4
3:14	39n57, 120n4, 145, 145n68
16:6-10	69n15
24:16	69n15
29:43	69n15
33-34	69n15
33	43, 61
33:20	43
33:23	43
40:34	69n15

Leviticus

17:11	206n115
18:5	207n119
25:47	205
25:48-49	205
25:49	206

Numbers

23:19	46n80
1:4	193n14

Deuteronomy

4:2	152n84
4:39	136n47
6:4	136n48, 143n64, 81n39
7:6	81n39
14:2	81n39

Scripture Index

Judge

10:18	193n74

2 Samuel

7	37n55
7:12-16	37n55
7:12	37
7:16	37, 87n52
7:23	146n71
23:5	51

1 Kings

22:19-23	149n76

2 Kings

19:15	136n47

Nehemiah

9:6-8	81n39
9:6	136n47

Job

10:5	58
11:7	42
23:13	51n96
33:4	156
35:10	147n73

Psalms

2:7	16n43, 156, 157
11:6	105n90
19:1	69n15
21:4	87
21:5	69n15
33:6	40, 135n45, 152n85, 156
33:11	52
38:18	104n88
40	102, 102n82
40:6-8	86n52, 97n70, 100, 101n81, 102, 109
40:6	101n81
69:27	104n88
75:8	105n90
78:70	87n52
86:10	136n48
89	87n52
89:2	110n102
89:3-4	16n43, 86n52
89:3	172n11
89:20	87n52
89:28-36	86n52
89:28-29	87n52
90:2	38, 38n57, 60
102	52n100
102:25-27	51n96
102:27	52n100
103:17	51
105:15	83n43
110	16n43
110:1	143n64, 162n112
116:13	105n90
149:2	147n73

Proverbs

8:22-30	40n60
8:23-24	40
8:23	86n52

Ecclesiastes

2:23	104n88
12:1	147n73

Isaiah

1:4-6	101n81
6	148
6:8-10	149

6:8	71n19, 148, 148n75
9:6	38n57, 68n12, 158n102
25:1	46
25:1b	73
31:3a	44
39:7	101n81
40:14	147n73
42:1	172n11
42:6	97, 97n71
42:8	70n15, 138n55
43:10	136n48, 138n52
43:13	56
44:6	136n48, 143n64
44:8	136n48
45:5-6	136n48
45:14	136n48
45:18	136n48
45:21-22	136n48
45:23	143n64
46:9	136n48
48:16b	72, 72n20
49:1-6	86n52
49:3	105n90
49:5-6	99
49:7	104n88
49:8	97
51:17	105n90
51:22	105n90
52:14	104n88
53	104n88, 105, 109
53:10-12	86n52
54:51	147n73
59:20-21	16n43

Jeremiah

1:5	173n14
10:10	52
10:11	139
25:15	105n90
31:33-34	115
32:38	115
34:18	82n39

Lamentations

3:37	62, 169

Ezekiel

23:31-33	105n90
36:25-27	115
37:24-25	102n82
37:26	88n55

Daniel

7:13	58

Hosea

1:11	193n74
3:5	102n82

Zechariah

3:9-13b	78n34
3:12-13	78n34
6:9-15	78n34
6:13	16n43, 16n44, 73, 73n21, 77, 77n33, 78n34, 88n55
6:15	77

Malachi

2:5	87
2:10	136n47
3:6	46n80, 51n96, 54

NEW TESTAMENT

Matthew

1:21	207n118
6:13	22n3
26:39	105n90

Mark

12	143n64
12:28-37	143n64
12:28-29	143n64
12:29-30	143n64
12:29	136n48

Luke

1:33	22n3
10:20	174
18:9-14	183n43
22:20	83n42
22:28-30	83n42
22:29	16n43, 83, 83n42, 83n43
23:25	172n11

John

1	69n15
1:1	26
1:14	53, 69n15, 156, 157
3:16	202n104
4:24	44, 44n72, 48
5:19-30	162n112
5:37	45
6:7	176n23
6:37	173n12
6:39	99, 173n12
6:64-65	173n12
8:58	39n57
10:30	11n25, 140, 141n61
10:38	141n61
12:23	70n15
12:40-41	148, 149
12:41	149n76
13:18	176
14-16	39n57
14:20	150n79
14:23	149, 150n79
14:26	72n20
14:28	11n25
15:24	162n112
15:26	72n20
15:28	162n112
16:7-8	72n20
17	16n43
17:3	136n48
17:4-5	138n55
17:6	173n12
17:12	173n12
17:24	51, 111n105
18:9	173n12
18:11	105n90

Acts

2:8-11	148n75
3:25	83n43
4:12	84
8:9-24	140n59
13:38-39	183n40, 183n40
13:48	173
15:11	183n40
17:28	137n50
20:27	76
20:28	211, 212, 212n132
28:25-26	148, 149
28:25	149n76

Romans

1:4	108n98
1:15-18	183n43
1:22	22n3
3:21-4:25	183n40
3:23	69n15
3:24	183n40, 184, 186
3:30	136n48
4	183n40

4:3	183
4:13-18	196
5	199n92
5:6	115, 115n114
5:8	115, 115n114, 202n104
5:10-11	183n40
5:12-21	198
5:14	198
5:18-19	183n40
5:19	183n40
6:15-23	183n40
8:9	103
8:33-34	183n40
8:33	174
9	112n105
9:5	22n3
9:11	112n105, 173n14
10:4	183n40
11:33-34a	42n66
11:36	22n3
14:10-11	143n64

1 Corinthians

1:30	70n16, 183n40
2:10-11	42n66, 74n25
2:10	109
3:16	150n79
4:3-4	183n40
6:11	183n40
8:4-6	136n48
8:6	135n45
11:3	161, 161n111
12:3	163
15	162n112, 199n92
15:22	200
15:24-28	162, 162n112
15:24	163
15:28	160n106, 163
15:45	198
15:47	198

2 Corinthians

4:6	70n15
5:17	96n67
5:18-19	96n67
5:18	95
5:21	183n40
11:31	22n3

Galatians

2:16	183n40, 191
3:10-11	207n118
3:16-17	194
3:16	195, 196, 197n87, 198
3:17	16n43, 195
4:4-5	207n118
4:4	71n19, 104n89

Ephesians

1	16n43
1:3-6	113
1:3-4	188, 189
1:3	86n52
1:4	88n55, 111n105, 174, 176, 194
1:6	113n110
1:7	70n16
1:9-10	170
1:11	6, 169n6
1:17-20	107n97
1:19-20	114
2:5	183n40
2:8	184
3:10	70n17
3:11	47, 51, 70n17
4:6	136n48
4:15-16	193n74
5:23-24	193n74
5:23	193
6:15	88n55

Philippians

2:5-11	53
2:6	43
2:7-8	103, 103n88, 104n88, 105, 109
2:7	53

(Phillipians continued)

3:7-9	183n40
3:8-9	183
4:3	174

Colossians

1:17	39
1:20	106n94
1:24-25	175n17
2:9	43

2 Thessalonians

2:13	98, 98n76, 109, 173n14, 174

1 Timothy

2:5	136n48, 201
3:9	135
3:16	99, 100n78, 183n40
6:3	88

2 Timothy

1:1	86n52, 87
1:9-10	16n43
1:9	86n52, 189
2:10	175n17
3:16	135n45

Titus

1:2	86n52, 87

Hebrews

1:3	138n55
2	208n121
2:10	208
2:14	208
5:8	211
6:13	82n39
7:2	88n55
7:9-10	189n63
7:22	16n43
7:26	209
9:14	107, 108n98
9:22	206n115
10	102
10:5-10	97n70, 100, 101n81, 109
10:5-9	102n82
10:5	101n81, 205
10:19-20	88n55
12:22	174
13:8	22n3

James

1:17	46n80, 51n96

1 Peter

1:2	98, 109, 153, 176
1:3	107n97
1:11	107
1:19	212n133
1:20	48n86, 111n105
1:24-25	51n96
2:4	172n11
3:18	106, 107, 107n96

2 Peter

3:8	58n110

1 John

2:1	209
3:5	209
4:2-3	99
4:10	202n104
5:7	151, 151n80, 152n84

Revelation

1:8	143n64	14:10	105n90
4:9	52	16:19	105n90
4:10	52	19-20	162n112
10:6	52	21-22	69n14
13:8	173, 174	21	70n15
		22:11	183n40

www.ingramcontent.com/pod-product-compliance
Lightning Source LLC
Chambersburg PA
CBHW070313240426
43663CB00038BA/2010